The Family in EU Law

Edited by

MARJA-LIISA ÖBERG

Lund University

ALINA TRYFONIDOU

University of Cyprus

CAMBRIDGE
UNIVERSITY PRESS

CAMBRIDGE
UNIVERSITY PRESS

Shaftesbury Road, Cambridge CB2 8EA, United Kingdom

One Liberty Plaza, 20th Floor, New York, NY 10006, USA

477 Williamstown Road, Port Melbourne, VIC 3207, Australia

314–321, 3rd Floor, Plot 3, Splendor Forum, Jasola District Centre, New Delhi – 110025, India

103 Penang Road, #05-06/07, Visioncrest Commercial, Singapore 238467

Cambridge University Press is part of Cambridge University Press & Assessment, a department of the University of Cambridge.

We share the University's mission to contribute to society through the pursuit of education, learning and research at the highest international levels of excellence.

www.cambridge.org
Information on this title: www.cambridge.org/9781009498821

DOI: 10.1017/9781009498838

First published 2024

A catalogue record for this publication is available from the British Library.

Library of Congress Cataloging-in-Publication Data
NAMES: Öberg, Marja-Liisa, editor. | Tryfonidou, Alina, editor.
TITLE: The family in EU law / edited by Marja-Liisa Öberg, Lund University; Alina Tryfonidou, University of Cyprus.
OTHER TITLES: Family in European Union law
DESCRIPTION: Cambridge, United Kingdom ; New York, NY : Cambridge University Press, 2024. | Includes bibliographical references and index.
IDENTIFIERS: LCCN 2024010393 (print) | LCCN 2024010394 (ebook) | ISBN 9781009498821 (hardback) | ISBN 9781009498791 (paperback) | ISBN 9781009498838 (epub)
SUBJECTS: LCSH: Domestic relations–European Union countries.
CLASSIFICATION: LCC KJE1105 .F39 2024 (print) | LCC KJE1105 (ebook) | DDC 346.2401/5–dc23/eng/20240317
LC record available at https://lccn.loc.gov/2024010393
LC ebook record available at https://lccn.loc.gov/2024010394

ISBN 978-1-009-49882-1 Hardback

Contents

Notes on Contributors

Albertina Albors-Llorens is Professor of EU Law at the Faculty of Law in the University of Cambridge and a Fellow of St John's College. Her research focuses on EU law and competition law, and she has lectured and published widely in these fields. She has been one of the editors of the *Cambridge Yearbook of European Legal Studies* (2012–2015), a note editor of the *Cambridge Law Journal* (2010–2020), and one of the editors of the *Yearbook of European Law* (2015–2022). She is currently a member of the editorial board of the *European Law Review*.

David Archard is Emeritus Professor of Philosophy at Queen's University Belfast, having previously taught at the Universities of Ulster, St Andrews, and Lancaster. He has published extensively in applied ethics, political philosophy, and philosophy of law. He is vice president of the Society for Applied Philosophy, was a member of the Human Fertilization and Embryology Authority and chair of the Nuffield Council on Bioethics, is chair of the Ethics Advisory Group of the 'Every Story Matters' exercise of the UK's COVID Public Inquiry, and a member of the Clinical Ethics Committee of Great Ormond Street Hospital.

Ségolène Barbou des Places is Professor of Public and European Law at the Sorbonne Law School, Paris 1 University. She is one of the joint editors of *European Papers: A Journal on Law and Integration*, and co-director of the GIS-Eurolab, an interdisciplinary network of 200 researchers on the European Union. Her research examines questions of substantive EU law with a particular focus on free movement law, EU citizenship, and migration law. She analyses the different forms of mobility organised at EU level, and she investigates the way in which EU law 'constructs the person' and the European society.

Michael Bogdan is Professor Emeritus at Lund University and Guest Professor at Charles University in Prague. He is the author of numerous books and articles, mainly in the fields of private international law, comparative law, law of international commerce, and private law. He is a member of the International Academy of Comparative Law, honorary member and former president of the Group européen de droit international privé, and emeritus member of the Institut de droit international.

Xavier Groussot is Professor of EU Law at Lund University and Visiting Professor at the European College of Paris, University Panthéon Assas (Paris II). He has previously been Visiting Professor at the Universities of Reykjavik, Nagoya, LUISS (Rome), ELTE (Budapest), and Bologna. He has published extensively in the fields of EU constitutional law, internal market law, procedural law, and legal theory. His current research focus is on the scope of application of the EU Charter of Fundamental Rights, the respect of the rule of law in Europe, and the concepts of emergency and solidarity in EU law.

Ruth Lamont is Reader in Child and Family Law at the University of Manchester. Her research focuses on the international movement of children and the legal regulation of child and family migration both in a modern and in a historical context. She has examined the role of the EU in relation to the family, particularly considering the impact of children's rights protections and the law relating to free movement of persons and EU private international family law affecting children. Her work has been cited by the Court of Justice of the European Union, and she has given evidence to the UK Parliament on the impact of Brexit on family law.

Alezini Loxa is a post-doctoral fellow in EU law at Lund University. She is a Greek lawyer (Athens Bar Association) and holds an LLB and an LLM in EU law from National and Kapodistrian University of Athens and a PhD in EU law from Lund University. She has been engaged academically and professionally in the field of human rights protection in Europe with a specific focus on EU law, social rights, and migrant and refugee protection.

Alice Margaria is Assistant Professor of Law and Reproduction and co-director of the interdisciplinary Research Priority Program 'Human Reproduction Reloaded' at the University of Zurich. Her research lies at the intersections of family law, diversity, and human rights. She is the author of *The Construction of Fatherhood: The Jurisprudence of the European Court of Human Rights* (Cambridge University Press 2019), and co-editor of *Leading Works in Law and Anthropology* (Routledge 2024).

Marja-Liisa Öberg is Associate Professor of EU Law at Lund University. Her research interests lie in the areas of EU constitutional and external relations law, third-country integration in the EU, the internal and external boundaries of EU integration, and interdisciplinary dimensions of EU integration. She is the author of *The Boundaries of the EU Internal Market: Participation without Membership* (Cambridge University Press 2020).

Nausica Palazzo is Assistant Professor at NOVA School of Law, Lisbon, and a 2024 JG McLeod Fellow at Western Law, London, Ontario. She is interested in queer approaches to family law and has published in top specialised journals such as *Columbia Journal of Gender & Law* and *Michigan Journal of Gender & Law*. Her book *Legal Recognition of Non-conjugal Families* came out with Hart Publishing (2021) and a co-edited collection on queer and religious alliances in family law was published by Anthem Press (2022).

Gunnar Thor Petursson is Professor at the School of Law, Reykjavik University and visiting professor at the Faculty of Law, Panthéon-Assas (Paris II). He was previously a director of the Internal Market Affairs Directorate at the EFTA Surveillance Authority (2017–2020). His research focuses on EU/EEA constitutional law, fundamental rights, and legal theory.

Jens M. Scherpe is Professor of Comparative Law at Aalborg University and founding director of the Nordic Centre for Comparative and International Family Law (NorFam). Until August 2022, he was professor of comparative law at the University of Cambridge and was the founding director of Cambridge Family Law. He is an emeritus fellow of Gonville and Caius College and the editor of the *International Journal of Law, Policy and the Family* (IJLPF).

Alina Tryfonidou is Assistant Professor of EU Law and Family Law at the University of Cyprus. She has previously worked at the Universities of Leicester (lecturer), Reading (lecturer, associate professor and professor), and Neapolis University Pafos (professor), and has held visiting positions at King's College London, the Institute of Advanced Legal Studies, the University of Reading, and the University of Bergamo. She has published extensively on issues related to EU free movement law and European family law, with special emphasis on the rights of sexual minorities. She has authored and co-authored studies commissioned by the European Parliament's Policy Department for Citizens' Rights and Constitutional Affairs at the request of the PETI Committee.

Geoffrey Willems is Professor at UCLouvain, Belgium. His teaching and research focuses mainly on family law, human rights applied to family law, and international and comparative family law. He has published extensively on issues related to personal autonomy, gender identity, sexual orientation, couple relationships, and assisted reproduction. In recent years, he has also developed a particular interest in the 'law and society' and 'law and literature' approaches.

Foreword

It is nearly twenty years since I wrote about families and the European Union (EU).[1] My aim then was to address two related debates: first, the concept of 'family', as it was developing across a range of fields of European law; and, second, what could be characterised as an emerging European 'family law'. What was surprising at that time was that while family law reforms at the national, Member State, level were usually the subject of heated political debate, legislative measures and judicial interpretations were progressing within the EU with comparatively little discussion. Indeed, the dominant impulse was towards a bureaucratic, harmonising, 'tidying' of disparate laws, with the risk of the lowest common denominator of what might constitute a 'family' becoming entrenched in Union laws, policies, and practices. Such approaches spanned many areas of activity, including international family law and codification of private law, with the danger being a concept of 'family' based on heterosexual marriage, biological children, and a gendered division of family and workplace labour.

It was in this light that I argued for a human rights foundation for any harmonisation or greater integration in the field of family law, with pluralism and diversity characterising any conceptualisation of what might constitute families and family life. This approach was, therefore, sceptical of further European integration of substantive family law, partly due to a sense that the real needs of families remained a vague and distant concern in the EU context, with economic and supra-political concerns dominating. I was also concerned at any potential 'erasure of difference', arguing that pluralism must shape not only the European polity generally but development of family concepts and family law particularly. These concerns were not particularly

1 C. McGlynn, *Families and the European Union: Law, Politics and Pluralism* (Cambridge University Press 2006).

original, and indeed drew on long-standing historical, political, and theoretical debates. Nonetheless, applying them to this particular context would, I hoped, generate debate and further analysis.

A further key driver was to examine what current law and future developments in this field might mean for the freedom, liberty, and equality of women and girls. I had come to the topic of 'families and the European Union' from examining the Union's equality and discrimination laws, concerned at the time to see a dominant ideology of motherhood running through equality law.[2] Such hegemonic ideologies of motherhood, and by implication of fatherhood and parenthood, constrained women and men's freedom and opportunities to choose how to live their lives. Conventional categories of 'family' acted in a similarly exclusionary and reductionist way, most particularly discriminating against same-sex relationships and marriage.

Reflecting now on the passage of nearly twenty years, as Jens Scherpe writes in his Epilogue to this book, over this time much has changed, but much has not.[3] This is most clear in relation to women's freedom and equality, where much has changed, but so much has not. While it is undoubtedly the case that the lives of *some* women and girls have become freer and more equal, there remains so much entrenched and structural inequality, including in relation to conventional familial roles and expectations. And for some women, particularly marginalised and minoritised communities, such as women identifying as LGBTQI, women with disabilities, and women from black and minoritised communities, equality is a veneer hiding the reality of their lives.

In fact, in the European context, we are arguably in a more dangerous place than twenty years ago, a place where freedoms once thought embedded are under serious challenge. The conservative ideology of some European countries, particularly though certainly not exclusively across eastern Europe, has resulted in women's freedom to live and choose their own lives, paths, and destinies, including creating their families at times of their own choosing and method, being seriously restricted and this is infecting much European discourse and legal developments. Populism and the resurgence online of hegemonic masculinities proliferates in all countries. These active forces, including Member State governments, are constraining EU action on women's human rights, and the elimination of violence against women, as well as on wider issues of family rights. Such forces are also enabling a

[2] C. McGlynn, 'Ideologies of motherhood in European Community sex equality law' (2000) 6 European Law Journal 29.

[3] See Chapter 13 by Jens M. Scherpe.

generation of incels and the proliferation of online misogyny that itself challenges fundamental rights such as women's freedom of expression, and threatens democracy by pushing women, and other vulnerable or marginalised communities, out of public life.

The same 'gender ideology' also has considerable adverse impacts on the rights of same-sex couples in a family context and LGBTQI rights in general. There was a strong feeling of inevitable progress, even if glacial, on these issues in previous decades. Any such optimism has been shattered. Discussion of concepts and ideals of 'family' in the European context must now be considered not just against a backdrop of apathy, which might once have characterised some cross-national debates, but one of real, active, antipathy, with proactive steps being taken to undermine any progress to date.

Similar antipathy is also evident in the legal and policy arenas of nationalism, immigration, and the connected questions of family and family life. While earlier debates may, in some respects, be characterised as moving progressively towards a more plural and liberal concept of family, this was partly due to the absence of any substantial debate in this field of the impacts and connections with law, policies, and practices on immigration, nationalism, and colonialism. My own writing, for example, lacked a sufficiently distinct and attentive discussion of intersectionality and the differing impacts of norms, judgments, and proposals on different communities.

It is in this climate that this new book edited by Marja-Liisa Öberg and Alina Tryfonidou is seeking to advance understanding and debate. It is a climate that is, on a scholarly level, more welcoming of debates on family and family law, in light of the sheer volume of EU law that now impacts on families. It is not possible for the institutions of the EU to avoid making institutional and legal decisions on definitions of family, and on the scope of laws and policies. There is, therefore, much to analyse and discuss, and this volume provides a thorough and thought-provoking engagement with so many of the key issues. It is an excellent example of scholarly inquiry which ensures we reflect on underlying principles, as well as analyse the detailed application of laws, policies, and practices. Across the chapters, we gain a clear sense of the significance of the EU engaging in this field, the depth of potential harms, and indications of a better way forward.

However, it is also a climate that, on a political level, as noted above, is polarised and toxic, with little apparent scope for compromise or debate. Many people in many Member States are not free to exercise their human rights to choose to live freely in their families of choice or to create the family they desire. Many are in fear of their families being separated; many are unable to live with their families.

In reflecting on developments over recent decades, it may also be worth considering what we would wish for in the next few years. What would we like our reflections to be in a further twenty years? While I would like to envision a pluralistic approach to families, family life, and family law, underpinned by human rights and a deep understanding and recognition of the vulnerabilities and structural inequalities facing some communities, I am not convinced that this is the current path. For many, the current path is one paved with fear, with inequality as integral to everyday life, and with high political stakes set on resisting progressive advancements. In such a supranational political climate, there are great risks in developing any common idea of a EU family law. Thus, while we analyse and debate the incremental changes, the often necessary decisions and choices, we must retain an eye and overarching review of the bigger picture of what more substantive changes and legislation might mean into the future. Perhaps greater competence and coherence in the field is not to be welcomed if it might be used to greater entrench discrimination against some communities.

Albert Camus wrote about 'unity and diversity, and never one without the other', being the core and 'secret' of European political communities.[4] It may be that in this field we need to focus more on preserving diversity, than in creating unity: the risk is that unity, at the level of concepts of family and family law, is at the expense of many marginalised and vulnerable communities.

Clare McGlynn

4 A. Camus, *Resistance, Rebellion and Death* (Wintage 1974).

Acknowledgements

This edited volume builds on a workshop held online on 1–2 July 2021. We are grateful for all the participants in the workshop as well as all authors who joined the project at a later stage for bringing this publication into life and contributing with invaluable insights. We would also like to thank Clare McGlynn for bridging this edited volume with the landmark publication in the field of EU family law – *Families and the European Union: Law, Politics and Pluralism* – which she published with Cambridge University Press in 2006; Xavier Groussot who was one of the initiators of the project; and the Rune and Lena Lavins Stiftelse for funding assistance. We are greatly indebted to Tom Randall, Marianne Nield, and Sharon McCann at Cambridge University Press for their support throughout the publishing process; to Kate McIntosh for compiling the index; and to the copy-editors for preparing the final manuscript.

Table of Cases

COURT OF JUSTICE OF THE EU

Court of Justice

Case 76/72 *Michel S. v Fonds national de reclassement social des handicapés* EU:C:1973:46
Case 8/74 *Dassonville* EU:C:1974:82
Case 36/75 *Rutili v Ministre de l'intérieur* EU:C:1975:137
Case 48/75 *Royer* EU:C:1976:57
Case 98/79 *Pecastaing v Belgian State* EU:C:1980:69
Case 163/82 *Commission v Italy* EU:C:1983:295
Case 184/83 *Hofmann v Barmer Ersatzkasse* EU:C:1984:273
Case 267/83 *Diatta* EU:C:1985:67
Case 222/84 *Johnston v Chief Constable of the Royal Ulster Constabulary* EU:C:1986:206
Case 59/85 *Reed* EU:C:1986:157
Case 222/86 *Unectef v Heylens and others* EU:C:1987:442
Case 5/88 *Wachauf* EU:C:1989:321
Case C-308/89 *Di Leo v Land Berlin* EU:C:1990:400
Case C-370/90 *Singh* EU:C:1992:296
Case C-97/91 *Oleificio Borelli v Commission* EU:C:1992:491
Case C-13/94 *P v S and Cornwall County Council* EU:C:1996:170
Case C-65/95 *The Queen v Secretary of State for the Home Department, ex parte Shingara* EU:C:1997:300
Case C-243/95 *Hill and Stapleton v The Revenue Commissioners and the Department of Finance* EU:C:1998:298
Case C-351/95 *Kadiman* EU:C:1997:205

Case C-85/96 *Martínez Sala v Freistaat Bayern* EU:C:1998:217
Case C-249/96 *Grant* EU:C:1998:63
Case C-218/98 *Abdoulaye v Renault* EU:C:1999:424
Case C-357/98 *The Queen v Secretary of State for the Home Department, ex parte Yiadom* EU:C:2000:604
Joined Cases C-122/99 P and C-125/99 P *D and Sweden v Council* EU:C:2001:304
Case C-413/99 *Baumbast* EU:C:2002:493
Case C-459/99 *MRAX* EU:C:2002:461
Case C-60/00 *Carpenter* EU:C:2002:434
Case C-117/01 *K.B.* EU:C:2004:7
Case C-452/01 *Ospelt and Schlössle Weissenberg* EU:C:2003:493
Case C-148/02 *Garcia Avello* EU:C:2003:539
Case C-200/02 *Zhu and Chen* EU:C:2004:639
Case C-373/03 *Aydinli* EU:C:2005:434
Case C-540/03 *Parliament v Council* EU:C:2006:429
Case C-1/05 *Jia v Migrationsverket* EU:C:2007:1
Case C-325/05 *Derin* EU:C:2007:442
Case C-267/06 *Maruko* EU:C:2008:179
Case C-353/06 *Grunkin-Paul* EU:C:2008:559
Case C-435/06 C EU:C:2007:714
Case C-453/07 *Er* EU:C:2008:524
Case C-127/08 *Metock* EU:C:2008:449
Case C-147/08 *Römer* EU:C:2011:286
Case C-310/08 *Ibrahim* EU:C:2010:1065
Case C-371/08 *Ziebell* EU:C:2011:809
Case C-480/08 *Teixeira* EU:C:2010:83
Case C-578/08 *Chakroun* EU:C:2010:117
Case C-14/09 *Genc* EU:C:2010:57
Case C-34/09 *Ruiz Zambrano* EU:C:2011:124
Case C-208/09 *Sayn-Wittgenstein* EU:C:2010:806
Case C-372/09 *Peñarroja Fa* EU:C:2011:156
Case C-391/09 *Runevič-Vardyn and Wardyn* EU:C:2011:291
Case C-542/09 *Commission v The Netherlands* EU:C:2012:346
Case C-149/10 *Chatzi* EU:C:2010:534
Case C-400/10 PPU *McB* EU:C:2010:582
Case C-430/10 *Gaydarov* EU:C:2011:749
Case C-617/10 *Åkerberg Fransson* EU:C:2013:105.
Case C-40/11 *Iida* EU:C:2012:691

Case C-83/11 *Secretary of State for the Home Department v Rahman* EU:C:2012:519
Case C-221/11 *Demirkan* EU:C:2013:583
Case C-249/11 *Byankov* EU:C:2012:608
Case C-256/11 *Dereci* EU:C:2011:734
Case C-300/11 *ZZ v Secretary of State for the Home Department* EU:C:2013:363
Joined Cases C-356/11 and C-357/11 *O. and S.* EU:C:2012:776
Case C-431/11 *United Kingdom v Council* EU:C:2013:589
Case C-529/11 *Alarape* EU:C:2013:290
Case C-583/11 *Inuit Tapiriit Kanatami and others v European Parliament and Council* EU:C:2013:625
Case C-656/11 *United Kingdom v Council* EU:C:2014:97
Case C-86/12 *Alokpa and Moudoulou* EU:C:2013:645
Case C-92/12 *HSE* EU:C:2012:255
Case C-167/12 *CD v ST* EU:C:2014:169
Case C-267/12 *Hay* EU:C:2013:823
Joined Cases C-293/12 and C-594/12 *Digital Rights Ireland and others* EU:C:2014:238
Case C-363/12 Z *v Government Department and the Board of Management of a Community School* EU:C:2014:159
Case C-370/12 *Pringle* EU:C:2012:756
Case C-423/12 *Flora Reyes* EU:C:2014:16
Case C-456/12 *O. and B.* EU:C:2014:135
Case C-457/12 *S v Minister voor Immigratie* EU:C:2014:136
Case C-81/13 *United Kingdom v Council* EU:C:2014:2449
Case C-138/13 *Dogan* EU:C:2014:2066
Case C-244/13 *Ogieriakhi* EU:C:2014:2068
Case C-437/13 *Unitrading Ltd v Staatssecretaris van Financiën* EU:C:2014:2318
Case C-165/14 *Rendón Marín* EU:C:2016:675
Case C-169/14 *Sánchez Morcillo v Banco Bilbao Vizcaya* EU:C:2014:2099
Case C-218/14 *Singh* EU:C:2015:476
Case C-222/14 *Maïstrellis* EU:C:2015:473
Case C-299/14 *Vestische Arbeit Jobcenter Kreis Recklinghausen v García-Nieto* EU:C:2016:114
Case C-362/14 *Schrems (I)* EU:C:2015:650
Joined Cases C-439/14 and C-488/14 *Star Storage* EU:C:2016:688
Joined Cases C-8/15 P to C-10/15 P *Ledra Advertising v Commission and ECB* EU:C:2016:701

Case C-115/15 *NA* EU:C:2016:487
Case C-133/15 *Chavez-Vilchez and others* EU:C:2017:354
Case C-205/15 *DGRFP v Toma and Biroul* EU:C:2016:499
Case C-231/15 *Prezes Urzędu Komunikacji Elektronicznej* EU:C:2016:769
Case C-401/15 Depesme and Kerrou EU:C:2016:955
Case C-428/15 *Child and Family Agency* EU:C:2016:819
Case C-443/15 *Parris* EU:C:2016:897
Case C-64/16 *Associação Sindical dos Juízes Portugueses* EU:C:2018:117
Case C-82/16 *K.A. and others* EU:C:2018:308
Case C-165/16 *Toufik Lounes* EU:C:2017:862
Case C-174/16 *H* EU:C:2017:637
Case C-451/16 *MB v Secretary of State for Work and Pensions* EU:C:2018:492
Case C-550/16 A. *and* S. EU:C:2018:248
Case C-673/16 *Coman and others* EU:C:2018:385
Case C-89/17 *Banger* EU:C:2018:570
Case C-335/17 *Neli Valcheva v Georgios Babanarakis* EU:C:2018:359
Case C-89/18 A *v Udlændinge- og Integrationsministeriet* EU:C:2019:580
Case C-94/18 *Chenchooliah v Minister for Justice and Equality* EU:C:2019:6930
Case C-129/18 *SM* EU:C:2019:248
Case C-311/18 *Facebook Ireland and Schrems (Schrems II)* EU:C:2020:559
Joined Cases C-518/18, C-624/18 and C-625/18 A.K. *(Independence of the Disciplinary Chamber of the Supreme Court)* EU:C:2019:982
Case C-519/18 *Bevándorlási és Menekültügyi Hivatal* EU:C:2019:1070
Case C-619/18 *Commission v Poland* (Independence of the Supreme Court) EU:C:2019:531
Case C-836/18 *Subdelegación del Gobierno en Ciudad Real v RH* EU:C:2020:119
Case C-181/19 *JD* EU:C:2020:794
Joined Cases C-245/19 and C-246/19 *État luxembourgeois contre B* EU:C:2020:795
Case C-817/19 *Ligue des droits humains* EU:C:2022:491
Case C-129/20 *Caisse pour l'avenir des enfants (Emploi à la naissance)* EU:C:2021:140
Case C-247/20 *VI* EU:C:2022:177
Case C-379/20 *B v Udlændingenævnet* EU:C:2021:660
Case C-379/20 Summary of the request for a preliminary ruling pursuant to Article 98(1) of the Rules of Procedure of the Court of Justice by Østre Landsret (Eastern High Court, Denmark), lodged on 11 August 2020

Case C-490/20 *V.M.A. v Stolichna obshtina, rayon 'Pancharevo'* EU:C:2021:1008
Case C-2/21 *Rzecznik Praw Obywatelskich* EU:C:2022:502
Order of the Court in Case C-2/21 *Rzecznik Praw Obywatelskich* EU:C:2022:502
Case C-156/21 *Hungary v Parliament and Council* EU:C:2022:97
Case C-157/21 *Poland v Parliament and Council* EU:C:2022:98
Action brought on 19 December 2022 in Case C-769/22 *Commission v Hungary* [2023] OJ C54/16

General Court

Case T-65/92 *Arauxo-Dumay* EU:T:1993:47
Case T-461/08 *Evropaïki Dynamiki v European Investment Bank* EU:T:2011:494
Case T-517/16 *Janoha and others v Commission* EU:T:2018:874
Case T-484/18 *XB v ECB* EU:T:2020:90
Case T-131/20 *IR v Commission* EU:T:2020:381

Opinions of Advocates General

Opinion of Advocate General Ruiz-Jarabo Colomer in Case C-65/95 *The Queen v Secretary of State for the Home Department, ex parte Shingara* EU:C:1996:451
Opinion of Advocate General Mischo in Joined Cases C-122/99 P and C-125/99 P *D and Sweden v Council* EU:C:2001:113
Opinion of Advocate General Geelhoed in Case C-413/99 *Baumbast and R* EU:C:2001:385
Opinion of Advocate General Stix-Hackl in Case C-60/00 *Carpenter* EU:C:2001:447
Opinion of Advocate General Kokott in Case C-480/08 *Teixeira* EU:C:2009:642
Opinion of Advocate General Sharpston in Case C-34/09 *Ruiz Zambrano* EU:C:2010:560
Opinion of Advocate General Bot in Case C-108/10 *Scattolon* EU:C:2011:211
Opinion of Advocate General Kokott in Case C-110/10 *Solvay v Commission* EU:C:2011:257
Opinion of Advocate General Mengozzi in Case C-249/11 *Byankov* EU:C:2012:380

Opinion of Advocate General Bot in Case C-300/11 *ZZ v Secretary of State for the Home Department* EU:C:2012:563

Opinion of Advocate General Kokott in Case C-167/12 *CD v ST* EU:C:2013:600

Opinion of Advocate General Wahl in Case C-363/12 Z *v Government Department and the Board of Management of a Community School* EU:C:2013:604

Opinion of Advocate General Mengozzi in Case C-423/12 *Flora May Reyes* EU:C:2014:16

Opinion of Advocate General Szpunar in Case C-202/13 *McCarthy and others* EU:C:2014:345

Opinion of Advocate General Szpunar in Case C-133/15 *Chavez-Vilchez and others* EU:C:2016:659

Opinion of Advocate General Wathelet in Case C-401/15 *Depesme and Kerrou* EU:C:2016:430

Opinion of Advocate General Wathelet in Case C-673/16 *Coman and others* EU:C:2018:2

Opinion of Advocate General Bobek in Case C-89/17 *Banger* EU:C:2018:225

Opinion of Advocate General Szpunar in Case C-335/17 *Valcheva v Babanarakis* EU:C:2018:242

Opinion of Advocate General Kokott in Case C-490/20 *V.M.A. v Stolichna obshtina, rayon 'Pancharevo'* EU:C:2021:296

EUROPEAN COURT OF HUMAN RIGHTS

Marckx v Belgium, Application no 6833/74

Johnston and Others v Ireland, Application no 9697/82

Christine Goodwin v the United Kingdom, Application no 28957/95

E v the United Kingdom, Application no 33218/96

Salgueiro Da Silva Mouta v Portugal, Application no 33290/96

Karner v Austria, Application no 40016/98

Odièvre v France, Application no 42326/98

Mata Estevez v Spain, Application no 56501/00

S.H. and Others v Austria, Application no 57813/00

Kozak v Poland, Application no 13102/02

P.B. and J.S. v Austria, Application no 18984/02

B and L v the United Kingdom, Application no 36536/02

EB v France, Application no 43546/02

L v Lithuania, Application no 27527/03

Sporer v Austria, Application no 35637/03
Zaunegger v Germany, Application no 22028/04
Schalk and Kopf v Austria, Application no 30141/04
Schlumpf v Switzerland, Application no 29002/06
X and Others v Austria, Application no 19010/07
Gas and Dubois v France, Application no 25951/07
Chapin and Charpentier v France, Application no 40183/07
YY v Turkey, Application no 14793/08
Vallianatos and Others v Greece [GC], Application nos 29381/09 and 32684/09
Godelli v Italy, Application no 33783/09
Aldeguer Tomás v Spain, Application no 35214/09
Hämäläinen v Finland, Application no 37359/09
Taddeucci and McCall v Italy, Application no 51362/09
Manenc v France, Application no 66686/09
Fedotova and Others v Russia, Application nos 40792/10, 30538/14 and 43439/10
Hallier and Others v France, Application no 46386/10
Bonnaud and Lecoq v France, Application no 6190/11
Boeckel and Gessner-Boeckel v Germany, Application no 8017/11
Oliari and Others v Italy, Application nos 18766/11 and 36030/11
Mennesson v France, Application no 65192/11
Labassee v France, Application no 65941/11
Paradiso and Campanelli v Italy, Application no 25358/12
Orlandi and Others v Italy, Application no 26431/12
AP, Garçon and Nicot v France, Application nos 79885/12, 52471/13 and 52596/13
Delecolle v France, Application no 37646/13
Pajic v Croatia, Application no 68453/13
Maymulakhin and Markiv v Ukraine, Application no 75135/14
Charron and Merle-Montet v France, Application no 22612/15
A.D.-K. and Others v Poland, Application no 30806/15
S.-H. v Poland, Application nos 56846/15 and 56849/15
D.B. and Others v Switzerland, Application nos 58817/15 and 58252/15
X and Y v Romania, Application no 2145/16 and 20607/16
Honner v France, Application no 19511/16
YT v Bulgaria, Application no 41701/16
R.F. and Others v Germany, Application no 46808/16
Przybyszewska and Others v Poland, Application nos 11454/17 and 9 others
AD and Others v Georgia, Application nos 57864/17, 79087/17 and 55353/19

D. v France, Application no 11288/18
C.E. and Others v France, Application nos 29775/18 and 29693/19
A.M. v Norway, Application no 30254/18
Concurring Opinion of Judge O'Leary in *A.M. v Norway*, Application no 30254/18
Dissenting Opinion of Judge Jelić in *A.M. v Norway*, Application no 30254/18
O.H. and G.H. v Germany, Application nos 53568/18 and 54741/18
Buhuceanu and Others v Romania, Application nos 20081/19 and 20 others
Callamand v France, Application no 2338/20

EFTA COURT

Case E-4/11 *Clauder* [2011] EFTA Ct. Rep. 216
Case E-26/13 *Gunnarsson* [2014] EFTA Ct. Rep. 254
Case E-28/15 *Yankuba Jabbi v The Norwegian Government* [2016] EFTA Ct. Rep. 575
Case E-4/19 *Campbell v The Norwegian Government* [2020] EFTA Ct. Rep. 21

INTER-AMERICAN COURT OF HUMAN RIGHTS

Advisory Opinion (Opinión Consultativa) 24/17 of 24 November 2017 in a case concerning Costa Rica <https://corteidh.or.cr/docs/opiniones/seriea_24_eng.pdf>

INTERNATIONAL COURT OF JUSTICE

Netherlands v Sweden (Application of the Convention of 1902 Governing the Guardianship of Infants) [1958] I.C.J. Reports 55.

CANADA

Halpern v Canada (AG), [2003] O.J. No. 2268 (10 June 2003)
Reference Re Same-Sex Marriage [2004] 3 S.C.R 698

FRANCE

Cour de Cassation, Assemblée plénière, Nos 619 and 620 of 3 July 2015
Cour de Cassation, 1ère Chambre Civile, Nos 824–827 of 5 July 2017

Advisory Opinion concerning the recognition in domestic law of a legal parent–child relationship between a child born through a gestational surrogacy arrangement abroad and the intended mother [GC], request no. P16–2018–001, French Court of Cassation, 10 April 2019

GERMANY

Verwaltungsgericht München 1.6.2006 – M 2 K 05.1595

REPUBLIC OF SOUTH AFRICA

Minister of Home Affairs and Another v Fourie and Another (CCT 60/04) [2005] ZACC 19

Lesbian and Gay Equality Project and Others v Minister of Home Affairs and Others [2005] ZACC 19

TAIWAN

Judicial Yuan Interpretation No. 748 of 24 May 2017

THE NETHERLANDS

Hoge Raad case no 463, 181.1980, Nederlands Jurisprudentie 1980, 1460

UNITED KINGDOM

Radmacher v Granatino [2010] UKSC 42

In Re E (A Child) (Care Proceedings: European Dimension) Practice Note [2014] EWHC 6 (Fam).

Re HA (A Child) (Brussels IIA Art. 15) [2015] EWHC 1310 (Fam).

Re J (Children) (Brussels II Revised: Article 15) [2016] UKSC 15

Re TT and YY [2019] EWHC 2384, 25 September 2019

R *(McConnell and YY) v Registrar General* [2020] EWCA Civ 559, 29 April 2020

USA

Obergefell v Hodges (576 U.S. _ (2015))

Table of Legislation

REGULATIONS

Council Regulation (EEC) No 1612/68 of 15 October 1968 on freedom of movement for workers within the Community [1968] OJ L257/2

Council Regulation (EC) No 1347/2000 of 29 May 2000 on jurisdiction and the recognition and enforcement of judgments in matrimonial matters and in matters of parental responsibility for children of both spouses [2000] OJ L160/1

Council Regulation (EC) No 2201/2003 of 27 November 2003 concerning jurisdiction and the recognition and enforcement of judgments in matrimonial matters and the matters of parental responsibility [2003] OJ L338/1

Council Regulation (EC, Euratom) No 723/2004 of 22 March 2004 amending the Staff Regulations of officials of the European Communities and the Conditions of Employment of other servants of the European Communities [2004] OJ L124/1

Regulation (EC) No 883/2004 of the European Parliament and of the Council of 29 April 2004 on the coordination of social security systems [2004] OJ L166/1

Regulation (EU) No 492/2011 of the European Parliament and of the Council of 5 April 2011 on freedom of movement for workers within the Union [2011] OJ L141/1

Regulation (EU) No 604/2013 of the European Parliament and of the Council of 26 June 2013 establishing the criteria and mechanisms for determining the Member State responsible for examining an application for international protection lodged in one of the Member States by a third-country national or a stateless person (recast) [2013] OJ L180/31

Regulation (EU) No 1303/2013 of the European Parliament and of the Council of 17 December 2013 laying down common provisions on the European Regional Development Fund, the European Social Fund, the Cohesion Fund, the European Agricultural Fund for Rural Development and the European Maritime and Fisheries Fund and laying down general provisions on the European Regional Development Fund, the European Social Fund, the Cohesion Fund and the European Maritime and Fisheries Fund and repealing Council Regulation (EC) No 1083/2006 [2013] OJ L347/320

Council Regulation (EU) No 2016/1103 of 24 June 2016 implementing enhanced cooperation in the area of jurisdiction, applicable law and the recognition and enforcement of decisions in matters of matrimonial property regimes [2016] OJ L183/1

Council Regulation (EU) No 2016/1104 of 24 June 2016 implementing enhanced cooperation in the area of jurisdiction, applicable law and the recognition and enforcement of decisions in matters of the property consequences of registered partnerships [2016] OJ L183/30

Council Regulation (EU) No 2019/1111 of 25 June 2019 on jurisdiction, the recognition and enforcement of decisions in matrimonial matters and the matters of parental responsibility and on international child abduction (recast) [2019] OJ L178/1

Regulation (EU, Euratom) No 2020/2092 of the European Parliament and of the Council of 16 December 2020 on a general regime of conditionality for the protection of the Union budget [2020] OJ L433/1

DIRECTIVES

Council Directive 64/221/EEC of 25 February 1964 on the co-ordination of special measures concerning the movement and residence of foreign nationals which are justified on grounds of public policy, public security or public health [1964] OJ L142/24

Council Directive 68/360/EEC of 15 October 1968 on the abolition of restrictions on movement and residence within the Community for workers of Member States and their families [1968] OJ L257/13

Council Directive 73/148/EEC of 21 May 1973 on the abolition of restrictions on movement and residence within the Community for nationals of Member States with regard to establishment and the provision of services [1973] OJ L172/14

Council Directive 75/117/EEC of 10 February 1975 on the approximation of the laws of the Member States relating to the application of the principle of equal pay for men and women [1975] OJ L45/19

Council Directive 79/7/EEC of 19 December 1978 on the progressive implementation of the principle of equal treatment for men and women in matters of social security [1979] OJ L6/24

Council Directive 90/364/EEC of 28 June 1990 on the right of residence [1990] OJ L180/26

Council Directive 90/365/EEC of 28 June 1990 on the right of residence for employees and self-employed persons who have ceased their occupational activity [1990] OJ L180/28

Council Directive 92/85/EEC of 19 October 1992 on the introduction of measures to encourage improvements in the safety and health at work of pregnant workers and workers who have recently given birth or are breastfeeding (tenth individual Directive within the meaning of Article 16 (1) of Directive 89/391/EEC) [1992] OJ L348/1

Council Directive 93/96/EEC of 29 October 1993 on the right of residence for students [1993] OJ L317/59

Directive 2000/31/EC of the European Parliament and of the Council of 8 June 2000 on certain legal aspects of information society services, in particular electronic commerce, in the Internal Market [2000] OJ L178/1

Council Directive 2000/78/EC of 27 November 2000 establishing a general framework for equal treatment in employment and occupation [2000] OJ L303/16

Council Directive 2003/86/EC of 22 September 2003 on the right to family reunification [2003] OJ L251/12

Council Directive 2003/109/EC of 25 November 2003 concerning the status of third-country nationals who are long-term residents [2004] OJ L16/44

Directive 2004/38/EC of the European Parliament and of the Council of 29 April 2004 on the right of citizens of the Union and their family members to move and reside freely within the territory of the Member States [2004] OJ L158/77

Directive 2006/54/EC of the European Parliament and of the Council of 5 July 2006 on the implementation of the principle of equal opportunities and equal treatment of men and women in matters of employment and occupation (recast) [2006] OJ L204/23

Directive 2006/123/EC of the European Parliament and of the Council of 12 December 2006 on services in the internal market [2006] OJ L376/36

Directive 2008/115/EC of the European Parliament and of the Council of 16 December 2008 on common standards and procedures in Member States for returning illegally staying third-country nationals [2008] OJ L348/98

Directive 2010/13/EU of the European Parliament and of the Council of 10 March 2010 on the coordination of certain provisions laid down by law, regulation or administrative action in Member States concerning the provision of audiovisual media services (Audiovisual Media Services Directive) [2010] OJ L95/1

Directive 2011/24/EU of the European Parliament and of the Council of 9 March 2011 on the application of patients' rights in cross-border healthcare [2011] OJ L88/4

Directive 2011/36/EU of the European Parliament and of the Council of 5 April 2011 on preventing and combating trafficking in human beings and protecting its victims, and replacing Council Framework Decision 2002/629/JHA [2011] OJ L101/1

Directive 2011/93/EU of the European Parliament and of the Council of 13 December 2011 on combating the sexual abuse and sexual exploitation of children and child pornography, and replacing Council Framework Decision 2004/68/JHA [2011] OJ L335/1

Directive 2011/95/EU of the European Parliament and of the Council of 13 December 2011 on standards for the qualification of third-country nationals or stateless persons as beneficiaries of international protection, for a uniform status for refugees or for persons eligible for subsidiary protection, and for the content of the protection granted (recast) [2011] OJ L337/9

Directive 2012/29/EU of the European Parliament and of the Council of 25 October 2012 establishing minimum standards on the rights, support and protection of victims of crime, and replacing Council Framework Decision 2001/220/JHA [2012] OJ L315/57

Directive 2013/33/EU of the European Parliament and of the Council of 26 June 2013 laying down standards for the reception of applicants for international protection (recast) [2013] OJ L180/96

Directive 2014/104/EU of the European Parliament and of the Council of 26 November 2014 on certain rules governing actions for damages under national law for infringements of the competition law provisions of the Member States and of the European Union [2014] OJ L349/1

Directive (EU) 2019/1158 of the European Parliament and of the Council of 20 June 2019 on work-life balance for parents and carers and repealing Council Directive 2010/18/EU PE/20/2019/REV/1 [2019] OJ L188/79

DECISIONS

Decision No 779/2007/EC of the European Parliament and of the Council of 20 June 2007 establishing for the period 2007–2013 a specific programme to prevent and combat violence against children, young people and women and to protect victims and groups at risk (Daphne III programme) as part of the General Programme Fundamental Rights and Justice

Council Decision (EU) 2015/1601 of 22 September 2015 establishing provisional measures in the area of international protection for the benefit of Italy and Greece [2015] OJ L248/80

Council Implementing Decision 2022/382 of 4 March 2022 establishing the existence of a mass influx of displaced persons from Ukraine within the meaning of Article 5 of Directive 2001/55/EC, and having the effect of introducing temporary protection [2022] OJ L71/1

EUROPEAN PARLIAMENT RESOLUTIONS

European Parliament Resolution of 18 December 2019 on public discrimination and hate speech against LGBTI people, including LGBTI free zones (2019/2933(RSP))

European Parliament Resolution of 11 March 2021 on the declaration of the EU as an LGBTIQ Freedom Zone (2021/2557(RSP))

Abbreviations

AA	Association Agreement
ART	assisted reproductive technology
AVMSD	Audiovisual Media Services Directive
CJEU	Court of Justice of the European Union
CoE	Council of Europe
CRD	Citizens' Rights Directive
EC	European Community
ECHR	European Convention on Human Rights
ECtHR	European Court of Human Rights
EEA	European Economic Area
EEC	European Economic Community
EFTA	European Free Trade Association
EU	European Union
EUCFR	European Union Charter of Fundamental Rights
MAP	medically assisted procreation
PACS	Pacte civil de solidarité
TCN	third-country national
TEU	Treaty on European Union
TFEU	Treaty on the Functioning of the European Union
UK	United Kingdom
UN	United Nations

1

Introduction

ALINA TRYFONIDOU AND MARJA-LIISA ÖBERG

1.1 THE 'FAMILY' AND THE LAW

The strong personal and societal relevance of 'The Family' has led to an iconic status in popular and 'official' discourses'.[1] On an individual plane, for most people, their family is the most important aspect of their life.[2] The questions that the interaction of law and the family give rise to are, thus, of enormous importance to the society as well as to the individual.[3] Considering two or more persons as constituting a family opens for them the door to a host of significant rights and privileges. Those groups of persons that have been denied the status of a family are not only refused the same rights and privileges but often face an additional stigma that is attached to relationships which have not received the stamp of approval of a 'familial relationship'.

Yet, despite its importance, there is no official or universal definition for the concept of 'family' in either its social or legal dimensions. In both contexts, variability and indeterminacy are its main characteristics.[4] The lack of an overarching definition reflecting a 'readily available and identifiable social construction of "family" to underpin' the law's understanding of this term has had crucial repercussions for the development of family law.[5] As noted by Herring, 'family' is presently a term that is 'of limited legal significance',[6] as it

1 A. Diduck, *Law's Families* (Cambridge University Press 2003) 1.
2 J. Bernardes, *Family Studies: An Introduction* (Routledge 1997) 1.
3 J. Herring, *Family Law* (Pearson 2021) 1.
4 J. Herring, R. Probert, and S. Gilmore, *Great Debates in Family Law* (Macmillan 2015), ch 1.
5 A. Brown, *What Is the Family of Law? The Influence of the Nuclear Family* (Hart Publishing 2019) 21.
6 Herring (n 3) 3.

is rarely used in national and international legal instruments.[7] In most instances, legal texts employ terms that denote a familial relationship (e.g. 'marriage', 'parent', 'child', 'descendant'), to determine whether individuals can derive rights or entitlements as a result of the relationship they maintain with another person. The courts are, therefore, more concerned with the interpretation of these terms than with determining the meaning of the notion of 'family'. Nonetheless, this does not detract from the continuing importance of the notion of 'family', which still determines the circle of the bearers of various rights: to this day, in many instances persons acquire and maintain certain rights only through their status as a family member of someone else.

Due to the fact that the social and legal understandings of the 'family' are directly influenced by the moral, religious, social, and political factors prevailing in a specific society, and given that these factors vary among different societies, there is great diversity in the family law systems around the world. This diversity is prevalent even within continents and regions which are considered rather homogeneous in political and social terms.[8] In fact, it is, exactly, because of this 'native character' that is imbued in the notion of the 'family' and – by extension – family law, that the latter has been considered an unsuitable subject for unification.[9]

Because the understanding of the 'family' is deeply influenced by the moral, religious, social, and political factors prevailing in each society, family law needs to keep abreast of the changes that take place with regard to these factors. Societal changes and medical advances affect the characteristics of today's families as well as put existing family law structures under considerable pressure. As noted by Scherpe:

> [t]oday we live in a world where marriages often end in divorce, where an increasing number of children grow up in families that do not conform to the 'traditional' view of what a family is; where categories of gender are not as fixed as they used to be; where persons legally classified as men can give birth to

[7] An exception to this is Article 8 of the European Convention on Human Rights (ECHR) which grants to individuals, inter alia, the right to respect for family life. In cases where this aspect of Article 8 ECHR is relied on, the European Court of Human Rights (ECtHR) is required to determine whether two or more persons enjoy 'family life' which means, essentially, whether they constitute a family, to be able to be covered by the protection offered by this provision.

[8] An obvious example that springs to mind here is the comparison in their approach towards same-sex marriage between Canada and the United States as well as the different approaches to this matter that could be observed within the United States, prior to the ruling in *Obergefell v Hodges* (576 U.S. _ (2015)).

[9] W. Müller-Freienfels, 'The unification of family law' (1968) 16 The American Journal of Comparative Law 175.

> children; where some persons are not legally classified as male or female; where children are not necessarily genetically related to (all) their legal parents and indeed may have three genetic parents, and even more social parents.[10]

Yet, as rightly explained by another commentator, '[t]he concepts of the law and the family do not seamlessly interact with one another',[11] as 'law is a clumsy tool for managing complex family problems'.[12] Accordingly, one of the greatest challenges for lawmakers is to recognise that family law needs to have moveable boundaries and that its goals should change over time to reflect and accommodate the lived realities of the families that it regulates. This creates significant tension by definition as it clashes with 'the law's desire for clarity and certainty'.[13]

Family law and the regulation of matters concerning families often have an impact on the human rights of individuals. While the legislator can and should take into account the moral, religious, social, and political factors prevailing in the society where a new piece of legislation affecting family relationships will apply, it must make sure that this will not result in a majority trumping the human rights of individuals who belong to vulnerable groups such as the members – or persons associated with members – of sexual or other minorities. In particular, as the European Court of Human Rights (ECtHR) has recently pointed out in a ruling concerning the legal recognition of same-sex relationships, '[t]he Court has consistently declined to endorse policies and decisions which embodied a predisposed bias on the part of a heterosexual majority against a homosexual minority'.[14] This demonstrates that the signatories to the European Convention on Human Rights (ECHR), which include all European Union (EU) Member States, are no longer bound by a mere negative obligation to refrain from interfering in the family lives of their citizens without justification. They are also bound by a positive obligation to respect and protect the family rights of individuals even if to do so requires them to ignore ingrained prejudice and stereotypical thinking on the part of the majority population.[15] Hence, the rights of individuals

[10] J. M. Scherpe, 'Breaking the existing paradigms of parent–child relationships' in G. Douglas, M. Murch, and V. Stephens (eds), *International and National Perspectives on Child and Family Law: Essays in Honour of Nigel Lowe* (Intersentia 2018) 344.

[11] Brown (n 5) 3.

[12] F. Kaganas and S. Day Sclater, 'Contact disputes: Narrative constructions of "good" parents' (2004) 12 Feminist Legal Studies 1, 6.

[13] Brown (n 5) 5.

[14] *Maymulakhin and Markiv v Ukraine*, Application no 75135/14, para 62.

[15] For an analysis of the positive obligations that the ECHR imposes on its signatory States with regard to, inter alia, the family rights that sexual minorities enjoy, see A. Tryfonidou, 'Positive state obligations under European law: A tool for achieving substantive equality for sexual minorities in Europe' (2020) 13 Erasmus Law Review 98.

that belong to families that do not conform to what is perceived to be the 'traditional family' in a certain society can no longer be side-stepped or, worse, violated, merely because the majority of the population ignores or condemns such families.

Having made these preliminary points regarding the concept of 'family' and its position in the law, we shall now proceed to place this discussion in the particular legal context with which this volume is concerned, namely, the EU legal framework.

1.2 THE 'FAMILY' UNDER EU LAW

The individual has been subject to extensive regulation in EU law. Initially, the focus was on the individual as the migrant economic actor,[16] since 1993 on the individual as the Union citizen,[17] and, more recently, on the individual as simply the bearer and enforcer of rights stemming directly from EU law. Nonetheless, as Scherpe reminds us in the Epilogue in this volume, the EU still does not have legislative competence in the area of family law, and it probably never will. The absence of EU legislative competence in the substantive[18] family law field has resulted in the relegation of the regulation of family relationships to the national level; however, national family laws need to be interpreted and applied in line with EU law in situations that fall within the scope of the latter.[19] The EU has, therefore, only been concerned with regulating family relationships in situations that come within the scope of EU

16 See, for instance, the essays in F. G. Jacobs (ed), *European Law and the Individual* (North Holland 1976).

17 There is a very long list of books and articles focusing on the status of a Union citizen. See, inter alia, S. O'Leary, *The Evolving Concept of Community Citizenship: From the Free Movement of Persons to Union Citizenship* (Kluwer 1996); the essays in D. Kochenov (ed), *EU Citizenship and Federalism: The Role of Rights* (Cambridge University Press 2017); F. Goudappel, *The Effects of EU Citizenship* (T. M. C. Asser Press 2010); E. Guild, C. J. Gortázar Rotaeche, and D. Kostakopoulou (eds), *The Reconceptualization of European Union Citizenship* (Brill Nijhoff 2014); J. Shaw, *The Transformation of Citizenship in the European Union* (Cambridge University Press 2007); H. Van Eijken, *EU Citizenship and the Constitutionalisation of the European Union* (Europa Law Publishing 2015).

18 As opposed to the procedural law field. It is well established that the Union does not have competence in the (substantive) family law field. However, Article 81(3) of the Treaty on the Functioning of the EU gives to the EU the competence to adopt measures 'concerning family law with cross-border implications'. This provision has been used as a legal base for a long list of private international family law measures. See C. Honorati and M. C. Baruffi, *EU Private International Law in Family Matters: Legislation and CJEU Case Law* (Intersentia 2022).

19 This has been reiterated by the Court of Justice of the EU (CJEU) in a number of its judgments. See, inter alia, Case C-267/12 *Hay* EU:C:2013:823, para 26; Case C-147/08 *Römer* EU:C:2011:286, para 38; and, most prominently, in Case C-673/16 *Coman and others*

law and where some other issue which falls within EU competence (e.g. in the areas of free movement, anti-discrimination, migration, and asylum) is predominant.

Thus, the notion of 'family' assumes relevance for EU law only as an auxiliary of the rights that Union citizens or – as explained by Öberg in Chapter 5 in this volume – third-country nationals (TCNs) derive from EU law. After all, there is no 'EU family law'.[20] Ultimately, it is the individual legal instruments adopted by the EU legislature in different policy areas (e.g. EU free movement law or anti-discrimination law) as well as the jurisprudence of the Court of Justice of the EU (CJEU) in those areas that demarcate the contours of the concept of 'family' (or, mainly, of related concepts) for the purposes of EU law. The legal understanding of 'family' has, thus, not been constructed in a systematic, structured, fashion. Rather, in EU law the notion 'family' has developed on an ad hoc basis determined by the main aims of the individual legislative instruments that (often implicitly) take this notion as a point of reference, and by the range of cases that have happened to reach the Court. As explained by Barbou des Places in this volume, there is, therefore, not a uniform category or definition of 'family' in EU legal norms but rather different conceptions of the 'family' for the purposes of different EU policy areas.

In recent years, increasing focus has been directed towards the way EU law addresses diverse family constellations in its laws and policies and how it manages the interaction of different national family law regimes in situations which fall within the EU's scope of application. In particular, there is significant uncertainty and controversy concerning the extent of the influence that EU law can – and should – have on the regulation of family-related matters, especially with respect to non-traditional family constellations that have often been ignored or condemned by the law. A plethora of complicated questions involving family-related matters have reached the CJEU concerning issues such as abortion, same-sex relationships, and surrogacy.[21] This has meant that the Court has been faced with the unenviable task of needing to carve out a

EU:C:2018:385, paras 37–38, and Case C-490/20 *V.M.A. v Stolichna obshtina, rayon 'Pancharevo'* EU:C:2021:1008, para 52.

20 For a detailed consideration of the long-term prospects for the development of EU family law, see C. McGlynn, *Families and the European Union: Law, Politics and Pluralism* (Cambridge University Press 2006), ch 7.

21 For an analysis, see, inter alia, N. Koffeman, *Morally Sensitive Issues and Cross-Border Movement in the EU: The Cases of Reproductive Matters and Legal Recognition of Same-Sex Relationships* (Intersentia 2015); F. Fabbrini, *Fundamental Rights in Europe: Challenges and Transformations in Comparative Perspectives* (Oxford University Press 2014), ch 5; A. Tryfonidou, 'Surrogacy in the ECHR and the European institutions' in K. Trimmings,

solution that can be equally welcomed – or, more accurately, tolerated – by all Member States. Although, as argued by Tryfonidou in this volume (see Chapter 2), EU law now recognises more family forms as 'family' than it did in the 1950s and 1960s, the influence of the nuclear family model[22] is still prevalent and thus, to this day, EU law does not sufficiently correspond to the individual and societal demands of contemporary family life as it continues to conceptualise all families through the prism of the nuclear family.[23]

It is of course true that challenges to the Court's upholding of the traditional nuclear family ideal have emerged in recent years with the adoption of the EU Charter of Fundamental Rights (EUCFR or 'the Charter')[24] and the case law of the CJEU. More specifically, recent rulings of the latter, such as *Coman* (2018)[25] and V.M.A. (2021)[26] – which are extensively analysed in this volume by Willems (Chapter 9) and Bogdan (Chapter 7) – confirm the path towards a more liberal view of the 'family' in the EU. However, the steps on this path have been taken rather diffidently. For instance, although the CJEU recognised in *Coman* that the term 'spouse' includes, for the purposes of Directive 2004/38,[27] the same-sex spouse of a Union citizen who has exercised free movement rights, it has emphasised throughout the judgment

S. Shakargy, and C. Achmad (eds), *Research Handbook on Surrogacy and the Law* (Edward Elgar Publishing 2024).

22 For an analysis of the historical and philosophical underpinnings of the nuclear family model, see Brown (n 5), ch 2.

23 For similar arguments, see Brown (n 5) 41–43; McGlynn (n 20); C. McGlynn, 'The Europeanisation of family law' (2001) 13 Child and Family Law Quarterly 35, 47; L. Woods, 'Family rights in the EU – Disadvantaging the disadvantaged?' (1999) 11 Child and Family Law Quarterly 17.

24 Charter of Fundamental Rights of the European Union [2012] OJ C 326/291.

25 See n 19. For an analysis, see, inter alia, J. J. Rijpma, 'You gotta let love move: ECJ 5 June 2018, Case C-673/16, *Coman, Hamilton, Accept v. Inspectoratul General pentru Imigrări*' (2019) 15 European Constitutional Law Review 324; A. Tryfonidou, 'The ECJ recognises the right of same-sex spouses to move freely between EU Member States: The *Coman* ruling' (2019) European Law Review 663; D. V. Kochenov and U. Belavusau, 'After the celebration: Marriage equality in EU law post-Coman in eight questions and some further thoughts' (2020) 27 Maastricht Journal of European and Comparative Law 549.

26 See n 19. For an analysis, see, inter alia, A. Tryfonidou, 'The ECJ recognises the right of rainbow families to move freely between EU Member States: The V.M.A. ruling' (2022) 47 European Law Review 534; D. Thienpont and G. Willems, 'Le droit à la libre circulation des familles homoparentales consacré par la Cour de justice de l'Union européenne' (2022) 132 Revue trimestrielle des droits de l'homme 925; L. Bracken, 'Recognition of LGBTQI+ parent families across European borders' (2022) 29 Maastricht Journal of European and Comparative Law 399.

27 Directive 2004/38/EC of the European Parliament and of the Council of 29 April 2004 on the right of citizens of the Union and their family members to move and reside freely within the territory of the Member States [2004] OJ L158/77.

that the cross-border recognition of (same-sex) marriages is required by EU law *only* for the purpose of granting EU family reunification rights to Union citizens who move. This means that once a married same-sex couple has established residency in the receiving Member State, EU law currently leaves them at the mercy of national law. Similarly, in *V.M.A.*, the CJEU held that the Member States are required to recognise the parenthood of the children of same-sex couples as established in another EU Member State, but this obligation is only imposed for the purpose of enabling Union citizens to exercise their free movement rights.

As noted by Petursson, Groussot, and Loxa in their chapter in this volume, CJEU case law, such as *Ruiz Zambrano*[28] and *Carpenter*,[29] provides evidence of the Court's 'timid use' of the provisions of the EUCFR to advance the protection of family life[30] in situations falling within the scope of EU law. The Court prefers to conclude that there is a violation of provisions within one of the 'core' policy areas of EU law (such as free movement, Union citizenship, or anti-discrimination law), rather than to establish a violation of fundamental human rights stemming from the Charter. If at all,[31] the Charter is usually only examined as a side issue forming part of the justification assessment at the end of the judgment. Yet, there is a silver lining in that. As argued by Albors-Llorens in her chapter in this volume, the principle of effective judicial protection laid down in Article 47 of the Charter has been effectively used by the CJEU in its case law involving the enforcement of the guarantees offered by EU law to Union citizens thereby achieving a higher standard of protection.

The above paragraphs demonstrate that when the CJEU has chosen to depart from the traditional nuclear family model, it has been anxious to emphasise the lack of EU competence – and the deference it shows to Member States – in the family law field. Being wary of possible accusations of exceeding the limits to its jurisdiction and of imposing its own views in relation to an area that is considered so close to the heart of the Member States and in which the latter zealously guard their policy autonomy, the CJEU has ensured that in situations which do not fall within the scope of EU law, Member States remain free to determine what types of relationship qualify as

[28] Case C-34/09 *Ruiz Zambrano* EU:C:2011:124.

[29] Case C-60/00 *Carpenter* EU:C:2002:434.

[30] For an analysis of the approach to the interpretation of the right to family life under EU law, see the essays in M. González Pascual and A. Torres Pérez (eds), *The Right to Family Life in the European Union* (Routledge 2018).

[31] In *Ruiz Zambrano* (n 28), the question of compliance with fundamental human rights was not examined at all.

familial ones. In turn, this means that the Member States' family laws remain widely divergent, as the issues they touch upon reflect historically, culturally, and ethically distinctive understandings of family composition and family life. This can be problematic, especially when, as argued by Lamont in this volume (Chapter 11), these differences are ignored by the EU legislature when it takes action to respond to problems in the family law field which have emerged or have become exacerbated as a result of the process of EU integration. Although the finding of a common EU approach is certainly difficult, it is nonetheless imperative due to the close connection of family matters with a number of core EU policies.

The same deference that has been exercised by the EU institutions and judiciary has, indeed, been shown by other international or regional organisations and courts when faced with the need to define the notion of 'family'. The ECtHR, for example, has recognised in its case law that same-sex couples with or without children can enjoy 'family life' and, thus, constitute a family.[32] Although this court has confirmed in its recent case law that *all* signatory States to the ECHR have a positive obligation stemming from Article 8 ECHR to introduce a status through which same-sex relationships will be legally recognised, it has nonetheless refrained from touching the hot potato of same-sex marriage. Instead, the ECtHR has ruled that under the current circumstances, the ECHR does not impose an obligation on States to introduce same-sex marriage in their territory.[33] Similarly, as is seen in Chapter 10 by Margaria in this volume, the ECtHR has ruled that the ECHR signatory States are obliged, when certain conditions are satisfied, to recognise the parent–child relationship between surrogate-born children and their intended parents as legally established in another country. Yet the same court has completely refrained from ruling on whether States should, in the first place, allow surrogacy in their territory and, if yes, how they should regulate it, given that it is a very controversial and, thus, delicate issue that falls squarely within the domain of national family law.

Accordingly, as argued by Archard in this volume (Chapter 3), there appears to be a general acknowledgement that different societies define what counts as a family and its members in different ways, and this is, to a great extent, respected by international and supranational organisations, including the EU. Nonetheless, as Palazzo explains in Chapter 12, recent developments

[32] *Schalk and Kopf v Austria*, Application no 30141/04, para 94; and *Gas and Dubois v France*, Application no 25951/07, para 32.

[33] *Oliari and Others v Italy*, Application nos 18766/11 and 36030/11; *Fedotova and Others v Russia*, Application nos 40792/10, 30538/14, and 43439/14; *Maymulakhin and Markiv v Ukraine* (n 14).

allow us to be hopeful that the constitutional relevance of the family can be increased in the EU in ways that could hardly have been predicted in the past, specifically by starting to include non-traditional families within the controversial area of the EU's common values. Hence, it is important to remember that although the EU does not have the competence to promulgate legislation in the substantive family law field and thus to harmonise the substantive family laws of the Member States, it nonetheless plays an important role in influencing the family laws and policies of the Member States. This is due to the fact that the instances in which the Union, mostly through its judiciary, will be called to take a stance on politically charged and controversial questions regarding familial ties and relationships are bound to increase, along with the expansion of the scope of application of EU law.

1.3 OVERVIEW OF THE BOOK

This edited volume results partly from the workshop 'The Family in EU Law', held on 1 and 2 July 2021, which explored how a family – a traditionally private-law governed institution – functions in the EU's supranational context and interacts with different legal regimes. This topic was first systematically explored by Clare McGlynn in her groundbreaking book *Families and the European Union* which was published in 2006.[34] As explained by Scherpe in the Epilogue of this volume, 'Much has happened since McGlynn's 2006 book, but some things have not changed.' The aim of this volume, therefore, is to provide an updated and comprehensive account of the concept of 'family' in EU law and its role in regulating relationship and shaping policies in Europe from the perspective of various legal and non-legal disciplines – philosophy, EU law, private international law, migration law, constitutional law, human rights law, comparative family law, and social anthropology. The result is an exciting mix of doctrinal and theoretical approaches which uncover the multitude of preconditions and determinants for family life under EU law. It must be acknowledged that the book does not – and cannot – exhaustively consider the role of the family in the EU nor does it attempt to offer a conclusive answer to the question of what constitutes a family under EU law. Nonetheless, we hope that the book will help stimulate thinking around the definition and role of one of the most fascinating, dynamic, and multifaceted concepts in contemporary national, European, and international law.

34 McGlynn (n 20).

The volume explores the family in EU law from four different angles. The first part of the book (Chapters 2–5) considers the philosophical and theoretical foundations of the family in law in general, and EU law in particular, including the definition of the family under EU law. The second part of the book (Chapters 6–8) provides an overview of the rights conferred upon the family by Union law and assesses whether these cater to the needs of all families (whether these are recognised as 'families' for the purposes of EU law or not). The third part of the book (Chapters 9 and 10) examines the EU family from the perspective of family diversity in comparison with the ECHR. Finally, the fourth part of the book (Chapters 11 and 12) offers insights into how EU law deals with some situations of crisis that are faced by families in the EU.

Part I of the volume opens with Chapter 2 by Alina Tryfonidou, which explores the questions of what is a 'family' in EU law and whether EU policies sufficiently address family diversity and its consequences. The chapter departs from the premise that the prevalence of the nuclear family model has traditionally meant that the only valid form of family in EU law was one consisting of an adult man and an adult woman who live together in a single-state context and produce their own biological children. This model is, also, based on the sexual division of labour: the man is the main breadwinner, whilst the woman is the homemaker. Nonetheless, in recent years, there is growing evidence of diversity in family forms. Moreover, there is an increasing departure from the traditional sexual division of labour. Although many EU Member States are already acknowledging this changing landscape of family life in their law and policy, the important question – for the purposes of this book – is whether the EU has been influenced by this: does EU law now sufficiently address family diversity and its consequences? This is the main question that is analysed in this chapter by examining the concept of 'family' employed across a spectrum of fields of substantive EU law.

Chapter 3 by David Archard explores, again, the notion of 'family', albeit from a philosophical perspective. Archard's point of departure is that EU family law recognises that there is such a thing as the family and that it does merit special legal protection. At the same time, there is an acknowledgment that different societies define what counts as a family, and its members, in different ways. He explains that the changes in family forms over the last hundred years have led some to argue 'the family' no longer exists, and, moreover, that it is not special. Archard, however, reviews and criticises those arguments, demonstrating that there can be a single concept of 'the family' and that the diversity of whatever falls under the concept does not of itself invalidate the continued usage of 'family' as a concept. The chapter argues that giving a special legal status to the family requires being satisfactorily able to define what it is, and offers a defence of a 'functional' definition. Archard then considers ways in which the family – as defined – might be thought uniquely valuable, critically reviewing appeals to the goods it provides and emphasising the key public good of families in rearing children. Archard's conclusion is that the probable impossibility of unifying EU family law does not mean that it is inconsistent to argue that a single concept of family encompasses many different national forms and that the family, in its diversity, continues to merit a special legal status.

In Chapter 4, Ségolène Barbou des Places, too, focuses on an exploration of the definition of the notion of 'family' but from an EU law perspective. The chapter first acknowledges the variable geometry of the family, and the absence of a uniform category of 'family' in EU legal norms. The chapter then shows that, despite the fragmentation of sources and the modulation of family circles, the way in which the EU characterises a person as a 'family member' obeys a form of logic and expresses a certain rationality. Borrowing from the work of Morgan[35] and his notion of 'doing family', the chapter demonstrates that in addition to the de jure family members, other persons are counted as family members on the basis of them 'behaving' like family members. Barbou des Places concludes that 'family members' is a defined category of EU law: it designates the groups of people who are assumed to perform – or asked to prove that they do perform – different functions like education, care, protection, and socialisation. It is subsequently emphasised that these roles are central because they contribute to a broader ambition, namely, participating in the cohesion of the whole of European society.

Part I of the volume is rounded off by Chapter 5 by Marja-Liisa Öberg, which takes as its point of departure the EU's close cooperation with third countries, especially in the EU's neighbourhood, which has erased a number of perceived boundaries between the EU and non-Member States. Whereas within the EU, family members are largely considered as natural beneficiaries of the free movement of persons with ensuing residence and social rights, it is less clear whether the same undisputed status of a family also applies beyond the EU's borders. The EU has concluded a number of association agreements with countries in its neighbourhood which comprise, to varying degrees, access to the EU's internal market including the free movement of workers. The *Polydor* doctrine of the CJEU has, however, established that similarly worded provisions in the EU Treaties and cooperation agreements concluded with third countries do not guarantee identical interpretation. With a focus on

[35] D. H. J. Morgan, *Family Connections* (Polity Press 1996).

Turkey, the European Economic Area, and the United Kingdom, the chapter analyses the conception of family and related rights in the EU's cooperation instruments, with an aim to establish to what extent non-EU families can be considered 'EU families'.

Part II of the book comprises three chapters, which focus on the different rights that families enjoy under EU law and their enforcement.

Chapter 6 by Xavier Groussot, Gunnar Thor Petursson, and Alezini Loxa begins by explaining that family rights have been protected under EU law long before the adoption of the Charter. In particular, the chapter argues that the CJEU consolidated the protection of family life through a free movement rationale, guided by the need to eliminate obstacles to the exercise of the fundamental freedoms guaranteed by the Treaty. The chapter then focuses on investigating how family rights are protected under EU law *today*. The authors first analyse the horizontal provisions of the Charter and how they can affect both the extent of protection and the substance of family rights. Subsequently, they look at how family rights have appeared in the Court's case law. Finally, the authors consider the interaction of family rights with the EU citizenship provisions. Exploring the connection between fundamental rights, free movement, and EU citizenship, the chapter concludes by signalling the timid use of Charter provisions to advance the protection of family life.

Chapter 7 by Michael Bogdan offers an elaborate analysis of three recent cases by the CJEU in the context of EU free movement law. The cases deal with the questions of whether and to what extent the EU Member States are obliged to accept a family status created abroad even when it is incompatible with their own family law (such as same-sex marriage and same-sex parenthood) or is a status totally unknown in their legal system (such as the Islamic *kafala*). Bogdan's argument is that the main approach chosen by the CJEU regarding same-sex marriage and same-sex parenthood created abroad, obliging the Member States to recognise them *for the purpose of free movement only*, may give rise to practical problems.

In Chapter 8, Albertina Albors-Llorens looks at the enforcement of the rights of free movement and residence provided by the Citizens' Rights Directive (Directive 2004/38) to Union citizens and their family members. In particular, the chapter examines the enforcement of these rights by members of the 'family' of the EU citizen – both 'core' members and 'other' family members according to the distinction created by the Directive under Articles 2(2) and 3(2), respectively – and, in particular, at how the CJEU has extended the application of the principle of effective judicial protection to these situations. This principle has been present in EU law since the early case law of the CJEU and is now entrenched in primary EU legislation in

Article 47 of the Charter but, in most areas of EU law, it has been interpreted in relation to the enforcement of substantive EU rights by the primary holders of these rights, that is, Union citizens. Albors-Llorens explains that Directive 2004/38 adds a different dimension to this by regulating the conditions that apply to the substantive rights that their family members *derive* from EU citizens and correspondingly introducing the necessity of effective legal protection of these rights. In a collection that seeks to explore the role of the 'family' in EU Law, this chapter specifically seeks to contribute an examination of how the guarantee of effective legal protection has taken hold in the interpretation of the provisions of the Directive as applied to family members.

Part III of the book examines questions of family diversity in EU law and the ECHR.

It begins with Chapter 9 by Geoffrey Willems offering an elaborate analysis of the position of same-sex couples and homoparental families under the ECHR and EU law. Addressing issues such as marriage and partnerships, parenthood and parental responsibility, but also social benefits, family reunification, and the legal recognition of family ties established abroad, the chapter takes the view that the recognition and protection of family relationships can follow multiple paths and that the ECtHR case law and EU law are mutually reinforcing for the benefit of the rights of same-sex couples and their children. It also acknowledges that subsidiarity considerations lead European bodies to favour a compromise approach, refraining from forcing states to abandon their traditional conception of family law's fundamental institutions: marriage and parenthood. The chapter, nevertheless, suggests that, at some point in the future, the increased visibility and legitimacy of same-sex couples and homoparental families should ultimately lead to imposing a European and inclusive understanding of these institutions.

In Chapter 10, Alice Margaria explores the approach of the European supranational courts towards one of the most controversial issues in the area of family law: surrogacy. The chapter focuses on the surrogacy case law of the CJEU and ECtHR to unravel the understanding of motherhood endorsed by the two judiciaries. It shows that legal motherhood continues to be tied to gestation and birth, thus placing intended mothers in a precarious legal position, especially compared to intended (genetic) fathers. As part of its effort to explain this gender imbalance, the chapter uses the experience of surrogacy as a window for a broader discussion on the gender of legal fictions governing the attribution of parenthood. Whilst the rule *mater semper certa est* remains one of the most immutable facts of European family laws, legal systems have generally demonstrated a certain flexibility and attention to context in determining legal fatherhood, at times departing from the marital presumption.

Margaria argues that this different attitude reflects a long-standing socio-legal fear of disaggregating motherhood, not only from gestation but also from care, in line with the gendered and higher expectations that legal systems have towards legal mothers if compared to legal fathers.

Part IV of the volume, which comprises two chapters, is devoted to a consideration of how EU law deals with situations of crisis faced by families.

In Chapter 11, Ruth Lamont explores the use by the Member States, of the EU private international family law rules designed to provide for the uniform assumption of jurisdiction over cross-border disputes, in the protection of children with links abroad from abuse or neglect by their family through the national child protection system. These measures include rules governing the assumption of jurisdiction over the parental responsibility of a child, including both private and public law measures. The chapter argues that the abused and neglected child was not a central focus when regulating the cross-border family and, as a consequence, legal borders between Member States' family law systems retain considerable significance for these children. Whilst each Member State has provision in place for public law child protection measures, the methods and approach adopted vary significantly between legal systems. The substantive outcomes for children in managing the risk posed by abuse may, thus, be significantly different, but the EU's private international family law rules are designed to obscure and ignore these differences and this has presented difficulties in supporting cross-national cooperation over the protection of a child. The political nature of these decisions has meant that the focus on the welfare of the child may consequently be lost in the management of public law proceedings between Member States.

Chapter 12 by Nausica Palazzo focuses on the role of the family in European culture wars. It analyses the ideological usage of the family by illiberal actors in Poland and Hungary and the EU's reaction to this kind of illiberal erosion. The chapter argues that recent developments seem to hold potential to increase the constitutional relevance of the family in the EU in ways that could hardly be predicted, by beginning to attract the (LGBTQ) family in the controversial area of the EU's common values. Palazzo claims that looking at the role of family in similar European culture wars and how it reflects on the constitutional relevance of the family in EU law is essential for understanding the contemporary movement.

The book concludes with an Epilogue (Chapter 13), written by Jens M. Scherpe. Using the changing legal bases for divorce, this chapter first canvasses how the traditional dividing lines between the so-called 'progressive North', consisting of predominantly protestant jurisdictions, and the 'conservative South' with predominantly catholic populations have faded away in family law – only to be replaced by a new dividing line between Eastern and Western European jurisdictions regarding the recognition of same-sex relationships and same-sex families. It then discusses whether 'the family' is part of the 'European Way of Life', proclaimed by the European Commission – headed by President Ursula von der Leyen – as one of the policy and strategy aims the EU should promote. However, the understandings of what a 'family' is still differ greatly within Europe, especially with regard to same-sex families, creating significant tensions. These tensions manifest, in particular, when the CJEU or the ECtHR pass down decisions which mandate the recognition of family forms, at least on specific issues, creating elements of an institutional European Family Law. The chapter concludes by expressing the hope that in the long term the tensions between different conceptions of family can be resolved within the existing frameworks in Europe and that a family in one country will also be a family in all other European countries.

PART I

The Family in EU Law: Concept and Context

2

What Is a 'Family' in EU Law?

Do EU Policies Sufficiently Address Family Diversity and Its Consequences?

ALINA TRYFONIDOU

2.1 INTRODUCTION

The family is recognised in national laws and international human rights and other instruments as being a fundamental group in society deserving of protection. It has no official or universal definition – it means different things to different people and meets different needs for different people.[1] Moreover, the concept of 'family' is not common across geographical spaces and its social and cultural understandings are constantly shifting – it is a 'highly elastic and changeable form'.[2] Accordingly, it is difficult – if not impossible – to provide a single, universal, definition for the notion of 'family' that encompasses the variety of relationships and forms of contemporary family life,[3] and, as noted by another commentator, 'we can never be quite sure what family means unless we can understand the context in which it is used'.[4]

This is the case even in the context of the European Union (EU).[5] Despite the fact that the EU Member States share some common values,[6] when it

[1] A. Diduck, *Law's Families* (Cambridge University Press 2003) 1.

[2] E. Leeder, *The Family in Global Perspective: A Gendered Journey* (Sage 2004), ch 1.

[3] A. Diduck and F. Kaganas, *Family Law, Gender and the State* (Hart Publishing 2012), ch 1.

[4] S. Coltrane, *Gender and Families* (Rowman & Littlefield 1998) 5. For an analysis of the concept of 'the family', see Chapter 3 by David Archard.

[5] It should be noted that, for ease of reference, the umbrella terms 'EU' and 'EU law' will be used throughout the chapter, even when referring to periods preceding the establishment of the EU in 1993.

[6] Article 2 of the Treaty on European Union (TEU) provides, 'The Union is founded on the values of respect for human dignity, freedom, democracy, equality, the rule of law and respect for human rights, including the rights of persons belonging to minorities. These values are common to the Member States in a society in which pluralism, non-discrimination, tolerance, justice, solidarity and equality between women and men prevail.'

comes to the question of what constitutes a 'family', there appears to be great divergence among them, especially with regard to specific matters such as same-sex relationships, cohabitation, registered partnerships, and parenting in situations which do not involve a man and a woman who are married and who are both biologically connected to their child(ren). It is not surprising, therefore, that family law and matters that touch on family life are areas that remain tightly controlled by the Member States, as the Court of Justice of the EU (CJEU) has repeatedly reminded us in its judgments.[7]

The EU does not have the competence to legislate in the area of family law,[8] and thus, in most instances, it falls on the Member States to determine whether a group of persons constitutes – in law – a family.[9] Nonetheless, there are certain EU legal instruments which require the existence of familial ties to apply or to bestow rights on persons whose situation falls within the scope of EU law. Accordingly, from the early days of the EU's existence, its legislature and judiciary have been confronted with the question of what constitutes a family for the purposes of EU law.

In the EU context, the prevalence of the nuclear family model – in secondary legislation and the case law interpreting it – has traditionally meant that the only valid form of family in EU law was one consisting of an adult male and an adult female who are married and live together in a single-state context and produce their own biological children. This model is also premised on the sexual division of labour: the man is the main breadwinner, whilst the woman is the homemaker.[10] Nonetheless, although this continues to be the 'gold standard' under the law, recent years have witnessed a growing visibility of diverse family forms, which include single-parent families, rainbow families, reconstituted families, and families consisting of more than two adults who together parent their (biological and non-biological) children.[11] There is, also, an increasing departure from the traditional sexual division of

7 See, for instance, Case C-148/02 *Garcia Avello* EU:C:2003:539, para 25; Case C-267/06 *Maruko* EU:C:2008:179, para 59; Case C-443/15 *Parris* EU:C:2016:897, para 59.

8 Apart from measures concerning family law with cross-border implications – see Article 81(3) of the Treaty on the Functioning of the EU (TFEU).

9 For this reason, as Clare McGlynn has noted, 'The Union's regulation of families is piecemeal and ad hoc and the development of family law is in its early stages': C. McGlynn, *Families and the European Union: Law, Politics and Pluralism* (Cambridge University Press 2006) 21.

10 For an explanation of the role of women in this model both in the past and the future (and especially for the purposes of social security), see V. Paskalia, *Free Movement, Social Security and Gender in the EU* (Hart Publishing 2007), ch 2.

11 L. Hodson, 'Ties that bind: Towards a child-centred approach to lesbian, gay, bi-sexual and transgender families under the ECHR' (2012) 20 International Journal of Children's Rights 501, 502. See, also, L. Carlson, L. Sz. Oláh, and B. Hobson, 'Policy recommendations: Changing families and sustainable societies: Policy contexts and diversity over the life course

labour, with women and men often equally engaging in earning as well as caring activities.[12] Moreover, the modern family is often characterised in terms of flux and fluidity. Many families conduct their lives across borders, live under different roofs or, even, in different countries. The above changes can be attributed to a combination of social and other trends, including shifting gender relations, globalisation, evolving employment patterns, and an increased acceptance of conjugal relationships outside marriage as well as of same-sex relationships.[13] Of course, to use the words of Advocate General Geelhoed pronounced twenty-three years ago in his Opinion in *Baumbast*, 'none of these phenomena are really new; it is merely that the intensity with which and the scale on which they now occur have become so considerable that the [EU] legislature must take account of them'.[14]

Some EU Member States are already acknowledging this changing landscape of family life in their law and policy. But has the EU been influenced by this? The aim of this chapter will be to consider whether the EU has remained faithful to the traditional ideology of the nuclear family or whether it has kept pace with recent developments by embracing a notion of the 'family' that is broad enough to encompass all diverse forms of family and goes beyond the male breadwinner / female carer model of heterosexuality. Moreover, I will consider whether the increasing (intra-EU) migration that has been brought about by European integration and – more broadly – the process of globalisation, with the resultant internationalisation of families and family life, has been taken into account by the EU when determining whether a group of persons can be considered a family for the purposes of EU law. To answer the above questions, there will be an examination of the concept of 'family' employed across a spectrum of fields of substantive EU law – free movement law, anti-discrimination law, and immigration law. The chapter does not claim to exhaustively cover all areas of EU law which demonstrate the EU's approach towards the notion of the 'family', nor does it cover the three fields of substantive EU law on which it focuses in their entirety; rather, a few of the most characteristic examples from each of the chosen areas have been

and across generations' (2017) FamiliesAndSocieties project consortium <www.familiesandsocieties.eu/wp-content/uploads/2017/06/WorkingPaper78.pdf>.

12 For a sociological analysis of this, see S. Irwin, 'Resourcing the family: Gendered claims and obligations and issues of explanation' in E. B. Silva and C. Smart (eds), *The New Family?* (Sage 1999).

13 See Opinion of Advocate General Szpunar in Case C-335/17 *Valcheva v Babanarakis* EU:C:2018:242, paras 28 and 29.

14 Opinion of Advocate General Geelhoed in Case C-413/99 *Baumbast and R* EU:C:2001:385, para 26.

selected. The chapter concludes that there is no single, overarching, definition of the family under EU law, but, rather, there are different definitions in different areas of EU law that are – still – underpinned by the traditional nuclear family model which has as its basis heterosexual marriage and genetic parenthood.[15]

2.2 THE TRADITIONAL NUCLEAR FAMILY MODEL UNDER EARLY EU LEGISLATION

The process of European economic integration began in the 1950s, taking the form of three economically orientated Communities.[16] Accordingly, just like with fundamental (human) rights for which the Treaties made no provision simply because it was unlikely that the promulgation and implementation of EU policies would give rise to their breach,[17] the founding Treaties were not concerned at all with the concept of 'family' or any related family rights or entitlements. This was for the simple reason that these were matters that were for the Member States to decide and in relation to which the EU had – and still has – no competence and, back at the time it was thought, no impact.[18]

The first time that EU law made provision for families was in the 1960s, with Regulation 1612/68.[19] The Regulation had as its main aim to bolster the free movement rights that were granted to workers by the European Economic Community (EEC) Treaty. For this purpose, it introduced the notion of 'family reunification', which required the Member State to which a worker moved to *automatically* accept certain of his/her family members within its territory without applying its immigration requirements. Provision for such family reunification rights was subsequently extended to other categories of

[15] See also Chapter 4 by Ségolène Barbou des Places.

[16] For more on the early steps in the history of the EU and, in particular, the creation of the three Communities, see P. Craig and G. de Búrca, *EU Law: Text, Cases and Materials (UK Version)* (Oxford University Press 2020) 3–5. See also L. Van Middelaar, *The Passage to Europe: How a Continent Became a Union* (Yale University Press 2014), ch 4.

[17] R. Schütze, *European Union Law* (Cambridge University Press 2018) 447.

[18] The CJEU still emphasises that family law and important family law questions such as a person's status which is relevant to the rules on marriage and parenthood are matters that fall within Member State competence. See, for instance, Case C-490/20 *V.M.A. v Stolichna obshtina, rayon 'Pancharevo'* EU:C:2021:1008, para 52.

[19] Council Regulation (EEC) No 1612/68 of 15 October 1968 on freedom of movement for workers within the Community [1968] OJ L257/2. Though, Berneri explains that, in fact, the first such piece of legislation was Regulation 15/1961 which was 'the first regulation of a three-step phase that culminated with Regulation 1612/1968/EEC and the full liberalisation of manpower': C. Berneri, *Family Reunification in the EU* (Hart Publishing 2017) 7 and 43.

free movers – the self-employed[20] and, in the 1990s, the economically inactive.[21]

Although the pieces of legislation that followed employed gender-neutral language or inclusive – albeit binary – language (by employing the pronouns 'he' and 'she') when referring to the migrant and his/her family members,[22] the first piece of legislation granting family reunification rights to migrant Member State nationals – Regulation 1612/68 – used the pronoun 'he' throughout when referring to the worker that would be joined by 'his' family. This way, it demonstrated the prevalence of the male breadwinner model.[23] The use of the male pronoun precisely demonstrates that the legislative drafters at the time could not envisage a situation whereby a woman would choose to move between the EU Member States for career purposes and her family would follow. The model treated 'women and children as the non-productive appendages of male workers'.[24] Of course, the Court has interpreted all the instruments providing family reunification rights to migrant Member State nationals (including Regulation 1612/68) as applying to both male and female 'sponsors' of family reunification rights, and, thus, no distinction has been drawn between men and women in the interpretation and application of these instruments.[25]

As regards categories of family members, provision for automatic family reunification rights in all instruments (apart from Directive 93/96, which only granted such rights to the spouse and the dependent children of the migrant Member State national and his/her spouse) was only made between the

[20] Council Directive 73/148/EEC of 21 May 1973 on the abolition of restrictions on movement and residence within the Community for nationals of Member States with regard to establishment and the provision of services [1973] OJ L172/14.

[21] Council Directive 90/364/EEC of 28 June 1990 on the right of residence [1990] OJ L180/26; Council Directive 90/365/EEC of 28 June 1990 on the right of residence for employees and self-employed persons who have ceased their occupational activity [1990] OJ L180/28; Council Directive 93/96/EEC of 29 October 1993 on the right of residence for students [1993] OJ L317/59.

[22] This, obviously, was the case for Directives 73/148 (n 20), 90/364 (n 21), 90/365 (n 21), 93/96 (n 21), but also the more recent Directives (which we shall mention in the next section) 2004/38 (n 45) and 2003/86 (n 46).

[23] G. Milios, 'Defining "family members" of EU citizens and the circumstances under which they can rely on EU law' (2020) Yearbook of European Law 293, 295. See also, I. Moebius and E. Szyszczak, 'Of raising pigs and children' (1998) 18 Yearbook of European Law 125.

[24] L. Ackers and H. Stalford, 'Children, migration and citizenship in the European Union: Intra-community mobility and the status of children in EC law' (1999) 21 Children and Youth Services Review 987, 990. See also, Paskalia (n 10), ch 3, for an analysis of female migration within the EU.

[25] See, for instance, Case C-1/05 *Jia v Migrationsverket* EU:C:2007:1, and Case C-40/11 *Iida* EU:C:2012:691.

migrant and (a) his/her spouse and their descendants under the age of twenty-one or dependants, and (b) dependent relatives in the ascending line of the migrant and his/her spouse.[26] The initial instruments covering the economically active, namely Regulation 1612/68 and Directive 73/148, also provided, respectively, that 'Member States shall facilitate the admission of any member of the family not coming within the provisions of paragraph 1 if dependent on the worker referred to above or living under his roof in the country whence he comes,'[27] and 'Member States shall favour the admission of any other member of the family of a national referred to in paragraph 1(a) or (b) or of the spouse of that national, which member is dependent on that national or spouse of that national or who in the country of origin was living under the same roof.'[28]

When it comes to adult conjugal relationships, only marriage was, initially, considered a family relationship which could give rise to automatic family reunification rights. At the time, the status of civil partnership was inexistent in Europe and beyond. Moreover, it would have been even less likely back in the 1950s and 1960s to recognise unmarried partners as constituting a 'family', given that cohabitation outside marriage was often, at the time, frowned upon. And even in the 1980s, in the *Reed* case,[29] when the CJEU was confronted with the question whether the unmarried partner of a migrant worker could be considered his 'spouse' and, thus, could *automatically* join him in the host Member State, the Court held that only marital relationships can fall within the notion of 'spouse' for the purposes of Article 10 of Regulation 1612/68. In the same case, nonetheless, the Court recognised that migrant workers would need to be allowed to be accompanied by their unmarried partners in the host Member State – in case this right was granted to the nationals of that State – to ensure they would not be discouraged from moving. This right to be joined by their unmarried partners was designated as a social advantage for the purposes of Article 7(2) of the same Regulation, which meant the host Member State would need to extend it to non-nationals if it already granted it to its own nationals. Alternatively, in situations where the host Member State did not grant to its own nationals the right to be joined by their unmarried partners – and, thus, Article 7(2) did not apply – the migrant worker would be able to rely on Article 10(2) of the Regulation to claim family reunification rights with 'any other member of the family' of the worker. However, this merely required the host Member State to 'facilitate'

[26] Article 10 of Regulation 1612/68 (n 19).
[27] Article 10(2) Regulation 1612/68 (n 19).
[28] Article 1(2) of Directive 73/148 (n 20).
[29] Case 59/85 *Reed* EU:C:1986:157.

admission of the family members who fell within those categories. The right was, thus, not automatic.

As regards 'descendants', that is, the children of the worker and his/her spouse, not much detail was provided in the legislation, apart from the fact that they should be either their dependants or under twenty-one years of age. The legislature, as well as the Court when interpreting the older pieces of legislation mentioned in this section, did not have the opportunity to clarify whether this would include children who were not biologically connected to either the migrant Member State national or his/her spouse, such as, for instance, adopted children or children conceived through assisted reproduction techniques where both the sperm and the egg were donated. McGlynn has pointed out that it would be 'repugnant' if the Court excluded such children from the scope of these provisions.[30] In any event, the Court had made clear that to be recognised as a 'descendant' it is not necessary that the child is biologically related to *both* spouses. In *Baumbast*, it was held that the step-children of the worker can also be considered as 'descendants' for the purposes of Article 10 of the 1968 Regulation. In this way, in one of the most important cases where the old legislative regime was interpreted, the notion of 'family' was extended to include reconstituted families which is already a departure from the traditional nuclear family model. This is notwithstanding the fact that, still, a marriage between a man and a woman forms the central relationship that bonds the family together.

In addition, in a series of cases, the Court devised the notion of the 'primary carer' that is, a third-country national who is the primary carer of a child who is either the direct beneficiary of free movement rights[31] or derives rights through his/her relationship with a Member State national who has exercised free movement rights.[32] From this case law, it can be observed that it is mainly women who were assigned the role of primary carer of children and other dependants despite the fact that some of them were equal or – even primary – contributors to the family finances. And this is so even in more recent case law.[33] This was also seen, albeit less explicitly, in the well-known *Carpenter* case where the Court did not employ the term 'primary carer' but may have based its reasoning on the fact that the wife of the Union citizen who was also the step-mother of his children needed to be allowed to stay in the United Kingdom to take care of her step-children so that her husband – a

30 McGlynn (n 9) 48.

31 Case C-200/02 *Zhu and Chen* EU:C:2004:639.

32 *Baumbast and R* (n 14).

33 Case C-310/08 *Ibrahim* EU:C:2010:1065, and Case C-480/08 *Teixeira* EU:C:2010:83; Case C-529/11 *Alarape* EU:C:2013:290; Case C-247/20 *VI* EU:C:2022:177.

Union citizen – could travel between Member States and offer his services in a cross-border context.[34]

In CJEU jurisprudence, it is thus women who have carried the double burden of labour market participation and expectations at home as the primary carers of children as well as homemakers.[35] Especially in the early years when the EU focused mainly on its market-building ambitions, taking care of the home and the children were not 'valued' as much as participation to the market and, thus, women who focused on home-building and child-care responsibilities were disadvantaged.[36] Moebius and Szyszczak noted back in 1998 that 'Community law maintains a rigid distinction between the market and the domestic sphere which perpetuates gender stereotyped roles for men and women and upholds discrimination in national laws'.[37]

It could be asked whether in the majority of cases it simply happened that it was the mother who was the primary carer of the child, and that if it had happened that the primary carer had been the father, the Court would have been equally willing to consider him a 'primary carer' and grant him a derivative right under EU law. This can be answered positively as, not only does the Court use gender-neutral terms when referring to the primary carer in its case law but, also, in *Rendon Marín*, it held that a father was the primary carer of his two minor children.[38] This way, the Court indicates that a man, too, can be considered as bearing that role. Moreover, the assignment of the

[34] See Case C-60/00 *Carpenter* EU:C:2002:434. This argument was actually explicitly rejected by the (female) advocate general in the case, Advocate General Stix-Hackl, in paras 102–106 of the Opinion: EU:C:2001:447. As noted by McGlynn, 'The apparent aim of Community law, therefore, is to privilege, and encourage the movement of, those families which provide the "infrastructure for men's mobility", that is, the availability of a (preferably full-time) wife': C. McGlynn, 'A family law for the European Union?' in J. Shaw (ed), *Social Law and Policy in an Evolving European Union* (Hart Publishing 2000) 225.

[35] For the same argument in relation to EU anti-discrimination law, see C. McGlynn, 'Ideologies of motherhood in European Community sex equality law' (2000) 6 European Law Journal 29. This approach has also been evident in the Court's older anti-discrimination case-law in situations where parental leave was only granted to women (i.e. the mother) and where this was held *not* to amount to discrimination the ground of sex (disadvantaging men): see, for instance, Case 163/82 *Commission v Italy* EU:C:1983:295; Case 184/83 *Hofmann v Barmer Ersatzkasse* EU:C:1984:273; Case C-243/95 *Hill and Stapleton v The Revenue Commissioners and the Department of Finance* EU:C:1998:298; Case C-218/98 *Abdoulaye v Renault* EU:C:1999:424.

[36] For an analysis of the EU's approach towards caregivers, see E. Caracciolo di Torella and A. Masselot, *Caring Responsibilities in European Law and Policy* (Routledge 2020).

[37] Moebius and Szyszczak (n 23) 133. See also, K. Scheiwe, 'EU law's unequal treatment of the family: The case law of the European Court of Justice on rules prohibiting discrimination on grounds of sex and nationality' (1994) 3 Social and Legal Studies 243.

[38] Case C-165/14 *Rendón Marín* EU:C:2016:675.

role of the 'primary carer' to the mother in the majority of cases can be attributable to the fact that it were the parties to the case themselves who claimed that the mother of the child was the primary carer. Hence, the Court's assignment of this role to the mother has been prescribed by the parties to the cases and cannot be attributed to perpetuated gender-stereotyped roles for men and women *maintained by the Court*.

Finally, by selecting to grant family reunification rights only to 'spouses', the old legislative regime excluded by default same-sex couples from automatic family reunification rights given that same-sex marriage was only introduced in 2001, and in only one EU Member State – the Netherlands. The same approach was followed by the Court when in two cases in the late 1990s and early 2000s it was confronted with the question of whether same-sex unmarried partners[39] and same-sex registered partners[40] should be treated as equivalent to opposite-sex spouses for the purposes of, respectively, EU anti-discrimination law and the EU staff regulations. In its judgments, the Court stated in a truly homophobic fashion that same-sex relationships, whether legally recognised or not, could not be treated as equivalent to opposite-sex relationships.[41]

From the above analysis, it can be concluded that the initial EU instruments which took into account familial ties for the purpose of bestowing rights stemming from EU law were based on a nuclear family model which only recognised as a family *married* couples and their parents and children. Hence, these persons were entitled to *automatic* family reunification rights. Of course, this rather narrow approach should be placed within the social and legal context in which the six founding EU Member States were operating. Admittedly, this context was more homogeneous than the EU of today whose membership has expanded to twenty-seven.[42] Hence, at a time when all Member State family laws made provision for marriage as the only legally recognised status for couples, it does not come as a surprise that the only status that turned two adults into a family for the purposes of EU law was marriage, which was available only between two persons of the opposite sex. At the time that the founding Community Treaties, as well as the European Convention on Human Rights (ECHR), were signed, even consenting sexual relationships among adult males remained a crime within many of the participating

39 Case C-249/96 *Grant* EU:C:1998:63.

40 Joined Cases C-122/99 P and C-125/99 P *D and Sweden v Council* EU:C:2001:304.

41 *Grant* (n 39), para 35; ibid, paras 33–40.

42 L. Hantrais, 'What is a family or family life in the European Union?' in E. Guild (ed), *The Legal Framework and Social Consequences of Free Movement of Persons in the European Union* (Kluwer 1999) 19.

countries,[43] and thus, legal recognition of same-sex relationships and the parenting rights of same-sex couples were not even contemplated when the original pieces of EU legislation that made provision for family reunification rights were drafted. Similarly, in the 1950s, and until not too long ago, the male breadwinner model was prevalent across the world including within the founding EU Member States and, hence, the assumption was made by the EU legislature that it would be the paterfamilias that would decide to move for economic purposes, and that it would be his wife and children that would need to move with him.

2.3 THE CURRENT EU LEGAL FRAMEWORK: A DEPARTURE FROM THE TRADITIONAL NUCLEAR FAMILY?

The question that this section aims to answer is whether the current EU legal framework has departed from the traditional nuclear family model. For this purpose, it will be examined whether the current legal framework covers same-sex spouses and the children of same-sex parents, whilst it will also be considered whether there is evidence of a departure from the traditional male breadwinner/female homemaker model.

Currently, there are only a few pieces of EU legislation that include the term 'family' as a concept which activates legal consequences. The term is not mentioned at all in the Treaty on European Union (TEU), whilst in the Treaty on the Functioning of the EU (TFEU) it is only used to refer to 'family law' or 'family reunification'.[44] In secondary legislation, the term 'family', either alone or with other terms, is used more widely. For instance, the terms 'family', 'family life', 'family members', 'family situation', and 'family relationship' are included in Directive 2004/38,[45] which has repealed and replaced all of the previous secondary law instruments governing the rights to free movement and residence of EU citizens (including family reunification rights), which were mentioned in the previous section. Similarly, Directive 2003/86,[46] which lays down the family reunification rights that third country nationals enjoy under EU law, makes extensive use of the terms 'family', 'family relationship', 'family life', 'family ties', and 'family members'.

43 Namely, Germany, Ireland, the UK, and Norway.

44 Articles 79 and 81 TFEU.

45 Directive 2004/38/EC of the European Parliament and of the Council of 29 April 2004 on the right of citizens of the Union and their family members to move and reside freely within the territory of the Member States [2004] OJ L158/77.

46 Council Directive 2003/86/EC of 22 September 2003 on the right to family reunification [2003] OJ L251/12.

Despite the replacement of the old legislative regime with new instruments which came into force in the wake of the new millennium, the traditional nuclear family remains the ideal of the family around which the majority of the existing legislation revolves. This is obvious, for instance, in the EU's immigration policy and, in particular, in Directive 2003/86, where recital 9 provides, 'Family reunification should apply in any case to members of the nuclear family, that is to say the spouse and the minor children.'[47] For other relationships, Member States maintain their discretion:

> It is for the Member States to decide whether they wish to authorise family reunification for relatives in the direct ascending line, adult unmarried children, unmarried or registered partners as well as, in the event of a polygamous marriage, minor children of a further spouse and the sponsor. Where a Member State authorises family reunification of these persons, this is without prejudice of the possibility, for Member States which do not recognise the existence of family ties in the cases covered by this provision, of not granting to the said persons the treatment of family members with regard to the right to reside in another Member State, as defined by the relevant EC legislation.[48]

Marriage between two persons of the opposite sex is still the law's 'gold standard' at both EU and Member State level, which means that anything resembling it may be recognised and regulated by the law insofar as it is performing similar societal functions. This becomes obvious when we look at the text of Directive 2004/38, which explicitly notes that registered partners are considered 'family members' of Union citizens only if the host Member State *treats registered partnerships as equivalent to marriages*.[49] In other words, only registered partnerships (whether opposite-sex or same-sex) which are treated – under the law – as marriages, deserve to be automatically recognised as a familial relationship for the purposes of EU law. Similarly, in 2018, the Court was in *Coman* called to clarify the meaning of the term 'spouse', for the purposes of the 2004 Directive.[50] It held that same-sex spouses are included

47 See also, Article 4(1) of Directive 2003/86 ibid.

48 Recital 10 and Articles 4(2) and (3) of Directive 2003/86 (n 46).

49 Article 2(2)(b) of Directive 2004/38 (n 45).

50 Case C-673/16 *Coman and others* EU:C:2018:385, paras 37–38. For an analysis, see, inter alia, J. J. Rijpma, 'You gotta let love move: ECJ 5 June 2018, Case C-673/16, *Coman, Hamilton, Accept v. Inspectoratul General pentru Imigrări*' (2019) 15 European Constitutional Law Review 324; A. Tryfonidou, 'The ECJ recognises the right of same-sex spouses to move freely between EU Member States: The *Coman* ruling' (2019) European Law Review 663; D. V. Kochenov and U. Belavusau, 'After the celebration: Marriage equality in EU Law post-Coman in eight questions and some further thoughts' (2020) 27 Maastricht Journal of European and

within the term 'spouses' for the purposes of Article 2(2) of the Directive and, thus, enjoy automatic family reunification rights. Hence, same-sex couples whose relationship conforms to the 'marriage ideal' are for the purposes of Directive 2004/38 brought within the scope of privileged relationships. Nonetheless, in *Coman*, the Court was also careful to emphasise the limitations attached to its pronouncement, ensuring that the interpretation of the term 'spouse' to include same-sex spouses is only applicable in cross-border situations and only for the purpose of granting family reunification rights. In this way, the Court avoided to appear as if imposing same-sex marriage on all Member States through the back door.[51]

When the members of a couple formalise their relationship either by marrying each other or by entering into a civil partnership which is equivalent to marriage, the EU legislator assumes that this constitutes sufficient evidence of their commitment to each other. Thus, formalising the relationship entitles the couple to automatic family reunification rights. As Alan Brown has noted, the extension of legal regulation to adult relationships which possess 'marriage-like' conjugality illustrates the significance of this idealised image of the nuclear family within the legal understanding of the family.[52]

Nonetheless, marriage and civil partnership are by no means the only models for partnership between adults who together form a family. Although, in view of the increase in cohabitation outside marriage, one would have expected that recent legislative initiatives would make provision for unmarried/unregistered couples, this has not been the case. Instead, a privileged position has been maintained for married couples or couples who, albeit not married, have chosen to formalise their relationship by making a commitment which is – perceived to be – equivalent to the commitment made by married couples. Hence, although Directive 2004/38 – unlike the previous legislative regime – makes an explicit reference to unmarried partners, it nonetheless relegates them to the less privileged Article 3(3) category, which does not grant *automatic* family reunification rights.

Hence, McGlynn's point from eighteen years ago still holds true today: 'While a marriage does not have to fulfil the *ideals* of marriage for there to be "family life", a non-marital relationship has to be proven to be the match, at least in ideal terms, of marriage. The marriage contract, therefore, acts as a barrier to further intrusion into the relationship, and the functions of marriage

Comparative Law 549. See also Chapter 7 by Michal Bogdan and Chapter 9 by Geoffrey Willems.

51 For an explanation of the limitations attached by the Court in this case, see Tryfonidou (n 50).

52 A. Brown, *What Is the Family of Law? The Influence of the Nuclear Family* (Hart Publishing 2019) 200.

are deemed to exist.'[53] This is reflected not only in the Court's approach towards marriage, which is, in all circumstances, considered to suffice for establishing family life (irrespective of the quality of the relationship) but also in its approach to situations where a marriage has broken down. In such instances, the Court has refrained from examining the particular circumstances of the case, noting that as long as the breakdown of the relationship is not officially established through a final divorce, the marriage is still considered as existing for the purposes of EU law.[54] This is so even if the spouses reside separately and with new partners,[55] the only exception being when the Union citizen from whom the rights are derived has left the host Member State prior to the issuance of the divorce.[56] This appears to be in contrast to the approach prevailing in the European Court of Human Rights (ECtHR) case law where all circumstances are taken into account to determine whether two or more persons enjoy family life together. As Stalford has observed, the CJEU has adopted a more 'formulaic approach' than the ECtHR, 'whereby the existence of genuine family *life* is irrelevant for the purposes of activating family rights under the free movement provisions' and what counts is 'the existence of a formal legal or biological link to confer the protection and entitlement of the free movement provisions'.[57]

Directive 2004/38 has also been interpreted by the Court as applying *only* to family members who are *joining or accompanying the Union citizen in the host Member State*.[58] This demonstrates that in the Court's view, families do not conduct family life across borders and a *disruption to enjoying family life which is conducted in a cross-border context* is incapable of impeding the free movement rights of Union citizens. This approach can be seen in the 2012 judgment in the case of *Iida*, where the Court refused to require a Member State (Germany) to grant the right of residence for the purposes of family reunification to a Japanese national whose wife and daughter had left Germany and moved to Austria where the wife worked.[59] One could have

53 McGlynn (n 9) 16.

54 See Case 267/83 *Diatta* EU:C:1985:67; Case C-370/90 *Singh* EU:C:1992:296; *Iida* (n 25), para 58.

55 Case C-244/13 *Ogieriakhi* EU:C:2014:2068, paras 37–38.

56 Case C-218/14 *Singh* EU:C:2015:476; Case C-115/15 *NA* EU:C:2016:487. Of course, Article 13 of Directive 2004/38 provides for a number of situations where the right of residence of the third country national spouse is maintained even after divorce.

57 H. Stalford, 'Concepts of family under EU law – Lessons from the ECHR' (2002) 16 International Journal of Law, Policy and the Family 410, 413. See also, Diduck and Kaganas (n 3) 39–41.

58 *Iida* (n 25), paras 61–63.

59 Ibid, paras 73–81.

argued that if Mr Iida had lost his right to reside in Germany and, thus, would need to leave that Member State, this could have interfered with the right to family life of his wife and daughter who were both Union citizens, and, as a result, impede their right to move to Austria.[60]

One can, of course, question the logic of the Court in cases like *Iida*. This is so especially in the light of *Coman*, which involved a married same-sex couple who had initially lived together for four years prior to their marriage but – due to the fact that they worked in different countries – they subsequently did not live in the same country, even after they married. In *Coman*, the Court held that the situation fell within the scope of EU free movement law and that family reunification rights should be granted because the couple claimed the right to move *together* to the Member State of nationality of one of them. In *Iida*, the third country national spouse wished to continue residing in the Member State of origin of the family, even after the family members who were Union citizens had moved to another Member State.

My argument is not that the Court should have refrained from granting family reunification rights in *Coman*. Rather, my argument is that Union citizens and their family members should not be deprived of family reunification rights in situations like the one in *Iida* simply because all the members of the family do not live in the same Member State. As Advocate General Wathelet noted in his Opinion in *Coman*,

> In a globalised world, it is not unusual for a couple one of whom works abroad not to share the same accommodation for longer or shorter periods owing to the distance between the two countries, the accessibility of means of transport, the employment of the other spouse or the children's education. The fact that the couple do not live together cannot in itself have any effect on the existence of a proven stable relationship . . . and, consequently, on the existence of a family life.[61]

Although the Court did not make any explicit statements regarding this point in *Coman*, it is clear from the judgment that it did not consider that the fact that the couple spent time living apart in different countries and even different continents precluded them from establishing family life. Accordingly, since the Court, in principle, appears to accept that family life can be conducted across borders, it should no longer insist that family reunification and

[60] A. Tryfonidou, '(Further) signs of a turn of the tide in the CJEU's citizenship jurisprudence: Case C-40/11, *Iida*, Judgment of 8 November 2012' (2013) 20 Maastricht Journal of European and Comparative Law 302, 317–320.

[61] Opinion of Advocate General Wathelet in Case C-673/16 *Coman and others* EU:C:2018:2, para 28.

related rights should only be granted if the family members *move* to the same Member State as the Union citizen.[62] If an obstacle to free movement can be proven to emerge as a result of a change in the 'status quo' of the family arrangements, this should suffice for finding a breach of EU law and for requiring the grant of family reunification rights.

Leaving aside conjugal relationships and moving on to consider the position of children, it will, again, be argued that the centrality of the nuclear family model means that, in general, the children who live in 'alternative families' often remain marginalised and largely excluded from many of the entitlements and benefits of Union membership.[63]

The last few years have shown a desire on the part of the EU to ensure that *all children* – irrespective of the family in which they live – should be treated in the same way under EU law. In 2019, for instance, the Court made it clear that children who are not biologically related to *either* of their (adoptive) parents can be considered as their parents' 'direct descendants' for the purposes of Directive 2004/38.[64]

More recently, the Court was invited to answer the more controversial question of the cross-border legal recognition of the familial ties among the members of rainbow families in a case which involved a baby girl whose parents were two persons of the same sex. Until recently, it was unclear whether Directive 2004/38 and, in particular, the terms 'direct descendant' and 'direct relatives in the ascending line' covered the members of rainbow families. This had given cause to Member States which do not recognise two persons of the same sex as the joint legal parents of a child, to refuse to recognise the legal ties among children and both of their (same-sex) parents – as these were established in another Member State – when families sought to claim rights deriving from EU law in their territory.[65] This issue was recently

[62] For another argument in favour of a broader approach to the scope of application of Directive 2004/38, in view of the increasingly cross-border nature of family relationships, see Opinion of Advocate General Szpunar in Case C-202/13 *McCarthy and others* EU:C:2014:345, paras 39–83.

[63] McGlynn (n 9) 22.

[64] Case C-129/18 *SM* EU:C:2019:248, para 54. See also Chapter 7 by Michal Bogdan.

[65] For a detailed analysis of this, see A. Tryfonidou, 'EU Free Movement Law and the children of rainbow families: Children of a lesser god?' (2019) 38 Yearbook of European Law 220. In 2020, NELFA (the Network of European LGBTIQ* Families Associations) produced a document which includes real life stories of rainbow families that have encountered obstacles in their (domestic and cross-border) legal recognition. The document is freely available online: <http://nelfa.org/inprogress/wp-content/uploads/2021/02/NELFA-fomcasesdoc-2021-1.pdf>. The obstacles to free movement faced by rainbow families in the EU have also been documented in a study commissioned by the European Parliament's Policy Department for Citizens' Rights and Constitutional Affairs at the Request of the PETI Committee of the

clarified by the Court in the V.M.A. case,[66] when it ruled that the term 'direct descendants' in Directive 2004/38 should be interpreted as including the children of same-sex couples who should, thus, enjoy automatic family reunification rights with the parent or parents who are Union citizens and exercise free movement rights.[67] Moreover, in the same case, the Court held that all EU Member States are required to recognise the parent–child relationship between a child and both of her same-sex parents, which was established in the host Member State where the family lives and was attested in a birth certificate issued by that State, for the purpose of permitting the child, who is an EU citizen, 'to exercise without impediment, with each of her two parents, her right to move and reside freely within the territory of the Member States'.[68] Hence, V.M.A. has established that the children of same-sex couples can enjoy – with both of their parents – *at least*[69] family reunification rights under EU law, in the same way that the children of nuclear families do. Children may either be 'sponsors' of these rights if they themselves are Union citizens, or beneficiaries through their Union citizen parent or parents.

Recently, marking a departure from the nuclear family model, the Commission has signalled its intention of securing the right of *all* children to have their relationship with their parents – as established in an EU Member State – legally recognised across the EU. In December 2022, the Commission submitted a proposal for a Regulation which lays down rules on international jurisdiction on parenthood determining which Member State's courts are competent to deal with parenthood matters; rules on the applicable law, which designate the national law that should apply to parenthood matters in cross-border situations; and rules on the recognition of judgments and official

European Parliament: see A. Tryfonidou and R. Wintemute, 'Obstacles to the Free Movement of Rainbow Families in the EU' (2021) <https://www.europarl.europa.eu/thinktank/en/document/IPOL_STU(2021)671505>.

66 V.M.A. (n 18). The Court affirmed its V.M.A. ruling in its Order in Case C-2/21 *Rzecznik Praw Obywatelskich* EU:C:2022:502. See also Chapter 9 by Geoffrey Willems.

67 For an analysis of the ruling, see, inter alia, A. Tryfonidou, 'The ECJ recognises the right of rainbow families to move freely between EU Member States: The V.M.A. ruling' (2022) 47 European Law Review 534; D. Thienpont and G. Willems, 'Le droit à la libre circulation des familles homoparentales consacré par la Cour de justice de l'Union européenne' (2022) 132 Revue trimestrielle des droits de l'homme 925; L. Bracken, 'Recognition of LGBTQI+ parent families across European borders' (2022) 29 Maastricht Journal of European and Comparative Law 399. See also Chapter 7 by Michal Bogdan and Chapter 9 by Geoffrey Willems.

68 V.M.A. (n 18), para 49.

69 For an explanation that the ruling can also be read more broadly, see Tryfonidou (n 67).

documents on parenthood issued in another EU Member State.[70] Although the proposed instrument applies to *all* families in situations where there is a cross-border element and, thus, obviously, families that fit the nuclear family model can benefit from it, it will in practice mostly be of interest to so-called 'alternative families'. This is due to the fact that it is mostly the latter type of families that face difficulties with the recognition of family ties among their members in cross-border situations.

Finally, since the 1970s, there has been a concerted effort to depart from the male breadwinner/female homemaker model by adopting measures aiming to achieve a reconciliation of professional and family lives, especially for women. The slow departure from this model is most recently reflected in Directive 2019/1158 on work–life balance for parents and carers, which came into force in 2019 and in which, also, the EU legislature made a conscious attempt to depart from the traditional nuclear family model albeit, as will be explained below, in a rather half-hearted manner.[71] It has been noted that the 'Directive aims to modernise the EU legal framework in order to allow parents and carers to better balance their life and work commitments, and to ensure equality between men and women regarding employment opportunities and treatment at work'.[72] The Directive acknowledges the existence of alternative families which do not conform to the nuclear family model. For example, it introduces the right to paternity leave for at least ten days upon the birth of a child for fathers *or equivalent second parents* but only where and insofar as recognised by national law; and it defines parental leave as leave that can be taken upon the birth or *adoption*, in this way removing any emphasis from the existence of genetic links between a child and their parents. However, the Directive states that the Member States 'have the competence to define marital and family status, as well as to establish which persons are to be

[70] European Commission, Proposal for a Council Regulation on jurisdiction, applicable law, recognition of decisions, and acceptance of authentic instruments in matters of parenthood and on the creation of a European Certificate of Parenthood COM(2022) 695 final. For an analysis of the proposal, see A. Tryfonidou, 'Cross-border recognition of parenthood in the EU: Comments on the Commission proposal of 7 December' (2023) 24 ERA Forum 149. See also the study commissioned by the European Parliament's Policy Department for Citizens' Rights and Constitutional Affairs at the Request of the PETI Committee of the European Parliament: A. Tryfonidou, 'Cross-border legal recognition of parenthood in the EU' (2023) <https://www.europarl.europa.eu/thinktank/en/document/IPOL_STU(2023)746632>.

[71] Directive (EU) 2019/1158 of the European Parliament and of the Council of 20 June 2019 on work–life balance for parents and carers and repealing Council Directive 2010/18/EU PE/20/2019/REV/1 [2019] OJ L188/79.

[72] European Commission, Directorate-General for Employment, Social Affairs and Inclusion, N. Picken and B. Janta, *Leave Policies and Practice for Non-traditional Families* (Publications Office 2020) 2 <http://data.europa.eu/doi/10.2767/276102>.

considered to be a parent, a mother and a father'.[73] Thus, when it comes to alternative families and, in particular, rainbow families, reconstituted families, and adoptive families, the Directive leaves it entirely up to the Member States to determine whether they will grant parental leave. This demonstrates the half-hearted approach of this instrument. Although the intention is to extend the availability of parental leave to alternative families, in practice, this is entirely dependent on the choice of the Member States.

2.4 CONCLUSION

EU family law now recognises that more family forms count as a family than it did in the 1950s and 1960s. Yet, as the above analysis has shown, the influence of the nuclear family ideal still prevails. This continuing centrality of the nuclear family model sits uneasily against the complex and diverse family forms that currently exist within the EU. Regardless of legislative reforms both at national and EU level, and changes in social demographics and the growing diversity of familial practices, the legal understanding of the 'family' under EU law continues to be centred around the traditional nuclear family model consisting of the nexus of the conjugal relationship and the parent–child relationship. In the meantime, it is still assumed that families live under the same roof and within the same Member State. Although an attempt has been made to slowly depart from the male breadwinner / female carer model, this model is still very much embedded within the societal and legal structure. Thus, despite the fact that there are bits and pieces of EU law that demonstrate acceptance of a greater diversity of family forms, the EU legal system continues to conceptualise all families through the prism of the nuclear family. This is problematic for the regulation of the diversity of family forms and practices in contemporary EU as it marginalises, excludes, and potentially discriminates against anyone who does not conform to this model.

[73] Recital 18 of Directive 2019/1158 (n 71).

3

What Makes the Family Special?

DAVID ARCHARD

3.1 INTRODUCTION: EU LAW AND THE FAMILY

Article 8 of the European Convention on Human Rights accords everyone the right to respect for their private and family life. Article 12 accords everyone of marriageable age the right to marry and found a family. The family is thus a significant and valuable social unit as far as the EU is concerned. However, inasmuch as under law a family is the locus of interrelated rights and responsibilities, as well being for its members a ground for benefits, it matters what counts as a family. Yet the European Union (EU) does not legislate on critical family issues such as divorce, the custody and guardianship of dependent children, and the financial responsibilities of spouses. The relevant laws are left to Member States although the EU does have rules, for instance, in those cases of spouses from different EU countries with different laws on divorce.

The EU also accords benefits to family members across different countries. These will be lost to UK citizens after Brexit in 2016.[1] Most centrally the EU guarantees freedom of movement between states. The Directive which accords this right to all EU citizens states that it should be extended to 'all family members irrespective of nationality'.[2] Yet in that case, enjoyment of these benefits broaches important questions of who counts as a member of a family.[3] There is an increasing body of case law by the Court of Justice of the

[1] H. Stalford, 'The UK referendum on membership of the EU: Whither social welfare and family law?' (2016) 38 Journal of Social Welfare and Family Law 115.

[2] Directive 2004/38/EC of the European Parliament and of the Council of 29 April 2004 on the right of citizens of the Union and their family members to move and reside freely within the territory of the Member States [2004] OJ L158/77.

[3] G. Milios, 'Defining "family members" of EU citizens and the circumstances under which they can rely on EU law' (2020) 39 Yearbook of European Law 293. See also Chapter 7 by Michael Bogdan and Chapter 9 by Geoffrey Willems.

EU (CJEU) defining what it is to be a family member, and which has been criticised for its presumed traditional view of a 'family' as a nuclear one.[4]

The problem facing EU law concerning the family is simple and understandable. The family is valuable and should be legally protected but there need be no agreement across different EU states as to what counts as a family and who its members are. This, in turn, reflects major social developments and extraordinary changes in family structures over the last hundred years. These have led many not simply to point out that the traditional nuclear family no longer predominates, but to doubt both whether it is even possible to think of a single concept of 'the family', and whether the family deserves any special legal protection. In what follows, I examine these changes and evaluate the claims that the concept of a family no longer has meaning and that the family should not be seen as meriting a special status in EU or indeed in any national law. In sum, I conclude that there is such a thing as a family but that there can be reasonable disagreement about what should be defined as a family. At the end I shall say something about this in the context of moves to harmonise or even unify EU family law.

The essential changes in family structure are evident in all EU countries.[5] However, they are nicely illustrated and evaluated in a recent UK Report. In September 2022, the UK's Children's Commissioner published Part One of a Review into Family Life commissioned by the government.[6] In its own words, it 'paints a unique and comprehensive picture of family life today. It focuses on what families look like in modern Britain, defines for the first time what exactly is protective about them, and looks at the unique experiences of children for whom the state is their parent.' The Review was informed by interviews with thousands of children and families across the country, an analysis of existing data sets, and conversations with stakeholders and experts as well as a review of the existing relevant literature.

The Review intends that this comprehensive survey of family life can and should inform law, policy, and the provision of appropriate services in respect of the family. Two key claims of the Review are as follows. First, the traditional two-parent family is in decline in the UK (as it is elsewhere in

4 H. Stalford, 'Concepts of family under EU law – Lessons from the ECHR' (2002) 16 International Journal of Law, Policy and the Family 410. See also Chapter 2 by Alina Tryfonidou.

5 K. Kiernan, 'Changing European families: Trends and issues' in J. Scott, J. Treas, and M. Richards (eds), *The Blackwell Companion to the Sociology of Families* (Blackwell 2004).

6 Children's Commissioner, *Family and its protective effect: Part I of the Independent Family Review* (2022) <www.childrenscommissioner.gov.uk/family/family-review/>.

Europe). Forty-four per cent of those born in the UK in 2000 will have spent some of their childhood up to the age of seventeen outside such a family compared with 21 per cent of children born in 1970. Second, what matters to their members is the quality of family relationships rather than the composition of the family.

From its survey of family members, four themes emerged: 'the emotional importance of connection within families; the importance of shared experience for family life; the unconditional support, both practical and emotional, from within families; and the strong, positive, and enduring relationships found in families. These factors were present in families of all shapes, sizes, and compositions.'

A simple summary might be as follows: the traditional family form is no longer the predominant one, but what is critical is whether and how the family, in whatever form it takes, is able to provide what it is that makes the family valuable and indeed special to its members. That claim is subject to two important critical responses: first, the multiplicity of family forms, of which the traditional family is only one, shows that there is no such thing as 'the family'; second, the family is neither unique nor special in providing what it is that is claimed to be its defining value. This double-headed response needs careful analysis not least because it would seem odd to deny both that there is such a thing as the family *and* that it is not special. What is 'it' if not 'the family'?

It is worth noting, first of all, that the Review lists the valued factors of family life in a chapter titled 'What defines family?' However, the word 'define' used here cannot mean identify or pick out what something is; rather it means what it is that makes something especially valuable. Yet, the counterpart to the summary claim quoted above, 'These factors were present in families of all shapes, sizes, and compositions' is 'These factors were nevertheless absent from some families of all shapes, etc.' This latter claim is not stated nor implied. But it is evidently true. Some families fail to provide the emotional support, connection, love, and enduring relationships that characterise other families. Hence, these features do not define what a family is; they do not hold true of all families. Rather they characterise what makes families that exhibit those features special. It also, importantly, motivates law and policymakers to support and facilitate the creation of those families that are special in the indicated sense.

The two elements of the response – that there is no such thing as the family and the family is not special – conjoin to subvert the importance the family assumes in law and policy. Expressed rhetorically and in a challenging manner, the response asks, why use legal and other measures to privilege and protect 'the family' which no longer exists and which, anyway, lacks whatever might justify its special treatment?

In what follows, I will examine the double response. First, I want to rebut the claim that there is no such thing as 'the family'; second, I want to defend the view that the family, minimally and functionally defined, is special. The first part has already been set out elsewhere, but I will summarise and further clarify my arguments in the following section.[7]

3.2 THE CONCEPT OF 'THE FAMILY'

As Raymond Williams showed in his 1976 work *Keywords*, 'family,' deriving from 'familiar' (from the Latin '*famulus*' which denotes a servant), was, initially, a household of servants and blood relations. After the seventeenth century and especially after the nineteenth, it came to connote the conjunction of a shared household or residence and 'kin' or blood relations. A family on this modern account is a set of consanguineous co-residential individuals. In its classic 'nuclear' form, the family comprises a married, heterosexual, couple with their biologically related offspring living in a single home.[8]

However, social, legal, demographic, and biological developments over the last hundred years – at least in the global North – have seen extraordinary changes in the family. This need no longer conform to the nuclear template. Its adult members may be single or plural; they need not be heterosexual, married, or in an intimate sexual relationship; the dependent children need not be biologically related to the adults; and there need not be a single shared residence.

The response from social science to these developments in family forms has been to resist the use of the term 'the family'. According to a now familiar sociological orthodoxy, we should not use the definite article. Instead, we should pluralise or abandon nominative usage in favour of adjectives and adverbs. Thus, rather than talk about *the* family, we should use the term 'families'.[9] Or we should speak of 'familial' practices and 'doing families'.[10] At best, according to some, we might retain the noun and its definite article

7 D. Archard, 'Family and family law: Concepts and norms' in E. Brake and L. Ferguson (eds), *Philosophical Foundations of Children's and Family Law* (Oxford University Press 2018).

8 R. Williams, *Keywords: A Vocabulary of Culture and Society* (Croom Helm 1976).

9 D. Gittins, *The Family in Question* (Macmillan 1985).

10 E. Dermott and T. M. Fowler, 'What is a family and why does it matter?' (2020) 9 Social Sciences 1. See Chapter 4 by Ségolène Barbou des Places.

but only with a qualifying and restrictive adjectival phrase, such as 'post-modern'[11] or 'post-familial'.[12]

I am unsympathetic to these moves and note that some sociologists have begun to criticise the orthodoxy.[13] But here are my reasons in brief, summarising and further clarifying what is argued in my 2018 chapter.

First, I see no reason to abandon the use of a single concept simply because it covers a multiplicity of different instances. No one proposes giving up the concept of 'house' because houses come in different sizes and shapes, and have various kinds of material composition. Indeed, there is something entirely self-defeating about arguing as follows: there is such a diversity of families that we must conclude that there is no such thing as a family. How do you estimate, and take account of, that diversity unless it is a diversity of different examples of the same sort of thing? Consider, by way of a parallel, the entirely rhetorical question, 'Since humanity exhibits such a diversity of individual humans, why should we speak of a single species *homo sapiens?*'

It might be argued, but I do not see this done even if it is sometimes suggested, that there are *so many* different kinds of families that the concept is stretched to a point where its boundaries are no longer clear. In this manner, it could be said, the concept somehow collapses under the weight of its multiplicity. Or, it is simply hollowed out of any content. It is a 'zombie' category, walking but dead and deprived of animating spirit. Yet why think this? The boundaries can remain clear between 'family' and other social category terms such as clan, tribe, friendship group, neighbourhood; the diversity – which is anyway surely not *that* extensive – can be celebrated as the richness of an ever-changing social form. Again, similarly, we might note and value the extraordinary variety of human beings without abandoning the species category.

Second, I do not see how giving up the noun in favour of the adjective ('familial') or verbal form ('to do families') helps. 'Familial' has to be construed as describing everything which is like a family. Yet those who commend its use are also saying that they are unable to pick out or identify what that thing which serves to identify alike instances is itself like. Or 'familial' is to be understood as whatever is of or shares the nature of a family. But, again, what is it that has such a nature if not something, constant and single, that merits the title of 'family'? Similarly, the awkward verbal construction, 'doing families,'

[11] J. Stacey, *Brave New Families: Stories of Domestic Upheaval in Late Twentieth Century America* (Basic Books 1990).

[12] E. Beck-Gernsheim, *Reinventing the Family: In Search of New Lifestyles* (Polity Press 2002).

[13] M. Gilding, 'Reflexivity over and above convention: The new orthodoxy in the sociology of personal life, formerly sociology of the family' (2010) 61 British Journal of Sociology 757.

presumably must be taken to mean that *something* is done. But those who use the phrase assert that it cannot pick out or identify *what* is being done.

Third, the conceptual challenge should be distinguished from a moral one. 'There is no such thing as the family' is a very different charge from 'there is no one thing the family should be'. It is certainly true that one response, that of conservative and traditionalist commentators, to the diversity of familial forms has been in the form of a lament for the disappearance or decline of the traditional family, the family as it should still be.[14] However, it should be obvious that one can reject this kind of normative claim and refuse to share in the bemoaning of a lost ideal, whilst still insisting that there is such a thing as the family.

One celebrated way to confuse the conceptual and the moral claims is by appeal to 'persuasive definitions.'[15] These are used by those who favour a particular understanding of what something ought to be. They do so by defining that thing in the terms they favour. In saying 'the family is to be defined as this sort of thing', they are actually saying, 'This is what the family *should* look like.' Thus, the family is by persuasive definition what they seek to persuade others it ought to be. Note that the chapter of the *Family Review* cited at the outset of this chapter might appear to answer its question, 'What defines family?', in persuasive terms.

Or those who use persuasive definition will argue that the family as they define it is what a 'real' or 'true' family looks like. However, persuasive definitions in whatever way they are constructed or employed can be exposed as such and resisted. Thus, it is perfectly possible to refuse to accept or endorse prejudicial or, indeed, honorific representations of the family. A conceptual claim should always be carefully distinguished from a normative one. Doing so permits drawing the conclusion that there are many kinds of family without favouring or rejecting any one kind over the others.

Fourth, one might try, as some have done, to ameliorate the confusing diversity of family forms by using certain adjectival qualifications. Raymond Williams, for instance, notes that 'nuclear' and 'extended' were used to distinguish between those family forms that took in many generations and that one which was restricted to parents and their children. In ordinary English usage, we often talk of our 'immediate' family to make a similar point. However, the adjectival usages recommended by some sociologists such as 'post-modern' and 'post-familial' have another purpose, namely that of deconstructing or subverting the noun that follows. It is a way of saying something

[14] B. Almond, *The Fragmenting Family* (Oxford University Press 2008).
[15] C. Stevenson, 'Persuasive definitions' (1938) 47 Mind 331.

like 'This is the family but not as we know it' such that we may take it that there is indeed no longer such thing as the family. Yet, once more, such an inference is unwarranted.

The statement in quotation marks alludes to the much-used remark (actually a misquotation) attributed to Dr Spock on encountering aliens in *Star Trek*, 'It's life, Jim, but not as we know it.'[16] But Spock does not deny that Jim has observed a life form; he only asserts that it is one that is unfamiliar to both of them. It *is* life, but one that is new and strange. Why then should we think that 'the family' as a concept cannot encompass even the dramatically different forms it now takes, and thus be prepared to accept that something is a family even if it is one we have not previously known?

Fifth, it is important to distinguish two questions. There is a general, conceptual, one that asks what distinguishes 'the family' from other social kind terms. The other is one of individuation and counting. This first question asks whether or not something falls under the concept of the family. The second asks whether or not something is a single instance of a family or in fact comprises several families. Thus, we can in some contexts ask – as an intelligible question – whether a given group of adults and children should count as one or more families.

For instance, a 'blended' (or 'bonus' or 'step') family is formed when adults take on a parental role for children previously raised by other parents. So, it might be difficult to decide how many families a child belongs to when their initial parents, one or both, enter into new relationships with adults who already have custodial responsibilities for other children. If Mark's father and mother separate, the latter creating a second family with her new partner and the partner's children, and if care for Mark is shared across his father, his mother, and partner, how many families is Mark, and indeed his mother, a member of?

That question makes good sense. However, the fact that it might appear to be a difficult question to answer does not yet give us a reason to abandon the concept of the 'family'. Rather, it prompts us to acknowledge that the diversity of familial forms allows in some cases for individuals to belong to more than one family, as well as to see how problematic it may be to count and agree on the number of some interlinked families. Yet for all those difficulties, we can still operate with an understanding of what a family is. We know what it means to say that Mark is a member of this or that family. It is merely that individuating each instance that falls under the conceptual category is more complex than it once was.

[16] E. Knowles, *Oxford Dictionary of Quotations* (Oxford University Press 2009).

Here is a nice comedic example from the movies. In the film *Help*, there is a scene in which its stars, the Beatles, are seen entering the front doors of what appear to be four adjacent relatively humble terrace houses and are commended by a neighbour for still being 'so natural'.[17] In fact, as we, the viewers, follow the Beatles inside, we are able to see that behind those separate doors is a single luxury space they all inhabit, albeit with distinguishable features and facilities peculiar to each of them. How many houses should we say there are then? Four or one? These questions can be asked, and puzzled over, without the need to stop employing the concept of a house.

Sixth, change in types and forms of family does not necessarily make a concept of family applicable at one time and inapplicable at another later time. It is wrong to claim, as one sociologist does, that, 'There is no single concept of the family which is true for all historical periods and in all places.'[18] What might be meant is that the kinds of family you would have seen several hundred years ago are not those that one sees now. But this is true of many things that change and evolve over time. These are yet further examples of things about which a Dr Spock may say that they are not 'as we know them'.

Certainly, some things change so significantly that the manner in which they were initially understood and defined is no longer adequate. Something can change its characteristics without ceasing to be the same thing. Here is a simple example. In 2019, Jaguar, the motor manufacturer, asked Oxford University Press to change its online dictionary definition of a 'car'. This was, 'A road vehicle, typically with four wheels, powered by an internal combustion engine and able to carry a small number of people.' The problem was that this excluded their electric motor–driven vehicles.[19]

What should be said of this example is that the original concept of a 'car' was poorly defined or managed in a manner that meant it was incapable of anticipating or accommodating change. We should not say that with the advent of the electric vehicle, something other than a car had been created, nor that there are different concepts of 'car' at different times. The essential idea of a self-powered, moving people carrier has been unchanged. There have always been cars from the first invention of the automobile, but their diversity is now such that we need a broader, more inclusive, concept. So it is, with changes in what remains recognisable as 'a family'.

[17] 'The Beatles at Home, from the Film *Help*!' <www.youtube.com/watch?v=Yx_7xjpySKo>.

[18] D. Cheal, *Sociology of Family Life* (Blackwell 2002) 4.

[19] R. Schreiber, 'Jaguar asks the Oxford English Dictionary to change its definition of "car"' (*Hagerty Media*, 15 August 2019) <www.hagerty.com/media/news/jaguar-oxford-english-dictionary-definition-of-car/>.

3.3 THE FAMILY OF FAMILY LAW

The foregoing only shows that there can be a single concept of the family and that the diversity of whatever falls under the concept does not of itself invalidate the continued usage of such a concept. It does not answer the question of how that concept is to be defined. Since the focus of this collection is 'the family in EU Law' we should address the question of what it is that the law regards as a family. This is important because the status of any family member is a source of obligations, rights, benefits, and exemptions. Thus, for instance, those who are parents have enforceable duties of care for their dependent children; children are legally protected against abuse and harm; families are the recipients of state benefits; family members are exempt from certain requirements (such as that of testifying in a criminal trial against another member); the inheritance of property takes account of familial relations; and so on. In EU law, the dependant members of a migrant worker's family have rights of entry into that state where the worker is employed.[20]

Herring has suggested that there are five possible ways for the law to understand and define a family: an ordinary, common-sense usage; an idealised definition; a functional definition; a formalistic definition whereby the family is identified as that which has certain properties; and a 'self-definition' approach whereby you are a family if you think you are.[21]

The problem with the first is that an appeal to ordinary language cannot solve familiar problems of how to understand what the law requires. Or it simply reduces any disagreements or conflicts concerning such requirements to disputes about what words, ordinarily and customarily, mean. An oft-used example is that of what 'vehicle' means as for instance in the case of *Garner v Burr*.[22] H. L. A. Hart used the hypothetical example, subsequently much quoted and used, of a legal rule that forbids you taking a vehicle into the public park. 'Plainly,' he said, 'this forbids an automobile, but what about bicycles, roller skates, toy automobiles? What about airplanes?'[23]

In response to these rhetorical questions, judges and legal commentators may move from an appeal to the indeterminacies of ordinary usage of words to an attempt to clarify what the purpose or original intention of any statute or law was: what were the vehicles that the park rule makers intended to forbid

20 Milios (n 4).

21 J. Herring, *Family Law* (Pearson 2017) 3–4.

22 *Garner v Burr* [1951] 1 KB 31.

23 H. L. A. Hart, 'Positivism and the separation of law and morals' (1958) 71 Harvard Law Review 593, 607.

entry to? We might thus insist that we need to know what the purpose of any instance of family law is if we are to clarify what exactly is the family that is its subject. In this manner, any appeal to ordinary language uses of family must ultimately be couched in terms other than that simply of what words mean and, for instance, consider what lawmakers intend a law of 'the family' to do. Words alone will not deliver what is needed.

The problem with the second, idealised, definition of 'family' is that it conflates a conceptual question of what a family *is* with an ethical question of what a family *ought to be*. As I argued earlier, the conceptual and normative issues at stake in discussions of the family need to be carefully separated and separately addressed. Above all, it is a mistake – made by those who use persuasive definitions – to answer the conceptual question in disguised normative terms, such that the family is what the definer thinks it should be.

The problem with the final definition, one of self-definition, is that it is simply unacceptably permissive and overinclusive. It allows anyone to define the family in any terms that suit them. Moreover, it will generate irresolvable problems of conflicting self-definition, whereby different individuals may disagree as to whether they are or are not members of one and the same family.

My own preference is for a minimal functional definition whereby a family is 'a multigenerational group, normally stably co-habiting, whose adults take primary custodial responsibility for any dependent children'.[24] I will not defend this definition here. However, I think it has the benefits of tolerating the diversity of familial forms noted, is morally neutral, and permits an independent evaluation of both what makes the family as such a valuable social institution and what makes some kinds of family better than others. It allows that evaluation to be made in terms of which familial forms better discharge the essential custodial role of rearing children. The definition thus honours the distinction between normative and conceptual matters, but permits an answer, without presuming what that is, to the question of what is good about the family and what counts as a good family.

3.4 FROM FAMILY TO INTIMACY

What is interesting about using a formal definition of the family is that it may reinforce what we could call the demoting of the concept of 'the family'. By 'demoting', I mean ceasing to regard the family as of special social worth. The use of the formal definition does this by raising the question of whether

[24] D. Archard, *The Family: A Liberal Defence* (Palgrave Macmillan 2010) 10.

or not what families have in common makes them uniquely valuable. To explain, if we fail to find a single unifying concept of the family in terms of its institutional structure (such as a particular set of relationships between its members), we might attend to those features of it that are appealing and attractive. Along these lines, we find the idea that families display certain qualities such as those of affectionate companionship, intimacy, and sharing. Remember that the Review into Family Life, cited at the outset, precisely defined the family in terms of an important emotional connection, shared experience, unconditional support, and enduring positive relationships between the members of families.

Yet such qualities can be found in other areas of the personal life of individuals. In this vein, Carol Smart's *Personal Life* argues that the family has no particular importance or centrality in a 'personal life' that encompasses 'all sorts of families, all sorts of relationships and intimacies, diverse sexualities, friendships and acquaintanceships'.[25]

What – it will be said – is valuable about the family are those properties exhibited by certain kinds of personal relationship. But these are not exclusively possessed by the family. What follows for family law is critical: the special privileges of legal recognition and protection afforded to 'the family' in virtue of those valued qualities, it will be argued, should be extended to these other non-familial relationships. We should thus move from the 'family' to 'familiarity'[26] and recognise at law 'households' 'not defined by either sexual partners or familial relationships, but rather by a shared emotional economy'.[27]

To summarise: the answer to the question of what makes the family special and merits its particular legal status is, roughly but nevertheless very startlingly simply, 'nothing'. First, there is no such thing as 'the family' (only 'familial' practices and 'doing families'). Moreover, second, what makes the 'familial' valuable does not make the family special. For what is true of the 'familial' is true also of the 'familiar', namely the intimacy and affectionate companionship of non-familial relationships such as friendship. The law should acknowledge this.

3.5 THE GOODS OF FAMILY

Thus far, I have tried to answer the first claim, namely that there is no such thing as 'the family'. I want now to attend to the second argument, namely that

25 C. Smart, *Personal Life: New Directions in Sociological Thinking* (Polity 2007) 188.

26 A. Diduck, 'Shifting familiarity' (2005) 58 Current Legal Problems 235.

27 A. Bottomley and S. Wong, 'Shared household: A new paradigm for thinking about the reform of domestic property relations', in A. Diduck and K. O'Donovan (eds), *Feminist Perspectives on Family Law* (Routledge 2006).

what makes the 'familial' valuable extends beyond the family to other personal relationships, and thus the law should give a special status to more than the family. I noted earlier the oddity of denying both that there is such a thing as the family *and* that it is special. But it is open to someone to accept even reluctantly that there is something meriting the title of 'the family' but refuse to accord it any special status.

Here is a schematic formulation of this second argument which I will express using the language of 'goods'. By goods I follow standard usage in Anglo-American political philosophy, and John Rawls in particular, by seeing them as those things that it is rational for individuals to want and to seek.[28] The argument to which I wish to respond then runs as follows: something (the family) is commended for legal recognition because it promotes certain goods. However, these goods are also promoted by other relationships. Thus, the law should recognise those relationships to the same extent that it already does the family.

To clarify further, it helps, if and when we talk about goods, to distinguish private, exclusive, goods and non-exclusive public goods. In simpler terms, the goods of relationships can be either private, that is enjoyed only by those in the relationship, or public in that everyone can enjoy them. They can of course be both; the fact that relationships have private goods does not exclude them from also having public goods. Take, for example, friendship: the intimacy, mutual support, and affection that characterises a friendship is valuable only to those who are the friends in question. However, if friendships can also underpin social solidarity, promote public health, assist compliance with the law, and support the economy, then friendship realises public goods enjoyed by all in society.[29]

Having clarified what is to be understood by goods, we can respond to the second argument (that non-familial relationships deserve the same special legal status as familial inasmuch as the former promotes goods to the same degree as the latter) by showing either that the private goods promoted by different relationships differ in their quality and value; or by showing that the family promotes particular public goods besides those private goods that might be of equivalent value with non-familial relationships.

Hence, in what follows I want, first, to concentrate on private goods and consider two ways in which one might argue that the private goods of family membership are different from those of other relationships such that the family is 'special' in the right way. I will then be able to show how the public

[28] J. Rawls, *A Theory of Justice* (Oxford University Press 1999) §15 and VII.

[29] E. J. Leib, 'Friendship and the Law' (2007) 54 UCLA Law Review 631.

goods of the family – if not the private goods alone – suffice to establish its special nature.

The first account of the putatively special nature of the private goods of the family is taken from Brighouse's and Swift's influential book on the family and justice, *Family Values*. They think that there is a particular, distinctive, and non-substitutable interest that adults have in acting as a parent, forming a relationship with a dependent child, and promoting that child's interests. This is a view they develop in offering a reason why a liberal egalitarian can reasonably think that the existence of families need not promote injustice. Its particular relevance in the present context is that, for them, the good of being a parent is both a private one and one that is not realised by other relationships such as friendship. I am thus not concerned with whether Swift and Brighouse do show that the existence of families can be congruent with justice, but rather with making use of their key idea that the family serves interests of a particular and, indeed, unique kind.

Swift and Brighouse argue that 'intimate relationships with others are essential for [people's] lives to have meaning'. Further, the intimate relationship of a parent with his/her child is 'sui generis', 'unique', and productive of 'a distinctive contribution to [a parent's] well-being'. 'Other intimate relationships have their own value, but they are not substitutes for a parenting relationship with a child.'[30]

This is a powerful and important claim but it does not show that the family is special in the way that is needed to accord the family its privileged legal status. Why? It is conceded by Brighouse and Swift that the private goods of parenthood are not goods for all adults:

> So the claim that the relevant relationship goods make a powerful contribution to the flourishing of the [individual] does not imply that those goods are good for everybody . . . [T]here may be people who do not need to be parents; those who . . . could indeed flourish fully without [parenting], and those whose lives would actually be diminished by their being parents.[31]

This is an important concession. And there are two elements to the concession. The first is that something's being of unique, non-substitutable, value to some does not mean that it is of such value to all persons: the goods of parenthood are not goods 'for everybody'. The second element of the concession is that those who do not value the goods in question need not thereby

[30] H. Brighouse and A. Swift, *Family Values: The Ethics of a Parent–Child Relationship* (Princeton University Press 2014) 87–88.

[31] Ibid 100.

suffer a shortfall of private goods: some individuals will 'flourish fully' without those goods of parenthood.

Taken together, the concession undercuts the claim that only the family can supply those valuable private goods that would justify according to it a status denied to other relationships. That would be the case if someone could not enjoy those goods that are necessary for a 'fully flourishing' life outside the family. Yet, some individuals do not derive value from the family *and* nevertheless live lives that are no less good in sum. For instance, some individuals will enjoy the same level of well-being as those who have families through securing the private goods of non-familial intimate relationships.

It may be true, as Brighouse and Swift aver, that other intimate relationships have their own value, but one that is no substitute for that of parenting. But something can be just as valuable as another thing without it having the same *kind* of value. For instance, there might be no substitute for the taste of truffles, but someone who dislikes that taste need not lack what is needed to have a complete gustatory meal experience; other, albeit different, tastes may suffice for a meal that is as satisfying to the diner as the one with truffles. A taste can be unique and non-substitutable without being one that is special in the sense of necessary for any fully satisfactory meal.

The sense in which Brighouse and Swift define the private good of parenthood does not suffice to show that the family should receive special legal protection. If other intimate relationships have equal, albeit not the same kind of, value as parenting, then the law should grant those relationships the same status as parenthood. That leaves unaccounted for the putatively public good of parenthood to which I will return.

The second account of why the family realises importantly different private goods than those of other relationships is noted by some sociologists who have been critical of the move to demote the family as a social institution. What such a demotion or 'circumvention' of the concept of family risks losing, they argue, is the powerful sense of belonging to a familial 'we' that individuals have and which they value highly. This feeling of who we are extends both into the past and into the future: 'a sense of responsibility, reverence and respect for ancestors that has both sociopolitical and spiritual components; and a sense of generational continuity that passes knowledge about previous generations down to future generations'.[32]

The British Broadcasting Corporation's (BBC) very popular series, *Who Do You Think You Are?* comprises episodes in which a well-known individual

[32] R. Edwards, J. McCarthy, and V. Gillies, 'The politics of concepts: Family and its (putative) replacements' (2012) 63 British Journal of Sociology 730, 736.

explores their ancestry. The results can be surprising and on occasion shocking. However, the programme's pleasure for the viewer lies in the reactions of the celebrities at the disclosures of a past they may not have previously known about but which on being found out matters greatly to them. That is the case even when a discovered ancestor is long dead. The programme is described by the broadcaster as follows: 'Lost connections and unfamiliar histories are revealed as celebrities trace their family trees. Discover stories of courage, joy, sacrifice and resilience – everyone has a tale to tell.'[33] That everyone does have a tale to tell is what makes the family of special value to its members.

Note, too, that this sense of temporal or historical continuity can be felt and valued by everyone inasmuch as we are all the children of parents, and all of us have ancestors even if some of us do not become parents. Moreover, those who do not themselves have children can still view the young within their extended family – our nephews and nieces, for instance – as giving them a sense of a 'future generation' that is special to them.

It is hard to see how this valued sense of 'having a tale to tell' about one's place in an ongoing history can be realised by non-familial relationships. Friendship, for example, does not, as the family does, extend back over time and forward across generations. Moreover, the value of what one could call a narrative identity would seem to be one that is both universal (we all value having such an identity) and unique in the sense of not having any equivalent outside the family. Here then is a way in which the private good of the family is both non-substitutable and, very plausibly, of greater value than any good of non-familial intimacy.

3.6 THE PUBLIC GOOD OF FAMILY

Moreover, this sense of continuous attachment to a past and a future can also be represented as a public good, in that such feelings of connection to the family can extend to our sense of belonging to the society in which our families flourish. Indeed, this was the claim of Edmund Burke who famously argued, 'To be attached to the subdivision, to love the little platoon we belong to in society, is the first principle (the germ as it were) of public affections. It is the first link in the series by which we proceed towards a love to our country, and to mankind.'[34] The family is just such a 'little platoon' by connection to

33 BBC, 'Who do you think you are?' <www.bbc.co.uk/programmes/b007t575>.

34 E. Burke, *Reflections on the Revolution in France* (first published 1790), (Penguin 1968) para 75.

which our affection to others is broadened to encompass our co-citizens and humanity as a whole.

Brighouse's and Swift's accounts may not suffice to show that the family serves private goods that other relationships cannot match. But they also see the family as having a public good. This is because it serves the interests of children as well as parents. Indeed, they believe that children should be raised by adults because that relationship of parenthood which is of value to the latter also serves the well-being of the former. They think that parenthood ought to promote the interests of children. Parents owe a fiduciary duty of care to dependent children and their rights are, in consequence, appropriately constrained.[35]

This suggests the most important way in which the challenge to the special status of the family can be met. This is especially so if the idea of the family as a 'little platoon' remains unpersuasive. We can grant that both friendships and intimate personal relationships do promote significant private and public goods. Nevertheless, we can and should insist that the family does something else, namely rear children. This is precisely what a functional definition of the family draws attention to. The family is essentially that social institution within which children are brought up. It is such an institution even if it also can and does provide affectionate companionship to its members.[36] In short, the family may not be able to compete with non-familial institutions if the standard of comparison is the quality of intimacy enjoyed but it will outrank those other relationships if what matters is the functional role the family uniquely fulfils.

It is worth adding that, although not an essential functional role, the family can and does often provide support and care across generations but in a reverse direction to that of rearing children. This is the case when the elderly parents are looked after by their adult children.

That primary functional role is important inasmuch as it ensures the graduation to adulthood of children and their eventual occupancy of those social roles – as citizen, worker, parent, and others – that ensures the stable reproduction of any society over time. Of course, in discharging that role the family is not beyond criticism. Indeed, it is subject to a range of familiar criticisms from psychoanalytic, Marxist, feminist, and countercultural commentators. It is probably best not to answer these criticisms by insisting that the family is a flawless social institution, every instance of which is ideal. Rather, we should attempt what I have described elsewhere as a 'Churchillian

[35] Brighouse and Swift (n 30) Part Three.

[36] D. Popenoe, 'American family in decline, 1960–1990' (1993) 55 Journal of Marriage and the Family 527, 529.

defence' of the family.[37] Winston Churchill famously said of democracy that 'it is the worst form of government, except for all the others'.[38] In similar fashion, we can say of the family that it is the worst institution in which to bring up children, apart from every other alternative. We can also allow that different familial forms serve the function of rearing children in better or worse ways.

Thus, the family provides a range of both private and public goods, and the former for both parents and children. Children benefit from being brought up in families, parents benefit from discharging their custodial duty of care, and society benefits from the inter-generational stability provided by inducting the next generation into their adult social roles. All of these goods are promoted by the family in ways and to an extent that is not true of non-familial intimate relationships. This, then, is the basic argument for the claim that the family deserves a legal status that is not merited by those other relationships.

However, one last point is in order. It is arguable – indeed it is highly plausible to think – that when the family displays those qualities that characterise the best of non-familial relationships, it is better at rearing children. These qualities are most obviously the strong bonds of affectionate companionship and reciprocal commitment. As we have seen, Brighouse and Swift think parents must fulfil the fiduciary duty of care for their children. That ensures that the children's well-being is at least good enough. But we can reasonably add that the well-being of children is advanced more if those adults who have custodial care of them are bound by a high degree of mutual commitment. This is persuasively argued by Anca Gheaus.[39]

If this claim is true, we have a reason not just to protect the family as a social institution but to promote those familial forms that can display these valued qualities. Arguing for this claim displays the merits of using a functional definition of the family and of clearly separating conceptual and normative issues. For we can agree that the concept of the family does capture a distinctive kind of social institution without at the same time begging normative questions of which are better or worse instances of the institution. Nevertheless, if the family is defined as an institution whose adult members have primary custodial care for the children, we can at least understand how we might go about evaluating two issues: first, whether the family does a better job of rearing children than other social institutions; and, second, which forms or kinds of family do a better job of rearing children than other forms.

[37] Archard (n 24) 68.
[38] W. Churchill, Speech in the House of Commons, Hansard (11 November 1947).
[39] A. Gheaus, 'Is the family uniquely valuable?' (2012) 6 Ethics and Social Welfare 120.

3.7 CONCLUSION

To conclude: the concept of 'the family' as functionally defined has survived momentous changes in society and endures across the multifarious forms it can take. The concept of 'the family' is not made redundant by these changes and is not a historical relic left behind by progress. It survives and indeed flourishes in its diversity. The family does have a unique and special value in the number and quality of goods it serves. The law – at both national and transnational levels – rightly protects that value and may seek to make of families the best that they can be in serving these goods and in discharging its indispensable functional role of rearing children.

At the outset I noted that EU law acknowledges that the family is a special social unit but has a problem with agreeing what shall count as a family and who are its members. It does so whilst worrying that the privileging of some familial forms might be counted as discriminatory. For instance, when defining who family members are for the purpose of extending the scope of the right to free movement to 'family members', who should count as a 'partner' – only a married spouse or could, and should, it also include a same-sex but unmarried partner?[40]

One way to resolve these problems would be by harmonising or indeed by unifying EU family law across all Member States. This has been extensively discussed but the prospects for such an institutional unification of substantive family law seem some way distant.[41] In the discussions, there is often emphasis on the fact that the family law of any Member State is indissolubly linked to a particular national culture (its 'sentiments and traditions') or to a stage of social development (assessed by reference to what is seen as a generally progressive arc of change). Whatever the explanation of the pessimistic assessment of the likelihood of its occurrence, any uniformity of family law across the EU would require the imposition on Member States from the 'top down'. This would be viewed as politically unacceptable and probably unworkable. Indeed, one reviewer of the prospects for harmonisation of family law notes that, in Europe, it could only mean political integration, and that, in consequence, 'Uniform family laws will signal the demise of the nation state, if not the end of politics.'[42]

[40] J. Guth, 'When is a partner not a partner? Conceptualisations of "family" in EU Free Movement Law' (2011) 33 Journal of Social Welfare and Family Law 193.

[41] W. Pintens, 'Family law in Europe: Developments and perspectives' (2008) 41 The Comparative and International Law Journal of Southern Africa 155.

[42] D. Bradley, 'Family Law' in J. M. Smits (ed) *Elgar Encyclopedia of Comparative Law* (Edward Elgar Publishing 2006) 269.

Nevertheless, it must be stressed that there is no inconsistency in a presumption underlying EU family law that the family does exist and does have value, whatever the various forms it assumes in different national jurisdictions. To repeat the essential claim of this chapter: the changes in the forms taken by the family should not and need not be taken as showing that there is no usable single concept of the family nor that it does not merit special legal protection.

4

Who Counts as a Family Member?

On the Importance of 'Doing Family' in EU Law

SÉGOLÈNE BARBOU DES PLACES

4.1 INTRODUCTION

'One of the first mental frameworks which informs the intelligibility of all life',[1] the family seems to be one of those common concepts that are immediately understandable. Ordinary definitions of the family refer to a group of persons united by the ties of marriage, blood, or adoption, forming a single household. These persons are assumed to interact with each other in their respective positions, usually those of spouses, parents, children, or siblings.[2]

Reading sociology and history, however, teaches us that the definition of the family is not as clear as it first seems. The notion of family has changed over time and its definition is the subject of intense controversy. For decades, the image of the family was based on marriage and implied a heterosexual relationship.[3] However, the narrowness of this definition, mainly based on patriarchal principles involving a male breadwinner and female homemaker,[4] has been increasingly criticised. Progressively the definition of family members has evolved, and in national, international, and European Union (EU) law, we find more encompassing conceptions of the family. However,

[1] E. Dubout, 'The European form of family life. The case of EU citizenship' (2020) 5 European Papers 3.

[2] See also Chapter 3 by David Archard.

[3] T. H. Hervey, 'A gendered perspective on the right to family life in European Community law' in N. Neuwahl and A. Rosas (eds), *The European Union and Human Rights* (Martinus Nijhoff 1995) 221. The Carpenter case (Case C-60/00 *Carpenter* EU:C:2002:434) is the best example of the EU consolidating the traditional notion of the wife at home.

[4] On the 'male breadwinner family model', see I. Moebius and E. Szyszczak, 'Of raising pigs and children' (1998) 18 Yearbook of European Law 125. See also L. Ackers, 'Citizenship, gender and dependency in the EU: Women and internal migration' in K. H. Hervey and D. O'Keeffe (eds), *Sex Equality Law in the European Union* (Wiley 1996) 221.

the controversy is not over, namely because 'rainbow' and other atypical forms of family are far from being on an equal footing with the traditional nuclear family.[5]

The purpose of this chapter is not to take a position in this debate, important as it is. Rather, its goal is to address another issue, based on the observation that the definition of 'family' is both uncertain and unstable in EU law. In certain parts of EU law, the family circle is limited to the nuclear family, or a slightly enlarged version of the family, while in other cases the family encompasses a broader group of persons. 'Family' is also defined on the basis of multiple and varying criteria. Comparing EU legal norms on free movement law, migration law, and private international law, one can only agree with Advocate General Mengozzi that the family is 'not a uniform category' in EU law.[6] Admittedly the same applies to national law, as the scope of the family varies according to the objective pursued by the legislator: to organise parental authority, to identify the legal heirs of a deceased person, to determine who are the creditors or debtors of child support, and so on. However, it is neither satisfactory nor convincing to assume that the definition of the family is purely functional in EU law.

It is not satisfactory because a totally fragmented regime does not sit well with the requirements of legal certainty which must guide the drafting and interpretation of EU law. Indeed, depending on whether or not someone is considered a 'family member', they may or may not have access to rights granted by EU law and be protected against breaches of other rights.[7] The fact that the holders of rights and obligations are designated without any apparent logic or coherence, sometimes even within the same policy area, can be considered problematic. Most importantly, the conclusion that the EU's definition of the family is purely functional is unconvincing because it tends to assume that EU law fulfils only a very limited role in family matters,

5 See A. Tryfonidou, 'EU Free Movement Law and the children of rainbow families: Children of a lesser god?' (2019) 38 Yearbook of European Law 220; N. Koffeman, *Morally Sensitive Issues and Cross-Border Movement in the EU: The Cases of Reproductive Matters and Legal Recognition of Same-Sex Relationships* (Intersentia 2015) 7–8; J. Rijpma and N. Koffeman, 'Free movement rights for same-sex couples under EU law: What role to play for the CJEU?' in D. Gallo, L. Paladini, and P. Pustorino (eds), *Same-Sex Couples before National, Supranational and International Jurisdictions* (Springer 2014); D. Kochenov, 'Gay rights in the EU: A long way forward for the Union of 27' (2007) 3 Croatian Yearbook of European Law and Policy 469. See also Chapter 2 by Alina Tryfonidou and Chapter 9 by Geoffrey Willems.

6 Opinion of Advocate General Mengozzi in Case C-423/12 *Flora May Reyes* EU:C:2014:16, para 33.

7 E. Caracciolo di Torella and A. Masselot, 'Under construction: EU family law' (2004) 29 European Law Review 32.

restricted by national traditions and cultures. Of course, there are reasons to believe that the EU's influence on national models of family life is restricted. In the absence of a sufficiently homogeneous social base, the EU would lack a basis for expressing a shared European conception of the family. In addition, the EU does not 'constitute' families:[8] it only recognises the variety of affiliation, and of conjugality that we find in the Member States' legislation,[9] hence building upon the families constructed at national level.[10] However, this reading is contradicted by the different works that, despite reaching opposite conclusions, all agree that EU law influences family patterns in Europe. Whether they argue that EU law 'undermines the family as a legal institution',[11] that the EU creates 'forms of family life',[12] or that the contribution of the Court of Justice of the EU (CJEU) to the protection of rainbow families is too weak,[13] EU law scholars are increasingly united around the idea that the EU's influence on national models of the family is real.[14]

[8] The 'family' is cursorily mentioned in only two treaty provisions: Article 79(2)a and Article 81 of the Treaty on the Functioning of the EU.

[9] In Case T-65/92 *Arauxo-Dumay* EU:T:1993:47, the Court of First Instance held that it 'does not consider that it is competent to widen the judicial interpretation of the specific terms used in the Staff Regulations in order to bring cohabitation within the definition of "marriage", or "'cohabitee" within that of "husband" or "wife"' (para 29).

[10] The most radical expression of the Member States' willingness to retain competence for family law is the Declaration on the Charter of Fundamental Rights of the European Union, in which the Republic of Poland declared that 'the Charter does not affect in any way the right of Member States to legislate in the sphere of ... family law'.

[11] For negative comments on the *Coman* judgment (Case C-673/16 *Coman and others* EU:C:2018:385) and of the *V.M.A.* ruling (Case C–490/20 *V.M.A. v Stolichna obshtina, rayon 'Pancharevo'* EU:C:2021:1008), see V. Stehlík, 'The CJEU crossing the Rubicon on the same-sex marriages? Commentary on Coman case' (2018) 18 International and Comparative Law Review 85. For a discussion on rainbow families' rights in EU countries in relation to right-wing populism, see A. Tryfonidou, 'The impact of right-wing populism on the family rights of sexual minorities in Europe' (2022) EU-POP Working Paper Series 2.

[12] Dubout (n 1).

[13] D. Kochenov and U. Belavusau, 'After the celebration: Marriage equality in EU law post-Coman in eight questions and some further thoughts' (2020) 27 Maastricht Journal of European and Comparative Law 549.

[14] Scherpe argues that while there is, at present, no comprehensive European family law, elements of an 'institutional European family law' have been created through decisions of the European Court on Human Rights and by the Court of Justice of the European Union as well as other EU instruments. At the same time an 'organic European family law' is beginning to emerge. The laws in many European jurisdictions have developed similarly and have 'grown together', not only as a result of the aforementioned institutional pressures, but also as a result of societal developments, and comparable reactions to medical and societal advances and changes: J. M. Scherpe, *The Present and Future of European Family Law* (Edward Elgar Publishing 2016). See also E. Pataut, 'La famille saisie par l'Union' in E. Bernard, M. Cresp, and M. Ho-Dac (eds), *La famille dans l'ordre juridique de l'Union européenne / Family within*

This chapter takes this idea as a starting point. It aims to show that, under the heterogeneous approach to the family, there is a rationale underpinning the EU's – apparently – variable and unstable approach to the family. It seeks to describe how the notion of 'family member' contained in EU legal provisions reflects the EU's perception[15] of what European society is (and what it should be). The notion of 'doing family', borrowed from sociology, will help to account for the reasoning of the EU legislator and judge. In EU law, there is no unitary definition of *what it is* to be a family member, but EU legal norms often tell us what it means to *act like* a family member. Some people, who cannot claim to have conjugal or parental bonds with rights' holders, are nevertheless referred to as 'family members' on the sole ground that they are *behaving* like family members. In characterising such people as family members, the EU values the family functions they are performing: protecting, caring, educating, and supporting the social integration of their family. However, this chapter will show that 'doing family' is a social fact, an objective social reality: it does not equate to 'feeling like' a member of the family. While the EU does not ignore feelings and the willingness to form a family, it relegates them to second place. This preference for a definition of family that is based on the social functions performed rather than on any self-definition is a political and ethical choice. The Union does not so much value the feeling of belonging to the family as the role that the constitution and preservation of family life plays in the service of European construction.

This chapter is divided into six sections. Sections 4.2 and 4.3 substantiate the idea that family is a variable geometry figure in EU law. Section 4.2 describes the variable scope of the family circle in EU legal instruments, and Section 4.3 shows that 'family' is a missing category of EU law. Thereafter, the chapter seeks to identify the rationale underpinning the delineation of the family members by EU legal norms. Section 4.4 presents the notion of 'doing family', borrowed from the work of David H. J. Morgan,[16] who focused on family practices. It shows the value of this notion for understanding the rationale of the EU approach. Section 4.5 invites nuance in the use of the notion of 'doing family' to describe EU law. The EU values the fact of 'doing family' but, in contrast with Morgan's work, there is no room for the self-definition of family members. Forming a family supposes that its members perform social functions, like providing care or contributing to the social

the Legal Order of the European Union (Bruylant 2020). See also Chapter 13 by Jens M. Scherpe.

15 Caracciolo di Torella and Masselot (n 7).

16 D. H. J. Morgan, *Family Connections* (Polity Press 1996) 186.

integration of its members. The rationale for this limitative definition of the family is explained in Section 4.6: family is a form of social membership that enables people to be part of a broader community: the European society. EU law models the definition of EU families on the EU project to construct a cohesive society. Section 4.7 concludes that despite the fragmentation of sources and the modulation of family circles, EU law projects a certain representation of the family. Even when unnamed, 'European families' exist.

4.2 THE VARIABLE SCOPE OF THE FAMILY CIRCLE

To illustrate the impossibility of accurately describing the 'European family', Strumia resorts to the notion of the 'variable geometry family'. The EU institutions rely 'on a flexible, pragmatic idea of family that leaves potential room to several models of cohabitation and reciprocal responsibility, and to a variety of underlying bonds, from the biological, to the legal, to the factual and affective'.[17] Apart from the members of the nuclear family – the spouses and children – who are systematically included in the group of 'family members', the precise boundary of the family circle is unstable and difficult to assess in EU law.

Several factors generate this instability. Time is the primary factor of variation. Since the 1950s, the definition of the family circle has evolved, espousing some of the social and legal changes in the Member States. This is visible in free movement law. Regulation 1612/68[18] on workers' mobility restrictively defined the family as being composed of the sole 'spouse', children, and the dependent relatives in the ascending line of the worker and *his*[19] 'spouse'. Three decades later, the 2004/38 Directive[20] included in the family circle the 'partner' with whom the Union citizen (a man or a woman) has contracted a registered partnership. Following the same logic, siblings and relatives who were not mentioned in the 1990 Dublin Convention[21] have

[17] F. Strumia, 'The family in EU law after the SM ruling: Variable geometry and conditional deference' (2019) 4 European Papers 389.

[18] Council Regulation (EEC) No 1612/68 of 15 October 1968 on freedom of movement for workers within the Community [1968] OJ L257/2.

[19] On the use of the masculine pronoun in different provisions of EU law, see V. Paskalia, *Free Movement, Social Security and Gender in the EU* (Hart Publishing 2007).

[20] Directive 2004/38/EC of the European Parliament and of the Council of 29 April 2004 on the right of citizens of the Union and their family members to move and reside freely within the territory of the Member States [2004] OJ L158/77.

[21] Convention determining the State responsible for examining applications for asylum lodged in one of the Member States of the European Communities – Dublin Convention [1997] OJ C 254/1.

been counted as members of the (extended) family by 'Dublin III' Regulation 604/2013.[22] The proposal for an Asylum and Migration Management Regulation confirms that the EU institutions are willing to retain this broad definition of the family circle.[23]

However, change over the course of time is not the only source of complexity. Even when adopting a static rather than a dynamic reading of the norms dealing with family life, it is hard to form a clear picture of the family. The fragmentation of legal sources is a second factor preventing the emergence of a uniform category of family in EU law. The perimeter of the family varies significantly from one text to another, even within one and the same policy field. A typical example is that of unmarried partners. Directive 2013/33 on the reception of applicants for international protection[24] is inclusive: its Article 2(c) designates as a family member 'the spouse of the applicant or his or her unmarried partner in a stable relationship'. Accordingly, Article 2(g) of the Dublin Regulation mentions the unmarried partners engaged in a durable relationship. Yet other texts, like the Family Reunification Directive[25] and the EU Citizens' Directive, are far less inclusive. They rely on a distinction between two groups of people, one named 'family members' which corresponds to the (slightly extended) traditional nuclear family, and the other one composed of people having other types of family ties. Unmarried partners fall into this second group.[26] The same logic applies for siblings and relatives. In most EU legal instruments, they are not included in the family circle. Article 6 of the Dublin III Regulation is an exception: it refers to a heterogeneous group composed of 'family members, siblings or relatives' of the unaccompanied minors. 'Relatives' are defined by Article 2(h) as 'the applicant's adult aunt or uncle or grandparent who is present in the territory of a Member State'.

[22] Regulation (EU) No 604/2013 of the European Parliament and of the Council of 26 June 2013 establishing the criteria and mechanisms for determining the Member State responsible for examining an application for international protection lodged in one of the Member States by a third-country national or a stateless person (recast) [2013] OJ L180/31.

[23] Proposal for a Regulation of the European Parliament and of the Council on asylum and migration management and amending Council Directive (EC) 2003/109 and the proposed Regulation (EU) XXX/XXX [Asylum and Migration Fund], COM(2020) 610 final.

[24] Directive 2013/33/EU of the European Parliament and of the Council of 26 June 2013 laying down standards for the reception of applicants for international protection (recast) [2013] OJ L180/96.

[25] Council Directive 2003/86/EC of 22 September 2003 on the right to family reunification [2003] OJ L251/12.

[26] In the Family Reunification Directive, the unmarried partner is not deemed to belong to the group of people who can rely on Article 4 which holds that Member States 'shall' authorise the entry and residence of the sponsor's spouse. See also Chapter 8 by Albertina Albors-Llorens.

These lists of family members may appear to have been composed at random and without any logic because the links between family members are very diverse. Parental and conjugal ties are predominant, but often EU law also recognises as family members people who interact from other circles and relationships. A recent example is that of the Council Implementing Decision 2022/382 of 4 March 2022 establishing the existence of a mass influx of displaced persons from Ukraine.[27] In addition to the spouse, the unmarried partner in a stable relationship, and minor unmarried children, Article 2 of the Decision designates as persons who shall be considered to be part of a family 'other close relatives who lived together as part of the family unit at the time of the circumstances surrounding the mass influx of displaced persons, and who were wholly or mainly dependent on the sponsor'. The 'other close relatives' is a vague category that serves to include, within the scope of the family, persons not having any predetermined legal family links but who depend on the sponsor. It will be remembered (from the previous paragraph) that the same category is mentioned in the Dublin Regulation but there 'relatives' refers to a different category of people: 'the applicant's adult aunt or uncle or grandparent who is present in the territory of a Member State' (Article 2(h)).

These examples, which attest to the categorical diversity of family in EU law, point to a third factor of variation in the definition of the family: the objective of the law. The family circle is defined according to the purpose of the EU norm under consideration. When the legislator's objective is to confer a legal status and to grant rights to individuals, the family circle tends to be narrowly defined. This is particularly apparent in the norms that distinguish between two categories of family members, who are accorded distinctive rights and treatment. Following its Article 3(1), the EU Citizen's Directive, which confers several important rights, 'shall apply' to the 'family' which is composed (under Article 2) of the spouse and registered partner, children, and ascendants in direct line. In contrast, under Article 3(2), the host Member States are only required to 'facilitate' entry and residence for the 'other family members' who are the persons not falling under the definition of Article 2 who are dependants or members of the household of the Union citizen. Accordingly, and despite the fact that he/she is not even named a 'family member', the 'partner with whom the Union citizen has a durable relationship, duly attested' is mentioned in Article 3(2)(b) as a person who 'may enjoy' facilitated access to entry and residence. The legislator has opted for the same approach

[27] Council Implementing Decision 2022/382 of 4 March 2022 establishing the existence of a mass influx of displaced persons from Ukraine within the meaning of Article 5 of Directive 2001/55/EC, and having the effect of introducing temporary protection [2022] OJ L71/1.

to family in concentric circles in the Family Reunification Directive. It distinguishes between a 'first family circle' including the sponsor's spouse and the minor children of the sponsor and spouse, composed of persons who have a right of entry and residence in the host State; and a 'second family circle' comprising first-degree dependent relatives in the direct ascending line of the sponsor or spouse, and adult unmarried children of the sponsor or spouse, composed of persons whose entry and residence is dependent on the host State being willing to welcome them.

These examples also show that the delineation of the family varies depending on the degree of harmonisation the legislator seeks to achieve. When adopting the EU Citizen's Directive, the legislator clearly sought to limit the Member States' discretion; hence the compilation of a rather precise and closed list of family members. In contrast, in the field of social security, preference was for a margin of appreciation left to national authorities. Logically, Article 1 of Regulation 883/2004[28] defines the 'member of the family' as '(i) any person defined or recognised as a member of the family or designated as a member of the household by the legislation under which benefits are provided …'.

It is clear from these examples that the definition of family – and the protection of family life – is often instrumental to achieving other objectives. This is not a novelty. Caracciolo di Torella and Masselot have argued that 'the regulation of the family has not been an end *per se*, but has been subsidiary to the successful completion of the "main building", namely the European Community (EC) common market. As a result, both soft law and binding measures were a bundle of *ad hoc* measures which did not support a coherent approach within this area.'[29] Given the multiple objectives pursued by the EU institutions in the different areas of EU law, the prospect of a clear and a priori definition of the family common to the different branches of EU law appears somewhat illusory.

4.3 THE FAMILY: A MISSING CATEGORY OF EU LAW?

It is not unreasonable to affirm that 'family' is an elusive category of EU law. Terminology confirms this idea. In the different secondary law instruments that organise family life, in particular in social law, free movement law, or private international law, the entity 'family' is rarely mentioned as such. The

[28] Regulation (EC) No 883/2004 of the European Parliament and of the Council of 29 April 2004 on the coordination of social security systems [2004] OJ L166/1.

[29] Caracciolo di Torella and Masselot (n 7).

preferred terms of the norms are 'family links', 'family relations', or 'family members', leading some scholars to consider that European law is constructed on the basis of, and for, individuals alone.[30] Some go as far as concluding that the 'European family' does not exist, at least in its traditional sense of a social institution.[31]

This description fits well with the analysis of free movement law, a domain in which the logic is 'of dissuasion or deterrence'.[32] Free movement law, Advocate General Bobek argues, is built on the premise that the Union citizen will be discouraged from moving, 'as those personally *close* to him will be barred from joining him'.[33] Given that social perceptions are changing and that there is an increasing range of forms of cohabitation, the definition of the persons who are 'close' to the Union citizen is not – and cannot be – defined a priori. Sometimes, the deterrence effect is even stronger with regard to a partner under Article 3(2) of Directive 2004/38 than it is with regard to some family members listed in Article 2. This is why Advocate General Bobek adds: 'I am simply suggesting that with regard to who is effectively "close" to a person, formal box-based generalisations are hardly appropriate.'[34]

It may be the same reluctance vis-à-vis 'formal box-based generalisations' that guided the legislator when adopting Regulation 2201/2003 concerning jurisdiction and the recognition and enforcement of judgments in matrimonial matters and matters of parental responsibility.[35] The text does not specify who are the persons holding parental responsibility and having the rights of access to the child defined in Article 2(10). Whether certain persons, such as grandparents, can be considered family members and have rights of access to their grandchild is not explained. This lack of clarity results from the negotiations of the time.[36] The legislator, pondering who may exercise parental responsibility, considered several options: limiting the persons concerned to one of the parents of the child or, conversely, imposing no limitations on

30 H. Fulchiron, 'Un modèle familial européen?' in H. Fulchiron and C. Bidaut-Garon (eds), *Vers un statut européen de la famille* (Dalloz 2014).

31 S. Barbou des Places, 'La famille du ressortissant d'Etat tiers: Une famille désinstituée?' in H. Fulchiron (ed), *La famille du migrant* (Lexis Nexis 2020). See also Chapter 3 by David Archard.

32 Opinion of Advocate General Bobek in Case C-89/17 *Banger* EU:C:2018:225. See also Chapter 7 by Michael Bogdan.

33 Opinion of Advocate General Bobek in Case C-89/17 *Banger* EU:C:2018:225, para 37.

34 Ibid.

35 Council Regulation (EC) No 2201/2003 of 27 November 2003 concerning jurisdiction and the recognition and enforcement of judgments in matrimonial matters and the matters of parental responsibility [2003] OJ L338/1.

36 See Opinion of Advocate General Szpunar in Case C-335/17 *Valcheva v Babanarakis*: C:2018:242.

specific persons whatsoever. Ultimately, the legislator opted not to provide for a limitation of the range of persons who may exercise parental responsibility. For Advocate General Szpunar, we can even infer from the legislator's silence that its goal was to extend the scope of Regulation 1347/2000.[37] The legislator contemplated all decisions concerning parental responsibility and rights of access 'irrespective of the nature of the persons who may exercise those rights'[38] and without excluding grandparents. There is no predetermination of what family could mean because flexibility was the preferred option. The legislator thus achieved the paradoxical outcome that, in a text governing parental responsibility, there is no trace of a definition, or even a conception, of the family.

The semantics employed by the different texts of EU law bring to light the conceptual confusion surrounding the notion of family. Different terms ('family members', 'other family members', 'relatives', 'other relatives', 'siblings', 'siblings and parents', 'parents') coexist to describe the persons having ties with the EU citizens or sponsors or person to be taken care of, often in an inconsistent manner. True, the rationale is to modulate the rights granted to the different categories of persons. But this mode of presentation and naming creates a conceptual ambiguity: Is it coherent to talk about a 'family' when some people are not even titled 'family members'[39] and others, named 'other family members', remain outside the scope of the provision that defines 'the family'?

Practical problems also arise from the inconsistent reference to the notion of 'family members'. The *Banger* case[40] illustrates the difficulties arising from the inconsistency in Directive 2004/38. Article 3(2) of the Directive grants a facilitation regime of mobility for the unmarried partner with whom the EU citizen has a durable and duly attested relationship but does not set out the specific procedural guarantees that shall accompany its implementation. Therefore, the judicial guarantees to be applied to unmarried partners, who are not on the list of 'family members' in Article 2, remain unclear. A difficulty emerged because Article 15 of the Directive on procedural guarantees refers to Union citizens and their 'family members' with no other indication. Both the

37 Council Regulation (EC) No 1347/2000 of 29 May 2000 on jurisdiction and the recognition and enforcement of judgments in matrimonial matters and in matters of parental responsibility for children of both spouses [2000] OJ L160/1, which was limited to disputes concerning parents.

38 Ibid, para 65.

39 This is the case of siblings and 'other relatives' who play an important part in the Dublin mechanism.

40 Case C-89/17 *Banger* EU:C:2018:570.

Commission and the UK government argued that the notion of Union citizens and their 'family members', which is legally defined in Article 2(2) of the Directive, does not include extended family members. Advocate General Bobek and the Court took another position. The Advocate General noted that the notion of 'family members' does not appear to be used consistently in the provisions of Directive 2004/38.[41] Since under Article 15 procedural safeguards shall apply 'to all decisions restricting free movement of Union citizens and their family members' without referring to Article 2, it is not unreasonable to consider that the procedural guarantees to apply to family mobility should not vary according to the type of conjugal bond. Following the same logic, the Court held that the procedural safeguards provided in Article 31(1) of Directive 2004/38 are applicable to the persons envisaged in Article 3(2)(1) of the directive. This approach must be welcomed insofar as procedural guarantees are accorded to members of the extended family. Yet it is not unreasonable to question the Court's logic, which assumes that a unitary category of family exists, despite the distinction that Directive 2004/38 makes among family members. At this stage, the legitimate question to be asked is whether the Court and the other EU institutions have a vision of the 'EU family' in mind. Is there a rationale underpinning their approach? These questions can be answered in the affirmative, provided that due consideration is given to the notion of 'doing family'.

4.4 DEFINING FAMILY MEMBERS AS THOSE WHO 'DO FAMILY'

Until now, the family has been described in this chapter as a category without substance. It is now time to take a new lens: instead of *who is in* the family or *what is* a family, we might instead ask *what makes* a family.[42] For Morgan,[43] family is a facet of social life: it represents a quality rather than a thing. Morgan's work is useful for our analysis because he has shifted sociological analyses from family as a structure to which individuals belong, toward understanding families as sets of activities, which take on a particular meaning, associated with family. This line of reasoning is insightful because it has proven to be quite impossible to find a unitary family structure in EU law. In EU legal norms, in contrast, one can identify different traces of 'family activities' and 'family practices'. It appears from various legal provisions that the EU recognises situations in which individuals 'behave' and 'act as family'

[41] Opinion of Advocate General Szpunar in *Valcheva v Babanarakis* (n 36), para 87.
[42] See also Chapter 9 by Geoffrey Willems.
[43] Morgan (n 16).

members. Often the individuals are granted rights when, or because, they perform one of the main social functions which are generally assigned to the family: to provide care, protection, and education, and to contribute to the social integration of its members.

True, the social functions generally assigned to the family are not valued equally. 'Doing family', in EU law, relates primarily to performing a caring function. The Court formulated this idea implicitly in the *Valcheva* case. Having noted that the legislator had left it undecided who could be a 'holder of parental responsibility', the Court then provided a defining criterion of 'parents': they are the persons 'with whom it is important for the child to maintain a personal relationship'.[44] In so judging, the Court has not emphasised a specific type of bond which would define a parent; a case-by-case analysis will be required to identify who the 'parents' are. Nevertheless, the Court has chosen to emphasise the importance of bonds in the interest of the minor.

In most free movement and migration norms, the caring function plays a more explicit role. Article 3(2) of the EU Citizen's Directive defines as 'other family members' the persons who 'are dependent or members of the household of the Union citizen having the primary right of residence, or where serious health grounds strictly require the personal care of the family member by the Union citizen'. The same logic guides the Dublin III Regulation, the Asylum Directives,[45] and the 2015 Relocation Decision:[46] people with no biological bonds and who are not de jure family members are nevertheless referred to as family members when they provide, or need, care. The most explicit provision is Article 4(2) of the Family Reunification Directive, which allows the Member States to authorise the entry and residence of: the first-degree relatives in the ascending line of the sponsor or his/her spouse, where they are dependent on them and do not enjoy proper family support in the country of origin; the adult unmarried children of the sponsor or spouse, where they are objectively unable to provide for their own needs on account of their state of health; the unmarried minor children as well as the adult unmarried children of the partner, when these children are objectively unable

[44] Case C-335/17 *Valcheva v Babanarakis* EU:C:2018:359, para 33.

[45] Directive 2013/33/EU (n 24); Directive 2011/95/EU of the European Parliament and of the Council of 13 December 2011 on standards for the qualification of third-country nationals or stateless persons as beneficiaries of international protection, for a uniform status for refugees or for persons eligible for subsidiary protection, and for the content of the protection granted (recast) [2011] OJ L337/9.

[46] Council Decision (EU) 2015/1601 of 22 September 2015 establishing provisional measures in the area of international protection for the benefit of Italy and Greece [2015] OJ L248/80.

to provide for their own needs on account of their state of health. The same logic guided the Council when adopting Implementing Decision 2022/382 which triggers the application of the Temporary Protection Directive for people from Ukraine.[47] In this text, the family includes the 'other close relatives' who lived together as part of the family unit 'and who were wholly or mainly dependent on the sponsor'.

The notions of 'need' and 'care' take on such importance in EU law that they have even led the Court, in the *Depesme and Kerrou* case,[48] to redefine the notion of 'children' and 'parent', despite the strict meaning of the notions under Regulation 492/2011.[49] Ms Depesme, Mr Kauffmann, and Mr Lefort each lived in a reconstituted family unit – living in France and Belgium – consisting of a biological mother and a stepfather. Each of them applied for a study grant on the basis that their stepfathers had worked in Luxembourg continuously for more than five years. Yet the Luxembourgish authorities refused their applications on the grounds that they were not legally the 'children' of frontier workers but merely the 'stepchildren'. The Luxembourgish government argued that the concept of 'child' had to be interpreted restrictively.[50] Following the AG, the Court confirmed the social value of providing maintenance and care. It held that the parent–child relationship has to be defined not in legal but in 'economic terms', in that the child of a step-parent with the status of migrant worker can claim a social advantage where the step-parent contributes to the child's maintenance. The centre of gravity of the judgment is not about membership or legal linkages, it is about performing a family role, day after day. 'Doing family' is a notion that comes in via the court's application to complement de jure family bonds.

On closer inspection, it appears that this conception has been at work for many years. Already in the *Carpenter* case, the Court had the concept of care

[47] Council Implementing Decision 2022/382 of 4 March 2022 establishing the existence of a mass influx of displaced persons from Ukraine within the meaning of Article 5 of Directive 2001/55/EC, and having the effect of introducing temporary protection [2022] OJ L71/1.

[48] Case C-401/15 *Depesme and Kerrou* EU:C:2016:955.

[49] Regulation (EU) No 492/2011 of the European Parliament and of the Council of 5 April 2011 on freedom of movement for workers within the Union [2011] OJ L141/1.

[50] *Depesme and Kerrou* (n 48), para 51. In contrast, Advocate General Wathelet argued that 'a strictly legal definition' of the parent–child relationship in the context of Article 7 of Regulation 492/2011 (n 49) would be inappropriate, considering the interpretation of 'family life' as protected by Article 7 of the Charter and Article 8 of the ECHR which has departed from the criterion of 'parental relationship', recognising the possibility of 'de facto family ties': Opinion of Advocate General Wathelet in Case C-401/15 *Depesme and Kerrou* EU: C:2016:430, para 59.

play a decisive role.[51] Accordingly, in *Ibrahim* and *Teixeira*,[52] the Court conferred a right of residence on a mother of a child in education on the basis of her being the primary carer for the child. In *Teixeira*, the Court even considered that the right of residence in the host Member State of the parent who is the primary carer for a child of a migrant worker ends, in principle, when the child reaches the age of majority unless the child continues to need the presence and care of that parent to pursue and complete his/her education.[53] Later, in *Alarape*,[54] the Court confirmed the possibility of the primary carer remaining on national soil as long as the child needs care. In so judging, the Court went beyond the limits of EU secondary law, which did not ground a right of residence on the sole fact of being a mother.[55] 'Acting like a parent' is what the Court takes into consideration. It serves either to replace – as in *Depesme and Kerrou* – or to complement – as in *Alarape* – de jure family ties.

In sum, when looking at EU secondary law and at CJEU case law through the lens of 'doing family', a more coherent picture of the family emerges. The 'family members' remain identified by the conjugal or kinship bonds they share with EU citizens or migrants. The extended family members, whether named 'other family members', 'other relatives', 'relatives' or unnamed altogether, are mainly identified by the family functions they fulfil or benefit from actively caring and protecting, or passively needing care and protection. This approach, however, is an objective social reality and 'doing family' should not be confused with 'feeling like a family'.

4.5 'DOING FAMILY' AS AN OBJECTIVE SOCIAL REALITY

When the *Coman* judgment[56] was handed down by the Court, very contrasting comments were made by EU legal scholars. Since the Court held that the mobility rights conferred by the EU citizenship Directive shall be granted to the same-sex spouse of an EU citizen, even without the requirement that the host Member State has established same-sex marriage, the judgment has been

[51] Case C-60/00 *Carpenter* EU:C:2002:434.

[52] Case C-310/08 *Ibrahim* EU:C:2010:1065, and Case C-480/08 *Teixeira* EU:C:2010:83.

[53] *Teixeira* (n 52), para 87.

[54] Case C-529/11 *Alarape* EU:C:2013:290.

[55] On caregiver's right of residence in free movement law, see K. Hyltén-Cavallius, 'Who cares? Caregivers' derived residence rights from children in EU free movement law' (2020) 57 Common Market Law Review 399.

[56] *Coman and others* (n 11). See also Chapter 2 by Alina Tryfonidou, Chapter 7 by Michael Bogdan, and Chapter 9 by Geoffrey Willems.

described as bold and progressive.[57] It was indeed legitimate to infer from the judgment that the Court was willing to interpret broadly the concept of EU citizens' family members,[58] and that the EU was progressively accepting new forms of families. However, a far less enthusiastic reading of the case emerged from sceptical scholars who denied that the Court had transformed the definition of family members. The outcome, they argue, was 'simply mandated by the language of the relevant legal provisions' since their inception, given that the term 'spouse' was 'purposefully gender-neutral in the Directive 2004/38'.[59] When families composed of a same-sex couple move to a Member State that does not recognise same-sex couples, they remain confronted with the possibility that the Member State will refuse to legally recognise the familial ties among the family members as these have been legally established elsewhere. The *Coman* ruling indeed creates an obligation to recognise such marriages but 'for the sole purpose of granting a derived right of residence to a third-country national'.[60]

This critical reading rightly underlines that even in *Coman*, a judgment that enshrines a more liberal view of the family, the family remains defined by stringent objective criteria. The Court in no way promotes a definition of the family that is self-defined or 'rooted in individual biographies'.[61] This contrasts with Morgan's approach which inferred from the notion of 'doing family' that social actors creatively constitute their own social world and that 'an individual's understanding of "my family" is subject to change over time'.[62] Morgan emphasises the fluidity, the diversity, and the multifacetedness of the family. Here lies the limit of Morgan's theory for the analysis of EU law. In EU secondary law and in CJEU case law, 'doing family' and 'feeling part of a family' are two separate things. 'Doing family' remains limited to performing a set of activities or actions: it is a matter of how people behave, not how they feel, how they think of themselves as a social group, or how they love.

In CJEU case law, the motivations or the reasons for 'doing family' are irrelevant. This appears clearly from the *Reyes* case,[63] in which the Court decided that for a twenty-one-year-old daughter of a Union citizen to be

57 See D. Kochenov and U. Belavusau, 'Same-sex spouses: More free movement, but what about marriage? Coman' (2020) 57 Common Market Law Review 227.

58 G. Milios, 'Defining "family members" of EU citizens and the circumstances under which they can rely on EU law' (2020) 39 Yearbook of European Law 293.

59 D. Kochenov and U. Belavusau (n 57).

60 *Coman and others* (n 11), para 46.

61 J. Finch, 'Displaying families' (2007) 41 Sociology 65.

62 Morgan (n 16).

63 Case C-423/12 *Flora Reyes* EU:C:2014:16.

regarded as being a 'dependant' of that citizen, the existence of a situation of real dependence must be established. That status can only be the result of a 'factual situation' characterised by the fact that material support for that family member is provided by the Union citizen who has exercised his right of free movement or by his spouse. The Court underlines that there is no need to determine 'the reasons' for that dependence or for the recourse to that support. The same rationale applies in *Depesme and Kerrou*. The national judge sought to clarify the extent to which emphasis had to be placed on the fact that the frontier worker 'continues to provide for the student's maintenance' without necessarily being connected to the student through a legal child–parent relationship, where a sufficient link of communal life can be identified. The Court replied that the status of dependent member of a family is 'the result of a factual situation, which it is for the Member State and, if appropriate, the national courts to assess'. The status of family member can be evidenced by 'objective factors', such as a joint household shared by that worker and the student. It is not necessary to determine the 'reasons for the frontier worker's contribution' to the maintenance of the student or make a precise estimation of its amount. 'Doing family' is an objective fact and the willingness to act as a parent is secondary. Such willingness can be inferred from the acts of 'parents' but needs to be proved.

Of course, the Court is not unaware of the emotional side to family life but feelings and emotions are not sufficient to 'constitute' the family. This is apparent in *Alarape*[64] – a case in which the national judge was asking whether, for a parent to qualify as a 'primary carer' so as to derive a right of residence from a child under Regulation 1612/68, it is necessary for that child to be dependent on such a parent, to reside in that parent's household, and to receive emotional support from that parent. The Court held that determining whether an adult child does or does not continue to need the presence and care of his parent supposes one should:

> take into account the particular circumstances and features of the main proceedings which might indicate that the need was genuine, such as, *inter alia*, the age of the child, whether the child is residing in the family home or whether the child needs financial or emotional support from the parent in order to be able to continue and to complete his education.[65]

Emotional ties are not ignored but they mainly serve to establish the children's dependency and are not central to the definition of family

[64] *Alarape* (n 54).
[65] Ibid, para 30.

ties.[66] In other words, it seems that recognising the importance of 'doing family' does not equate to giving individuals the choice to decide for themselves who counts as family members. Rather, because the family is the 'basic cell' of European society, its definition is modelled after the EU's goal to create a cohesive society.

4.6 THE ROLE OF 'DOING FAMILY' IN THE DESIGN OF EUROPEAN SOCIETY

Among EU law scholars, the story increasingly told is one of the EU making space for greater individual emancipation and self-determination but leading to a society in which the sense of community and membership is frustrated.[67] This reading is well established among those who believe in the negative influences of the EU on family law. The EU supposedly destabilises the family order, accentuating the tendency towards individualism and the break-up of the family institution. The *Coman* judgment, and the recent *Pancharevo* ruling,[68] may have increased the impression that in promoting subjective rights and overvaluing the interest of the individual at the expense of the socially dominant conception of the family, the Court contributes to the overall phenomenon of relegation of the family as a legal institution.

There is, however, another narrative to be taken seriously. It tells that EU law strives to convert European individuals into members of the social and institutional spheres that prevail in their Member State of residence. The family is one of the 'collective entities' which individuals are destined to

[66] See Berneri who regrets the limited application of the concept of 'emotional dependency' elaborated in the *Ruiz Zambrano* judgment: C. Berneri, 'Family reunification between static EU citizens and third country nationals' (2018) 20 European Journal of Migration and Law 289.

[67] See A. Somek, 'The individualisation of liberty: Europe's move from emancipation to empowerment' (2013) 4 *Transnational Legal Theory* 258; A. Somek, 'Alienation, despair and social freedom' in L. Azoulai, S. Barbou des Places, and E. Pataut (eds), *Constructing the Person in EU Law: Rights, Roles, Identities* (Hart Publishing 2016) 5; A. Menendez, 'Which free movement? Whose free movement?' in S. Borelli and A. Guazzarotti (eds), *Labour Mobility and Transnational Solidarity in the European Union* (Jovene editore 2019) 7.

[68] In which the Court ruled that a child who has same-sex parents according to a birth certificate drawn up by the host Member State must be issued an identity card or a passport by the Member State of her nationality and must be able to exercise her freedom of movement in the EU with each of her parents. With these judgments, the CJEU is said to have removed at least the most obvious legal barriers that had stood in the way of rainbow families' free movement. See A. Tryfonidou, 'The ECJ recognises the right of rainbow families to move freely between EU Member States: The V.M.A. ruling' (2022) 47 European Law Review 534. See also Chapter 9 by Geoffrey Willems.

belong to.[69] Azoulai argues that family membership is of particular importance because it is 'a proxy for social membership':[70] families are not 'mini-societies' but entities which are central to the construction of a cohesive European society, hence the importance accorded by the EU to situations in which individuals 'do family'. Caring and protecting, participating in the construction of stable communities are all some of the individual acts that contribute to the construction of a broader social community.

Different factors support this social membership narrative. It can be observed that in various provisions and judgments, family members are encouraged to play two main roles that are decisive for the cohesion of European society. The first role is to provide material and emotional support to the most fragile and vulnerable members of the society. This aspect is central in the rules on the family reunification of refugees. Special attention is given to the possibility for refugees to recreate a family: being vulnerable people, they need to enjoy a sphere of solidarity. This is why, in the *TB* case,[71] and in the A.S. case,[72] the Court has restated the importance of family reunification as a necessary way of making family life possible, 'which is of particular importance for refugees on account of the reasons which obliged them to flee their country'.[73] Children being fragile and vulnerable individuals, the Court also values the role of their caregivers. As mentioned earlier, this led the Court in *Depesme*, *Teixeira* or *Chavez Vilchez* to characterise the

69 L. Azoulai, 'The European individual and collective entities' in L. Azoulai, S. Barbou des Places, and E. Pataut (eds), *Constructing the Person in EU Law: Rights, Roles, Identities* (Hart Publishing 2016).

70 Ibid.

71 Case C-519/18 *Bevándorlási és Menekültügyi Hivatal (TB)* EU:C:2019:1070. The Court held that Article 10(2) of Council Directive 2003/86/EC must be interpreted 'as not precluding a Member State from authorizing the family reunification of a refugee's sister only if she is, on account of her state of health, unable to provide for her own needs, provided that: – first, that inability is assessed having regard to the special situation of refugees and at the end of a case-by-case examination taking into account all the relevant factors, and; – secondly, that it may be ascertained, having regard to the special situation of refugees and at the end of a case-by-case examination taking into account all the relevant factors, that the material support of the person concerned is actually provided by the refugee, or that the refugee appears as the family member most able to provide the material support required.': para 77.

72 Case C-550/16 A. *and* S. EU:C:2018:248. The Court held that Article 2(f) of Directive 2003/86, read in conjunction with Article 10(3)(a), must be interpreted as meaning that a third-country national who is below the age of eighteen at the time of entry into the territory of a Member State and of the introduction of asylum application in that State, but who, in the course of the asylum procedure, attains the age of majority and is thereafter granted refugee status must be regarded as a 'minor' for the purposes of that provision.

73 Case C-129/18 SM EU:C:2019:248, para 32. Here the court borrows from the text of Council Directive 2003/86/EC of 22 September 2003 on the right to family reunification [2003] OJ L251/12.

stepfather as a 'parent' despite the absence of legal links, solely on the basis of the assistance provided. In the *SM* case,[74] the Court also decided that a child under a legal guardianship system such as Algerian *kafala*, although cannot be regarded as a 'direct descendant' of a Union citizen for the purposes of Directive 2004/38, can be defined as one of the 'other family members' referred to in Article 3(2)(a).[75] The words employed in Article 3(2)(a) are indeed capable of covering the situation of a child placed with citizens of the Union under the *kafala* system 'in respect of whom those citizens assume responsibility for its care, education and protection'. In these different cases, the family was always conceived as the social entity best suited to provide protection and adequate care for the most fragile individuals.

Family members are called on to perform a second social function: to contribute to the stability of social relations. *Coman* is an interesting example because the argument which grounded the judge's decision to grant same-sex spouses the right to move in the EU is the importance of protecting the family life that was created 'or strengthened' in another Member State. In so doing, the Court emphasises the individual's need for stability, a social reality that is expected to benefit both individuals and society. In other cases, the Court values the actions taken by 'family members' which ensure the continuity of children's education and integration in the host society. This is noteworthy in cases in which mothers (as in *Chavez Vilchez*) or stepfathers (as in *Depesme*) stand in for the children's defaulting father by paying for maintenance and education in his stead. These persons deserve to be called 'family members' because giving children the opportunity to attend school and pursue further education is 'a condition for the best possible integration of children of migrant workers in the social life of the host member State,' Advocate General Kokott explained[76] The mother–child or stepfather–stepchild tie is not reducible to a form of universal human relation, based on legal ties or on feelings. It is based on specific relational links that contribute to the European project of creating a cohesive society. 'Family members' can thus be described as the active persons whose presence and care are required for the purposes of integration and stability. They are defined by the specific role they are destined to play in the common interest. Being a family member is a role given to the individual as part of broader relations with others embedded in European society. Performing useful social functions is what makes a family in EU law.

[74] Case C-129/18 *SM* EU:C:2019:248.
[75] See further Chapter 7 by Michael Bogdan.
[76] Opinion of Advocate General Kokott in Case C-480/08 *Teixeira* EU:C:2009:642, para 62.

4.7 CONCLUSION

It is very tempting to believe that EU law fulfils only a limited role in family matters, restricted by national traditions and cultures. There are good reasons to believe that the (possible) influence of the EU on national models of family life is limited. In the absence of a general EU competence clause, there can be no real family law. In the absence of a sufficiently homogeneous social base, the EU would lack a basis for expressing a shared European conception of the family. In other words, the EU would not substitute its own value and representation.

However, this chapter has revealed that this description fails to account for the power of the EU's language which contributes to modelling 'the way we live and conceive our lives'.[77] It has been shown that despite the apparent variable geometry of the family, and the absence of a uniform category of 'family', the way in which the EU characterises a person as a 'family member' obeys a form of logic and expresses a certain rationality. Despite the fragmentation of sources and the modulation of family circles, rights and obligations are not randomly distributed; EU law projects a certain representation of the family. We have observed that in addition to the de jure family members, other persons are counted as family members on the basis of their 'behaving' like family members. Even when unnamed, European families exist: they are the groups of people who are assumed to perform – or asked to prove that they do perform – different functions, like education, care, protection, and socialisation. These roles are central because they contribute to a broader ambition – participating in the cohesion of the whole of European society, which is composed not of isolated individuals, but of social groups related by strong human bonds, and not only economic ties. This can be viewed as a limited contribution to the emergence of European society or, on the contrary, as the sign that EU integration is progressively taking on a more human face.

[77] Dubout (n 1).

5

One Big Happy 'European Family'? An External Perspective

MARJA-LIISA ÖBERG

5.1 INTRODUCTION

Since the early days of European integration, the European Union (EU) has been concluding association agreements (AAs) with countries in its neighbourhood.[1] In addition to EU citizens who derive rights and obligations directly from the EU Treaties, an increasing number of non-EU citizens have been granted similar free movement rights in the internal market which places them in between the categories of 'citizens' and 'foreigners'.[2] A situation both similar and different has been created by Brexit which altered the EU's territorial scope and removed EU citizenship status from United Kingdom (UK) citizens.

The fact that non-EU member states, undertakings, and individuals are directly affected by the EU legal space raises questions as to what parameters, beyond the formal criteria, can distinguish between EU Member States and non-Member States, individuals holding citizenship of the respective countries,[3] and families.[4] With a focus on Turkish, European Economic Area

[1] The first in line were the Agreement establishing an association between the European Economic Community and Greece [1963] OJ L26/294, and the Agreement establishing an association between the European Economic Community and Turkey [1964] OJ L217/3685.

[2] D. Thym and M. H. Zoetewij-Turhan, 'Introduction: Free movement between membership and partnership' in D. Thym and M. H. Zoetewij-Turhan (eds), *Rights of Third-Country Nationals under EU Association Agreements* (Brill 2015) 2.

[3] For studies on 'European individuals', see, for example: L. Azoulai, 'Transfiguring European citizenship: From Member State Territory to Union Territory, in EU citizenship and federalism: The role of rights' in D. Kochenov (ed), *EU Citizenship and Federalism* (Cambridge University Press 2015); M.-L. Öberg, 'From EU citizens to third country nationals: The legacy of *Polydor*' (2016) 22 European Public Law 97. For an analysis of the 'peoples of Europe', see Editorial Comments, 'Who are the "peoples of Europe"?' (2023) 60 Common Market Law Review 305.

[4] Thym and Zoetewij-Turhan (n 2) 2.

(EEA), and Brexit (UK and EU) families, the chapter attempts to answer the principal question of whether the families of third-country nationals (TCNs) who exercise their free movement within the Union enjoy a similar level of recognition as do the families of EU citizens. There is no clear definition of what or who constitute an 'EU family'.[5] For the purposes of this chapter, the 'EU family' is understood as composed of an EU citizen and their family members of any nationality, who enjoy rights under EU primary and secondary law, including free movement, non-discrimination, and political citizenship rights under the EU Treaties and the right to private and family life under the EU Charter of Fundamental Rights (EU Charter) and the European Convention on Human Rights (ECHR); whose integration capability in the host Member State society is assumed; and whose family life stability is protected by the host society.

In EU free movement law, families are the natural corollaries of the freely moving individual and contribute to the achievement of the internal market. Family life is supported by the rights of family reunification and of EU citizenship, as well as EU anti-discrimination law and social policy regulations. Whereas citizenship status is restricted to the nationals of EU Member States, the rights enjoyed by EU citizens, with the exception of political rights, are not exclusive and can be granted to TCNs, including as direct right holders.[6] However, in the case of AAs providing such rights to non-EU citizens, the scope of the rights is conditioned by the less ambitious aims of AAs as compared to the EU Treaties. This affects the situation of the non-EU families making use of the rights granted by AAs in the EU as well as the perception of the role of 'family' in the construction of the internal market. Unveiling the relevance accorded to family relationships in the external dimension of EU integration – as compared to integration within the EU – enables a deeper understanding not only of the individual conditions of freely moving families but also of the significance of the 'family' in the European integration process.

Section 5.2 discusses the role played by families in EU integration: initially, as facilitators and enablers of free movement and, later, as anchored in the

[5] See further Chapter 4 by Ségolène Barbou des Places.

[6] Kochenov and van den Brink have identified five categories of such persons, including TCN long-term residents in the EU under Directive 2003/109/EC, and TCNs benefitting from the agreements their country of origin has concluded with the EU whereby the individuals receive enforceable rights, including the EEC-Turkey AA, the EEA Agreement, and the Withdrawal Agreement: D. Kochenov and M. van den Brink, 'Pretending there is no Union: Non-derivative *Quasi*-citizenship rights of third-country nationals in the EU' in D. Thym and M. H. Zoetewij-Turhan (eds), *Rights of Third-Country Nationals under EU Association Agreements* (Brill 2015) 68.

fundamental status of EU citizenship. Section 5.3 explores the situation of Turkish families in the EU through the lens of 'conditional', 'qualifying', and 'associated' family statuses. Section 5.4, in contrast, explores the situation of EEA families as 'equivalent' families in relation to the EU families. Section 5.5 delves into integration as an objective under EU law and a qualifying tool vis-à-vis TCN families. Section 5.6 deals with the special case of Brexit families in the mixed EU–non-EU setting where the 'integration-family rights'-axis is reversed. In Section 5.7, the chapter concludes that whereas a clear distinction can be made between EU families and some non-EU families, and the perception of the role of the family in the EU's external instruments varies, the concept of the 'EU family' is, nevertheless, inherently flexible and open for conversion from the status of 'non-EU family' to 'EU family'.

5.2 FAMILY RIGHTS AS COROLLARY TO FREE MOVEMENT IN THE INTERNAL MARKET

The freely moving individual has been accompanied by family members since the early days of the European Economic Community (EEC). The right to free movement of workers provided residence rights in the host Member State for the worker's spouse, descendants under the age of twenty-one or dependent on the worker parent, and the dependent relatives in the ascending line of any nationality; the spouse and dependent ascendants and descendants were allowed to take up employment in the host Member State.[7] The ancillary residence rights of family members were regarded as an auxiliary to achieving the free movement of workers and, thereby, realising the internal market.[8] Due to the Member States' immigration concerns, however, this process of liberalisation was not unlimited vis-à-vis family reunification with TCN family members.[9]

The scope of the rights of the 'EU family' in another Member State depends on whether the freely moving EU citizen's family members are Union citizens or not. TCN family members are 'derivative addressees of EU law': their rights are based on their relationship with the primary addressee of EU law.[10] For the family to come into the scope of EU law, the primary

[7] Article 10(1) of Council Regulation (EEC) No 1612/68 of 15 October 1968 on freedom of movement for workers within the Community [1968] OJ L257/2. See also C. Berneri, *Family Reunification in the EU* (Hart Publishing 2017) 7.

[8] G. Barrett, 'Family matters: European community law and third country national family members' (2003) 40 Common Market Law Review 369, 375–376.

[9] Berneri (n 7).

[10] Barrett (n 8) 371. See also Chapter 8 by Albertina Albors-Llorens.

addressee – the EU citizen – must hold an 'activity or status' that makes the application of EU law relevant.[11]

The introduction of EU citizenship with the Maastricht Treaty in 1993 solidified EU integration: by directly linking citizens to the EU, the Union could now foster the creation of an 'EU identity' distinct both from the Member States and from third countries.[12] For families in the EU, EU citizenship changed the playing field profoundly. The initial foundation of economic interests embraced by the establishment of the internal market was replaced by a rights-based and more general approach to the fundamental freedoms.[13] Article 21(1) of the Treaty on the Functioning of the EU (TFEU) grants EU citizens a 'right to move and reside freely within the territory of the Member States', including rights that are 'self-standing', that is, rights which persist in the absence of a cross-border element and protect potential future movement.[14] EU citizenship grants wide protection to EU citizens' family members regardless of whether the latter themselves have exercised free movement within the EU.[15] As a complement, citizenship rights have been further substantiated by EU family law measures facilitating free movement and creating a 'common judicial area'.[16]

EU citizenship embodies a process in which political rights have been strengthened, integration deepened, and a common identity built among the peoples of the EU. This process is reflected in the Spanish memorandum 'Towards a European Citizenship', which states that an EU citizen is 'not just a privileged foreigner but also a fundamental actor in the life of the European institutions'.[17] By means of comparison, family members of any nationality supporting an EU citizen in exercising their free movement rights in another Member State equally assume the role of fundamental actors facilitating the use of free movement rights,[18] and are, thus, not merely foreigners privileged with the possibility to reside in the Union. By analogy, the achievement of the aims of AAs which grant free movement rights to TCNs is facilitated by family members who enable a TCN to exercise those rights. Since TCNs are not EU citizens, however, the question of whether the rights of non-EU families

[11] Barrett (n 8) 377.
[12] Conclusions, Fontainebleau European Council of 25–26 June 1984, 6 Bulletin of the European Communities (1984).
[13] Barrett (n 8) 418.
[14] Berneri (n 7) 4 and 93.
[15] Ibid 88.
[16] R. Lamont, 'Not a European family: Implications of Brexit for international family law' (2017) 29 Child and Family Law Quarterly 267, 270.
[17] 'Towards a European citizenship', Europe Documents No 1653, 2 October 1990.
[18] Case C-60/00 *Carpenter* EU:C:2002:434.

warrant alignment with those enjoyed by EU citizens is contingent on whether a deeper notion of European identity and purpose in relation to the internal market and the European integration project can be assigned to TCN families.

5.3 THE 'CONDITIONAL', 'QUALIFYING', AND 'ASSOCIATED' TURKISH FAMILY

The profundity of the aims of opening up the internal market to participation by non-Member States, which in some cases includes the free movement of workers, varies from one (usually) AA to another, from mostly economic exchanges in the 1963 AA concluded between the EEC and Turkey (EEC-Turkey AA)[19] to deep cooperation in the area of the internal market and beyond as an alternative to membership in the EEA Agreement.[20] The variation among the aims of AAs resembles the development of free movement rights in the EU, from market integration to beyond.[21]

The EEC-Turkey AA set out to 'promote the continuous and balanced strengthening of trade and economic relations between the Parties by, among others, establishing a customs union covering all trade in goods',[22] and 'progressively securing freedom of movement for workers'.[23] Despite the long duration of the agreement, the latter has not yet been fully attained.[24] In terms of residency and other related rights, a Turkish worker's family in the EU is, compared to an EU family, a 'step-by-step qualifying family'. Pursuant to Decision 1/80 of the Association Council[25] which complements the AA with more specific rules on free movement, Turkish workers gain access to the labour market as well as some associated residence rights. However, it is within Member State competence to lay down rules for the first entry and residence of Turkish workers and their family members.[26]

Similarly to the EU families' free movement rights being subject to certain conditions, the right of Turkish workers to free access to employment and other related rights within the scope of the Decision can be limited on

[19] See n 1.
[20] Agreement on the European Economic Area [1994] OJ L1/3.
[21] F. Wollenschläger, 'A new fundamental freedom beyond market integration: Union citizenship and its dynamics for shifting the economic paradigm of European integration' (2011) 17 European Law Journal 1, 34.
[22] Article 2 EEC-Turkey AA.
[23] Article 12 EEC-Turkey AA.
[24] Case C-81/13 *United Kingdom v Council* EU:C:2014:2449, para 57.
[25] Decision 1/80 of the Association Council of 19 September 1980.
[26] Barrett (n 8) 416–417.

grounds of public policy, public security, or public health,[27] whereas the limitation must be 'indispensable to safeguard that interest'.[28] As a general rule, a Turkish worker's family members do not enjoy self-standing rights in the host Member State. The purpose of their right of residence is limited to ensuring family unity[29] in order not to 'discourage' the Turkish worker from exploiting the possibility to work in an EU Member State.[30] With the duration of their legal residence in the host Member State, the rights of the family members of a Turkish worker to take up employment in the host Member State gradually increase. Family members gain access to the employment market after three years of lawful residence upon 'authorisation' to join a Turkish worker in a Member State subject to, during the first five years, priority given to workers from the EU.[31] Differently from the children of EU citizens, the possibility of the children of Turkish workers to join their parents in the host Member State is subject to conditions established by the Member State.[32] However, after one of their parents has been legally employed in a Member State for at least three years, the situation of Turkish children who have completed a course of vocational training in the host Member State becomes more advantageous than that of other family members. They may take up employment without being subjected to any additional time restrictions.[33]

The situation of Turkish children has been called an 'association citizenship' – a status sharing similarities with EU citizenship 'while at the same time maintaining distinct limitations and some prerogatives'.[34] In *Derin*, the Court of Justice of the EU (CJEU) concluded that there are 'significant differences between the respective legal situations' of the children of Turkish workers and EU citizens.[35] Yet, the fact that the 'significant differences' are not only to the detriment of the Turkish children render the situations 'ultimately incomparable'.[36]

Overall, the Turkish family is an 'association family'. Similarly to AAs, which cover a large variety of aims and mechanisms some of which replicate

27 Article 14 of Decision 1/80.
28 Case C-371/08 *Ziebell* EU:C:2011:809, para 86.
29 Case C-351/95 *Kadiman* EU:C:1997:205, paras 34–36.
30 J. Beqiraj and F. Ippolito, 'Conceptualizing an 'association citizenship' for children of Turkish workers' in D. Thym and M. H. Zoetewij-Turhan (eds), *Rights of Third-Country Nationals under EU Association Agreements* (Brill 2015) 279.
31 Article 7 of Decision 1/80.
32 See further in Section 5.5.
33 Article 7 of Decision 1/80.
34 Beqiraj and Ippolito (n 30) 278.
35 Case C-325/05 *Derin* EU:C:2007:442.
36 Beqiraj and Ippolito (n 30) 292.

EU law and others not,[37] the legal situation of a Turkish family in terms of residency and access to the labour market comes close to that of an EU family but cannot be equated thereto. This owes largely to the humble aims of the EEC-Turkey AA as compared to the EU Treaties. The differences between the EEC-Turkey AA and other agreements, such as the EEA Agreement, became particularly explicit in judgments in the three cases *United Kingdom v Council*, which provided the CJEU with the opportunity to compare – and contrast – the objectives of the EEA Agreement,[38] the Agreement between the European Community (EC) and Switzerland on the Free Movement of Persons,[39] and the EEC-Turkey AA,[40] respectively. The judgments elucidate the differences in objectives and context of the agreements in question which, in accordance with the so-called *Polydor*-doctrine,[41] impact the interpretation of the substantive provisions of the agreements, especially those which are worded identically to EU acquis.

In comparison with the other two agreements,[42] the CJEU stated that the objectives of the EEC-Turkey AA are narrower than the fullest possible realisation of the free movement of persons, stating merely the wish of the contracting parties to secure between them the freedom of movement for workers in progressive stages.[43] As established in cases such as *Demirkan*[44] and *Ziebell*,[45] no general freedom of movement including for long-term residents equivalent to EU citizenship is in place between the EU and Turkey. Neither is the freedom of movement for workers as established in the EU applicable to the EEC-Turkey AA.[46] Such interpretations are not supported by the 'exclusively economic'[47] character of the AA.[48] The differences in aims between the EEC-Turkey AA and the EU Treaties uphold the fundamental distinction between the rights provided to Turkish workers and their families as compared to their EU counterparts.

[37] See, for example, M.-L. Öberg, 'Internal market acquis as a tool in EU external relations: From integration to disintegration' (2020) 47 Legal Issues of Economic Integration 151.

[38] Case C-431/11 *United Kingdom v Council* EU:C:2013:589.

[39] Case C-656/11 *United Kingdom v Council* EU:C:2014:97.

[40] Case C-81/13 *United Kingdom v Council* (n 24).

[41] See Öberg (n 3).

[42] See further in Section 5.4.

[43] Case C-81/13 *United Kingdom v Council* (n 24), paras 43 and 45.

[44] Case C-221/11 *Demirkan* EU:C:2013:583.

[45] Case C-371/08 *Ziebell* (n 28).

[46] Case C-81/13 *United Kingdom v Council* (n 24), para 50.

[47] S. Ganty, 'Silence is not (always) golden: A criticism of the ECJ's approach towards integration conditions for family reunification' (2021) 23 European Journal of Migration and Law 176, 186.

[48] Kochenov and van den Brink (n 6) 97.

Despite the numerous limitations, the Turkish family is nevertheless not a forever qualifying family in the EU. In *Er*, the CJEU asserted that once a person has satisfied the conditions set out in Decision No 1/80, the Member States cannot adopt measures that would defeat the person's ability to exercise the rights arising therefrom.[49] After the conditions have been satisfied and regardless of whether the Turkish family constitutes a burden on the social security system, the Turkish family has 'qualified' into the host Member State. This 'qualification' is also exemplified by Article 7(2) of Decision 1/80 whereby the child of a Turkish worker retains the right to take up employment in the host Member State even after their worker parent has left either employment or the host Member State altogether.[50] Article 14, furthermore, precludes automatic expulsion of Turkish nationals following a criminal conviction.[51]

Once in the process of qualifying or having already qualified, the Turkish family is also a 'protected family'. First, in respect of decisions concerning the granting and renewing of residence permits and expulsion decisions, the EU standards of protection of fundamental rights apply,[52] including the right to respect for private and family life by virtue of Article 7 of the EU Charter and Article 8(1) ECHR. Second, the 'standstill' clause in Article 41(1) of the EEC-Turkey AA provides stability for the family situation of Turkish families. The standstill clause precludes the Member States when regulating Turkish nationals' first entry from adopting new restrictions to their establishment and residence in their territories compared to what applied at the time when the Additional Protocol entered into force.[53] This means that even though the situation of Turkish workers and their family members in the EU is not comparable to that of EEA European Free Trade Association (EFTA) nationals as discussed in the next section, their legal situation is stable and foreseeable over time.

5.4 THE 'EQUIVALENT' EEA FAMILY

The EEA Agreement, which entered into force in 1994, provides more comprehensive free movement rights to TCNs than any other AA. The

49 Case C-453/07 *Er* EU:C:2008:524.

50 Beqiraj and Ippolito (n 30) 284.

51 Case C-373/03 *Aydinli* EU:C:2005:434, para 12.

52 Case C-256/11 *Dereci* EU:C:2011:734.

53 Additional Protocol, signed in Brussels on 23 November 1970 and annexed to the Agreement establishing an Association between the European Economic Community and Turkey [1977] OJ L361/60.

general objective of the EEA Agreement is to create a 'homogeneous European Economic Area' based on equal conditions of competition and respect for the same rules in view of promoting 'continuous and balanced strengthening of trade and economic relations'.[54] As specified by the CJEU in *Council v UK*,[55] the EEA Agreement shall provide 'for the fullest possible realisation of the free movement of goods, persons, services and capital within the whole EEA, so that the internal market established within the European Union is extended to the EFTA States'.[56]

The EEA Agreement covers nearly the entire spectrum of the internal market, including the free movement of persons.[57] Directive 2004/38,[58] which complements the Treaty provisions governing the free movement of persons by, inter alia, setting out the limitations and conditions attached to the rights to free movement enjoyed by Union citizens, has been incorporated in the EEA Agreement.[59] By means of the Directive, the right of residence in the territory of the EEA is granted to workers holding the nationality of an EU Member State as well as Iceland, Liechtenstein, and Norway, their family members, students, pensioners, and persons with sufficient financial resources.

Save for Articles 20 and 21 TFEU, which are not incorporated in the EEA Agreement, the scope of free movement rights under the EEA Agreement with the applicable exceptions is equivalent to the free movement of EU citizens in the EU, including the coordination of social security systems. For example, the CJEU has deemed that the aims of the EEA Agreement as well as 'the level of integration already attained'[60] support extending the scope of Regulation 883/2004[61] to the EEA and thereby ensuring the same social conditions for the exercise of the free movement rights for EU citizens and EEA EFTA States' nationals alike.[62] A clear distinction is made with regard to

[54] Article 1(1) EEA Agreement.

[55] Case C-431/11 *United Kingdom v Council* (n 38), recalling Case C-452/01 *Ospelt and Schlössle Weissenberg* EU:C:2003:493, para 29.

[56] Case C-431/11 *United Kingdom v Council* (n 38), para 50.

[57] Articles 28 and 29 EEA Agreement.

[58] Directive 2004/38/EC of the European Parliament and of the Council of 29 April 2004 on the right of citizens of the Union and their family members to move and reside freely within the territory of the Member States [2004] OJ L158/77. The Directive is applicable in the EEA with certain terminological modifications as EU citizenship does not apply to the EEA EFTA States.

[59] EEA Joint Committee, decision of 7 December 2007 no 158/2007 amending Annex V (Free movement of workers) and Annex VIII (Right of establishment) to the EEA Agreement.

[60] Case C-431/11 *United Kingdom v Council* (n 38), para 57.

[61] Regulation (EC) No 883/2004 of the European Parliament and of the Council of 29 April 2004 on the coordination of social security systems [2004] OJ L166/1.

[62] Ibid, paras 50 and 58.

Turkey.[63] The fact that the Regulation does not apply to Turkish workers has profound consequences for the conditions under which the latter can exercise their free movement in the EU. To Turkish workers, instead, Decision No 3/80 of the Association Council[64] applies, providing only limited rights.[65]

Similarly to the EU, free movement in the EEA is 'to be exercised under objective conditions of freedom and dignity' and also to be 'granted to their family members, irrespective of nationality'.[66] Similarly to the case of Turkey, the right of residence of family members – either EU citizens in the EEA EFTA States or EEA EFTA State nationals in the EU – is a derived right dependent upon the EEA citizen who is the primary rights holder and intended not to 'discourage' the primary rights holder with family ties from exercising free movement.[67] In certain cases, such as divorce or when the Union citizen dies or leaves the host EEA state, a family member's right to reside may become autonomous.[68]

In terms of free movement rights, the situation of EEA families is largely comparable to EU families. This owes to the extensive aims of the EEA Agreement, the broad catalogue of free movement and corollary rights provided therein, as well as the generous, homogeneity-driven case law of the EFTA Court.[69] In a string of significant case law, the EFTA Court has gone to lengths to grant Directive 2004/38 in the EEA the same effect as in the EU, despite the different citizenship contexts.

The first case in the sequence, *Clauder*, concerned the family reunification of a German citizen who had been a long-time resident in Liechtenstein, with his wife, also a German citizen.[70] Both of them being non-economically active (pensioners), the reunification was claimed to cause an additional burden on the host state's social assistance system. The issues at hand were the right to free movement and the right to family life. The EFTA Court confirmed the right of EEA nationals to move and reside freely within the territory of the EEA states regardless of economic activity, thereby protecting the right to family life as the necessary corollary to the right to free movement. In the following judgment in *Gunnarsson*, the EFTA Court confirmed the

63 Case C-81/13 *United Kingdom v Council* (n 24), para 57.
64 Decision No 3/80 adopted by the Association Council on 19 September 1980.
65 Case C-81/13 *United Kingdom v Council* (n 24), para 24.
66 Recital 5, Preamble to Directive 2004/38/EC (n 58).
67 Case C-86/12 *Alokpa and Moudoulou* EU:C:2013:645, para 22.
68 Recital 15, Preamble and Articles 12, 13 and 18 of Directive 2004/38/EC (n 58).
69 See C. Tobler, 'Free movement of persons in the EU v. in the EEA: Of effect-related homogeneity and a reversed Polydor Principle' (2018) 3 European Papers 1429.
70 Case E-4/11 *Clauder* [2011] EFTA Ct. Rep. 216.

equivalence of the scope of free movement rights in the EEA with the free movement right of Union citizens irrespective of economic activity.[71]

The EFTA Court has been criticised for stretching the scope of rights granted to EEA nationals too far, going beyond the level of corresponding rights and obligations under EU law.[72] Nevertheless, with *Jabbi*,[73] the EFTA Court continued the line of homogeneity-securing case law. In the case, the EFTA Court bypassed the CJEU's interpretation in *O. and B.* of Directive 2004/38.[74] In *O. and B.*, the CJEU interpreted Directive 2004/38 as not providing a derived right of residence to a family member of a Union citizen returning to their Member State of origin because in the EU context, Article 21(1) TFEU is instead applicable. This is, however, different with regard to the EEA. Via the controversial techniques of 'effect-related homogeneity',[75] or 'reverse *Polydor* principle',[76] the EFTA Court found that Directive 2004/38 shall be applied by analogy to a situation where an economically non-active EEA citizen returns with their TCN spouse to the EEA citizen's home country. In *Jabbi*, the same result was achieved, in essence, as in *O. and B.* but by different – and controversial – interpretational means. Whether all of the examples mentioned above will be upheld by the CJEU in the EU-pillar of the EEA is left to be seen. At this point, the interpretation of the EU's free movement rules in the EEA, especially by the EFTA Court, essentially follows the essence of the CJEU's ruling in *Metock*,[77] in which the Court established the 'protection of the family life' of Member State nationals as a necessary corollary to 'eliminat[ing] obstacles to the exercise of the fundamental freedoms' provided by the Treaties – an aim that goes beyond achieving economic aims by means of the free movement of workers. It is, thus, possible to say that the objectives and substantial provisions of the EEA Agreement regarding the extension of the EU internal market to the EEA EFTA States as well as their subsequent interpretation strongly uphold homogeneity in the situation of EEA families as compared to EU families.

[71] Case E-26/13 *Gunnarsson* [2014] EFTA Ct. Rep. 254.

[72] Advokatfirmaet Simonsen Vogt Wiig AS, 'Legal study on Norway's obligations under the EU Citizenship Directive 2004/38/EC' (4 January 2016) 139. <www.udi.no/globalassets/global/forskning-fou_i/annet/norways-obligations-eu-citizenship-directive.pdf>

[73] Case E-28/15 *Yankuba Jabbi v The Norwegian Government* [2016] EFTA Ct. Rep. 575, para 77.

[74] Case C-456/12 *O. and B.* EU:C:2014:135. The EFTA Court gave an equivalent ruling in Case E-4/19 *Campbell v The Norwegian Government* [2020] EFTA Ct. Rep. 21.

[75] C. Burke and Ó. Í. Hannesson, 'Citizenship by the backdoor? *Gunnarsson*' (2015) 52 Common Market Law Review 1111.

[76] Tobler (n 69).

[77] Case C-127/08 *Metock* EU:C:2008:449, para 56.

5.5 THE 'INTEGRATED FAMILY'?

The free movement of persons in the EU frequently collides with the interests of the Member States, including with regard to economic, social, and identity-related matters. Within the EU, tensions in the internal market concerning the free movement of persons are exemplified, for instance, by the transitional arrangements that restrict the free movement of workers from new Member States for a limited period of time, as well as the conditions that apply to the free movement of persons such as engagement in work or studies, or possession of sufficient funds. In the context of the free movement of persons, immigration concerns are considered but predominantly for the purpose of protecting the national social welfare systems. In the context of external migration, the conflict between the aim of enabling the free movement of workers and family reunification, on the one hand, and control over migration, integration, and the protection of national identity, on the other, is significantly more pronounced.[78]

The EU is set out to constitute a space unifying differences between peoples, societies, and states on the basis of shared values, which are reflected in the terminology of integration in EU law: 'belonging, membership, common values and solidarity'.[79] With the notable exception of developed countries including the EEA EFTA States and Switzerland, the assumption of a shared basis of common values does not apply to non-Member States nor to their nationals who can be subject to civic integration requirements in the EU.[80] Civic integration requirements are a perfect exemplification of the tensions inherent to family reunification. Whereas the economic development of the Union calls for the free movement of workers including from outside the EU, the introduction of civic integration requirements assumes that the cultural differences between the third country and the EU are significant and that the integration of TCNs into the EU Member States' societies necessitates additional conditionality.

Traditionally, integration has been an issue determined by national laws controlling access to citizenship and, thereby, distinguishing the 'perfect

[78] P. Dąbrowska-Kłosińska, 'The right to family reunion vs integration conditions for third-country nationals' (2018) 20 European Journal of Migration and Law 251.

[79] S. Barbou des Places, 'The integrated person in EU law' in L. Azoulai, S. Barbou des Places, and E. Pataut (eds), *Constructing the person in EU law: Rights, roles, identities* (Hart Publishing 2016) 196.

[80] S. Carrera and A. Wiesbrock, 'Civic Integration of Third-Country Nationals: Nationalism versus Europeanisation in the Common EU Immigration Policy', CEPS 2009.

citizens' from the 'foreigners'.[81] Integration has entered the realm of EU law as a result of the 'Europeanisation of immigration policy', which gives EU the role of controlling integration[82] via, for example, residency and family reunification rights. The increasing attention to integration in the EU is accentuated by the creation in 2019 of the alarmistic-sounding post of a Commissioner and Commission vice-president for 'Protecting our European Way of Life'.

The aim of family reunification is to facilitate family life as well as help ensure the family's integration in the host Member State subject to restrictions laid down in law but is, as previously mentioned, not unconditional. Directive 2003/86 allows the Member States to reject an application of family reunification on grounds of public policy, public security, or public health.[83] Furthermore, a Member State may, while considering the child's best interests, set up additional requirements for 'overriding reasons in the public interest' regarding the family reunification of a TCN worker parent with minor-age children; the requirements include the consideration of ensuring successful integration, that the parent worker (1) has resided in the Member State for less than two years; (2) has an appropriate dwelling; (3) has sufficient income to support for themselves and their family; and (4) complies with integration-related measures established by the Member State.[84]

Under certain conditions, Member States are permitted under Article 15(3) of Directive 2003/109 to establish integration requirements, such as those of civic integration for TCNs under national law.[85] When the conditions set by one Member State are met, the requirements are automatically satisfied within the entire EU.[86] 'Once' a TCN is integrated in one Member State, he or she is, thus, 'always' integrated in the entire EU notwithstanding the fact that integration is ultimately a matter of degree rather than absolute quantity.[87]

[81] S. Carrera, *In Search of the Perfect Citizen?* (Martinus Nijhoff 2009) 440–441. For criticism on how integration requirements perpetuate prejudices, see D. Kochenov, 'Mevrouw de Jong Gaat Eten: EU citizenship and the culture of prejudice' EUI Working Paper RSCAS 2011/06 <https://cadmus.eui.eu/handle/1814/15774>, 7.

[82] Carrera (n 81) 441.

[83] Article 6(1) of Council Directive 2003/86/EC of 22 September 2003 on the right to family reunification [2003] OJ L251/12.

[84] See a summary of legislation and CJEU case law in Case C-379/20 Summary of the request for a preliminary ruling pursuant to Article 98(1) of the Rules of Procedure of the Court of Justice by Østre Landsret (Eastern High Court, Denmark), lodged on 11 August 2020, para 15.

[85] Council Directive 2003/109/EC of 25 November 2003 concerning the status of third-country nationals who are long-term residents [2004] OJ L16/44.

[86] Editorial Comments (n 3) 306.

[87] Barbou des Places (n 79) 189.

The CJEU has interpreted the lawfulness of the Member States' integration requirements on multiple occasions, often in the context of the EEC-Turkey AA. In *Dogan*, the CJEU considered the compatibility of a German requirement of basic language skills as a precondition for family reunification with the standstill clause in the EEC-Turkey AA. The Court recognised that the grounds put forward by the German government – the prevention of forced marriages and the promotion of integration – can constitute overriding reasons in the public interest but that German law goes beyond what is necessary to attain the objective as the dismissal of the application is automatic and does not allow for consideration of the specific circumstances of individual cases.[88]

Another case, *Genc*,[89] concerned a Danish rule restricting the reunification in Denmark of TCN children above the age of fifteen with their sponsor parent, a TCN worker, after two years of legal residency unless justified by 'particularly compelling reasons', including 'regard for family unity'.[90] The rationale behind the Danish rule is to prevent granting residence rights to minor-age children who have had most of their upbringing and schooling in their country of origin and whose chances of successful integration in the Danish society are, therefore, low. Because of the lack of individual assessment of the applicants' integration potential on the basis of 'sufficiently precise, objective and non-discriminatory criteria',[91] the Court deemed the rule to breach the standstill clause in the EEC-Turkey AA. The focus of the national rule is on the individual with little integration potential rather than on the family as a whole. In the absence of a possibility of family reunification with minor children, however, the entire family may be less likely to integrate fully into the host Member State society. In *Genc*, the Court upheld the standstill clause and, thereby, the function of families as supporting elements of integration in the host society.

In the more recent case *B*,[92] the Court considered whether the age limit of fifteen years below which the child of a Turkish worker residing legally in the host Member State may apply for family reunification constitutes a 'new restriction' prohibited by the standstill clause in the EEC-Turkey AA, and, if so, whether it could be justified by the objective of ensuring successful integration of the TCN which could constitute an overriding reason in the public interest. In this case, the Court decided that since practice did not provide evidence of the Danish authorities 'systematically refusing' applications for family reunification from children aged fifteen and above, the

88 Case C-138/13 *Dogan* EU:C:2014:2066.
89 Case C-14/09 *Genc* EU:C:2010:57.
90 Para 9(13) of the Law on aliens (Udlændingeloven).
91 *Genc* (n 89), para 66.
92 Case C-379/20 *B v Udlændingenævnet* EU:C:2021:660, para 18.

provision did violate the standstill clause but could be justified on legitimate grounds and was proportional to the aim pursued. A careful consideration of individual cases, thus, justifies restrictive national rules on family reunification. It is also implied that the supporting role of family members in achieving the aims of free movement of workers can be subject to the integration potential of individual family members. Family members with potential integration difficulties, such as a spouse with insufficient command of the official language of the Member State in question, or a child considered too old to successfully acquire the language, values, and professional or academic skills, are not considered to have the prospects of being able to sufficiently contribute to the Member State's society and labour market. They are not regarded as supporting the integration of the Turkish worker in the host Member State and, thereby, helping achieve the predominantly economic aims of the EEC-Turkey AA to a degree that would outweigh the potential costs for the host society.

Another important question to consider is whether, and to what extent, TCN families can maintain connections to and be successfully integrated in more than one country. In A, the Court held that the relationships that individuals can have with different countries, including EU Member States and third countries, are 'not mutually exclusive' and that the attachment of a third country (in this case Turkish) national to their country of origin cannot determine their prospects of integration.[93] A national provision based on a contrary claim was thus not considered suitable for achieving the aim of integration in the host society.[94] The question of an individual's attachment to more than one Member State is equally relevant in a purely EU or even national context,[95] with less at stake in terms of free movement rights than the effect of the distribution of rights.[96] Only in exceptional circumstances such as expulsion does it become acutely pertinent to establish a Member State to which the individual is primarily integrated.[97] Directive 2004/38 exemplifies the correlation between integration and rights. A similar correlation in the form of time scales, which indicate certain rights becoming available, applies to the qualifying periods of the family members of Turkish workers in an EU Member State's labour market.

It is generally accepted that EU citizens have connections to and are integrated in different Member States. Free movement, which has the effect

[93] Case C-89/18 A *v Udlændinge- og Integrationsministeriet* EU:C:2019:580, para 39.

[94] Ibid, para 42.

[95] Ganty (n 47) 178.

[96] See Barbou des Places (n 79) 183.

[97] Ibid, 182–183.

of leading to integration in different Member States, is strongly encouraged. Initially, participation in the labour force of the host Member State's society and contributing thereto in the form of paying taxes constituted a test of integration.[98] However, the emergence of a specific 'objective' of integration in EU law whereby rights are expected lead to the integration of an individual in the host Member State[99] has marked a departure from the economic foundation of free movement rights.[100] It is, thus, relevant in the EU's external and internal contexts alike.

The possibilities of family reunification and the independent rights of the Turkish workers' family members are limited by the predominantly economic rationale of the EEC-Turkey AA. Against the backdrop of the long period of stagnation in the Turkish EU accession process, there are currently no indications of a sudden deepening of the relationship between the EU and Turkey that would warrant a new impetus for the free movement of Turkish workers in the EU and the accompanying rights of family members.

The overall situation of Turkish workers and their families in the EU is comparable to long-term guests at a hotel. Turkish families are provided entry into the EU, but their key cards open the door to one room only – the one Member State in which the long-term residency under Directive 2003/109 is granted. The Turkish family is not considered part of the family (the 'collectively constituted society in a deeper sense')[101] and cannot move themselves freely in the entire house ('the EU's full territory in a geographical sense').[102] Yet the Turkish family is welcome to contribute to the society by participating in the labour force and demonstrating willingness and capability of integration into the society, upon the formal achievement of which – the acquisition of citizenship of an EU Member State by any of the family members – it can become a genuine 'EU family'.

5.6 THE 'REMOVED' BREXIT FAMILIES

Brexit has brought about a dramatic change in the status of EU families in the UK, and British families in the EU. Solving the situation of the families

98 Case C-542/09 *Commission v The Netherlands* EU:C:2012:346, para 65.

99 Barbou des Places (n 79) 181.

100 Recital 4, Preamble to Council Directive 2003/109/EC (n 86) provides that 'The integration of third-country nationals who are long-term residents in the Member States is a key element in promoting economic and social cohesion, a fundamental objective of the Community stated in the Treaty.'

101 Editorial Comments (n 3) 306.

102 Ibid.

finding themselves on the 'other' (but – importantly – not 'wrong') side of the EU-UK border was one of the priorities in the countless rounds of withdrawal negotiations. The importance of families in the midst of the Brexit turmoil is reflected in the Preamble to the Withdrawal Agreement, which recognises the necessity 'to provide reciprocal protection for Union citizens and for United Kingdom nationals, as well as their respective family members, where they have exercised free movement rights' before the end of the transition period.[103] The fact that the EU's AAs scarcely mention families highlights the significance of families (duly defined) in the unusual legal relationship between the EU and the UK as a former Member State.

Brexit families are distinct from the Turkish and the EEA families in that the emphasis in the comparison of their legal situation with that of EU families is on the differences rather than similarities. Putting an end to the free movement of persons was one of the main arguments in the Brexit debate that ended in the UK leaving the Union.[104] Yet, citizenship rights have been extended to individuals and families directly affected by Brexit with certain important distinctions. In the context of Brexit families, it is pertinent to ask how the former or sustained connection to the EU affects their legal situation.

Article 9(a) of the Withdrawal Agreement provides a broad definition of family members. A Brexit family is comprised of persons 'irrespective of their nationality' who are 'family members of Union citizens or family members of United Kingdom nationals as defined in point (2) of Article 2 of Directive 2004/38/EC' or other persons 'whose presence is required by Union citizens or United Kingdom nationals in order not to deprive those Union citizens or United Kingdom nationals of a right of residence'.

As a former Member State, the relationship of the UK with the EU is substantially different from both Turkey and the EEA EFTA States. The focus in the Brexit process and in the reconstruction of a legal and political relationship post-Brexit has not (yet) been on strengthening ties, but rather on finding a satisfactory solution to protecting the individuals and families affected by the UK's withdrawal and enabling them to maintain the

[103] Recital 6, Preamble to the Agreement on the withdrawal of the United Kingdom of Great Britain and Northern Ireland from the European Union and the European Atomic Energy Community [2019) OJ C 384/1.

[104] See, for example, A. Łazowski, 'When *Cives Europae* became bargaining chips: Free movement of persons in the Brexit negotiations' (2018) 18 ERA Forum 469.

relationships and ties of integration to their states of residence and origin, as well as to their habitual lives, families, communities, and identities.[105]

The Withdrawal Agreement contains provisions on EU citizens who have exercised their right to reside in the UK, UK citizens who have exercised that right in the EU before the end of transition period, as well as their family members including children born or adopted in the future.[106] Article 13 allows continued residence rights in the UK for EU nationals, EU national family members, and TCN family members, based indirectly on Directive 2004/38 and conditional upon participation in the labour force, being a student, having sufficient funds, or being a family member of a worker – hence, belonging to a qualified category.

More severely affected by Brexit are vulnerable persons falling outside of the qualified categories, such as family members with insecure career paths or working periods intertwined with periods of absence from the labour market.[107] These and other categories of people who, within the EU, would have been caught by the safety net of EU citizenship and the limited manifestation of financial solidarity are, in the post-Brexit reality, left without protection.[108]

Under Article 15(3) of the Withdrawal Agreement, five years of legal residency grants EU and UK citizens and their family members a right to permanent residency on the conditions provided by EU free movement law; periods before as well as after the transition period shall be included. Under Directive 2004/38, the status of permanent residency can be lost after two years of absence from the host state whereas the Withdrawal Agreement allows for a five-year period of absence.[109] The status is not lost if either the EU or UK citizens or their family members change status, with the exception of family members whose rights of residence depend on the primary right holder after the end of the transition period and who cannot become primary right holders.[110] This is a significant difference from Turkish workers who lose

[105] According to Spaventa, since UK citizens have built lives in the EU, as former EU citizens they should be treated at least as favourably as former family members: E. Spaventa 'Mice or horses? British citizens in the EU 27 after Brexit as "former EU citizens"'(2019) 44 European Law Review 589.

[106] Articles 10(1)(a) and 10(1)(e) of the Withdrawal Agreement.

[107] M. Dougan, 'So long, farewell, aufwiedersehen, goodbye: The UK's withdrawal package' (2020) 57 Common Market Law Review 631.

[108] C. O'Brien, 'Between the devil and the deep blue sea: Vulnerable EU citizens cast adrift in the UK post-Brexit' (2021) 58 *Common Market Law Review* 431, 439; For further examples, see Dougan, ibid 671–674.

[109] Article 15(1) of the Withdrawal Agreement.

[110] Article 17(1) of the Withdrawal Agreement.

residency rights upon leaving the host Member State for a significant, but undefined, period of time without a valid reason such as maternity leave or sickness.[111] Whereas efforts have, thus, been made to ensure stability in their residence situation, Brexit has disrupted the previously relatively unbureaucratic life of EU-UK families. The Withdrawal Agreement provides a possibility for the respective host States to require EU or UK citizens and their family members to apply for a new residence status – the 'settled status' – which entails rights under the Agreement,[112] but which has also been subject to severe criticism.[113]

In stark contrast to the limitations applying to the family members of Turkish workers, the family members of EU or UK citizens holding the right of residence or permanent residence in the UK or the EU, respectively, enjoy an unconditional right to take up employment or self-employment in the host State.[114] In situations where a family is separated by the primary carer of the children of an EU or UK worker leaving the host State, certain stability is ensured for the remaining family members. The children retain a right of residency until they reach the age of majority, or longer if the child continues their studies and needs 'the presence and care of the primary carer',[115] hence not disrupting the daily lives of the family members.

Under EU law, the divided but not necessarily broken family receives special attention. By virtue of EU citizenship, individuals as well as families enjoy the freedom to choose how and where to conduct their family life. This is, for example, reflected in Regulation 883/2004, which enables the payment of family benefits and tax credits by the host Member State for the EU workers' children residing abroad.[116] The Regulation also applies in the EEA. The EU family can choose to be spread out across the Union, and beyond. The EU family has the freedom not to cohabit but to nevertheless function as an economic and social family unit, and also to reunite at will. By the powerful statement of the European Commissioner for Employment, Social Affairs, Skills and Labour Mobility, there are no 'second-class workers in the EU', and no 'second-class children'.[117] The payment of family benefits by a Member

[111] Article 6 of Decision 1/80.

[112] Article 18(1) of the Withdrawal Agreement.

[113] See O'Brien (n 108).

[114] Article 24(2) of the Withdrawal Agreement.

[115] Ibid.

[116] For statistics, see S. Kennedy, 'Child Benefit and Child Tax Credit for children resident in other EEA countries' Research Briefing, SN06561 <https://commonslibrary.parliament.uk/research-briefings/sn06561/>.

[117] European Commission, 'Indexation of family benefits: Commission opens infringement procedure against Austria' Press release, IP/19/462 (24 January 2019) <ec.europa.eu/commission/presscorner/detail/en/IP_19_463>.

State for children residing in another Member State reaffirms the status of a family that does not cohabit on a daily, weekly, or even a monthly basis. Not bringing a family along to the host Member State constitutes, if it represents the choice of the family, an alternative means of supporting free movement in the EU.[118] If the family members of an individual exercising their free movement right did not wish to or could not move from their Member State of origin, considering the family as a unit only if sharing a household on a permanent basis would obstruct the freely moving individual. The flexible approach to the physical location of individual family members offers space for individual considerations of the best interests of the family.

Brexit families are, overall, 'removed' families – not necessarily due to their rights gained under EU (citizenship) law but, potentially, due to their identity as 'EU families'. Differently from the Turkish and the EEA families, the Brexit families have a sustained and genuine connection to the EU, either via citizenship or place of residence, but the maintained rights of individuals and family members are not intended to reinforce integration, specifically. Instead, the sustained connection to the host State society via rights of residency and taking up employment as well as access to the social security systems serve the purpose of maintaining pre-existing family relationships. The rationale of the derived rights of family members in the cases of the Turkish and the EEA families to support the achievement of economic or further integration aims, respectively, is, thus, reversed in the case of Brexit.

5.7 CONCLUSION

On the basis of the expansion of EU integration beyond the Union's borders providing free movement rights to many groups other than EU citizens and accompanying rights to their family members, is it possible to conclude that an all-encompassing 'European family' is about to emerge? The examples of Turkish, EEA, and Brexit families indicate large variations in the situations and scope of rights of family members of freely moving workers based on whether the respective non-Member State's cooperation with the EU is based on predominantly economic rationales, guided by the aim of achieving deeper integration, or focused on maintaining a former status. However, the boundaries

[118] In contrast, the CJEU interpreted Directive 2004/38 as not granting a right to long-term residence in Germany to a Japanese citizen whose wife had moved to Austria together with their child, and from whom he is now separated: Case C-40/11 *Iida* EU:C:2012:691. See also A. Tryfonidou, '(Further) signs of a turn of the tide in the CJEU's citizenship jurisprudence: Case C-40/11, *Iida*, Judgment of 8 November 2012' (2013) 20 Maastricht Journal of European and Comparative Law 302; and Chapter 2 by Alina Tryfonidou.

between 'EU families' and their 'non-EU' counterparts are more or less opaque depending on the legal arrangement. The mutually strong efforts on behalf of the EU as well as the EEA EFTA States and, in particular, the EFTA Court are leading to increasingly homogeneous conditions for the purpose of exercising free movement rights by EU and EEA families. Furthermore, over time, as witnessed by the 'qualifying' Turkish families, the dissimilarities between the rights of EU and non-EU families become less distinct. This is different in the case of Brexit families whose family status is conserved with a focus not on deepening but on maintaining rights previously enjoyed.

As noted above, to appreciate whether the conditions of non-EU families in the EU should warrant alignment with the situation of EU families, it is necessary to consider the extent to which TCNs carry a deeper notion of European identity and purpose. In the EU, TCN workers and, indirectly, their families contribute to achieving both the core aim of the EU integration project – the creation of the internal market – and its expansion to non-Member States. The role of the freely moving workers and their families is instrumental to achieving the latter. Furthermore, there is no reason to assume that a TCN individual cannot foster a sense of belonging and identity towards an EU Member State to a level comparable to an EU citizen exercising their right to free movement. Brexit constitutes a distinctive example of truly mixed identities across the EU–UK borders.

It is important to bear in mind that differently from an 'individual' or 'citizen', the concept of an 'EU family' or a 'non-EU family' is inherently flexible. A 'non-EU family', too, is a flexible category in that a family is to certain extent autonomous from its country of origin. One or more members of a family can make use of free movement rights, take up work in an EU Member State, become a permanent resident, and, eventually, assume that Member State's citizenship, thereby becoming an EU citizen and granting the entire family the status of an 'EU family'. During this process, on the individual level, the economic rationale of a TCN to work in the EU is replaced by a level of identity with the host society and integration therein. The 'EU family' is, thus, a concept less closely tied to the processes of membership, accession, and withdrawal from the EU and per definition more open to welcoming new members.

PART II

The EU Family and Rights

6

The Fundament of the Fundaments?

Family Rights and the EU Charter of Fundamental Rights

XAVIER GROUSSOT, GUNNAR THOR PETURSSON,
AND ALEZINI LOXA

6.1 INTRODUCTION

Similarly to other conventional fundamental rights, the right to respect for family life[1] was not mentioned in the European Union (EU) Treaties from the outset. The right of families of economically active EU nationals (workers) has been protected through secondary legislation already since the 1960s.[2] However, as emphasised by the Court of Justice of the EU (CJEU) in *MRAX*,[3] the protection of the family life of EU Member State nationals was related to a primary objective, namely to 'eliminate obstacles to the exercise of the fundamental freedoms guaranteed by the Treaty'. This point had also been emphasised in *Carpenter*,[4] which was delivered in the same month as *MRAX*.

The strong link between the right to family life and free movement is not surprising, and the question we will examine in the following pages is to what extent this link remains essential when invoking the right to respect for family life under the EU Charter of Fundamental Rights (the Charter).[5] Can the Charter provisions extend the protection of family life under EU law? Or is a free movement element necessary for the activation of the Charter provisions? Moreover, how does the protection of family life under the Charter interact with the EU citizen status?

1 On the right to family life in general, see, for example, C. McGlynn, *Families and the European Union Law, Politics and Pluralism* (Cambridge University Press 2006); M. Pascual and A. Torres Pérez (eds), *The Right to Family Life in the European Union* (Routledge 2018).

2 See, for example, Council Regulation (EEC) No 1612/68 of 15 October 1968 on freedom of movement for workers within the Community [1968] OJ L257/2.

3 Case C-459/99 *MRAX* EU:C:2002:461, para 53.

4 Case C-60/00 *Carpenter* EU:C:2002:434, paras 38–39.

5 Charter of Fundamental Rights of the European Union [2012] OJ C 326/391.

Investigating the link between free movement, family rights, and EU citizenship is essential for the following reason. The right to family life, which is often used in case law to interpret the free movement and citizenship provisions of the Treaty on the Functioning of the EU (TFEU), relates – using a federal jargon – to the issues of localism and the moral values of national communities.[6] In the EU, this means that the interpretation and limitation of the right is dictated by the Charter's horizontal clauses that guide the 'competence valuation', which takes place between the centre and the periphery, that is, between the EU and its Member States.[7] Whether family rights can be protected at the EU level or at the national level can have far-reaching consequences, especially for families that do not fit within the traditional heteronormative ideal. In the context of rule of law backsliding in some Member States,[8] strengthening the link between family rights and EU citizenship can consolidate the protection of queer families.

In this chapter, we examine how family rights are protected in EU law. Section 6.2 discusses the relationship between the horizontal provisions of the Charter and family rights. In this section, we highlight that the horizontal provisions of the Charter affect both the extent of protection of family life (depending on whether a claim falls within the scope of EU law) and the substance of the right (what the scope of the right can be).

In Section 6.3, we turn to the specific provisions related to the right to family life (Article 7 and its attached rights such as Article 9 on the right to marry, Article 21 on non-discrimination, Article 24 on the best interests of the child, and Article 33 on the protection of family life) and we examine how the protection they afford has been developed in the case law of the Court.

In Section 6.4, we look at the interaction of family rights with the citizenship provisions under Articles 20 and 21 TFEU. The analysis shows how the CJEU has at times protected family rights without reference to the Charter, but through embedding such rights in the protection afforded by the EU citizen status. More recent case law developments have pointed to a stronger link between the Charter and the citizenship provisions. Section 6.5 concludes our investigation, by suggesting that the EU citizenship provisions have

6 C. Joslin, 'Federalism and family status' (2015) 90 Indiana Law Journal 787.

7 See X. Groussot and G. T. Petursson, 'The EU Charter of Fundamental Rights five years on – The emergence of a new constitutional framework' in S. de Vries, U. Bernitz, and S. Weatherill (eds), *The EU Charter of Fundamental Rights as a Binding Instrument – Five Years Old and Growing* (Hart Publishing 2015).

8 See pending Case C-769/22 *Commission v Hungary* regarding the violation of the rights of LGBT people and closed infringement case INFR(2021)2115 on the Polish 'LGBT free' zones. See also Chapter 12 by Nausica Palazzo.

shown more potential for the protection of family life than the Charter provisions on family rights.

6.2 FAMILY RIGHTS AND THE HORIZONTAL PROVISIONS OF THE EU CHARTER

Since the entry into force of the Charter, the right to respect for family life is protected under Article 7 which stipulates that 'Everyone has the right to respect for his or her private and family life, home and communications'. Further, Article 6 of the Treaty on European Union (TEU) provides that the Charter has 'the same legal value as the [EU] Treaties'. By virtue of this Article, the right to respect for family life has been augmented to the level of primary law. This repositioning of fundamental rights in EU law was both timely and welcomed,[9] as it marked a new stage in the process of European integration.[10]

At the same time, it has been maintained that – within the scope of EU law – the Charter is to be the *starting point and reference legislation* for any legal analysis involving fundamental rights.[11] The Charter is, thus, the fundament for fundamental rights protection in EU law – it impacts and steers the review of EU law in light of fundamental rights. Relatedly, the protection offered under Article 7 of the Charter is dependent on and conditioned by the applicability of the Charter.

Before analysing the substantive scope of Article 7 of the Charter and related rights under the Charter in Section 6.3, it is, first, important to lay down and explain the circumstances under which the Charter is applicable. Second, since the Charter rights and principles are applied on the basis of a methodology that is impacted by the horizontal provisions found in Title VII of the Charter, this section will also address the main elements of the horizontal provisions and their implications for the right to family life.

9 See Groussot and Petursson (n 7).

10 K. Lenaerts, 'Exploring the limits of the EU Charter of Fundamental Rights' (2012) 8 European Constitutional Law Review 375. See also P. Eeckhout, 'The EU Charter of Fundamental Rights and the federal question' (2002) 39 Common Market Law Review 945.

11 In their Joint Declaration of January 2011, the presidents of the Strasbourg and Luxembourg courts stated that '[T]he Charter has become the reference text and the starting point for the CJEU's assessment of the fundamental rights which that legal instrument recognises.' Opinion of Advocate General Bot in Case C-108/10 *Scattolon* EU:C:2011:211, para 108 states: 'Since the Charter now occupies a central place in the system of protection of fundamental rights in the Union, it must, ... constitute the reference legislation each time the Court is called upon to rule on the compliance with an EU measure or a national provision with the fundamental rights protected by the Charter.'

When analysing the case law of the CJEU, where fundamental rights play a role, three main categories of cases emerge: (1) cases that deal with actions of the EU institutions,[12] including annulment cases under Article 263 TFEU; (2) cases that deal with the implementation of EU law at the national level, that is, the situation when Member States are implementing and applying EU secondary law at the national level;[13] and (3) review of Member State actions in light of fundamental Treaty provisions/principles, such as the citizenship provisions, free movement provisions, or other fundamental provisions of EU law.[14] Each of these categories represents an 'entry point' through which the EU Charter, with all that follows, may enter the scene of EU law.

For the first category of cases, Charter rights may be used to review the legality of EU secondary norms. Examples of such cases include *Digital Rights Ireland*,[15] and *Schrems I* and *Facebook Ireland and Schrems (Schrems II)* cases,[16] where Articles 7 and 8 of the Charter played an important role in gauging the validity of EU secondary norms. The first case where the CJEU referred to the Charter revolved around family rights. This was *Parliament v Council*,[17] a case that concerned the European Parliament's (unsuccessful) claim for the annulment of the final subparagraph of Article 4(1), Article 4(6), and Article 8 of Directive 2003/86 on the right to family reunification.[18]

In the second category of cases, we have the situation where EU secondary norms are to be interpreted in light of fundamental rights when implemented and applied at the national level. This category features the largest number of cases, which concern, for example, deportation and family reunification regulated in secondary law, the national application of which must be compliant with fundamental rights. Many examples relate to the application of Directive 2004/38,[19] and other instruments, such as Regulation 2201/2003

[12] Case C-370/12 *Pringle* EU:C:2012:756. On the limitations of the scope, see Joined Cases C-8/15 P to C-10/15 P *Ledra Advertising v Commission and ECB* EU:C:2016:701.

[13] Case 5/88 *Wachauf* EU:C:1989:321. See also Case C-817/19 *Ligue des droits humains* EU:C:2022:491, paras 86–87.

[14] Principle of non-discrimination or Article 19 TEU.

[15] Joined Cases C-293/12 and C-594/12 *Digital Rights Ireland and others* EU:C:2014:238.

[16] Case C-362/14 *Schrems (I)* EU:C:2015:650, and Case C-311/18 *Facebook Ireland and Schrems (Schrems II)* EU:C:2020:559.

[17] Case C-540/03 *Parliament v Council* EU:C:2006:429.

[18] Council Directive 2003/86/EC of 22 September 2003 on the right to family reunification [2003] OJ L251/12.

[19] Directive 2004/38/EC of the European Parliament and of the Council of 29 April 2004 on the right of citizens of the Union and their family members to move and reside freely within the territory of the Member States [2004] OJ L158/77. See Recital 31, Preamble: 'This Directive respects the fundamental rights and freedoms and observes the principles recognised in

concerning jurisdiction and the recognition and enforcement of judgments in matrimonial matters and the matters of parental responsibility.[20]

In the third category of cases, we have the application of Treaty provisions in review of Member States' measures. In this category, we find the typical free movement situations such as in *Carpenter*, where the right to family life is a threshold over which Member States need to go to successfully justify a restriction to free movement. In this category, we would place cases that are based on the fundamental provisions found in the Treaty, namely Article 20 and/or Article 21 TFEU on EU citizenship and the rights of EU citizens to move and reside freely in the territory of member states.[21] The cases concerning citizenship and fundamental rights, in particular the right to family life, can broadly be fleshed out in three main areas: firstly, situations where Union citizens are being deported from a host member state; secondly, claims that involve the Union citizen's identity;[22] and, thirdly, cases that concern the right to respect for family life.[23] In sum, fundamental rights – and more precisely EU Charter rights and principles – operate in varying situations within EU law.

On the relationship between the right to family life and the horizontal provisions of the Charter, this right applies following Article 51 of the Charter to the actions of the EU institutions, and to the Member States, 'when implementing Union law'.[24] When falling within the scope of EU law, a

particular by the Charter of Fundamental Rights of the European Union.' See also Case C-127/08 *Metock* EU:C:2008:449.

[20] Council Regulation (EC) No 2201/2003 of 27 November 2003 concerning jurisdiction and the recognition and enforcement of judgments in matrimonial matters and the matters of parental responsibility [2003] OJ L338/1. See Case C-400/10 PPU *McB* EU:C:2010:582.

[21] Case C-34/09 *Ruiz Zambrano* EU:C:2011:124 is an ideal example apart from the fact that, surprisingly, the EU Charter is not applied in the case. In more recent cases, the CJEU is using the EU Charter also in the citizenship realm; see analysis in Section 6.4. Similar reasoning is also applied in relation to Article 19 TEU in the context of the rule of law, such as Case C-64/16 *Associação Sindical dos Juízes Portugueses* EU:C:2018:117, and Case C-619/18 *Commission v Poland* (Independence of the Supreme Court) EU:C:2019:531.

[22] See, for example, Case C-208/09 *Sayn-Wittgenstein* EU:C:2010:806; Case C-391/09 *Runevič-Vardyn and Wardyn* EU:C:2011:291.

[23] See N. Nic Shuibhne, 'The right to move and reside: Disentangling the dual dynamics of fundamental rights in EU citizenship law' in S. Douglas-Scott and N. Hatzis (eds), *Research Handbook on EU Law and Human Rights* (Edward Elgar Publishing 2017) 105.

[24] Case C-617/10 *Åkerberg Fransson* EU:C:2013:105. In the case, the Court noted that it had no competence to examine the compatibility of national law with the Charter, if it was 'lying outside the scope of European Union law'. However, if the national legislation was falling within the 'scope of European Union law', the Court explained that that would not constitute a scenario where fundamental rights would not be applicable, since 'applicability of European Union law entails applicability of the fundamental rights guaranteed by the Charter' (see paras 20 and 21).

situation involving the application of Article 7 of the Charter should pay particular consideration to the non-absolute nature of the right to family life and to its close relationship to Article 8 ECHR.

The very substance of a fundamental right, such as the right to family life, is very much linked to the extent of the acceptable limitations to that right under Article 52(1) of the Charter. It should be highlighted that EU fundamental rights are not only limited or balanced against each other, they may, and very often do, act in a complementary way. A case in point is Article 47 of the Charter that is often linked with a substantive fundamental right.[25] Article 52 (1) of the Charter is a specific limitation clause, to be applied 'horizontally' throughout the Charter.[26]

Importantly, the EU right to family life is also a corresponding right to Article 8 ECHR following Article 52(3) of the Charter and the explanations to the Charter.[27] In Article 52(3) of the Charter, we find a *homogeneity*-type clause,[28] which states that insofar as the Charter contains rights, which correspond to rights guaranteed by the ECHR, the meaning and scope of those rights shall be the same as laid down in the ECHR. However, the same provision also states that this shall not prevent Union law from providing more extensive protection. Even if many attempts were made during the drafting of the Charter to include a direct reference to the case law of the European Court of Human Rights (ECtHR), no such reference is found in the Charter.[29] However, as held by Groussot and Gill-Pedro, by giving the Charter binding force as primary EU law, the EU is committing to protecting rights guaranteed by ECHR, where an equivalent is found in the Charter. This means, in their

[25] Joined Cases C-245/19 and C-246/19 *État luxembourgeois contre B* EU:C:2020:795, para 52: 'In the present instance, however, the three fundamental rights involved are not liable to be at odds with each other but are complementary in their application. The effectiveness of the protection that Article 47 of the Charter is intended to confer on the holder of the right guaranteed thereby cannot be expressed or assessed other than in relation to substantive rights, such as those referred to in Articles 7 and 8 of the Charter.'

[26] Article 52(1) of the Charter states: 'Any limitation on the exercise of the rights and freedoms recognised by this Charter must be provided for by law and respect the essence of those rights and freedoms. Subject to the principle of proportionality, limitations may be made only if they are necessary and genuinely meet objectives of general interest recognised by the Union or the need to protect the rights and freedoms of others.'

[27] Explanations Relating to the Charter of Fundamental Rights [2007] OJ C303/17.

[28] Opinion of Advocate General Kokott in Case C-110/10 *Solvay v Commission* EU:C:2011:257, para 95.

[29] X. Groussot and E. Gill-Pedro, 'Old and new human rights in Europe – The scope of EU rights versus that of ECHR rights' in E. Brems and J. Gerards (eds), *Shaping the Rights in ECHR – The Role of the European Court of Human Rights in Determining the Scope of Human Rights* (Cambridge University Press 2013) 247.

view, protecting the rights 'as defined by the ECtHR'.[30] Article 52(3) of the Charter will also have to be read, applied, and interpreted in light of Article 53 of the Charter. Indeed, in the *Explanations to the Charter*, the following is stated regarding Article 7:

> The rights guaranteed in Article 7 correspond to those guaranteed by Article 8 of the ECHR. To take account of developments in technology the word 'correspondence' has been replaced by 'communications'. In accordance with Article 52(3), the meaning and scope of this right are the same as those of the corresponding article of the ECHR. Consequently, the limitations which may legitimately be imposed on this right are the same as those allowed by Article 8 of the ECHR . . . .[31]

This view on the substantive scope of Article 7 of the Charter and its strong link with Article 8 ECHR was also clearly confirmed by the CJEU in the O. *and* S. case, where the Court described Article 7 of the Charter as 'containing rights corresponding to those guaranteed by Article 8(1) [ECHR]'.[32] Similarly, in *Carpenter*, which was delivered prior to the entry into force of the EU Charter, the Court relied solely on Article 8 ECHR.

6.3 PROTECTION OF FAMILY LIFE IN THE CHARTER AND THE CASE LAW OF THE COURT

The protection of family life in the Charter appears in Article 7, but the scope of protection of the right is also related to Article 9 on the right to marry, Article 21 on non-discrimination, Article 24 on the best interests of the child, and Article 33 on the right to family and professional life.

The latter Article, while mentioned in case law, has not had any effect on expanding the protection of family life in EU law. Specifically, Article 33(1) refers to the protection of family under EU law 'as a unit to be protected in its own right, rather than exploited in the pursuit of other goals'.[33] Despite the potential of the provision as argued by Costello,[34] Article 33(1) of the Charter has only been invoked in disputes related to EU staff benefits and the Court has not elaborated on its scope of protection and relation to Article 7 of the

[30] Ibid 250.

[31] Explanations relating to the Charter of Fundamental Rights (n 27).

[32] Joined Cases C-356/11 and C-357/11 O. *and* S. EU:C:2012:776, para 76.

[33] C. McGlynn, 'Families and the European Union Charter of Fundamental Rights: Progressive Change or Entrenching the Status Quo' (2001) 26 European Law Review 582, 587.

[34] C. Costello, 'Article 33 Family and Professional Life' in S. Peers, T. Hervey, and A. Ward (eds), *The EU Charter of Fundamental Rights: A Commentary* (Hart Publishing 2014) 917.

Charter.[35] Article 33(2) of the Charter refers to the right to reconciliation of family and professional life. In essence, this provision refers to existing entitlements under secondary law.[36] Accordingly, the relevant case law refers to the right protected under Article 33(2) of the Charter next to secondary law which gives expression to it.[37] Nevertheless, the right has not been used as a basis for expanding reconciliation policies and extending the protection of families.[38]

Contrary to the mere reference of Article 33 in case law, the Court has elaborated a lot more on the relation of Article 7 with Articles 21 and 24 of the Charter to extend the protection offered by EU law to queer families. Specifically, the case law on queer families had been developed with reference to the importance of the principle of non-discrimination even before the adoption of the Charter.[39] No use has yet been made of Article 9 on the right to marry, as the Court has held that the civil status of marriage and all the benefits that are connected to it are part of the competence of the Member States.[40] However, when Member States exercise their competence, they should comply with the principle of non-discrimination.[41] This line of reasoning is still present in the Court's case law even after the adoption of the Charter.

In the early case of *K.B.*, the Court took a progressive approach to the right to marry of trans individuals, by linking the protection of the right to family life to non-discrimination.[42] The case concerned the pension rights of the trans partner of a worker, K.B., a cis woman, who was in a relationship with a trans man who could not officially register his gender reassignment. As a result, they were unable to marry, which meant that K.B.'s partner was not entitled to her widower's pension. The protection of the right of trans people to marry was ensured in this case by reference to Article 12 ECHR and the *Goodwin v the*

[35] Case T-131/20 *IR v Commission* EU:T:2020:381; Case T-484/18 *XB v ECB* EU:T:2020:90; Case T-517/16 *Janoha and others v Commission* EU:T:2018:874.

[36] C. McGlynn, 'Reclaiming a feminist vision: The reconciliation of paid work and family life in European Union law and policy' (2001) 7 Columbia Journal of European Law 262.

[37] Case C-149/10 *Chatzi* EU:C:2010:534, para 37; Case C-222/14 *Maïstrellis* EU:C:2015:473, para 39; Case C-174/16 *H* EU:C:2017:637, para 32; Case C-129/20 *Caisse pour l'avenir des enfants (Emploi à la naissance)* EU:C:2021:140, para 44.

[38] For arguments as to how this could be done, see Costello (n 34) 919–924.

[39] A model that is privileged by both political and judicial institutions: S. Choudhry, 'Right to Respect for Private and Family Life (Family Life Aspects)' in S. Peers, T. Hervey, and A. Ward (eds), *The EU Charter of Fundamental Rights: A Commentary* (Hart Publishing 2014) 207; McGlynn (n 33) 586. See Case C-267/06 *Maruko* EU:C:2008:179, para 59 analysed below.

[40] *Maruko* (n 39); Case C-443/15 *Parris* EU:C:2016:897, para 59; Case C-673/16 *Coman and others* EU:C:2018:385, para 37.

[41] *Maruko* (n 39), para 59; Case C-443/15 *Parris* EU:C:2016:897, para 58.

[42] Case C-117/01 *K.B.* EU:C:2004:7.

UK case of the Strasbourg Court.[43] More specifically, the CJEU held that this case gave rise to inequality of treatment, not in relation to the enjoyment of EU rights, but with respect to the necessary precondition thereof, which is the capacity to marry.[44] By extrapolating the ECtHR standards of protection to the EU legal order, the Court found that the relevant national legislation, which precluded K.B. and her trans partner from marrying and, thus, benefitting from widower's pension, was both in breach of Article 12 ECHR and EU law.[45]

While *K.B.* added a significant layer of protection for trans rights,[46] a more restrictive approach was taken in relation to same-sex couples in *Grant*[47] and *D and Sweden v Council*.[48] The former case, in particular, has been criticised for the 'lack of any real commitment to fundamental rights'.[49] Ms Grant was a worker who claimed a travel concession for her same-sex partner. Her employer refused to grant this benefit on the ground that such concessions were only provided to unmarried partners of opposite sex. The Court had to address the question of whether such refusal constituted discrimination prohibited by EU law.[50] The Court referred to the ECtHR case law of the time, which excluded same-sex relationships from protection under Articles 8 and 12 ECHR to justify the unequal treatment suffered by Ms Grant by her employer.[51]

D and Sweden v Council, too, concerned a worker, who claimed household allowance under the Council Staff Regulations. The benefit was granted to D's married colleagues but was denied to him because his registered same-sex partnership was not considered equivalent to a marriage. Even though the Charter was not binding at the time, Advocate General Mischo took Article 9 into account in his Opinion, and pointed to its inherent limitations. Specifically, he highlighted that the explanations to the Charter are clear in that 'Article 9 neither prohibits nor requires the grant of the status of marriage to relationships between persons of the same sex'.[52] To the Advocate General,

43 Ibid, para 33; *Christine Goodwin v the United Kingdom*, Application no 28957/95.

44 *K.B.* (n 42), para 30.

45 Ibid, para 36.

46 In line with Case C-13/94 *P v S and Cornwall County Council* EU:C:1996:170, para 94.

47 Case C-249/96 *Grant* EU:C:1998:63.

48 Joined Cases C-122/99 P and C-125/99 P *D and Sweden v Council* EU:C:2001:304.

49 See McGlynn (n 1) 142.

50 Under Article 119 EC Treaty on equal pay and Council Directive 75/117/EEC of 10 February 1975 on the approximation of the laws of the Member States relating to the application of the principle of equal pay for men and women [1975] OJ L45/19.

51 *Grant* (n 47), paras 33–34.

52 Opinion of Advocate General Mischo in Joined Cases C-122/99 P and C-125/99 P *D and Sweden v Council* EU:C:2001:113, para 97.

this confirmed the difference in treatment between marriage and same-sex partnerships.

The Court followed the Opinion of the Advocate General by affirming that marriage should be taken to imply a relationship 'within the traditional meaning of the term'.[53] What is more, the Court confirmed the decision of the Court of First Instance, which had held that long-term same-sex relationships are not covered by the right to private life under Article 8 ECHR.[54] Even though there was no legal possibility for D to contract a marriage at the time, the Court found that the situations of marriage and same-sex partnership were not comparable, thus confirming the finding in *Grant*.[55] As a result, D could not claim a violation of the principle of equal treatment.[56]

In *Maruko*, the Court took a different approach from *D and Sweden v Council* finding that same-sex partnerships and marriage could be treated as comparable.[57] Maruko was in life partnership with a person of the same sex. After the partner's death, he claimed widower's pension, but his claim was rejected because the two had not been married. The Court did not examine the case under the prism of the right to private life or the right to marry. It confirmed that issues of civil status and the benefits connected to it are matters of national competence.[58] However, the Court reminded that, in the exercise of such competence, Member States need to comply with non-discrimination provisions. Of relevance to the resolution of the case under a non-discrimination lens was also the fact that national law established same-sex partnership and provided for gradual equivalence of marriage and partnership in relation to social security rights.[59]

The next development for same sex couples came with *Coman*.[60] In this case, the referring court made explicit reference to Article 9 of the Charter as relevant for the adjudication of the case.[61] However, Advocate General Wathelet pointed out that Article 9 becomes irrelevant by virtue of the explanations to the Charter.[62] These limit the scope of protection that the Union can

53 *D and Sweden v Council* (n 48), para 11.
54 Ibid, paras 14 and 60.
55 Ibid, para 51.
56 Ibid, paras 51–52.
57 *Maruko* (n 39).
58 Ibid, para 59.
59 Ibid, paras 67–69.
60 *Coman and others* (n 40). See also Chapter 9 by Geoffrey Willems.
61 *Coman and others* (n 40), para 17.
62 Opinion of Advocate General Wathelet in Case C-673/16 *Coman and others* EU:C:2018:2, para 43.

offer and confirm – as does the case law – that the Member States are entirely free to arrange issues related to marital status.

Hence, what defined *Coman* was the protection offered by Article 7 of the Charter. The connection of Article 7 of the Charter with free movement and the right to non-discrimination necessitated the recognition of same sex unions for the purposes of exercising free movement rights under EU law. Contrary to the Advocate General, the Court did not make an explicit reference to the link between Articles 7 and 21 of the Charter. Instead, it referred to the evolution of ECtHR case law[63] and proceeded to declare that same-sex relationships do fall within the notion of private and family life.[64] The Court eventually resolved the case by connecting the protection of private and family life under Article 7 of the Charter to the effective exercise of free movement rights.[65] The case has been celebrated in scholarship for many reasons.[66] Among these is the fact that it provided 'a federal path for the recognition of the marriage status for the purposes of residence in the EU countries still hanging behind institutionalization of same-sex unions'.[67] Contrary to previous case law which revolved around employment benefits, this case was central in extending the reach of EU fundamental rights protection through a free movement rationale.

The issue of protection of queer families returned to the Court's docket in the V.M.A. case, which concerned the cross-border recognition of same-sex parenthood.[68] In that case, we see more clearly the impossibility of using Article 9 of the Charter as a tool to advance a broader conception of family life under EU law. Advocates General Wathelet and Mischo are proven right in their Opinions on earlier cases that it must be impossible for the Court to use Articles 9 and 7 of the Charter as tools to expand protection of queer families under EU law.[69] Instead, Article 9 can be used to reinforce national restrictive

63 *Orlandi and Others v Italy*, Application no 26431/12, and *Vallianatos and Others v Greece* [GC], Application nos 29381/09 and 32684/09.

64 *Coman and others* (n 40), para 50.

65 Ibid, paras 47–51.

66 A. Tryfonidou, 'The ECJ recognises the right of same-sex spouses to move freely between EU Member States: The Coman Ruling' (2019) 44 European Law Review 663; D. V. Kochenov and U. Belavusau, 'After the celebration: Marriage equality in EU law post-Coman in eight questions and some further thoughts' (2020) 27 Maastricht Journal of European and Comparative Law 549.

67 D. Kochenov and U. Belavusau, 'Same-sex spouses: More free movement, but what about marriage? Coman' (2020) 57 Common Market Law Review 227, 239.

68 Case C-490/20 *V.M.A. v Stolichna obshtina, rayon 'Pancharevo'* EU:C:2021:1008. See also Chapter 9 by Geoffrey Willems.

69 Opinion of Advocate General Mischo in *D and Sweden v Council* (n 52) ECLI:EU:C:2001:113, and Opinion of Advocate General Wathelet in *Coman and others* (n 62).

conceptions of family. Specifically, in *V.M.A.*, the referring court invoked Article 4(2) TEU in conjunction with Article 9 of the Charter as a potential basis for justifying national competence on the conception of family and parentage. The Court confirmed once again that EU law, and the Charter in particular, cannot affect the discretion of Member States in the recognition of same sex marriage or parenthood in purely internal situations.[70] Avoiding unnecessary engagement with Article 9 of the Charter, the Court had recourse to Articles 7 and 24 to establish the protection of queer families and the cross-border recognition of same-sex parenthood as means to ensure the effective exercise of the free movement rights enjoyed under Article 21 TFEU.[71]

In this context, it is important to reflect on the two central issues which characterise the relation between Articles 7 and 9 of the Charter and the protection of queer families: competence and the link with free movement. First, in all of the cases discussed, the Court expressly stated that the civil status of marriage and the benefits tied thereto fall under Member States' competence. A similar reasoning, albeit from the premise of human rights law, has been followed by the ECtHR. The ECtHR has held that Article 12 ECHR does not impose an obligation to grant same-sex couples the right to marry.[72] Member States are entirely free to choose whether they allow same-sex marriage or not, the conditions under which they regulate same-sex unions, and whether they recognise them as equivalent to marriage or not. This is in line with the localist conception of sovereignty in US federalism, which maintains that marriage should be regulated at local level as it promotes 'a shared moral vision of the good family life'.[73] Further, it confirms the danger that Weiler pointed in the early 2000s regarding the risk that Charter regresses the status quo: 'each time an innovative concept were argued before the European Court, it would be pointed out that a proposal to that effect was considered in the drafting of the Charter and failed. It would be much harder for the Court to crystallise a Community right when such was considered and rejected by a political constituent assembly.'[74] The categorical nature of the

70 Case C-490/20 *V.M.A. v Stolichna obshtina, rayon 'Pancharevo'* EU:C:2021:1008, paras 51–52.

71 See also Order of the Court in Case C-2/21 *Rzecznik Praw Obywatelskich* EU:C:2022:502 which repeated the Court's reasoning in V.M.A.

72 This obligation cannot derive from either Article 12 alone or from Article 14 in conjunction with Article 8. See *Schalk and Kopf v Austria*, Application no 30141/04; *Chapin and Charpentier v France*, Application no 49183/07.

73 See A. Dailey, 'Federalism and families' (1995) 143 University of Pennsylvania Law Review 1787, 1790.

74 J. Weiler, 'Editorial: Does the European Union truly need a Charter of Rights?' (2000) 6 European Law Journal 95.

explanations on Article 9 of the Charter precludes the possibility of ever using it to extend the protection of queer families.

This brings us to the second issue of links with free movement. Unable to use the substantive provisions of the Charter, the Court extends the protection of the right to family life by emphasising the need for effective exercise of free movement rights. After ascertaining that EU law does not affect Member State competence on marital issues, the Court reminds that the Member States should exercise their competence in compliance with the principle of non-discrimination and the free movement provisions. In essence, the Court extends the protection provided by the Charter to queer families by using the effective exercise of free movement rights as a 'trump card'.[75] The effective exercise of free movement rights enjoyed not only by workers, but also by EU citizens under Article 21 TFEU has also been behind the extensive protection of family life. The more specific way in which this takes place and the reluctance of the Court to refer to the Charter when extending such protection will be analysed in the following section.

6.4 FAMILY RIGHTS AND EU CITIZENSHIP

Family rights have often been discussed in EU law within the study of the citizenship case law, which has created a 'bundle of rights'.[76] The relationship between the issue of citizenship and fundamental rights has never been simple.[77] Following *Martínez Sala*,[78] the CJEU started to progressively

[75] A. Loxa, 'Analysis: "Cross-border recognition of parenthood for rainbow families"' (*EU Law Live*, 14 December 2021) <https://eulawlive.com/analysis-cross-border-recognition-of-parenthood-for-rainbow-families-by-alezini-loxa/>. See also A. Tryfonidou, 'The ECJ recognises the right of rainbow families to move freely between EU Member States: The V.M.A. ruling' (2022) 47 European Law Review 534, on the gaps that remain following VMA.

[76] The term 'bundle of rights' refers to the sociological understanding of citizenship suggested by T. H. Marshall, according to whom citizenship is a process of accumulation of bundles of civil, political, and social rights by people: see T. H. Marshall, *Citizenship and Social Class, and Other Essays* (Cambridge University Press 1950). This understanding of citizenship has been taken on by different scholars to conceptualise what the EU citizenship status could imply: see C. Schönberger, 'European citizenship as federal citizenship, some citizenship lessons of comparative federalism' (2007) 19 European Review of Public Law 63. See also R. Koslowski, 'A constructive approach to understanding the European Union as a federal polity' (1999) 4 Journal of European Public Policy 561.

[77] See S. Adam and P. Van Elsuwege, 'EU citizenship and the European federal challenge through the prism of family reunification' in D. Kochenov (ed), *EU Citizenship and Federalism – The Role of Rights* (Cambridge University Press 2017) 443. Most EU citizenship cases are linked to family reunification; see, for example, Case C-578/08 *Chakroun* EU:C:2010:117, paras 61–64.

[78] Case C-85/96 *Martínez Sala v Freistaat Bayern* EU:C:1998:217.

develop case law tying citizenship and EU fundamental rights, in particular the right to family life protected by Article 8 ECHR, through the general principles of EU law.

Moreover, the Court has on many instances employed Article 24 of the Charter on the rights of the child, thereby extending the protection of family life under EU law. In the early stages of the Court's case law, the protection of children's rights 'remain[ed] parasitic on the migrant; rights [were] granted to children instrumentally in order to ensure economic success'.[79] However, as noted by McGlynn, the Charter marked an evolution in the EU legal order 'from the instrumentalism which characterizes the fields of free movement, to the protectionism of policies on violence and trafficking, to a recognition of children's independence and autonomy'.[80] Children were no longer seen as potential 'consumers' or 'appendages to economic actors'.[81] Instead the Court's case law elevated them to 'persons of their own right'.[82]

Initially, the Court was reluctant to use the Charter as the legal basis of protection of the rights of children holding an EU citizenship. Instead, the protection of children as autonomous bearers of rights was based on the citizenship provisions. In the seminal ruling in *Chen*,[83] the Court adjudicated that the protection of the best interests of the Union child can be the basis of a derivative residence right for the child's third-country national parent. This conclusion was made by reference to the need for an effective enjoyment of the rights conferred by Union citizenship to children. The Charter was not applicable at the time of adjudication and the principle of the best interests of the child was not referred to by the Court.

In a similar vein, *Ruiz Zambrano* confirmed the protection of children's rights and the reluctance of the Court to employ the Charter.[84] In this case, the national court invoked the Charter as a basis for review of the national legislation at stake.[85] Advocate General Sharpston similarly suggested that the relevant questions be examined from a human rights angle by reference to the right to family life and the Charter.[86] However, the Court failed to take Article 24 of the Charter into account in its decision, demonstrating a 'lack of

79 See McGlynn (n 1) 49. Indicatively Case 76/72 *Michel S. v Fonds national de reclassement social des handicapés* EU:C:1973:46; Case C-308/89 *Di Leo v Land Berlin* EU:C:1990:400.

80 McGlynn (n 1) 67.

81 McGlynn (n 33) 584.

82 McGlynn (n 1) 74.

83 Case C-200/02 *Zhu and Chen* EU:C:2004:639; McGlynn (n 1) 56.

84 *Ruiz Zambrano* (n 21).

85 Ibid, para 35.

86 Opinion of Advocate General Sharpston in Case C-34/09 *Ruiz Zambrano* EU:C:2010:560, paras 151–177.

confidence in human rights arguments'.[87] Instead, once more, it ensured the protection of Union children as autonomous bearers of rights under the citizenship provisions by reference to Article 20 TFEU and the 'substance of rights' test. The ruling in *Ruiz Zambrano* is very progressive, but the reasoning of the CJEU is minimal and excludes any reference to the application of the Charter and EU fundamental rights. In this ruling, we see a 'constitutional challenge'[88] posed by the extension to fundamental rights in the citizenship case law which confirms Iglesias Sanchez' suggestion that 'the intersection between European citizenship and fundamental rights is extremely complex to articulate without pushing the contours of one of them beyond the carefully built-up constitutional balances, since their underlying rationales give rise to significant tensions and difficulties when assessing the possible ways forward'.[89]

Generally, post-*Zambrano* case law reflects and confirms the *malaise* of the Court to use the Charter in parallel with citizenship provisions.[90] Yet, following *Rendón Marín*,[91] new developments may herald a new era in the intersection between EU citizenship and EU fundamental rights. In *Rendón Marín*, the CJEU applied a 'slightly looser test' in its interpretation of Article 20 TFEU by relying on the concept of dependency and the EU Charter.[92] The case concerned a third-country national from Colombia with a criminal record. As a father, Mr Rendón Marín was responsible for the primary care of two children, one of Polish and the other of Spanish nationality, who were both schooled in Spain. The Court had to assess the refusal of a residence permit by the Spanish authorities based on reasons of public policy and public security having the possible consequence for Mr Rendón Marín moving back to Colombia. Was the effectiveness of the two children's EU citizenship in danger here? For the Court, the situation at issue was capable of resulting in their deprivation of the genuine enjoyment of the substance of rights conferred by the status of Union citizenship. For that, the Court found that the case fell within the scope of EU law.[93] Relatedly, the assessment of Mr Rendón Marín's situation should take into account the right to respect

87 McGlynn (n 1) 73.

88 J. Snell, 'Do fundamental rights determine the scope of EU law?' (2018) 43 European Law Review 475.

89 S. Iglesias Sanchez, 'Fundamental rights and citizenship of the Union at a crossroads: A promising alliance or a dangerous liaison?' (2014) European Law Journal 107.

90 See Case C-86/12 *Alokpa and Moudoulou* EU:C:2013:645; Case C-115/15 NA EU:C:2016:487.

91 Case C-165/14 *Rendón Marín* EU:C:2016:675.

92 D. Ferri and G. Martinico, 'Revisiting the Ruiz Zambrano doctrine and exploring the potential for its extensive application' (2021) 27 European Public Law 685.

93 *Rendón Marín* (n 91), para 80.

for private and family life (Article 7 of the Charter), read in conjunction with the obligation to take into consideration the child's best interests under Article 24(2) of the Charter.[94] The interpretation of the CJEU on Article 20 TFEU follows a logic borrowed from the free movement case law, the Court first evaluating the potential breach of EU primary law like in *Dassonville*,[95] and thereafter assessing the restriction to primary law in light of the Charter and EU fundamental rights like in *Carpenter*.

After *Rendón Marín*, the crucial question was whether the interpretation of Article 20 TFEU in light of the Charter would be applied consistently in cases with similar factual situations. The CJEU provided a clear positive answer in two Grand Chamber cases: *Chavez-Vilchez*[96] and *KA*.[97] *Chavez Vilchez* concerned third-country national mothers of children with EU nationality who had applied for social assistance and child benefits in the Netherlands. Their applications were refused because the mothers had no residence rights at the time. The national court inquired whether the mothers can derive a right of residence from Article 20 TFEU.[98] In his Opinion, Advocate General Szpunar took the principle of the best interests of the child as a starting point.[99] Contrary to the Opinion of the Advocate General, however, the Court based the rights of irregular migrants who were parents of Union children on the 'genuine enjoyment of the substance of rights conferred by Article 20 TFEU' test. In this test, the Court deferred the resolution of the case to the national courts and pointed out that an assessment of the genuine enjoyment test should take place in connection to the right to respect for family life under Article 7 of the Charter and the obligation to take into account the best interests of the child under Article 24(2) of the Charter.[100] This highlighted the importance of fundamental rights protection as procedural limits to Member State action.

In *KA*, the Belgian courts asked the CJEU about the compatibility of national provisions and administrative practice with Article 20 TFEU and the Return Directive.[101] These provisions made it possible for immigration

[94] Ibid, para 81.

[95] Case 8/74 *Dassonville* EU:C:1974:82.

[96] Case C-133/15 *Chavez-Vilchez and others* EU:C:2017:354.

[97] Case C-82/16 K.A. *and others* EU:C:2018:308.

[98] Ibid, para 39.

[99] Opinion of Advocate General Szpunar in Case C-133/15 *Chavez-Vilchez and others* EU:C:2016:659, para 42.

[100] *Chavez-Vilchez and others* (n 96), para 70.

[101] Directive 2008/115/EC of the European Parliament and of the Council of 16 December 2008 on common standards and procedures in Member States for returning illegally staying third-country nationals [2008] OJ L348/98.

authorities to refuse to examine applications for family reunification made by TCNs based on existing entry bans, and lead to the impossibility to determine on a case-by-case basis the relationship of dependency between an EU citizen and their TCN family member. Following the Opinion of Advocate General Sharpston,[102] the Court considered that Article 20 TFEU precludes a national practice that consists of not examining an application for residence for the purposes of family reunification by a TCN family member of a Union citizen who is a national of that Member State and who has never exercised his/her right to freedom of movement.[103] In assessing the existence of a relationship of dependency capable of justifying a derived right of residence under Article 20 TFEU, the national authority must take account Articles 7 and Article 24(2) of the Charter.[104] The Court also elaborated on the concept of dependency by delineating a clear line between situations involving minor and adult EU citizens. For the Court, in situations where the EU citizen is an adult, dependency is conceivable 'only in exceptional circumstances' where the separation of the EU citizen and the TCN family member is not possible.[105] Overall, *KA* constitutes an important addition to the case law because it clarified the concept of dependency in the use of the 'substance of rights test' and the evaluation of a potential breach of the effectiveness of EU citizenship by national authorities.

New positive developments on the right to family life can also be seen in relation to the interpretation of Article 21 TFEU. The *Lounes* case is of particular interest, although it does not explicitly mention Article 7 of the Charter.[106] In this case, the Court had to decide whether a Spanish national, Ms Ormazabal, who moved to the UK and became a British citizen, while keeping her Spanish nationality, could be treated in the same way as a person in a purely domestic situation. The CJEU refused to follow this path, which would have undermined the effectiveness of Article 21(1) TFEU,[107] and considered that a dual national who has exercised her freedom to move to a Member State other than her Member State of origin, may rely on the rights pertaining to Union citizenship, in particular the rights provided for in Article 21(1) TFEU.[108] In doing so, the Court underlined in a clear fashion that the

[102] *K.A. and others* (n 97), para 76.
[103] Ibid, para 62.
[104] Ibid, para 76.
[105] Ibid.
[106] See Case C-165/16 *Toufik Lounes* EU:C:2017:862. Mr Lounes, an Algerian national, had married Ms Ormazabal in London four years after his illegal entry to the UK.
[107] Ibid, para 53.
[108] Ibid, para 51.

rights which Member State nationals enjoy under that provision include the right to lead a normal family life in the host Member State together with their family members.[109] Although this paragraph does not expressly refer to Article 7 of the Charter, it is this specific provision that the Court has in mind when it mentions the right to lead a normal family life.[110] As put by Réveillère, 'the Court is attaching the right to lead a normal family life to Article 21 TFEU, as it has attached the right not to suffer discrimination on grounds of nationality to Article 20 TFEU in *Martínez Sala*'.[111] *Lounes* clarifies the sibylline language of the star case *Baumbast*, where it was stated more than twenty years ago that Article 21 TFEU can be legitimately restricted only if the restriction is proportionate and in accordance with the general principles of EU law.[112]

Lounes, *Chavez-Vilchez* and *KA* are central for interpreting Articles 20 and 21 TFEU in light of the Charter and, thus, understanding and viewing EU fundamental rights and the Charter as they should be – instruments of EU primary law that should be used consistently for interpreting not only EU secondary legislation but also Treaty provisions having a primary rank.[113] The situation had become unclear following the *Ruiz Zambrano* ruling, but the most recent cases of the CJEU demonstrate a new ambitious judicial strategy of the CJEU in its use of EU fundamental rights.[114]

6.5 CONCLUSION

The Court's case law from recent years has shown substantive and positive developments in the protection of family life which are noticeable particularly due to the increasing use of the Charter. However, it also follows from our analysis that the Court has always been very careful in its use of the Charter to extend the protection of family rights under EU law. The citizenship case law has provided a good illustration of the 'hiding effect' of EU family rights in relation to the 'substance of rights test' and Article 20 TFEU. The Court has in many cases avoided explicit reference to Charter provisions on the protection

[109] Ibid, para 52.

[110] Ibid, in particular, para 56, which refers to *Metock* (n 19), para 62. *Metock* makes reference to *Carpenter* (n 4) and *MRAX* (n 3) that are discussed in the introduction of this chapter.

[111] V. Réveillère, 'Family rights for naturalized EU citizens: Lounes' (2018) 55 Common Market Law Review 1855.

[112] Case C-413/99 *Baumbast* EU:C:2002:493, paras 72 and 94. According to para 72: 'Regulation No 1612/68 must be interpreted in the light of the requirement of respect for family life laid down in Article 8 of the European Convention. That requirement is one of the fundamental rights which, according to settled case law, are recognised by Community law.'

[113] In that respect, see also Case C-817/19 *Ligue des droits humains* EU:C:2022:491, paras 86–87.

[114] See also Case C-181/19 *JD* EU:C:2020:794.

of family life. Instead, it has reinforced the protection of the right to family life by embedding it to the 'substance of rights' to be enjoyed by EU citizens. The same holds true in relation to the timid use of Article 9 of the Charter, which has now been stripped of all potential in the litigation on same-sex partnerships. From a general perspective, it seems difficult to deny that family rights are closely associated to the exclusive competence of the Member States and their most profound moral values and constitutional identities. This makes the penetration of the progressive Charter rights very difficult at the national level. In this area, localism and subsidiarity are high on the agenda of the Member States.

7

The Status of Family Member as a Pre-condition of the Free Movement in the EU

MICHAEL BOGDAN*

7.1 INTRODUCTION

Article 21(1) of the Treaty on the Functioning of the European Union (TFEU) gives every citizen of the European Union (EU) the right, subject to very few exceptions, to move and reside freely within the territory of the Member States. This freedom of movement means not only that the Member States must not impose direct restrictions in the form of administrative requirements such as visas and residence permits, but also that they must not deter EU citizens from moving by indirect obstacles, including those following from differences of family law. For example, an EU citizen might hesitate to use his/her freedom of movement to another Member State if that State would not recognise his/her marriage or his/her parental relation to his/her adopted children. Similarly, an EU citizen would probably refrain from moving if he/she could not be accompanied by close family members who are not citizens of the EU. Family law is thus of great relevance for the free movement of persons. This applies, in particular, to cross-border family law issues, such as the recognition in the host Member State of a family status created abroad.

This chapter deals with some aspects of the delimitation of the categories of those non-EU citizens who are entitled to move to and reside in an EU Member State in their capacity of family members of an EU citizen (the

* This chapter is an extended and updated version of an article originally published by Charles University (Prague) in (2020) 4 Acta Universitatis Carolinae Iuridica 85. The author wishes to thank the original publisher for approving the re-publication.

primary right holder).[1] The free movement of such persons is in principle regulated by the EU Directive 2004/38 of 29 April 2004 on the right of citizens of the Union and their family members to move and reside freely within the territory of the Member States.[2] Article 2(2) of the Directive defines family members as the spouse, the partner with whom the EU citizen contracted a registered partnership on the basis of the legislation of a Member State (provided the host Member State treats registered partnerships as equivalent to marriage), direct descendants who are under the age of twenty-one or are dependents, and dependent direct relatives in the ascending line (such as parents and grandparents).

Article 3 declares the listed family members to be indirect beneficiaries of free movement rights, but goes further than that by adding additional categories of persons whose entry and residence, in accordance with the national legislation and subject to an extensive examination of the personal circumstances of the persons concerned, the Member States are obliged to 'facilitate'; these categories comprise certain persons with weaker family ties to the EU citizen concerned, such as 'any other family members' who, in the country from which they have come, are dependents, members of the household, persons requiring personal care by a family member, or partners having a duly attested durable relationship with the EU citizen (the last-mentioned group, comprising mainly *de facto* cohabitees, is in some Member States, such as Sweden,[3] regarded as a legitimate family form regulated by law). However, the right of these persons to have their entry and residence 'facilitated' is much weaker than the entry and residence rights of family members listed in Article 2(2).

As opposed to the criteria of being a dependent, member of household, or a person requiring personal care by the EU citizen, which are basically mere matters of fact, the status of belonging to one of the categories of family members mentioned specifically in Article 2(2) of the Directive (spouse, registered partner, direct descendant, or direct ascendant) is a legal issue, to be answered in principle on the basis of the family law of the host Member State, including its rules of private international law.[4] Only exceptionally there are uniform rules of EU private international law regarding family law status,

[1] This issue is closely related, but not identical, to the right of third-country nationals residing lawfully in the EU to be joined by their family members pursuant to Council Directive 2003/86/EC of 22 September 2003 on the right to family reunification [2003] OJ L251/12.

[2] [2004] OJ L158/77.

[3] See the Swedish Cohabitees Act (2003:376).

[4] Persons having a duly attested durable relationship with the EU citizen constitute a borderline category, because different Member States may have different statutory definitions of legally relevant cohabitation that can be duly attested.

such as the provisions on the recognition of divorces and marriage annulments in the EU Regulation 2019/1111 (known as Regulation Brussels IIb).[5] There are presently no EU regulations or directives on the validity of marriages, validity and dissolution of registered partnerships, paternity and other parenthood, and adoptions.[6]

This gives rise to the question whether the Member States have full discretion to deal with these issues or must, to comply with Article 21(1) TFEU and the above-mentioned Directive 2004/38, respect family relationships created abroad pursuant to foreign law. This is of particular interest whenever the family status in question is in the Member State where it is relied on considered reprehensible or is totally unknown.

This question has arisen, and was to some extent answered, in three recent judgments of the Court of Justice of the European Union (CJEU). The importance of the three decisions is underlined by the fact that all of them have been rendered by the Court's Grand Chamber. The purpose of this chapter is to subject the three judgments to a critical analysis, regarding both the conclusions and the reasoning of the CJEU.

7.2 THE CASE OF SAME-SEX MARRIAGE

The first judgment, *Coman v Inspectoratul General*, was rendered on 5 June 2018.[7] It concerned two persons of the same sex who had married in Belgium in accordance with Belgian law. One of the members of the couple lived at that time in Belgium and was an EU citizen (he possessed both American and Romanian nationality), while the other held only American citizenship and continued to live in the United States. After some time, the couple wished to move together to Romania, but the Romanian authorities refused to grant the American spouse long-term residence rights on grounds of family reunion pursuant to EU law, because in accordance with Article 227 of the Romanian Civil Code 'marriages between persons of the same sex entered into or contracted abroad by Romanian citizens or by foreigners shall not be

[5] Council Regulation (EU) No 2019/1111 of 25 June 2019 on jurisdiction, the recognition and enforcement of decisions in matrimonial matters and the matters of parental responsibility and on international child abduction (recast) [2019] OJ L178/1.

[6] On 7 December 2022, the European Commission submitted a proposal for a Council regulation on jurisdiction, applicable law, recognition of decisions, and acceptance of authentic instruments in matters of parenthood and on the creation of a European Certificate of Parenthood, COM(2022) 695 final.

[7] Case C-673/16 *Coman and others* EU:C:2018:385. See also Chapter 2 by Alina Tryfonidou and Chapter 9 by Geoffrey Willems.

recognised in Romania'. The applicants argued that this provision was contrary to the Romanian Constitution, so the matter was referred to the Romanian Constitutional Court which, in turn, had doubts about the proper interpretation of the EU Directive 2004/38 and turned to the CJEU for a preliminary ruling.

To start with, it must be noted that the case did not, in fact, fall directly within the scope of application of Directive 2004/38. The CJEU had on several previous occasions interpreted this Directive, in accordance with its wording,[8] as to mean that it governs only those situations where an EU citizen and his family members who are third-country nationals want to enter and reside in a Member State other than that of the EU citizen's nationality. Consequently, it does not confer a derived right of residence on third-country nationals who intend to accompany or join their EU relative in the latter's own Member State.[9] However, the full effect of the freedom of movement granted to EU citizens by Article 21(1) TFEU presupposes that an EU citizen can bring his close family with him also when he returns to his own Member State, since he would otherwise be discouraged from exercising that freedom by leaving his State. The third-country family members of an EU citizen who moves to his own Member State, even though not entitled to a derived right of residence pursuant to Directive 2004/38, can thus be granted such right directly on the basis of Article 21(1) TFEU. The conditions for obtaining such right must not, according to the CJEU, be stricter than those stipulated in Directive 2004/38, which means that the Directive is to be applied by analogy even in the situation dealt with in the *Coman* judgment.

The CJEU went on to admit that a person's marital status is a matter that falls within the competence of the Member States, which are thus free to decide whether or not to allow marriage for persons of the same sex in their domestic law. However, the exercise of that competence must comply with EU law. To permit the Member States to accord or refuse residence rights to third-country nationals who lawfully married an EU citizen in another Member State where the EU citizen genuinely resided at that time, would make the freedom of movement of EU citizens vary from one Member State to another depending on the forum Member State's attitude towards same-sex marriages. Furthermore, a refusal of residence rights could in its consequences

[8] Article 3(1) of Directive 2004/38 (n 2) provides that '[t]his Directive shall apply to all Union citizens who move to or reside in a Member State *other than that of which they are a national* and to their family members...' (emphasis added).

[9] See, for example, the Grand Chamber judgment in Case C-457/12 *S v Minister voor Immigratie* EU:C:2014:136.

amount to denying the EU citizen his right to return to his own Member State together with his spouse.

A restriction on the freedom of movement may, nevertheless, be justified if it is based on objective considerations of public interest, is proportionate to its legitimate objective, and does not go beyond what is necessary to attain that objective. Some Member States submitted observations to the CJEU referring to the fundamental nature of the institution of marriage as a bond between a man and a woman and claimed that even if a refusal to accept same-sex marriages might constitute a restriction of the rights under Article 21(1) TFEU, such a restriction is justified on grounds of public policy and national identity protected by Article 4(2) TFEU.

This reasoning was, however, not accepted by the CJEU, which stated that any restrictions imposed on a fundamental right such as the freedom of movement under Article 21 TFEU must be interpreted strictly and cannot be determined unilaterally by each Member State without control by the EU. The public policy exception may be relied on only if there is a genuine and sufficiently serious threat to a fundamental interest of society. The obligation of a Member State to recognise a same-sex marriage 'for the sole purpose of granting a derived right of residence to a third-country national' does not, according to the CJEU, undermine the institution of marriage in that Member State. Neither does it undermine the national identity there or pose a threat to the public policy. Furthermore, any national restrictions on the freedom of movement must be consistent with the fundamental rights protected by the Charter of Fundamental Rights of the EU,[10] including its Article 7 guaranteeing protection of private and family life. That Article must be understood in the same way as the corresponding Article 8 of the European Convention for the Protection of Human Rights and Fundamental Freedoms (ECHR), which is interpreted by the European Court of Human Rights (ECtHR) as to apply to both same-sex and opposite-sex couples.[11]

The CJEU concluded, therefore, that Article 21(1) TFEU gives a third-country national of the same sex as his EU spouse, who married in accordance with the law of the Member State where the EU spouse had genuine residence at that time, the right to move to and reside in the Member State of which the EU spouse is a national irrespective of the fact that the marriage

[10] [2007] OJ C303/1.

[11] The attitude of the ECtHR towards same-sex couples is demonstrated, for example, by its judgment in the case *Orlandi and Others v Italy*, Application no 26431/12, where the Court held that States are still free to restrict access to marriage to different-sex couples, but acknowledged that same-sex couples are entitled to such legal recognition and protection that does not leave them in a legal vacuum.

is not recognised there. As mentioned above, this derived right of residence must not be subjected to conditions that are stricter than those stipulated in Directive 2004/38.

While the outcome of the *Coman* case, protecting the right to family life of same-sex married couples, can hardly be objected to, some parts of the reasoning and terminology used by the CJEU seem to be more controversial. It is noteworthy that the Court repeatedly affirms the obligation for a Member State to 'recognise a marriage between persons of the same sex', even though merely for the sole purpose of granting a derived right of residence to a third-country national.[12] This obligation to recognise the marriage is not mentioned in the holding itself and it is almost certainly not meant to imply the duty to consider the couple to be actually married. Considering the same couple to be married for some purposes only creates a situation where the question of whether they are married cannot be answered by a simple 'yes' or 'no'. It is true that limping marriages are a well-known phenomenon in private international law, but they normally concern marriages that are recognised in some countries only, and not marriages that are recognised and unrecognised in the same country depending on the context.

It is interesting that in the *Coman* judgment the CJEU, when applying Article 21(1) TFEU in the light of analogies borrowed from Directive 2004/38, relied on the Directive's Article 2(2) and discussed whether the same-sex marriage could be recognised with the effect that the third-country citizen involved would be considered a 'spouse' for the purposes of a derived right of residence. The Court did not discuss the possibility of analogous application of Article 3(2) of the Directive, that might probably qualify the same-sex spouse as an 'other family member' or at least as a partner with whom the EU citizen had 'a durable relationship, duly attested'. The probable main reason of the Court's choice on this point is that whereas Article 2(2) grants the same-sex spouse an almost automatic right of entry and residence, Article 3(2) would place him in a much weaker position, merely obliging the Member State concerned to undertake an extensive examination of his personal circumstances to conclude whether his family life was of such a kind that would entitle him to family unification pursuant to the national legislation of that Member State. It is true that a decision refusing the right of entry or residence would even in such a case have to provide justification and comply with Article 7 of the Charter of Fundamental Rights of the EU and Article 8 ECHR, but the compulsory extensive examination of personal circumstances

[12] See *Coman and others* (n 7), paras 45 and 46.

could take time and the outcome would be much more uncertain, thus subjecting same-sex couples to discrimination.

One may also question the wisdom of limiting the holding of the *Coman* judgment explicitly to situations where the same-sex marriage has been concluded in an EU Member State pursuant to its law, an additional condition being that the EU citizen concerned must have been a genuine resident there at the time. The arguments used by the CJEU in support of its decision should reasonably carry the same weight even if the same-sex marriage in question had been concluded in the United States pursuant to American law during the EU citizen's short visit there. There are fortunately no reasons to interpret the Court's holding *e contrario* as to mean that under such circumstances the outcome would be different. It is submitted that the CJEU simply chose to limit the holding of its judgment to the circumstances in the case at hand and refrained from expressing an opinion on other situations.

It follows clearly from the wording of the *Coman* judgment that the CJEU did not intend to oblige the Member States to give same-sex marriages concluded in another Member State full effects under private law, for example as to maintenance, marital property regime, or inheritance. This remains an open question though, since even differences between Member States regarding such issues may conceivably discourage a couple from making use of the freedom of movement within the EU, especially in view of the increasing application of the law of the country of habitual residence.[13] Theoretically, it is also possible that a refusal to recognise the married status as such might in some cases be deemed to constitute an unlawful restriction on free movement, for example, if the refusal by a Member State to recognise same-sex couples as married carries such a social stigma that it deters such couples from moving there.

7.3 THE CASE OF ISLAMIC *KAFALA*

The second judgment, *SM v Entry Clearance Officer*, was rendered on 26 March 2019.[14] It differs from the *Coman* case in two very important aspects. First, the disputed family member status was created in and pursuant to the law of a non-Member State, and second, the status itself was of a kind

[13] It is noteworthy that the CJEU has held that the mere fact of having different surnames in different Member States could create serious inconveniences constituting an obstacle to free movement. See, for example, Case C-353/06 *Grunkin-Paul* EU:C:2008:559.

[14] Case C-129/18 *SM* EU:C:2019:248.

unknown in the law of the Member State to which the third-country citizen intended to move.

The judgment involved a French married couple residing in the UK, which at the relevant time was an EU Member State. An Algerian court assigned to them the parental responsibility for an abandoned child under the Algerian *kafala* system. This institution, based on Islamic law, gave the couple parental authority and responsibility which was in some respects similar to adoption. The couple undertook, *inter alia*, to give the child an Islamic education, keep her fit morally and physically, supply her needs, look after her teaching, treat her like natural parents, protect her, defend her before judicial instances, and assume civil liability for her detrimental acts. They were also authorised to receive family allowances, subsidies, and other benefits; to sign any administrative and travel documents; and to take the child out of Algeria. Furthermore, the child's surname was officially changed to that of the couple.[15]

If deemed to be an adopted child of the French couple, the Algerian child would be classified as their direct descendant and, as such, would enjoy the right of entry and residence in the UK as their family member pursuant to Article 2(2) of Directive 2004/38.[16] Nevertheless, the British authorities refused to clear the child for entry to the UK as an adopted child, on the ground that *kafala* was not recognised as adoption under UK law.

After the matter was referred to the CJEU, the Court pointed out that Article 2(2) does not designate the law determining the meaning and scope of the concept of 'direct descendant' and that under such circumstances the need for a uniform application of EU law and the principle of equality require that the concept must normally be given an independent and uniform interpretation throughout the EU. According to the CJEU, the concept of 'direct descendant' commonly refers to the existence of a direct parent–child relationship between the two persons concerned. The concept must be construed broadly, so that it includes both the biological and the adopted children, since it is established that adoption creates a legal parent–child relationship. Where there is no parent–child relationship, the child cannot, according to the Court, be described as a direct descendant for the purposes of the Directive.

The Court examined the legal effects of *kafala* and noted, *inter alia*, that unlike adoption, which is forbidden by Algerian law, the placing of a child under a *kafala* guardianship does not mean that the child becomes the guardian's heir. Furthermore, a *kafala* relationship comes to an end when

15 See ibid, paras 27 and 28.

16 In this case, as opposed to the *Coman* judgment, Directive 2004/38 was directly applicable, since the UK was not the Member State of the couple's nationality.

the child attains the age of maturity and may even be revoked at the request of the biological parents or of the guardian. The Court concluded that as opposed to adoption, *kafala* does not create such a parent–child relationship between the child and its guardian that would qualify the child as direct descendant in the sense of Article 2(2) of Directive 2004/38.

However, the Court did not stop there but went on to point out that the child, even though not a direct descendant under Article 2(2), could, depending on its personal circumstances in the individual case, be entitled to a privileged treatment pursuant to Article 3(2), that is, to have its entry 'facilitated'. Recital 6 of Directive 2004/38 mentions that to maintain the unity of the family 'in a broader sense', the situation of persons who do not enjoy an automatic right of entry and residence since they are not family members should be examined by the Member State concerned on the basis of its own national legislation, taking into consideration their relationship with the EU citizen and any other relevant circumstances, such as their financial or physical dependence on the same. The examination should be extensive and, in the event of a negative decision, provide justification by stating the reasons for the refusal. The CJEU confirmed that the Member States have a wide discretion as regards the selection of the factors to be taken into account at this examination, but stressed that in accordance with Recital 31 of Directive 2004/38, their discretion must be exercised in the light of and in line with the provisions of the Charter of Fundamental Rights of the EU, whose Article 7, recognising the right to respect for private and family life, has the same meaning and scope as Article 8 ECHR.

The CJEU found it apparent that the actual relationship between a child placed under the *kafala* system and its guardians may, depending on all the current and relevant circumstances of the case, constitute a family tie falling within the definition of family life protected by these provisions. According to the CJEU, the assessment by the authorities of the Member State concerned must be balanced and reasonable and take into consideration, *inter alia*, the age at which the child was placed under the *kafala* system, whether the child has lived with its guardians since its placement, the closeness of the personal relationship between them, and the extent to which the child is legally and financially dependent on its guardians. The risk that the child will become a victim of abuse, exploitation, or trafficking must also be taken into account, but if it is established that the child and its *kafala* guardians will lead a genuine family life, the best interests of the child demand, in principle, that it be granted the rights of entry and residence to live with its guardians in the Member State where they reside.

It might seem close at hand to understand the CJEU judgment as to mean that the Court, while refusing to equal *kafala* to adoption,[17] has recognised it as a valid family-law status *sui generis*, with legal consequences of its own. Such interpretation would, however, be incorrect. It is true that the Court considered the child to belong to the category of 'any other family members' under Article 3(2) of Directive 2004/38, but this is a very wide and vague category with no family law effects at all. Belonging to this 'extended family' gives no automatic right of entry or residence, unless the third-state national in question fulfils additional conditions such as being a dependent or a household member.

There is, of course, nothing preventing Member States from equalling *kafala* to adoption in their domestic family law and/or in their private international law for purposes other than the interpretation of the EU Directive 2004/38. The recognition of *kafala*, as an institution intended to protect orphans and abandoned children, could as such hardly be considered to violate the public policy of the host Member State.[18] In this respect, *kafala* differs not only from a same-sex marriage but also from, for example, polygamous marriages.

A polygamous marriage appears, in fact, to be a particularly problematic example, since it questions the whole concept of spouse and family life prevailing in practically all EU Member States. It is very doubtful whether a Member State, even if recognising, in principle, the validity of polygamous marriages concluded abroad,[19] must or can treat the parties to such marriages as spouses under Article 2(2) of Directive 2004/38 or as partners with a duly attested durable relationship under Article 3(2) of the same. In any case, Article 27 of the Directive allows Member States to restrict the freedom of movement and residence on grounds of public policy. Regarding the possibility of direct application of Article 21(1) TFEU, it is submitted that its interpretation should be based on an analogous application of Article 4(4) of Directive 2003/86 on the right to family reunification,[20] which provides that in the event of a polygamous marriage, where the third-country national

[17] It is worth mentioning that Article 4(b) of the 1996 Hague Convention on Jurisdiction, Applicable Law, Recognition, Enforcement and Co-operation in Respect of Parental Responsibility and Measures for the Protection of Children, ratified or acceded to by all EU Member States, excludes adoption from the Convention's scope of application, whereas its Article 3(e) covers explicitly 'provision of care by *kafala* or an analogous institution'.

[18] This does not necessarily apply to all of *kafala*'s purported legal effects, such as the obligation of the guardians to give the child an Islamic education.

[19] This was the position of Sweden prior to 1 July 2021, provided that at the time of the conclusion of the marriage none of the parties was a Swedish citizen or habitual resident.

[20] See n 1.

residing in the EU already has a spouse living with him, the Member State concerned 'shall not authorise the family reunification of a further spouse'. There are no reasons to treat, in this respect, the right to reunification with an EU citizen more generously than reunification with a third-country national residing lawfully in the EU.

7.4 THE CASE OF SAME-SEX PARENTHOOD

The third judgment, *V.M.A. v Stolichna obshtina, rayon 'Pancharevo'*, was rendered on 14 December 2021.[21] The case concerned a child of a married same-sex couple, consisting of a British and a Bulgarian citizen. The child was born and resided in Spain and its Spanish birth certificate listed both parents as 'Mothers'. The Bulgarian parent applied to Bulgarian authorities for a Bulgarian birth certificate, such certificate being necessary for obtaining a Bulgarian identity card and a Bulgarian passport. The application was rejected because the applicant refused to provide information about the identity of the child's biological mother and the fact that the recording of two mothers on a birth certificate was contrary to the public policy of Bulgaria. Besides, the Bulgarian birth certificate form did not provide for the option of two mothers. On the other hand, the Bulgarian court requiring a CJEU preliminary ruling seems to have assumed that the child was in fact a citizen of Bulgaria (and thereby also of EU), probably because under the Bulgarian Constitution, a child is a Bulgarian citizen if at least one of the parents is a Bulgarian national.

The CJEU noted that an identity card or a passport were necessary to enable the child to exercise the right to move and reside within the territory of the Member States guaranteed by Article 21(1) TFEU.[22] The Court confirmed that a person's status, such as parentage, is a matter within the competence of the Member States, which are thus free to decide whether or not to allow joint parenthood for persons of the same sex under their national law. However, in exercising that competence, each Member State must comply with EU law, including the obligation to recognise the parent–child relationship between the child and each of the same-sex parents in the context of the child's exercise of its rights under Article 21(1) TFEU. The CJEU

[21] Case C-490/20 *V.M.A. v Stolichna obshtina, rayon 'Pancharevo'* EU:C:2021:1008. The same issues were dealt with by the CJEU in Case C-2/21 *Rzecznik Praw Obywatelskich* EU:C:2022:502, which was decided on 24 June 2022 by a mere order instead of a judgment, since the ruling could be clearly deduced from the existing case law, namely the *V.M.A.* judgment. See also Chapter 2 by Alina Tryfonidou and Chapter 9 by Geoffrey Willems.

[22] In fact, Article 4(3) of Directive 2004/38 (n 2) obliges the Member States to issue to their own nationals an identity card or passport stating their nationality.

added that this does not pose a threat to the public policy of the Member States, which are not required to recognise the child–parent relationship for purposes other than the exercise of the rights derived from EU law, such as for claims to inheritance or maintenance. The judgment followed much of CJEU's reasoning in the *Coman* case, which need not be repeated here.

The situation in the *Pancharevo* case differs from that in the other two judgments above, because in *Pancharevo* it was common ground that the child in question was an EU citizen and, as such, a primary (as opposed to derivative) holder of the right to free movement within the EU. Nevertheless, the effective exercise of this right depended on the possession of an identity card or a passport issued by the Member State of the child's nationality. The refusal of that State to provide such documents due to its refusal to recognise joint parenthood of a same-sex couple would deprive the child of its rights under EU law. This was understandably found unacceptable by the CJEU. On the other hand, an official document confirming the joint parenthood without indicating that this is for the sole purpose of free movement may be abused, for example, if it is used abroad for the purpose of claiming inheritance or other such right.

7.5 CONCLUSION

The discussed judgments can be understood as to mean that the nationals of the EU Member States have not merely both national and EU citizenship but even a double personal status, namely one for the enjoyment of rights under EU law and another for purposes governed by national law such as maintenance or inheritance. This may create some confusion, since neither the national legal systems nor the perception of the law by the populations of the Member States reckon with situations where the same person is at the same time both married and single, or both a parent and a stranger in relation to the same child.

It would, therefore, be preferable to leave the recognition of family status as such to national law (including its private international law rules to the extent that they have not been unified by the EU) and disconnect, in these cases, the issue of family status from the specific consequences of that status. By doing so, even officially unrecognised and invalid status can be given selected substantive effects, for example, regarding the right to free movement pursuant to EU law. In the meantime, the risk of confusion could, at least in theory, be avoided by requesting the Member States to produce model document forms indicating whether the status stated therein is limited to certain purposes only.

8

Family Members and the Citizens' Rights Directive

Broadening the Scope of the Principle of Effective Judicial Protection

ALBERTINA ALBORS-LLORENS

8.1 INTRODUCTION

Directive 2004/38/EC[1] (CRD) coalesced in one single legislative Act, the regulation of the right to free movement and residence of European Union (EU) citizens and their family members set out in the primary provisions of EU law[2] and removed the 'sector-by-sector, piecemeal approach'[3] to this right that had theretofore prevailed.[4] This measure shares with its predecessors the underlying principle that the right of residence and free movement of EU citizens would not be effective unless extended to their close family members

[1] Directive 2004/38/EC of the European Parliament and of the Council of 29 April 2004 on the Right of Citizens of the Union and their Family Members to Move and Reside freely within the Territory of the Member States (hereinafter CRD) [2004] OJ L158/77.

[2] See Articles 45 and 20(2)(a) TFEU and Article 45(1) of the EU Charter of Fundamental Rights.

[3] Recital 4, Preamble to the CRD.

[4] See Council Regulation (EEC) No 1612/68 of 15 October 1968 on freedom of movement for workers within the Community [1968] OJ L257/2 (repealed by Regulation (EU) No 492/2011 of the European Parliament and of the Council of 5 April 2011 on freedom of movement for workers within the Union [2011] OJ L141/1) and other measures (repealed by the CRD) such as Council Directive 68/360/EEC of 15 October 1968 on the abolition of restrictions on movement and residence within the Community for workers of Member States and their families [1968] OJ L257/13; Council Directive 73/148/EEC on the abolition of restrictions on movement and residence within the Community for nationals of Member States with regard to establishment and the provision of services [1973] OJ L172/14; Council Directive 90/364/EEC of 28 June 1990 on the right of residence [1990] OJ L180/26; Council Directive 90/365/EEC of 28 June 1990 on the right of residence for employees and self-employed persons who have ceased their occupational activity [1990] OJ L180/28; and Council Directive 93/96/EEC of 29 October 1993 on the right of residence for students [1993] OJ L317/59. On the issue of restrictions to the right of entry and residence, Directive 64/221/EEC [1964] OJ L142/24 (repealed by the CRD) was the immediate predecessor of the CRD.

because, otherwise, EU citizens would be seriously discouraged from exercising their free movement rights.[5]

The academic literature has discussed in great detail the *substantive* dimension of the rights provided in the CRD and its evolution through the case law.[6] However, this chapter will look at something different, namely, at the *enforcement* of these rights by members of the 'family' of the EU citizen – both 'core' members and 'extended' family members according to the division created by the Directive[7] – and, in particular, at how the Court of Justice of the EU (CJEU) has applied the principle of effective judicial protection to these situations.

It is, of course, understood that whenever a substantive right exists, there should be an effective remedy that allows for its enforcement. The principle of effective judicial protection has been present in EU law through the case law of the CJEU[8] and is now entrenched in primary EU legislation through Article 47 of the EU Charter of Fundamental Human Rights and Article 19 of the Treaty on European Union (TEU).[9] In most areas of EU law, this principle has been interpreted in relation to the enforcement of substantive EU rights by the *primary* holders of these rights[10] – that is, Union citizens. However, the CRD adds a different and interesting dimension to this landscape by also addressing the rights that family members *derive* from mobile EU citizens. From a legal perspective, these family members are therefore not considered as entities in

5 As Advocate General Sharpston eloquently expressed it in her Opinion in Case C-34/09 *Ruiz Zambrano* EU:C:2010:560, para 128: '. . . when citizens move, they do so as human beings, not as robots. They fall in love, marry and have families. The family unit, depending on circumstances, may be composed solely of EU citizens, or of EU citizens and third country nationals, closely linked to one another. If family members are not treated in the same way as the EU citizen exercising rights of free movement, the concept of freedom of movement becomes devoid of any real meaning.'

6 See, among others, C. Barnard, *The Substantive Law of the EU* (Oxford University Press 2022), 336–375; E. Guild, S. Peers, and J. Tomkin, *The EU Citizenship Directive: A Commentary* (Oxford University Press 2019). On family reunification, see C. Berneri, *Family Reunification in the EU* (Hart Publishing 2017). See also Chapter 7 by Michael Bogdan.

7 See Section 8.2 on the different status of these two types of family members.

8 Case 222/84 *Johnston v Chief Constable of the Royal Ulster Constabulary* EU:C:1986:206, para 18; Case 222/86 *Unectef v Heylens and others* EU:C:1987:442, para 14; Case C-97/91 *Oleificio Borelli v Commission* EU:C:1992:491, para 14.

9 Thus, Article 47 of the EU Charter of Fundamental Rights requires the effective protection of EU rights and Article 19 TEU obliges Member States to provide remedies to ensure effective legal protection in areas covered by EU law. Article 19 TEU is very relevant in our field of study because most restrictions of the rights to free movement – such as for instance expulsion decisions – will derive from the actions of national authorities and claimants will be natural persons who will bring proceedings to challenge these restrictions before the national courts.

10 This terminology has been used before in the academic literature and in the case law of the Court. See G. Barrett, 'Family matters: European community law and third country family members' (2003) 40 Common Market Law Review 369, 370–371.

their own right – unless they are also primary holders of EU rights as EU citizens – but as *deriving* any legal protection under EU law from the EU citizen entitled to free movement rights. This translates into a degree of remoteness and uncertainty insofar as the safeguard of their rights is concerned because these are contingent on the vicissitudes of fortune experienced by the primary holder of the EU rights. The unpredictability that flows from the subsidiary nature of the rights of family members is true both in relation to 'core' and 'extended' family members but, in relation to the latter, is further compounded by the fact that the CRD, as we shall see, imposes vaguer obligations on Member States than in relation to the former. Consequently, the precariousness of the substantive rights of family members means that the effective judicial protection of these rights – when established – becomes a matter of essential concern not only in assessing critically the level of protection offered by the CRD but also in considering the overall position of family members under EU law.

In a collection that seeks to explore the role of the family in EU law, this chapter aims to contribute an examination of how the guarantee of effective judicial protection has taken hold in the interpretation of the provisions of the CRD when applied to family members of an EU citizen. To this end, it will examine first the legal system of protection, both substantive and procedural, articulated by the CRD and then will analyse the evolution of the principle of effective judicial protection in relation to the family members of EU citizens. In particular, it will argue that the procedural safeguards included in the CRD to protect EU citizens and their families from restrictions on their right to entry or reside in a host Member State have been increasingly interpreted with primary and direct reference to the principle of effective judicial protection as configured in Article 47 of the Charter. This has enabled the Court to draw from a richer and broader body of case law and to bolster the protection offered by that principle rather than, as it had been historically the case, using the principle to *infuse* the interpretation of those guarantees within the narrow parameters of the CRD itself – or of Directive 64/221,[11] its immediate predecessor. Ultimately, the effect of this shift has been that a higher standard of protection has emerged in the case law.

8.2 THE LEGAL SYSTEM OF PROTECTION ARTICULATED IN THE CITIZENS' RIGHTS DIRECTIVE

The CRD provides that certain family members of an EU citizen, as defined in Article 2(2) CRD, are full beneficiaries of the protection of the Directive

[11] See n 4.

when they accompany or join the EU citizen.[12] These 'core' family members are: the spouse of the Union citizen; the partner with whom the Union citizen has contracted a registered partnership in a Member State – if the legislation of the host Member State treats registered partnerships as equivalent to marriage; the direct descendants who are under the age of twenty-one or are dependants and those of the spouse or partner; the dependent direct relatives in the ascending line and those of the spouse or partner.[13] The protection that they receive encompasses the right to free movement and residence and other related rights such as entitlement to take up employment or self-employment in the host State[14] and the right to equal treatment,[15] as well as the application of substantive and procedural safeguards against restrictions of the right to entry to and expulsions from a host State on grounds of public policy, public security, and public health.[16]

By contrast, according to Article 3(2) CRD, the rights of entry and residence of *other* family members and of the partner with whom the EU citizen has durable relationship, duly attested, only have to be 'facilitated' by the host Member State.[17] In its glorious open-endedness, the use of the term 'facilitated'[18] has predictably yielded an interesting body of case law in relation to this 'extended family members' that has clarified the content of this 'facilitation' obligation.[19]

[12] Article 3(1) CRD.

[13] There is an exception in relation to EU citizens who are students in Article 7(4) CRD. This narrows the circle of 'family members' to their spouse, the registered partner in the sense of Article 2(2) CRD, and dependent children in relation to the right to reside in a host Member State for more than three months.

[14] Article 23 CRD.

[15] Article 24 CRD. See also Article 10 of Regulation 492/2011 (n 4), which sets out the right to educational, apprenticeship, and vocational courses for workers' children.

[16] Articles 27–33 CRD.

[17] Article 3(2) CRD.

[18] In this respect, see Recital 6 of the Preamble to the CRD, which provides: 'In order to maintain the unity of the family in a broader sense and without prejudice to the prohibition of discrimination on grounds of nationality, the situation of those persons who are not included in the definition of family members under this Directive, and who therefore do not enjoy an automatic right of entry and residence in the host Member State, should be examined by the host Member State on the basis of its own national legislation, in order to decide whether entry and residence could be granted to such persons, taking into consideration their relationship with the Union citizen or any other circumstances, such as their financial or physical dependence on the Union citizen.'

[19] See Case C-83/11 *Secretary of State for the Home Department v Rahman* EU:C:2012:519, paras 18–26. As Advocate General Bobek lucidly summarised in his Opinion in Case C-89/17 *Banger* EU:C:2018:225, the decision in *Rahman* developed three dimensions of the 'facilitation regime' in Article 3(2) CRD: '(i) the absence of an automatic right of entry and residence; (ii) the obligation to enact a facilitation regime according to national law for which

We therefore see that the CRD bifurcates the protection given to the 'family' of an EU citizen into two categories: 'core' family members and 'extended' family members. The dividing line between these two groups is ultimately one that separates the *automatic* entitlement to the rights in the Directive (for those listed in Article 2(2) CRD) from the *discretionary* grant of these rights by the host Member State (for those listed in Article 3(2) CRD) – although an obligation falls on this State to grant the latter group of family members 'a certain advantage' over other third-country nationals.[20] In other words, while the circle of 'core' family members drawn by Article 2(2) CRD is slightly wider than the one in Regulation 1612/68, one of its predecessors,[21] the family unit deserving of full protection by the CRD still seems to be mostly based on 'legal marriage, biological links and economic dependency'.[22] The case law of the CJEU has developed the key notions of 'spouse',[23] 'direct descendants and dependent ascendants',[24] and 'other family members'[25] in the context of the right to entry and residence under EU law, as well as its application to some internal situations on the basis of primary EU law.[26] However, the two-pronged approach to the family of the EU citizen entrenched in the legislative framework of the CRD has remained.

The system put in place by the CRD seeks to regulate in more detail than the Treaties the substantive rights that pertain to EU citizens and their family members. In relation to family members, whose position is not explicitly regulated in the primary Treaty provisions, the Directive develops their right of departure from[27] and entry to[28] a Member State; the conditions for their right to reside in a host Member State[29] for up to three

Member States enjoy a margin of discretion and (iii) the fact that that discretion is not unlimited', at para 51 of his Opinion and see also paras 52–60.

[20] *Secretary of State for the Home Department v Rahman* (n 19), para 21.

[21] See n 4.

[22] See E. Caracciolo di Torella and A. Masselot, 'Under construction: EU family law' (2004) 29 European Law Review 32, 38), referring to the model of family that emerged from Regulation 1612/68. See also Chapter 2 by Alina Tryfonidou.

[23] Case C-673/16 *Coman and others* EU:C:2018:385, paras 48–50.

[24] Case C-1/05 *Jia v Migrationsverket* EU:C:2007:1, paras 34–37; Case C-490/20 *V.M.A. v Stolichna obshtina, rayon'Pancharevo'* EU:C:2021:1008, para 68; Case C-129/81 *SM* EU:C:2019:248, paras 44–73.

[25] *Secretary of State for the Home Department v Rahman* (n 19) paras 27–40.

[26] Case C-34/09 *Ruiz Zambrano* EU:C:2011:124.

[27] Article 4(1) CRD.

[28] Article 5(1) CRD.

[29] In this respect, the case law has also determined the right to residence can also be granted to family members in the Member State where the EU citizen is a national if this EU citizen carries out an economic activity with a cross-border element (like the regular provision of services across a frontier or travelling daily to work in another Member State) if the refusal to

months,[30] for more than three months,[31] upon the death or departure of the Union citizen or divorce,[32] and their right to permanent residence.[33] Furthermore, it also outlines related rights such as the right to take up employment and self-employment[34] and the right to equal treatment.[35]

It is evident that, in the system of legal protection set out by the CRD, the rights of entry to and residence in a host Member State occupy a central position. For the purposes of this chapter, it is equally important to note that these are not absolute rights, but subject to limitations imposed by the Treaty and secondary legislation. These limitations apply to the mobile EU citizen who is the primary holder of these rights, but they can also inherently affect their family members, whose rights to entry and residence are, as we saw earlier, dependent on those of the EU citizen, particularly when they are third-country nationals.[36]

Treaty-based limitations include those on grounds of public policy, public security, and public health.[37] The Directive adds some further restrictions to the right to reside on other grounds, notably where a temporary right to residence comes to an end because an EU citizen or a family member no longer satisfies the conditions set out for that temporary right in Articles 6 and

grant that right of residence would discourage the EU citizens from exercising their rights to free movement (see Case C-60/00 *Carpenter* EU:C:2002:4340 and Case C-457/12 *S v Minister voor Immigratie* EU:C:2014:136, where the Court reached this conclusion through the interpretation of the primary Treaty provisions - Articles 49 and 45 TFEU respectively).

30 Article 6(1) CRD.

31 Article 7(1)(d) and 7(2) CRD. Articles 9 and 10 regulate those administrative formalities and the issue of residence cards for family members who are third-country nationals.

32 Articles 12 and 13 CRD.

33 Article 16(2) CRD.

34 Article 23 CRD.

35 Article 24(1) CRD. This right to equal treatment extends to entitlement to social assistance – but see the limitation provided in Article 24(2) CRD and the line of case law that excludes family members of workers and self-employed EU citizens from it (Case C-299/14 *Vestische Arbeit Jobcenter Kreis Recklinghausen v García-Nieto* EU:C:2016:114 at para 44) – as well as the right to schooling of children of migrant workers, provided in Article 10 of Regulation 492/2011 (n 4).

36 As the Court has explained, 'the Treaty provisions on citizenship of the Union do not confer any autonomous right on third-country nationals. Any rights conferred on third-country nationals are not autonomous rights of those nationals, but rights derived from those enjoyed by a Union citizen': Case C-836/18 *Subdelegación del Gobierno en Ciudad Real v RH* EU:C:2020:119, para 38. By contrast, family members who are themselves EU nationals may enjoy the protection of EU law as primary holders of EU rights as well as being derivative beneficiaries of that protection.

37 See Article 45(3) TFEU (workers); Article 52 TFEU (self-employed); Article 62 TFEU (services); Article 21 (1) TFEU (citizenship).

7 CRD.[38] These apply, for instance, to non-economically active EU citizens (unless they have acquired the right to permanent residence) who lack sufficient resources in the sense that they might become an unreasonable burden on the social assistance system of the host Member State or do not have comprehensive sickness insurance coverage.[39] More specifically, while the Directive gives 'core' family members a general right to reside in a host Member State in the event of the death or departure of the Union citizen or in the event of divorce, annulment, or termination of a registered partnership, it also places some important limitations on the retention of this right, which are more severe in the case of family members who are third-country nationals.[40] Additionally, Article 35 CRD allows the refusal, termination, or withdrawal of rights under the CRD in cases of abuse of rights or fraud, such as marriages of convenience. All these limitations can lead to situations where an EU citizen and their family members might be deprived of their right of entry and residence, something, which as acknowledged in the preamble to the Directive 'can seriously harm persons, who having availed themselves of the rights and freedoms conferred on them by the Treaty, have become genuinely integrated into the host Member State'.[41]

It is therefore unsurprising that the CRD should develop the conditions pertaining to these restrictions in quite some detail. In particular, Chapter VI of the Directive contains an array of substantive principles[42] and procedural safeguards that Member States must respect when restricting the rights of entry and residence on grounds of public policy, public security, and public health. The latter include the right of mobile EU citizens and their family members to be notified of decisions depriving them of their right to entry or residence (Article 30 CRD) and the right to access to judicial and, where appropriate, to administrative redress procedures and the right to appeal against decisions taken against them (Article 31 CRD). These central provisions are supplemented by Articles 32 and 33 CRD, which cover, respectively, limitations on the use of exclusion bans and the prohibition of automatically using expulsion

[38] Case C-94/18 *Chenchooliah v Minister for Justice and Equality* EU:C:2019:6930, para 74.

[39] See Article 14(1) CRD in relation to the right to reside in the territory of a host Member State for up to three months and Article 7(1)(b) in relation to the right to residence for more than three months and less than five years.

[40] See the conditions imposed on family members who are themselves EU citizens in the case of death or departure of the Union citizen or in the event of divorce before they can acquire the right to permanent residence (Article 12(1) CRD) and 13(1) CRD) and those more restrictive conditions imposed on family members who are third-country nationals that find themselves on the same situation (see Article 12(2) and (3) CRD and Article 13(2) CRD).

[41] Recital 23, Preamble to the CRD.

[42] See Articles 27–29 CRD, which have generated a very abundant body of case law.

as a criminal penalty. Likewise, Article 15 of the CRD extends, by analogy, those procedural safeguards to cases where the right to residence is restricted on other grounds,[43] as does Article 35 CRD in relation to situations involving an abuse of rights.

While the substantive principles contained in Articles 27–29 CRD reflect the principle frequently emphasised by the Court, that derogations to free movement are to be interpreted strictly,[44] the procedural safeguards in Articles 30–31 CRD have now been increasingly interpreted by the Court by primary reference to the right to an effective remedy enshrined in Article 47 of the EU Charter in situations where mobile EU citizens and their family members are expelled or refused entry to a host Member State.[45] It is, therefore, in this context that the right to effective judicial protection of family members of EU citizens has come strongly to the fore. In the sections that follow, we will consider the interpretation of this right in relation to both 'core' and 'extended' family members of EU citizens.

8.3 THE PRINCIPLE OF EFFECTIVE JUDICIAL PROTECTION OF FAMILY MEMBERS UNDER THE CITIZENS' RIGHTS DIRECTIVE

The CRD shored up and extended the procedural guarantees provided in Articles 6–8 of Directive 64/221[46] – the original Directive that regulated restrictions to free movement. Recitals 25 and 26 of the CRD neatly illustrate this by making it clear, respectively, that procedural safeguards of the rights of Union citizens and their family members in the event of their being denied leave to enter or reside in another Member State should ensure a high level of protection of these rights and that judicial redress procedures should be available to Union citizens and their family members who have been refused leave to enter or reside in another Member State. This stance has been robustly endorsed by the CJEU, when applying Articles 30 and 31 CRD, with the result that the principle of effective judicial protection has begun to emerge strongly in some cases as the *primary* and *explicit* guide in the

43 See further, *Chenchooliah v Minister for Justice and Equality* (n 38) where the Court clarified at paras 81–82 that the expression 'by analogy' was to be interpreted as meaning that while the same essential safeguards would apply where the right to free movement was restricted on other grounds, some specific safeguards contained in those provisions (Article 30(2), the third indent of Article 31(2), and Article 31(4) CRD) were, by nature, confined exclusively to expulsions based on grounds of public policy, public security, and public health.

44 Case 36/75 *Rutili v Ministre de l'intérieur* EU:C:1975:137, para 27.

45 Case C-300/11 *ZZ v Secretary of State for the Home Department* EU:C:2013:363, para 50.

46 See n 4 and further, Barnard (n 6) 490–494, and Guild, Peers, and Tomkin (n 6) 291–304.

interpretation of these provisions rather than taking a more implicit role by pervading the application of the specific procedural guarantees set out in the Directive.

In the following sections, we will explore both this phenomenon and its extension to the rights of family members under the CRD. To this end, we will first consider some examples of how the principle was used in earlier case law under Directive 64/221[47] and then we will look at more recent case law that illustrates neatly the shift described above.

8.3.1 *The Procedural Guarantees against Decisions Refusing Entry and Expulsion Decisions in the Earlier Case Law: The Underlying Force of the Principle of Effective Judicial Protection*

As indicated above, Directive 64/221[48] laid down a significantly lower level of procedural protection than the CRD in cases of refusals to entry or expulsion decisions against EU citizens and their families. Article 8 of Directive 64/221 provided that EU mobile citizens and their family members had the right to the '*same legal remedies*' in relation to expulsion orders or denials of entry to a host Member State as were available to nationals of a host State in respect of acts of the administration. This implied the possibility that such remedies might either be unavailable or not be entirely effective in a particular situation. Article 9 of Directive 64/221 attempted to address some of the deficiencies in Article 8. Thus, it provided in Article 9(1) that: (a) where no right of appeal to a court of law were available, or (b) available only in respect of the legal validity of the decision or (c) where an appeal would not have suspensory effect, a person concerned by an expulsion decision could at least exercise their right to defence before a competent authority which was not the same as the authority that adopted the restrictive measures. The object of Article 9 of the Directive was, in the words of the Court, 'to ensure a *minimum* procedural safeguard'[49] for persons affected in the three situations provided in Article 9(1).

On the one hand, these provisions were clearly imbued by the spirit of securing that those subject to restrictive measures should have access to a legal remedy. On the other, as we have just seen, they ultimately reflected access only to *adequate* legal remedies[50] rather than fully satisfying the requirements

[47] See n 4.

[48] Ibid.

[49] Case 98/79 *Pecastaing v Belgian State* EU:C:1980:69, para 15.

[50] In fact, Recital 3 of the Preamble to Directive 64/221 (n 4) provided that 'nationals of other Member States should have adequate legal remedies available to them in respect of decisions of administration in such matters'.

of the principle of effective judicial protection by guaranteeing both access to *judicial* redress and the right to an *effective*, and not just adequate, remedy. As Advocate Ruiz-Jarabo Colomer argued in his Opinion in *ex parte Shingara*,[51] such limitations, while perhaps acceptable at the time when this early Directive was adopted, were soon no longer consistent with the parameters of the principle of effective judicial protection which began to be developed by the Court in its general body of case law and was later consolidated in Article 47 of the Charter.

It is therefore unsurprising that, while the wording of Articles 8 and 9 of Directive 64/221 remained unchanged until eventually superseded by the higher standards of protection ushered by Articles 30 and 31 CRD, the case law interpreting those provisions not only clarified their scope but also embodied a drive towards higher levels of procedural protection. Thus, cases like *Royer*[52] and *ex parte Shingara*,[53] fostered an alignment of the case law within the specific framework of Directive 64/221 with the evolution of the general case law on national remedies to ensure the maximum latitude and effectiveness possible of the remedies provided within the somewhat restrictive parameters of the Directive. Those cases interpreted the meaning of the entitlement of persons subject to a restrictive measure to the 'same legal remedies' as nationals of the host State had in relation to restrictive measures adopted by the administration.

In *Royer*,[54] the Court held that a decision ordering the expulsion of an EU citizen or their family members could not be executed, except in duly justified cases of urgency, until the combined set of remedies provided in Articles 8 and 9 had been exhausted. In turn, in *ex parte Shingara*,[55] the Court took the view that the guarantees applicable to the three situations detailed in Article 9(1) in relation to expulsion decisions also applied to the application of Article 9(2) covering refusals to issue a first residence permit or ordering expulsion before the issue of a first permit.[56] This approach continued in *ex parte Yiadom*,[57] where the national authorities of a host Member State argued that the default

[51] Opinion of Advocate General Ruiz-Jarabo Colomer in Case C-65/95 *The Queen v Secretary of State for the Home Department, ex parte Shingara* EU:C:1996:451, paras 70–103.
[52] Case 48/75 *Royer* EU:C:1976:57.
[53] Case C-65/95 *The Queen v Secretary of State for the Home Department, ex parte Shingara* EU:C:1997:300.
[54] *Royer* (n 52).
[55] *The Queen v Secretary of State for the Home Department, ex parte Shingara* (n 53).
[56] Ibid, paras 33–37.
[57] Case C-357/98 *The Queen v Secretary of State for the Home Department, ex parte Yiadom* EU:C:2000:604.

procedural guarantees provided in Article 9(1) and (2) did not apply to a situation where an EU citizen had been granted temporary admission to a host Member State. They averred that this was outside the scope of Article 9(1) and (2), which *literally* covered expulsion decisions, those refusing the renewal of a residence permit, those refusing the issue of a first residence permit, and those ordering expulsion before the issue of a first residence permit. The Court, however, held that in the light of the general principles interpreting the Directive, an EU citizen who had been temporarily admitted to the territory of a Member State should be entitled to the procedural safeguards in Article 9.[58] While the Court did not explicitly invoke the principle of effective judicial protection in these cases and appeared to draw its interpretation from the principles emanating within the narrow confines of the Directive, it is clear that the spirit of that principle guided the conclusions reached.[59] By contrast, the Opinions of some Advocates General at the time were more vocal both in acknowledging the emergence and growing influence of the principle of effective judicial protection in the general body of case law and also in supporting the *explicit* extension of the full guarantees embodied in that principle to the restrictions of free movement contemplated in Directive 64/221.[60]

In some of the earlier cases following the entry into force of the CRD, the principle of effective judicial protection continued to underline the interpretation followed by the Court, greatly facilitated by the higher level of procedural protection entrenched in Articles 30–33 CRD. Nonetheless, allusions to that principle still seemed to be mostly cautious and indirect. For instance, in some cases calling for the interpretation of the procedural safeguards attached to the legality of national administrative prohibitions on leaving the territory of Member States, the Court used Article 32 CRD and applied the traditional combination of the principles of procedural autonomy, effectiveness, and non-discrimination, thus consolidating a pattern of interpretation drawn within the narrow confines of the CRD itself.[61] In a few cases, the right to an effective judicial remedy began to be expressly mentioned.[62]

58 Ibid, para 38.

59 In some of the later cases interpreting Directive 64/221 (n 4), there were, however, some direct references to the principle of effective judicial protection (see Case C-459/99 *MRAX* EU:C:2002:461, para 101).

60 See the Opinion of Advocate Ruiz-Jarabo Colomer in *The Queen v Secretary of State for the Home Department, ex parte Shingara* (n 51).

61 Case C-249/11 *Byankov* EU:C:2012:608, paras 67–82. By contrast, see the Opinion of Advocate General Mengozzi in the same case (EU:C:2012:380, para 32), where he made a direct reference to the right to an effective remedy as underlying the guarantees in the CRD.

62 Case C-430/10 *Gaydarov* EU:C:2011:749, para 41.

To sum up, a consideration of the historical case law under Directive 64/221 –which offered only a minimum standard of legislative procedural protection – and of the cases decided in the early years after the CRD was adopted, reveals the growing but still mostly implicit influence of the principle of effective judicial protection. Against that backdrop, and as we shall see in the next section, more recent cases have reflected an open shift towards the explicit priority of that principle in interpreting the procedural guarantees accorded to EU citizens and to their family members.

8.3.2 *The Emergence of the Principle of Effective Judicial Protection as a Primary Interpretative Guide*

The rise to prominence of the principle of effective judicial protection as primary interpretative tool in this area mirrors recent developments in other areas of EU law, where Article 47 of the Charter, either alone[63] or in conjunction with Article 19(1) TEU,[64] has taken centre stage in influencing the shape of national remedies.[65] In the context of the CRD, *ZZ v Secretary of State for the Home Department*[66] provides a clear example of the use of Article 47 of the Charter in this way. The case concerned the interpretation of Article 30(2) CRD, which stipulates that those affected by a decision restricting the right of entry or residence 'must be informed, precisely and in full of the public policy, public security or public health grounds on which the decision taken in their case is based *unless* this is contrary to the interests of State security [emphasis added]'. On the facts of the case, an EU citizen, who had resided lawfully in the UK for fifteen years – and hence acquired the right of

[63] See, for instance, Case C-205/15 *DGRFP v Toma and Biroul* EU:C:2016:499; Case C-231/15 *Prezes Urzędu Komunikacji Elektronicznej* EU:C:2016:769; Joined Cases C-439/14 and C-488/14 *Star Storage* EU:C:2016:688; Case C-169/14 *Sánchez Morcillo v Banco Bilbao Vizcaya* EU:C:2014:2099, and Case C-437/13 *Unitrading Ltd v Staatssecretaris van Financiën* EU:C:2014:2318.

[64] Case C-64/16 *Associação Sindical dos Juízes Portugueses* EU:C:2018:117; Joined Cases C-518/18, C-624/18, and C-625/18 A.K. *(Independence of the Disciplinary Chamber of the Supreme Court)* EU:C:2019:982.

[65] In this sense, there has been an argument that the standards of protection derived from applying Article 47 of the Charter seem more stringent than those emanating from the application of the principles of effectiveness and non-discrimination (see K. Gutman, 'The essence of the fundamental right to an effective remedy and to a fair trial in the case law of the Court of Justice of the European Union: The best is yet to come?' (2019) 20 German Law Journal 884, 895 and the literature cited therein).

[66] *ZZ v Secretary of State for the Home Department* (n 45).

permanent residence in the UK[67] – was subject to an expulsion measure on grounds of public security, without having been informed of the grounds justifying this measure, either in detail or in summary form. This was because, in accordance with national law, the disclosure of this information was deemed to be contrary to the interests of State security. The national court considering the appeal against the exclusion order made a reference to the Court of Justice asking whether the principle of effective judicial protection required that the Union citizen should be at least informed in this situation of the essence of the grounds against him.

Although the national court referred to the principle of effective judicial protection 'set out in Article 30(2)' of the CRD,[68] the Court used Article 47 of the Charter instead as the primary interpretative source. This is significant because it enabled it to draw from a wider body of case law than that limited to a piecemeal interpretation of the provisions in the CRD. An insular and literal interpretation of the letter of Article 30(2) CRD would have probably justified the complete refusal to disclose the grounds for expulsion for reasons of State security. However, a longstanding line of case law of the Court set out that the right to an effective remedy included the right of the person concerned to know the reasons upon which a decision had been taken against them.[69] The Court approached the ZZ case in the light of this line of case law and weighed the interests of State security on the one hand and the right to an effective remedy of EU citizens on the other.

Ultimately, the balance struck by the Court emphasised the power of Article 47 of the Charter. The Court explained that this provision imposes a duty on the national court in these circumstances to ensure, first, that the refusal to disclose the information in full to the EU citizen concerned is *strictly necessary* and, second, that the EU citizen is, in any event, informed of the *essence* of the grounds justifying the expulsion while taking into account 'the necessary confidentiality of the evidence'.[70] In other words, the Court firmly highlighted the importance of the rights of the defence even in cases where the interests of State security were at stake. The extent of the duty imposed on national courts to comply with those requirements cannot be underestimated. It reflects a high level of intrusion of the principle of

67 See Article 16(1) CRD and the special protection against expulsion for those who have acquired the right to permanent residence in Article 28 (2) and (3) CRD.

68 *ZZ v Secretary of State for the Home Department* (n 45), para 34.

69 See Case C-372/09 *Peñarroja Fa* EU:C:2011:156, para 63, and – in the context of the CRD – Case C-430/10 *Gaydarov* (n 62), para 41.

70 *ZZ v Secretary of State for the Home Department* (n 45), para 68.

effective judicial protection on decisions of national competent authorities either refusing entry or restricting the right to residence of mobile Union citizens and their families.

8.3.3 *The Expansion of the Reach of the Principle of Effective Judicial Protection to Cover 'Extended' Family Members under the CRD*

As seen in the previous section, the decision in *ZZ*[71] highlighted the use of Article 47 of the Charter as the primary source to give effect to the principle of effective judicial protection when applied to the interpretation of the specific procedural guarantees in the CRD. The claimant in that case was an EU national married to a British national – at a time when the UK was still a Member State of the EU – and hence was entitled to the protection of the CRD both as a primary holder of the substantive rights and, derivatively, as a 'core' family member under the CRD. The decision, therefore, made it clear that the enhanced protection offered by Article 47 clearly extended both to EU nationals and to those family members in Article 2(2) CRD. The entitlement to the right to an effective remedy to family members under the CRD is also justified by Recital 31 to the Directive, which provides that the Directive 'respects the fundamental rights and freedoms and observes the principles recognised in particular by the Charter of Fundamental Human Rights of the European Union'. It follows from this that 'core' family members are automatically included in that protection given their position as full beneficiaries of the CRD.

However, the issue of whether the *same* protection would be afforded to the 'extended' family members set out in Article 3(2) CRD, whose claim to the enjoyment of the substantive rights under the CRD is much less certain, remained unresolved. The decision in *Banger*[72] shed light on that question. There, Ms Banger, a South African national, and her partner, a UK national, had lived in the Netherlands, where Ms Banger was issued with a residence permit. When the couple moved to the UK, the competent authorities declined to provide Ms Banger with a residence permit on the basis that the UK was her partner's *home* Member State and that the domestic legislation transposing Article 3(2) CRD only applied to extended family members of Union citizens *from other Member States*. The national court made a

71 *ZZ v Secretary of State for the Home Department* (n 45).

72 Case C-89/17 *Banger* EU:C:2018:570, paras 45–50. The need to clarify this arose because some provisions of the CRD expressly mention extended family members (such as Article 10 CRD) but others do not. On the possible rules of interpretation of this dimension of the CRD, see Guild, Peers, and Tomkin (n 6) 82–86.

preliminary reference to the Court of Justice that covered the interpretation of both substantive and procedural rights under the CRD.

On the substantive issues, the national court essentially asked whether the principles established by the ruling of the Court in *Singh*[73] or in the CRD itself could be understood to protect the position of extended family members of an EU citizen who having exercised their right to free movement in another Member State returns to their *home* Member State. The Court of Justice relied primarily on a teleological interpretation of Article 21(1) TFEU to derive an obligation on a Member State to *facilitate* the provision of residence permit for a third-country national who is the unregistered partner of an EU national returning to their *home* Member State.[74]

On the procedural front, the national court raised the very important question of the scope of judicial protection required by EU law for 'extended' family members. This was a point not covered by the CRD. Under the law of England and Wales, Ms Banger did not have the right to appeal against the decision of the national competent authority, with judicial review being the only remedy available to her. Ms Banger contended that the system of judicial review under national law did not allow for a full review of the facts in question. By contrast, had she been a 'core' family member she would have had the right to appeal, with the opportunity of a fuller judicial scrutiny. In essence, the key issue was whether the judicial protection safeguards contained in Articles 15 and 31 CRD applied to 'extended' family members of the mobile EU citizen in the same manner as they applied to 'core' family members, which are the natural beneficiaries of the full protection of the CRD.

In his leading Opinion, Advocate General Bobek considered the complexion of the right to an effective judicial remedy for extended family members in the light of two converging interpretative sources. These were, first, the provisions of the CRD itself and, second, the requirements emanating from Article 47 of the Charter and from the classical remedial principles of effectiveness and non-discrimination.[75] In the application of the former, he acknowledged that a literal interpretation of Article 15 CRD meant that only 'core' family members would be clearly protected but that such textual interpretation was transparently contrary to the spirit of the CRD because the refusal of a residence card to extended family members could be construed as a 'restriction to free movement rights of the Union citizen himself'.[76]

[73] Case C-370/90 *Singh* EU:C:1992:296.

[74] *Banger* (n 72), paras 27–35.

[75] Ibid, para 82.

[76] Ibid, para 88.

However, it was the use of Article 47 of the Charter[77] that provided him with a solid platform to conclude that, even if the CRD did not explicitly apply the relevant procedural safeguards to extended family members, that provision required not only access to judicial redress but also a full judicial scrutiny of the broad discretion granted to Member States under Article 3(2) CRD. Advocate General Bobek concluded that it was ultimately for the national court to ascertain whether the national system of judicial review did satisfy those requirements.

The judgment of the Court, while terser in its reasoning than the Opinion of the Advocate General, reached the conclusion that the provisions of the CRD had to be interpreted in the light of Article 47 of the Charter and that this meant that a national court should be able to ascertain whether a decision refusing a residence permit to an extended family member is based on a sufficiently solid factual basis and is compliant with procedural safeguards, which would include the obligation of the national competent authority to undertake an extensive examination of the applicant's personal circumstances and to justify any denial of entry or residence.[78]

The decision in *Banger* thus demonstrated that 'extended' family members were entitled to the procedural protection offered by the CRD, a result that was achieved through the primary application of the principle of effective judicial protection enshrined in Article 47 of the Charter to the interpretation of Articles 31 and 15 CRD.

8.4 CONCLUSIONS

The principle of effective judicial protection, first recognised in the case law of the CJEU, acquired ultimate visibility by taking its place among the provisions of the EU Charter of Fundamental Rights which, by its own admission, aims to 'strengthen the protection of fundamental rights'.[79] While this principle has remained intertwined with the traditional remedial principles of national procedural autonomy, effectiveness, and non-discrimination,[80] the use of Article 47 of the Charter as an interpretative platform in

[77] Ibid, para 48.
[78] Ibid, paras 51–52.
[79] See Recital 4 of the Preamble to the Charter.
[80] Commentators have highlighted the broader scope of the principle contained in Article 47 of the Charter. See, S. Prechal and R. Widdershoven, 'Redefining the relationship between "Rewe-effectiveness" and effective judicial protection' (2011) 4 Review of European Administrative Law 41, 50.

cases concerning the legality of national procedural rules has become commonplace in the case law on national remedies. Of course, this seems a natural evolutionary step considering the proclamation of the Charter as a solemn political declaration at the time of the Treaty of Nice and its subsequent entry into force with the Treaty of Lisbon. However, the direct allusion to Article 47 of the Charter has represented much more than a cosmetic change. This is because it has yielded a body of case law that has bolstered the potential of this principle, offering a broader range of protection to those whose substantive rights under EU law might have been infringed.[81]

This chapter has sought to argue that the approach in the general case law on national remedies has recently found a reflection in the specific appraisal by the CJEU of the procedural rights of family members of mobile EU citizens under the CRD. Both the CRD and the measures preceding it have taken as a starting point for the entitlement to free movement rights – and for the assessment of the legality of any restrictions to them – the notion that family members are not entities on their own right but merely recipients of derivative rights. Against that unpromising backdrop, the case law of the CJEU has neatly illustrated both a teleological approach to the configuration of the substantive rights to free movement of family members[82] and a rise to prominence of the principle of effective judicial protection as the primary interpretative tool shaping the procedural guarantees available in cases where the rights to entry and residence have been restricted.

The case law interpreting the minimum standard of procedural protection offered by Directive 64/221, as well as the early case law considering the more generous ones contained in the CRD, mostly reflected an approach wedded to the insular confines of those pieces of legislation which was progressively infused by the need to ensure the maximum effectiveness of the available remedies. However, cases like *ZZ*[83] and *Banger*[84] exemplified a much bolder leap by using Article 47 of the Charter to deploy the full force of the principle of effective judicial protection in cases where even the more generous parameters of the CRD might not have allowed for the protection sought by the EU citizen and their family members. This is significant on three counts. First, because it means that the case law in this area is no longer out of step with the evolution of the general body of case law on national remedies given that it confirms a shift towards the primary interpretative role of Article 47 of the

[81] See n 63.
[82] See Section 8.2.
[83] *ZZ v Secretary of State for the Home Department* (n 45).
[84] *Banger* (n 72).

Charter in securing the right to an effective remedy under EU Law. Second, because, in this context, the force of Article 47 of the Charter is applied to the construction of procedural guarantees articulated by *EU secondary legislation*. Until now, much of the case law illustrating the potent effect of that provision has referred to scenarios where the effectiveness of *national* procedural rules has been at stake.[85] This move thus neatly reflects the two-pronged effect of Article 47 on both national and EU-derived remedies. Finally, and more importantly for the purposes of this collection, the approach of the Court in this area does much to address, at the level of enforcement of EU rights, the uncertain position of 'core' and, particularly, 'extended' family members under the CRD. Such a trend should be welcomed so that the commitment of the EU to the rights to free movement and family life is fully realised.

[85] That said, Article 47 of the Charter has also been used in the context of the interpretation of the conditions applying to the centralised system of EU remedies provided in the TFEU. There, the Court has in some areas shown a reluctance to go beyond the letter of the Treaties to give full effect to the principle. This is, for example, the case in relation to the case law interpreting the standing requirements of private parties under Article 263(4) TFEU (see Case C-583/11 *Inuit Tapiriit Kanatami and others v European Parliament and Council* EU:C:2013:625, para 98). However, in other areas, the employ of Article 47 of the Charter has filled some gaps in the system of legal protection provided in the Treaties (see Case T-461/08 *Evropaïki Dynamiki v European Investment Bank* EU:T:2011:494, para 118). Furthermore, recent EU harmonising legislation in the field of remedies like Directive 2014/104/EU of the European Parliament and of the Council of 26 November 2014 on certain rules governing actions for damages under national law for infringements of the competition law provisions of the Member States and of the European Union [2014] OJ L349/1, also shows the explicit influence of Article 47 of the Charter (see Recitals 4–5 of the Preamble to the Directive).

PART III

The EU Family and Family Diversity

9

All Paths Lead to Equality?

Same-Sex Couples and Rainbow Families under European Law

GEOFFREY WILLEMS

9.1 INTRODUCTION

The European landscape remains very fragmented as regards recognition and protection of same-sex couples and rainbow families.[1] As regards couples, only twenty Council of Europe (CoE) States allow same-sex marriages,[2] whereas nine others recognise and protect same-sex relationships only through registered partnerships.[3] In the remaining jurisdictions, same-sex couples have no possibility of formalising their relationship[4]. As regards parent–child relationships, only nine States provide for a 'true' same-sex parenthood regime, similar to that applied to different-sex parents,[5] whereas twenty-one systems allow the establishment of adoptive same-sex parenthood at least in some cases.[6] In sixteen CoE States, same-sex partners may use assisted reproductive

[1] The figures below are based on ILGA-Europe, 'Rainbow Map and index 2023' <https://www.ilga-europe.org/report/rainbow-europe-2023/>.

[2] The Netherlands (2002), Belgium (2003), Spain (2005), Norway (2009), Sweden (2009), Portugal (2010), Iceland (2010), Denmark (2012), France (2013), the UK (2014), Luxembourg (2015), Ireland (2015), Germany (2017), Finland (2017), Malta (2017), Austria (2019), Slovenia (2022), Switzerland (2022), Andorra (2023), Estonia (2024).

[3] Czech Republic (2006), Hungary (2009), Liechtenstein (2011), Croatia (2014), Cyprus (2015), Greece (2015), Italy (2016), San Marino (2019), Montenegro (2021). A law on same-sex civil unions was passed in 2023 by the Latvian Parliament and is expected to enter into force on 1 July 2024.

[4] Albania, Armenia, Azerbaijan, Bosnia and Herzegovina, Bulgaria, Georgia, Lithuania, the Republic of Moldova, North Macedonia, Poland, Romania, Serbia, Slovakia, Turkey, and Ukraine.

[5] Austria, Belgium, Denmark, Malta, the Netherlands, Portugal, Spain, Sweden, and the UK.

[6] Andorra, Austria, Belgium, Croatia, Denmark, Estonia, Finland, France, Germany, Iceland, Ireland, Luxembourg, Malta, the Netherlands, Norway, Portugal, Slovenia, Spain, Sweden, Switzerland, and the UK.

technology (ART) to found a family.[7] Against this background, this chapter aims to describe and analyse the role of the European Court of Human Rights (ECtHR) and EU law in the developing movement towards full recognition and protection of same-sex couples and rainbow families; it highlights the idea that their different and complementary approaches complement and consolidate each other in a way that appropriately leads to a gradual increase of the requirement for equal treatment of all families, regardless of sexual orientation.

First, Section 9.2 specifically considers the growing recognition and protection of same-sex couples. Significantly, it was only in 2010 that the ECtHR affirmed that same-sex parents enjoy a 'family life' within the meaning of Article 8 of the European Convention on Human Rights (ECHR).[8] The section contemplates a series of questions including the central issue of same-sex marriage, alternative forms of recognition and protection, allocation of couple-related social benefits, family reunification, and cross-border recognition of same-sex marriage.

In Section 9.3, a similar panoramic view of European developments is proposed as regards the progressive recognition and protection of rainbow families. Starting with the fundamental question of same-sex parenthood and same-sex adoption, it will also consider parental responsibility as an alternative way of offering some protection and recognition to same-sex parents and their children and social benefits as a significant dimension of family policy, before – finally – turning to the issues of family reunification and cross-border recognition, which have recently given rise to substantial developments.

As a whole, the developments below emphasise that recognition and protection of same-sex relationships and rainbow families can follow multiple paths and that the ECtHR case law and EU law (including EU legislation and the CJEU case law) are mutually reinforcing for the benefit of the rights of same-sex couples and their children. They also reflect the fact that, while the consecration of the right to same-sex marriage and same-sex parenthood may be considered as the final objective to be achieved, subsidiarity considerations necessarily lead European bodies to favour, at least temporarily, more modest ways.

7 Austria, Belgium, Denmark, Finland, France, Iceland, Ireland, Luxembourg, Malta, the Netherlands, Norway, Portugal, Spain, Sweden, Switzerland, and the UK.

8 *Schalk and Kopf v Austria*, Application no 30141/04, para 94.

9.2 SAME-SEX COUPLES

9.2.1 *Same-Sex Marriage: A Renewed Interpretation of the Right to Marry?*

At the time of the adoption of the ECHR in 1950, marriage was understood in the traditional sense of a union between a man and a woman. Accordingly, Article 12 ECHR unequivocally affirms that 'men and women of marriageable age have the right to marry and to found a family'.[9] The ECtHR case law confirmed that this provision was designed to protect the right to marry a person of the opposite gender even if, in *Goodwin*,[10] the Court precised that the terms man and woman did not necessarily refer to 'a determination of gender by purely biological criteria'. Similarly, in *D and Sweden*, the CJEU notoriously considered that 'according to the definition generally accepted by the Member States, the term marriage means a union between two persons of the opposite sex'.[11] At the time these decisions were issued, the Netherlands was the only jurisdiction allowing same-sex marriages.

The Charter of Fundamental Rights of the EU (the Charter) adopted in 2002[12] suggests a new approach to marriage. Article 9 of the Charter guarantees the right to marry without any reference to gender. The Charter official commentary explains that this reflects a deliberate choice to 'broaden the scope' of the right to marriage considering the 'diversity of domestic regulations on marriage' and, notably, the evolution in Dutch and Belgian law.[13] A few years later, in its landmark *Schalk and Kopf v Austria* decision, the Strasbourg Court strongly relied on the more 'modern',[14] or 'liberal',[15] wording of Article 9 of the Charter to deliver a 'renewed' interpretation of Article 12 ECHR. Based on the developments in EU law, the Court affirmed that it 'would no longer consider that the right to marry enshrined in Article

9 See, however, for a detailed analysis: K. Waaldijk, 'The gender-neutrality of the international right to marry: Same-sex couples may still be excluded from marriage, but their exclusion – and their foreign marriages – must be recognised' (23 July 2018) <https://papers.ssrn.com/abstract=3218308>. The author argues that the *travaux préparatoires* of the ECHR do not seem to include any indication that these words were specifically intended to exclude or include same-sex couples from the right to marry and that they should rather be read as emphasising the dimension of equality between men and women.

10 *Christine Goodwin v the United Kingdom*, Application no 28957/95, para 100.

11 Joined Cases C-122/99 P and C-125/99 P *D and Sweden v Council* EU:C:2001:304, para 34.

12 Charter of Fundamental Rights of the European Union [2012] OJ C326/2.

13 *Schalk and Kopf v Austria* (n 8), para 25.

14 Explanations relating to the Charter of Fundamental Rights [2007] OJ C303/02.

15 P. Murat, 'Article II-69' in L. Burgorgue-Larsen, A. Levade, and F. Picod (eds), *Traité établissant une Constitution pour l'Europe. Commentaire article par article. Partie II: La Charte des droits fondamentaux de l'Union* (Bruylant 2005) 165.

12 must in all circumstances be limited to marriage between two persons of the opposite sex' and that, as a consequence, 'it [could not] be said that Article 12 is inapplicable to the applicants' complaint'.[16]

However, both the Commentary and *Schalk and Kopf* underline that the decision to allow same-sex marriage belongs to national authorities. According to the Explanation relating to the Charter of Fundamental Rights, 'Article [9] neither prohibits nor imposes the granting of the status of marriage to unions between people of the same sex.'[17] Similarly, *Schalk and Kopf* affirmed that 'marriage has deep-rooted social and cultural connotations which may differ largely from one society to another' and that 'it must not rush to substitute its own judgment in place of that of the national authorities'.[18] The ECtHR decision has been rightly criticised as the Court did not engage in a true proportionality review. More specifically, it did not explain the relative weight of the applicants' right and the 'social and cultural connotations' put forward by the government nor why the latter should trump the former.[19] Having decided that Article 12 did not require State Parties to allow same-sex marriages, the Court also refused to discuss the matter under Articles 8 and 14 as 'the Convention is to be read as a whole'.[20]

The subsequent case law of the CJEU and the ECtHR confirms this subsidiary approach leaving the issue of same-sex marriage to the discretion of national authorities. The CJEU has frequently recalled that 'a person's status, which is relevant to the rules on marriage, is a matter that falls within the competence of the Member States and EU law does not detract from that competence'.[21] In the same vein, the ECtHR has repeatedly confirmed that 'while it is true that some Contracting States have extended marriage to same-

16 *Schalk and Kopf v Austria* (n 8), para 61.

17 Explanations relating to the Charter of Fundamental Rights (n 14) 21.

18 *Schalk and Kopf v Austria* (n 8), para 62.

19 See, in contrast, the review carried out with regards to the marriage of transsexuals (*Christine Goodwin v the United Kingdom* (n 10), paras 97–103) or the marriage between a father-in-law and his daughter-in-law (*B and L v the United Kingdom*, Application no 36536/02, paras 34–41).

20 *Schalk and Kopf v Austria* (n 8), para 101. This 'systemic' approach, which subordinates the interpretation of Article 8 to that of Article 12, is certainly well established in the Court's case law (see *Johnston and Others v Ireland*, Application no 9697/82, para 57) but has recently been called into question by Judge Angelika Nussberger. In her view, reading the Convention 'as a whole' implies understanding the right to marriage in the light of the rapid transformations of family life, rather than corseting the interpretation of Article 8 by aligning it with the perhaps overly restrained interpretation of Article 12 (*Delecolle v France*, Application no 37646/13, separate opinion of Judge Nussberger, 17).

21 Case C-267/06 *Maruko* EU:C:2008:179, para 59; Case C-443/15 *Parris* EU:C:2016:897, para 58; Case C-673/16 *Coman and others* EU:C:2018:385, para 37. See also Chapter 6 by Xavier Groussot, Gunnar Thor Petursson, and Alezini Loxa.

sex partners, Article 12 cannot be construed as imposing an obligation on the Contracting States to grant access to marriage to same-sex couples' and even specified that 'it enshrines the traditional concept of marriage as being between a man and a woman'.[22] This reiterated reference to the heterosexual nature of marriage might be considered as a step backward in comparison with the more open-ended considerations expressed in *Schalk and Kopf*.

However, some positive trends may be observed in the recent case law of both courts. In its landmark decision in *Coman v Inspectoratul Genral Pentru imigrari*,[23] the CJEU delivered a progressive interpretation of the term 'spouse'. In the Court's view 'the term "spouse" within the meaning of Directive 2004/38 is gender-neutral and may therefore cover the same-sex spouse of the Union citizen concerned'.[24] For its part, in *Orlandi and Others v Italy*, the ECtHR slightly amended its way of referring to State Parties' discretion regarding the issue of same-sex marriage by affirming that they 'are *still* free ... to restrict access to marriage to different-sex couples' (emphasis added).[25] This might be considered as a first tangible indication of a possible tightening of European control linked to the evolution of national legislations.[26]

[22] *Hämäläinen v Finland*, Application no 37359/09, para 96; *Chapin and Charpentier v France*, Application no 40183/07, para 37.

[23] *Coman and others* (n 21). See A. Caiola, 'Une acception large de la notion de "conjoint" pour garantir la liberté de séjour des citoyens européens' (2018) Revue des affaires européennes 335; E. Bribosia and I. Rorive, 'L'arrêt Coman: Quand la Cour de justice contribue à la reconnaissance du mariage homosexuel' (2018) n 253 Journal de droit européen 344–347; M. Fallon, 'Observations sous CJUE, 5 juin 2018, Gr. Ch., Coman, C-673/16, EU: C:2018:385' (Cahiers de l'EDEM, June 2018) <http://uclouvain.be/fr/instituts-recherche/juri/cedie/actualites/observations-sous-cjue-5-juin-2018-gr-ch-coman-c-673-16-eu-c-2018-385.html>; H. Fulchiron, 'Citoyenneté européenne, liberté de circulation et reconnaissance des situations familiales créées dans un État membre: Un petit pas pour de grandes enjambées?' (2018) Recueil Dalloz 1678; P. Hammje, 'Obligation de reconnaissance d'un mariage entre personnes de même sexe conclu dans un État membre aux fins d'octroi d'un droit de séjour dérivé' (2018) Revue critique de droit international privé 816; A. Tryfonidou, 'An analysis of the ECJ ruling in Case C-673/16 Coman: The right of same-sex spouses under EU law to move freely between EU Member States' (2019) Research report prepared for NELFA <http://nelfa.org/inprogress/wp-content/uploads/2019/01/NELFA-Tryfonidou-report-Coman-final-NEW.pdf>; G. Willems, 'Le droit au regroupement familial des époux homosexuels consacré par la Cour de justice de l'Union européenne' (2018) La semaine juridique (édition générale). See also Chapter 7 by Michael Bogdan.

[24] *Coman and others* (n 21), para 35.

[25] *Orlandi and Others v Italy*, Application no 26431/12.

[26] See J.-Y. Carlier. 'Vers un ordre public européen des droits fondamentaux – L'exemple de la reconnaissance des mariages de personnes de même sexe dans l'arrêt Coman', (2019) Revue trimestrielle des droits de l'homme 220.

9.2.2 *Transgender Spouses: A Particular Case of Same-Sex Marriage*

In recent years, both the ECtHR and the CJEU have had to deal with a particular configuration of the claim for authorising same-sex marriage, arising from situations where individuals married to a different sex spouse have subsequently changed their gender identity.

In the ECtHR case *Hämäläinen v Finland*,[27] the applicant was a trans woman denouncing the fact that she could not be officially registered as a woman without ending her marriage with the woman whom she had married before her transition because, at the time, Finland did not allow same-sex marriage. She could either divorce or consent to her marriage being converted into a registered partnership. In its 2014 decision, the Court considered that such alternative was not in breach of the ECHR, considering the lack of European consensus on allowing same-sex marriage or dealing with the pre-existing marriage of trans persons.[28] The Court also endorsed the government's view that when a marriage was 'converted' into a registered partnership 'the original legal relationship [continued] with only a change of title and minor changes to the content of the relationship'.[29] The Court finally considered that 'the effects of the conversion of the applicant's marriage into a registered partnership would be minimal or non-existent as far as the applicant's family life is concerned'[30] and that no separate issue arose under Article 12 of the ECHR.[31] These explanations equating marriage with registered partnership can hardly be reconciled with the Court's classic rhetoric that 'marriage confers a special status on those who enter into it'.[32] This contradiction arguably makes the whole reasoning unsatisfactory as it biased the proportionality test. Indeed, three dissenting judges found it very problematic to force the applicant to choose between having her gender identity recognised and keeping her civil status. In their opinion, persons in the applicant's situation should be allowed to remain married after the acknowledgment of the acquired gender. This is one of the very rare occasions where Strasbourg judges expressly took a position in favour of (a very specific type of) same-sex marriage.

A few years later, in *M.B. v Secretary of State for Work and Pensions*,[33] the CJEU was faced with a similar situation but in the context of Directive 79/7/

[27] *Hämäläinen v Finland* (n 22).
[28] Ibid, para 74.
[29] Ibid, para 84.
[30] Ibid, para 85.
[31] Ibid, para 97.
[32] See, for example, *Gas and Dubois v France*, Application no 25951/07, para 68.
[33] Case C-451/16 *MB v Secretary of State for Work and Pensions* EU:C:2018:492.

EEC on the progressive implementation of the principle of equal treatment for men and women in matters of social security.[34] The applicant in the main proceedings was a trans woman who was faced with the same cruel alternative as Mrs Hämäläinen, before same-sex marriage was introduced in the UK in 2014. For religious reasons, she decided to remain married with her wife and renounced having her acquired female gender officially registered. However, when she reached the age of sixty at which women were entitled to retirement pension, the applicant applied for such a pension but was refused. Referring, among others, to *Maruko*[35] and *Coman*[36], the Court admitted that 'EU law does not detract from the competence of the Member States in matters of civil status and legal recognition of the change of a person's gender'.[37] Differently from *Hämäläinen*, the applicant 'only' claimed entitlement to a retirement pension rather than the recognition of gender as such. Accordingly, the Court ruled that Article 4 of Directive 79/7 that prohibits sex-based discrimination precluded national legislation obliging a transgender person to end their marriage to benefit from a retirement pension at the age corresponding to their new identity.

This case demonstrates how, through the specifics of EU law, the ECtHR decision allowing a State to require dissolution of marriage as a condition for gender recognition is somewhat softened by a CJEU decision providing the persons who refuse to end their marriage with at least some of the benefits associated with the unrecognised acquired gender.

9.2.3 *Registered Partnerships: Official Recognition as a Basic Right*

While the CJEU does not consider itself legitimate to impose on states the creation of a legal status accessible to same-sex couples, the Strasbourg Court has recently confirmed that such a positive obligation exists under Article 8 ECHR.

Already in 2001, the CJEU found in *D and Sweden v Council of the European Union*, that 'since 1989 an increasing number of Member States have introduced, alongside marriage, statutory arrangements granting legal recognition to various forms of union between partners of the same sex or of the opposite sex and conferring on such unions certain effects'.[38] At the time,

[34] Council Directive 79/7/EEC of 19 December 1978 on the progressive implementation of the principle of equal treatment for men and women in matters of social security [1979] OJ L6/24.

[35] *Maruko* (n 21).

[36] See *Coman and others* (n 21).

[37] *MB v Secretary of State for Work and Pensions* (n 33), para 29.

[38] *D and Sweden* (n 11), para 35.

the Court considered that this did not imply that registered partners could be covered by the term 'married official' used in the Community Staff Regulations.[39] Since then, the EU has extended the benefits associated with marriage to registered EU officials as far as they do not have access to marriage.[40] However, in *Parris v Trinity College Dublin*,[41] the Court recalled that 'Member States are … free to provide or not provide … an alternative form of legal recognition of [same-sex relationships], and, if they do so provide, to lay down the date from which such a marriage or alternative form is to have effect'.[42] This is an obvious consequence of 'the lack of EU competence with regard to these matters which … means that the EU cannot legislate in order to require all EU Member States to afford legal recognition to the familial ties among the members of rainbow families in their own territory'.[43]

The ECtHR, however, has progressively affirmed the right for same-sex couples to an alternative legal status. In *Schalk and Kopf*, the ECtHR considered that states enjoyed a margin of appreciation 'in the timing of the introduction of legislative changes'[44] as well as 'as regards the exact status conferred by alternative means of recognition'.[45] As the European consensus on partnerships grew stronger, the Court reconsidered its initial position. In the 2015 *Oliari and others v Italy* decision,[46] the ECtHR ruled that the lack of any form of official registration available to same-sex partners was in breach of the right to family life guaranteed by Article 8 ECHR. The Court insisted that 'same-sex couples … are in a relevantly similar situation to a different-sex couple as regards their need for legal recognition and protection of their relationship'.[47] It also underlined that, given the impossibility to

39 Ibid, para 39.

40 Council Regulation (EC, Euratom) No 723/2004 of 22 March 2004 amending the Staff Regulations of officials of the European Communities and the Conditions of Employment of other servants of the European Communities [2004] OJ L124/1.

41 *Parris* (n 21).

42 Ibid, para 59.

43 A. Tryfonidou and R. Wintemute, 'Obstacles to the free movement of rainbow families in the EU'. Study requested by the European Parliament PETI Committee (2021) <www.europarl.europa.eu/supporting-analyses>.

44 *Schalk and Kopf v Austria* (n 8), para 105.

45 Ibid, para 108.

46 *Oliari and Others v Italy*, Application nos 18766/11 and 36030/11. See also A. Hayward, 'Same-sex registered partnerships – A right to be recognized' (2016) 75 Cambridge Law Journal 27; V. J. Marzano, 'Oliari and the European Court of Human Rights: Where the court failed' (2017) Pace International Law Review 241; S. Ragone and V. Volpe, 'An emerging right to a "gay" family life? The Case Oliari v. Italy in a comparative perspective' (2016) 17 German Law Journal 451.

47 *Oliari and Others v Italy* (n 46), para 165.

marry, same-sex couples had a 'particular interest' in an alternative status providing them 'core rights' relevant to a couple and endowed with an 'intrinsic value' irrespective of its specific legal effects.[48] In the Court's view, the Italian Government failed to indicate the 'community interest' that would have justified the absence of a statute.[49] Moreover, the Court considered that while a wide margin of discretion must be recognised as to the 'exact status' conferred, such large margin did not apply to the 'general need' for legal recognition, especially in a European context where legal recognition of same-sex couples was rapidly gaining ground.[50]

Since *Oliari* was based on several very specific aspects of the Italian context,[51] it was not clear whether it imposed a positive obligation on all CoE States to create an alternative form of union.[52] In 2017, the CoE Commissioner for Human Rights, Nils Muižnieks, observed that 'it is difficult to read the Oliari judgment, and concurring opinion, as anything else than placing a positive obligation on states parties to the ECHR to provide legal recognition to same-sex couples as a way to protect their right to family life'.[53] This positive obligation to provide a legal framework was confirmed by the Court in *Fedotova and others v Russia*, first in a chamber judgment issued on 13 July 2021,[54] and subsequently in a Grand Chamber decision issued on 17 January 2023.[55]

9.2.4 *Social Benefits: Piercing the Veil of Marriage*

While lacking the legitimacy to require States to set up registered partnership formulas, the CJEU has proven particularly committed to the defence and development of the rights of registered partners. In several cases, the Court has considered, on the basis of the Employment Equality Directive (Directive

48 Ibid, para 174.
49 Ibid, para 176.
50 Ibid, paras 177–178.
51 The Constitutional Court and the Court of Cassation had both affirmed the need to recognise and protect same-sex couples (ibid, para 180), in line with the sentiment of the Italian population as reflected in official surveys (ibid, para 181).
52 Hayward (n 46).
53 Commissioner for Human Rights, 'Access to registered same-sex partnerships: It's a question of equality' (Council of Europe 2017) <www.coe.int/en/web/commissioner/-/access-to-registered-same-sex-partnerships-it-s-a-question-of-equality>.
54 *Fedotova and Others v Russia* (Chamber judgment), Application nos 40792/10, 30538/14 and 43439/10, para 56.
55 *Fedotova and Others v Russia* (Grand Chamber judgment), Application nos 40792/10, 30538/14 and 43439/10, para 178. See also *Buhuceanu and Others v Romania*, Application nos 20081/19 and 20 others, Maymulakhin and Markiv v. Ukraine, Application no. 75135/14, and *Przybyszewska and Others v. Poland*, Applications nos. 11454/17 and 9 others.

2000/78/EC),[56] that same-sex couples who could not marry but only enter into a registered partnership should be granted the same social benefits as different-sex spouses. First, in *Maruko* and *Römer*,[57] the Court decided that German *Lebenspartners* should be able to benefit from a survivor's or retirement pension under the same conditions as heterosexual spouses. It emphasised, however, that its ruling only applied to partnerships that, as the German status, were reserved for same-sex couples and provided effects very similar to those associated with marriage. However, this approach was expanded, in *Hay v Crédit Agricole*,[58] to partnerships available to both different-sex and same-sex couples and less close to marriage regarding legal effects, as the French *Pacte civil de solidarité* (PACS). In this case, the Court indeed decided that a gay employee entering into a PACS with a person of the same sex should be entitled to the same bonus and leave as those provided to heterosexual persons on the occasion of their marriage. This string of case law constitutes an important step forward for same-sex couples by implying that same-sex registered partners deprived of access to marriage must as a minimum enjoy the same benefits as spouses. Nevertheless, its scope remains limited to situations where same-sex partners have access to at least some form of official registration.

For its part, the ECtHR was prompt to require equal rights for same-sex and different-sex *de facto* partners, but durably allowed States to favour different-sex spouses over unmarried same-sex partners deprived of access to marriage.

In 2003, the Court decided in *Karner*[59] that a surviving same-sex *de facto* partner should have the right to continue his deceased partner's tenancy in the same way as a surviving different-sex *de facto* partner. Considering that the issue fell into the ambit of the protection of 'home' under Article 8 ECHR (as the Court did not yet recognise that same-sex couples can enjoy 'family life' as such), the Court stated that differences in treatment on the basis of sexual orientation must be justified by 'particularly serious reasons'[60] and that the aim of protecting the traditional family was legitimate but 'rather abstract' and pursuable through 'a broad variety of concrete measures'.[61] In the Court's

[56] Council Directive 2000/78/EC of 27 November 2000 establishing a general framework for equal treatment in employment and occupation [2000] OJ L303/16.

[57] Case C-147/08 *Römer* EU:C:2011:286.

[58] Case C-267/12 *Hay* EU:C:2013:823. See F. Lambinet and S. Gilson, 'Arrêt "Hay": Les partenaires (de même sexe) pacsés doivent-ils être traités comme des (hétérosexuels) mariés' 2014 Journal de droit européen 243.

[59] *Karner v Austria*, Application no 40016/98. See also *Kozak v Poland*, Application no 13102/02; *P.B. and J.S. v Austria*, Application no 18984/02.

[60] *Karner v Austria* (n 59), para 37.

[61] Ibid, para 41.

view, Austria did not demonstrate the necessity to exclude same-sex partners to achieve that aim. This requirement that unmarried couples be treated equally, regardless of their sexual orientation, was confirmed in subsequent decisions, such as *Kozak v Poland*[62] and *P.B. and J.S. v Austria*.[63]

However, when the ECtHR was faced with the question of whether same-sex partners deprived of the possibility of marrying should be granted the same social benefits as married opposite-sex couples, it was not as bold as the CJEU and refused – for *de facto* partners as well as for registered partners – to pierce the veil of marriage. In *Manenc v France*[64] and *Mata Estevez v Spain*,[65] the Court indeed accepted the State's choice to provide a survivor's pension only to spouses, even if that implied that same-sex partners were necessarily deprived of such pension as, at the time, it was impossible for them to marry. The Court thus failed to recognise the discrimination based on sexual orientation hiding behind the distinction based on civil status. Despite strong criticism,[66] this approach has also been applied later in *Gas and Dubois*, as regards access to adoption.[67] Fortunately, it seems to have been abandoned in the *Taddeucci and McCall*[68] decision relating to family reunification, in which the court decided that same-sex *de facto* partners who cannot marry should have the same right to family reunification as different-sex

[62] *Kozak v Poland* (n 59), para 43 (eviction from the deceased partner's social housing).

[63] *P.B. and J.S. v Austria* (n 59), para 43 (extension of sickness and accident insurance for civil servants).

[64] In its decision in *Manenc v France* (Application no 66686/09) issued on 21 September 2010, the ECtHR decided that France could, without infringing Article 14 of the ECHR, refuse to grant a survivor's pension to a homosexual man after the death of his partner with whom he had entered into a civil partnership five years earlier. The Court emphasised that the PACS remained 'alien to marriage' and that the fact that France did not allow same-sex marriage 'could not of itself suffice to place the applicant in a situation analogous or comparable to that of a surviving spouse' with regard to the right to a pension. (The law on *mariage pour tous* was adopted in 2013.)

[65] In its *Mata Estevez v Spain* decision (Application no 56501/00) issued on 10 May 2001, the Court ruled that Spain could, without violating the Convention, deny a homosexual man whose de facto partner had died the benefit of a survivor's pension, since this benefit was reserved for spouses, even though homosexuals were not able to marry (the ley on *matrimonio igualitario* was adopted in 2005).

[66] Lambinet and Gilson (n 58); C. Tobler, 'Equality and non-discrimination under the ECHR and EU law: A comparison focusing on discrimination against LGBTI persons' (2014) 74 Heidelberg Journal of International Law 521.

[67] *Gas and Dubois v France* (n 32), paras 66-71.

[68] *Taddeucci and McCall v Italy*, Application no 51362/09; See N. Koffeman, 'Taddeucci and McCall v. Italy: Welcome novelty in the ECtHR's case-law on equal treatment of same-sex couples' (*Strasbourg Observers*, 27 July 2016) <https://strasbourgobservers.com/2016/07/27/taddeucci-and-mccall-v-italy-welcome-novelty-in-the-ecthrs-case-law-on-equal-treatment-of-same-sex-couples/>.

spouses.[69] It shall be seen whether the Court will, in the future, transpose this new reasoning to the issue of social benefits that was at stake in *Manenc* and *Mata Estevez*. In such case, the ECtHR case law would provide a useful complement to the *Hay* case law by expanding its egalitarian dynamic to *de facto* partners.

It should be mentioned, finally, that, in two decisions issued in 2016, the CJEU as well as the ECtHR still refused to extend spouses' survivor's pension rights to same-sex partners, even if the specificity of these cases may limit their significance. In *Parris v Trinity College Dublin*,[70] the CJEU decided that the denial of a survivor's pension to the applicant's same-sex registered partner on the ground that at the time of his retirement in 2010 such pension was reserved for spouses was not in breach of the provisions of Directive 2000/78/EC, even if at that time same-sex couples could not marry (Ireland allowed same-sex marriage in 2015). In *Aldeguer Tomas v Spain*,[71] the ECtHR similarly ruled that the denial of a survivor's pension to a surviving same-sex *de facto* partner on the ground that at the time of the death in 2002 such pension was reserved for spouses was not in breach of the ECHR, even if at that time same-sex couples could not choose to marry (Spain allowed same-sex marriages in 2005). As mentioned above, the relevance of both cases is arguably limited due to their specific circumstances. Indeed, both Spain and Ireland had in the meantime taken effective steps to expand the right to a survivor's pension to same-sex partners either through the institution of a civil partnership scheme providing for a survivor's pension (Ireland)[72] or through access to marriage and all associated benefits (Spain). Thus, the courts might take a different approach in cases where the State has not taken such steps in view of guaranteeing equality between couples in the enjoyment of social benefits.

[69] *Taddeucci and McCall v Italy* (n 68), para 83.

[70] *Parris* (n 21); A. Tryfonidou, 'Another failed opportunity for the effective protection of LGB rights under EU law: Dr David. L. Parris v. Trinity College Dublin and Others' (*EU Law Analysis*, 1 December 2016) <http://eulawanalysis.blogspot.com/2016/12/another-failed-opportunity-for.html>.

[71] *Aldeguer Tomás v Spain*, Application no 35214/09.

[72] It should be mentioned, in this respect, that Mr Parris did not benefit directly from this evolution. In 2011, registered partnership was introduced and the survivor's pension scheme was extended to the registered partner, but only if the beneficiary of the pension had entered into a registered partnership with his/her same-sex partner prior to turning sixty. Mr Parris, who was already sixty-five in 2011, did and could obviously not meet this requirement. However, the Court found that this did not amount to discrimination on the basis of sexual orientation or age.

9.2.5 *Family Reunification: The Strong Protection of the Partners' Core Right to Simply Be Together*

In the spectacular *Coman* judgment issued on 5 June 2018, the CJEU decided that, to determine the beneficiaries of the right to family reunification of EU citizens, the term 'spouse' referred to in Article 2(2)(b) of the 2004/38 directive on the right of citizens of the Union and their family members to move and reside freely within the territory of the Member States[73] must be understood as including same-sex spouses as well as different-sex spouses, even if the host state does not allow same-sex marriages. Accordingly, Romania must provide a residence permit to the American spouse with whom a Romanian citizen had been validly married in Brussels where they effectively resided together before moving to Romania. This does not amount to a full recognition of the marriage as it must only be taken into account in the application of EU family reunification law. The judgment is, nevertheless, significant in clearly recognising the right to family reunification for same-sex spouses of EU citizens in all EU Member States. In particular, the Court stressed that the concept of spouse was gender-neutral and had to be interpreted in the light of the aim of directive 2004/38 and of Article 7 of the Charter providing for the right to respect for private and family life. From this perspective, the right of same-sex couples to live together in the Member State of which one of them is a national outweighs the Member States' desire to protect their 'public order' or 'national identity'. Based on *Coman*, this right is only recognised with respect to EU citizens who have entered into a same-sex marriage in another Member State. The future will tell whether its scope can be extended to foreigners legally residing in the Union via Directive 2003/86 and to marriages concluded outside the EU.[74]

Quite interestingly, in the context of this contribution, the ECtHR case law provides very significant additions to the protection offered by *Coman*. While Directive 2004/38 only protects same-sex couples who are married or in a registered partnership equivalent to marriage, the ECtHR decided in *Pajic*[75] and *Taddeucci and McCall* that same-sex *de facto* partners without access to marriage should benefit from family reunification under the same conditions as different-sex *de facto* partners and different sex-spouses. In *Pajic*, the Court

[73] Directive 2004/38/EC of the European Parliament and of the Council of 29 April 2004 on the right of citizens of the Union and their family members to move and reside freely within the territory of the Member States [2004] OJ L158/77.

[74] Tryfonidou, 'An analysis of the ECJ ruling in Case C-673/16 Coman: The right of same-sex spouses under EU law to move freely between EU Member States' (n 23) 14 and 16.

[75] *Pajic v Croatia*, Application no 68453/13.

applied the established *Karner* case law on the requirement that same-sex *de facto* partners be granted the same rights as different-sex *de facto* partners. Accordingly, the Croatian legislation allowing the reunification of heterosexual *de facto* partners only was in breach of articles 8 and 14 of the ECHR. *Taddeucci* goes much further. It departs from the approach taken in *Manenc*[76] and *Mata Estevez*[77] and considers that, as regards marriage-associated benefits, same-sex *de facto* partners who do not have access to marriage *are not* in a situation analogous to that of different-sex *de facto* partners who have the possibility of contracting marriage. However, the Italian legislation treated them in the same way by denying the right to family reunification to all *de facto* partners. Such similar treatment of different situations is in breach of the ECHR unless the defending State adduces 'particularly convincing and weighty reasons'. In the Court's view, the 'margin of appreciation enjoyed by the States in protecting the traditional family' invoked by the government did not meet this standard.[78]

9.2.6 *Recognition of Marriages Celebrated Abroad: Partnerships as a Way of Compromise*

The *Coman* judgment cautiously recalls that 'a person's status, which is relevant to the rules on marriage, is a matter that falls within the competence of the Member States'[79] and only affirms 'an obligation to recognise [same-sex] marriages for the sole purpose of granting a derived right of residence to a third-country national'.[80] It has been suggested, however, that, at some point, the *Coman* dynamic may lead to a more general principle of recognition of same-sex marriage celebrated abroad. Indeed, it remains to be seen to what extent it will or will not be 'sustainable'[81] to confine the recognition of marriage to the sole question of family reunification. It is unclear whether host states, when required to grant residence permits to same-sex spouses, will be able to refuse the latter all the benefits normally deriving from marriage. It is reasonable to think that this first form of 'targeted recognition'[82] will give

76 *Manenc v France* (n 64).
77 *Mata Estevez v Spain* (n 65).
78 *Taddeucci and McCall v Italy* (n 68), paras 92–93.
79 *Coman and others* (n 21), para 37.
80 Ibid, para 46.
81 Bribosia and Rorive (n 23) 347.
82 Fulchiron, 'Citoyenneté européenne, Liberté de circulation et reconnaissance des situations familiales créées dans un État membre: Un petit pas pour de grandes enjambées?' (n 23) 1678.

rise to others, for example regarding the social and/or fiscal effects of marriage[83] by way of a kind of 'contagion or percolation' effect.[84] *Coman* might thus be auguring a trend towards a larger or even a full recognition of same-sex marriages across EU Member States: if more and more rights arise from marriages celebrated abroad it may become increasingly difficult to justify a refusal of the title of 'spouses'. Considering the current position of the CJEU on the Member States' competence regarding marriage, it is however unlikely that such an obligation of full recognition will be affirmed in the near future.

Recently, the ECtHR arrived at a compromise approach. In *Orlandi v Italy*,[85] the Court found that Italy could not, without violating the Convention, deny any form of recognition to foreign same-sex marriages. The applicants were same-sex couples married in Canada, the United States, and the Netherlands complaining that various local administrations in Italy had refused to officially register their marriages. The Court stated that the recognition of a person's 'real marital status' was a matter of personal and social identity and 'psychological integrity'.[86] The Court also pointed out that since *Schalk and Kopf*, the right to marry was applicable to same-sex couples wishing to marry and that it followed that Article 12 ECHR also applied to same-sex couples already married in another legal order.[87] Nevertheless, states were 'still free' to reserve marriage for heterosexuals[88] and may legitimately aim to prevent their nationals from having recourse abroad to institutions refused in their legal order.[89] Against this background, the Court noted that the lack of recognition had not deprived the applicants either of the rights they had previously enjoyed in Italy or the rights acquired in the country where they had married.[90] Moreover, Italy was allowed a comfortable margin of appreciation since, despite the rapid movement in favour of the recognition of same-sex couples

83 Hammje (n 23) 833.

84 Fallon (n 23).

85 *Orlandi and Others v Italy* (n 25). H. Fulchiron, 'La CEDH et la reconnaissance des mariages entre personnes de même sexe célébrés à l'étranger: Avis de tempête ou signal brouillé?' (2018) Recueil Dalloz 446; J. Lievens, 'EHRM opent deur naar Europese erkenning homohuwelijk' (2018) Juristenkrant 1; C. Poppelwell-Scevak, 'Oliari, Orlandi and Homophobic dissenting opinions: The Strasbourg approach to the recognition of same sex marriages' (*Strasbourg Observers*, 2 February 2018) <https://strasbourgobservers.com/2018/02/02/oliari-orlandi-and-homophobic-dissenting-opinions-the-strasbourg-approach-to-the-recognition-of-same-sex-marriages/>.

86 *Orlandi and Others v Italy* (n 25), para 144.

87 Ibid, para 145.

88 Ibid, para 192.

89 Ibid, para 207.

90 Ibid, para 208.

in Europe, America, and Australasia,[91] there was no consensus among the states refusing same-sex marriage on the recognition of marriages celebrated abroad.[92] However, the Court held that domestic authorities, without having to recognise the marriages as such, should have taken them into consideration as civil unions. Indeed, the absence of any recognition and the subsequent legal vacuum disregarded the social reality of the applicants' situation without compelling justification.[93]

9.3 RAINBOW FAMILIES

9.3.1 *Same-Sex Parenthood: A Matter of National Identity?*

The ECtHR has dealt with the question of same-sex adoption in two significantly different cases. The first case, *Gas and Dubois*,[94] concerned two women who lived together in a registered partnership in France. They had travelled to Belgium to conceive a child through assisted reproductive technology (ART) and wanted the child to be adopted in France by the birth mother's partner. However, such adoption was impossible as intra-family adoption was reserved to spouses, and marriage to different-sex couples only. In the second case, X. *and others v Austria*,[95] two women living together in a *de facto* relationship and raising the child that one of them had conceived during a previous heterosexual relationship wanted the child to be adopted by the mother's partner. Such adoption was impossible as intra-family adoption was only allowed for different-sex *de facto partners* but not for same-sex *de facto* partners.

Beyond the difference regarding the circumstances of the child conception, the main contrast between *Gas and Dubois* and X. *and others* was that, in the

[91] Ibid, para 204.

[92] Ibid, para 205.

[93] Ibid, para 209.

[94] *Gas and Dubois v France* (n 32).

[95] *X and Others v Austria*, Application no 19010/07, para 137. See N. Rodean, 'Adoption and same-sex couples: New rights in European constitutional space after the ruling X and Others v. Austria' (2014) 29 Direitos Fundamentais & Justiça 30; G. Puppinck, 'X. and Others v. Austria (Part I): Had the woman been a man ...' (*Strasbourg Observers*, 4 March 2013) <https://strasbourgobservers.com/2013/03/04/x-and-others-v-austria-part-i-had-the-woman-been-a-man/>; S. Smet, 'X. and Others v. Austria (Part II): A narrow ruling on a narrow issue' (*Strasbourg Observers*, 6 March 2013) <https://strasbourgobservers.com/2013/03/06/x-and-others-v-austria-part-ii-a-narrow-ruling-on-a-narrow-issue/>; P. Martens, 'L'égalité dans l'adoption' (2013) Revue de jurisprudence de Liège, Mons et Bruxelles 1404; G. Willems, 'Orientation sexuelle et adoption : L'Autriche condamnée par la Cour européenne des droits de l'homme' (2013) Revue trimestrielle des droits de l'homme 1037.

former, the applicants could not adopt because adoption was reserved for spouses (and marriage was reserved for opposite-sex couples), whereas in the latter, the couple could not adopt because adoption was reserved for opposite-sex couples, either married or not. In the former case, therefore, the difference based on sexual orientation was somehow 'hidden' behind a distinction made on the basis of matrimonial status whereas in the latter, it was 'blatant', as adoption was available to different-sex *de facto* partners but not same-sex *de facto* partners.

In both cases, the Court accepted that there existed a family life between the two women and the child which is protected by Article 8 ECHR. Beyond this, the Court ruled very differently. In *Gas and Dubois*, the Court considered that the applicants were treated by France exactly like opposite-sex registered partners who could not adopt and could not be compared to opposite-sex spouses as 'marriage confers a special status on those who enter into it'.[96] In some sense, the ECtHR refused to see that it was the applicants' sexual orientation that prevented them from marrying which – in turn – prevented them to proceed to the adoption. The Court disregarded the forbidden discrimination based on sexual orientation poorly concealed behind an admissible distinction on the basis of the status of a couple. Things turned out very differently in X. *and others*. Since the distinction was clearly based on the applicants' sexual orientation, the Court referred to *Salgueiro Da Silva Mouta*[97] and *E.B. v France*[98] to recall that 'differences based solely on considerations of sexual orientation are unacceptable under the Convention'.[99] The protection of the traditional family was considered 'a weighty and legitimate reason which might justify a difference in treatment' although it was 'rather abstract' and could be pursued by 'a broad variety of concrete measures'.[100] As the government admitted that 'same-sex couples may be as suited for second-parent adoption as different-sex couples', the Court concluded that Austria did not adduce 'particularly strong and convincing reasons' to justify the disputed distinction and that there had been a breach of Articles 8 and 14 ECHR.[101] X. *and others* undoubtedly constituted a big step forward for lesbian and gay parents but its importance is undermined by the circular reasoning relied on in *Gas and Dubois* by which the right to adoption is only guaranteed where *de facto* partners may adopt.

96 *Gas and Dubois v France* (n 32), para 68.
97 *Salgueiro Da Silva Mouta v Portugal*, Application no 33290/96.
98 *EB v France*, Application no 43546/02.
99 *X and Others v Austria* (n 95), para 99.
100 Ibid, para 138–139.
101 Ibid, para 151.

Fortunately, *Taddeucci and McCall* dismissed the *Gas and Dubois* approach and logically considered that the 'specificity of marriage' argument cannot be used against those who cannot marry,[102]. One can thus hope that this updated reasoning will be applied in future same-sex adoption cases and that the ECtHR will accordingly affirm an explicit right to same-sex adoption based on the idea put forward in X. *and others* that 'same-sex couples [are] as suited for ... adoption as different-sex couples'.[103]

While favourable developments may thus be expected as regards adoption,[104] the ECtHR may remain more reluctant to affirm the right to 'direct' (as opposed to 'adoptive') same-sex parenthood established through a legal presumption or acknowledgement of 'co-maternity' or 'co-paternity'. To our knowledge, the ECtHR has delivered only one decision on the matter – *Boeckel and Gessner-Boeckel.*[105] In this case, two German women were living together in a *Lebenspartnerschaft* and one of them gave birth to a son. Two years after the birth, the German court allowed a second parent adoption, by the mother's life partner. The applicants subsequently requested the court to change the child's birth certificate, as, in their view, the presumption automatically designating the mother's husband as the child's legal father should have been applied *mutatis mutandis* in their situation. The ECtHR found, however, that same-sex registered partners and opposite-sex spouses were not in a comparable situation in this respect. According to the Court, the presumption was based on the idea that 'the man who was married to the child's mother at the time of birth was indeed the child's biological father ... [even if] this legal presumption might not always reflect the true descent' whereas, in contrast, 'in case one partner of a same-sex partnership gives birth to a child, it can be ruled out on biological grounds that the child descended from the other partner'.[106]

[102] *Taddeucci and McCall v Italy* (n 68). See Koffeman (n 68).

[103] *X and Others v Austria* (n 32).

[104] See, nevertheless, *C.E. and Others v France*, Application nos 29775/18 and 29693/19 where the Court decided that the impossibility for a woman to adopt her former same-sex partner's child was not in breach of the right to respect for private and family life. The significance of this case may be limited as it focuses on the situation of ex-partners and as the Court took in consideration positive developments arising in French law in the context following the revision of bioethic laws in 2021. See C. Derave and H. Ouhnaoui, 'C.E. & al. v. France: Legal recognition of intended parenthood from previous same-sex relationships (between women)' (*Strasbourg Observers*, 7 October 2022) <http://strasbourgobservers.com/2022/10/07/c-e-al-v-france-legal-recognition-of-intended-parenthood-from-previous-same-sex-relationships-between-women/>.

[105] *Boeckel and Gessner-Boeckel v Germany*, Application no 8017/11.

[106] Ibid, para 30.

In the very recent *V.M.A. v Stolichna obshtina* case,[107] the CJEU similarly emphasised that 'a person's status, which is relevant to the rules on marriage and parentage, is a matter that falls within the competence of the Member States' and that they 'are thus free to decide whether or not to allow marriage and parenthood for persons of the same sex'.[108] In her Opinion, Advocate General Kokott more specifically noted that among the Member States that allow same-sex marriage, 'only some provide for the 'automatic' parenthood of the wife of the biological mother of a child'[109] and that 'the rules on parentage determine the family relationships which are at the heart of family law' and 'represent the essence of the conception which the [State] is seeking to protect as its national identity'.[110]

Currently, another case concerning the issue of same-sex parenthood, *R.F. and others v Germany*,[111] is pending before the ECtHR. Differently from the *Boeckel* case, here one of the women gave birth while the other provided the eggs. Accordingly, both women may claim to be – in some sense – the child's biological mother. In light of the recent confirmation by the CJEU that the recognition of same-sex parenthood is a matter that should be left to the states, it remains to be seen whether this double biological connection with the child will lead the court to take a different approach than the one taken in *Boeckel* and rule in favour of the applicants.

9.3.2 *Assisted Reproductive Technology: The Cross-Border Dimension*

The ECtHR has never had the opportunity to address clearly the question of whether same-sex couples could have an ECHR-guaranteed right to found a family via ART techniques. In *Gas and Dubois*, the applicants had travelled to Belgium for insemination but the Court was not seized of the question of access to ART but only of the subsequent issue of adoption. The Court nevertheless noted that 'while French law provides that … insemination is available only to heterosexual couples it also states that it is to be made available for therapeutic purposes only'. From this therapeutic perspective, the applicants' situation cannot be compared to that of infertile heterosexual couples and they cannot be said to be discriminated against.[112] *Gas and*

[107] Case C-490/20 *V.M.A. v Stolichna obshtina, rayon 'Pancharevo'* EU:C:2021:1008.
[108] Ibid, para 52.
[109] Opinion of Advocate General Kokott in Case C-490/20 *V.M.A. v Stolichna obshtina, rayon 'Pancharevo'* EU:C:2021:296, para 75.
[110] Ibid, para 105.
[111] *R.F. and Others v Germany*, Application no 46808/16.
[112] *Gas and Dubois v France* (n 32), para 63.

Dubois was followed by another French application – *Charron and Merle-Montet*[113] – to the ECtHR. The application concerned the fact that lesbian couples had no access to insemination in France but was considered inadmissible as the applicant had not exhausted the domestic remedies.[114] In any case, it must be kept in mind that the ECtHR has proven very reluctant to impose any obligation on State Parties as regards medically assisted procreation (MAP) even in situations involving opposite-sex couples.[115] In the foreseeable future, the Court is therefore very unlikely to take serious steps in favour of same-sex partners who want to become parents through ART.

Due to the fact that ART constitutes medical services under EU law these are to be considered 'services' within the meaning of Article 57 TFEU insofar as they are carried out legally and in return for payment, and 'health care' within the meaning of directive 2011/24/EU on patient mobility.[116] EU law thus generally allows individuals to move within the Union to benefit from ART techniques, even when these techniques are prohibited in their State of origin. It seems that a 'considerable flow of patients' crosses borders between European states for reproductive purpose, either because of 'legal restrictions based on prohibition of the technique per se, or because of inaccessibility due to the characteristics of the patients (like age, sexual orientation or civil status)'.[117]

[113] *Charron and Merle-Montet v France*, Application no 22612/15.

[114] See J.-P. Marguénaud, 'Le refus de la procréation médicalement assistée à un couple d'homosexuelles mariées ou la subsidiarité otage de la proportionnalité'. (2018) Revue trimestrielle de droit civil 349.

[115] See A. Lebret, 'The European Court of Human Rights and the framing of reproductive rights' (2020) Droits fondamentaux <www.crdh.fr/revue/n-18–2020/the-european-court-of-human-rights-and-the-framing-of-reproductive-rights/>; G. Willems, 'Droits de l'homme et procréation médicalement assistée: La Cour de Strasbourg face aux évolutions biomédicales et aux mutations de la filiation' in N. Massager (ed), *Procréation médicalement assistée et gestation pour autrui: Regards croisés du droit et de la pratique médicale* (Anthemis 2017); B. Pastre-Belda, 'La Cour européenne des droits de l'homme, entre promotion de la subsidiarité et protection effective des droits' (2013) Revue trimestrielle des droits de l'homme 256.

[116] Directive 2011/24/EU of the European Parliament and of the Council of 9 March 2011 on the application of patients' rights in cross-border healthcare [2011] OJ L88/4. See N. Koffeman, 'Legal responses to cross-border movement in reproductive matters within the European Union' (IACL World Congress – Constitutional Challenges: Global and Local, Oslo, April 2014) <https://scholarlypublications.universiteitleiden.nl/access/item%3A2854771/view>. See also W. Van Hoof and G. Pennings, 'Extraterritorial laws for cross-border reproductive care: The issue of legal diversity' (2012) 19 European Journal of Health Law 187.

[117] F. Shenfield and others, 'Cross border reproductive care in six European countries' (2010) 25 Human Reproduction 1367.

However, the freedom to provide services protected by the TFEU is not absolute and states may try to prevent their nationals from crossing borders to resort to domestically prohibited techniques.[118] Directive 2011/24/EU indeed stipulates that none of its provisions 'should be interpreted in such a way as to undermine the fundamental ethical choices of Member States'.[119] In this respect, it is worth mentioning that in her Opinion in *V.M.A. v Stolichna obshtina*, Advocate General Kokott included human reproduction among 'the fundamental institutions of family law'. In her view, 'national rules governing marriage (or divorce) and parentage (or even reproduction) define the family relationships which are at the heart of this field'.[120]

Similarly, in the *Mennesson* case, the ECtHR decided that a state could legitimately seek 'to deter its nationals from having recourse to methods of assisted reproduction outside the national territory that are prohibited on its own territory'.[121] On a different note, however, it must be kept in mind that in *S.H. and others v Austria*, the Court explicitly noted that restrictions to access to ART were 'more acceptable' if nationals could easily seek the desired treatments abroad.[122] There may be a form of paradox or at least tension here, since, while states may thus seek to discourage 'reproductive tourism', the Court sometimes considers state bans to be less problematic when the denied services can be accessed in another country.

9.3.3 *Shared Parental Responsibility and Contacts: A Favourable, Yet Timid, Evolution*

Currently, the EU has no competence to regulate adoption and parenthood, and the ECtHR is not (yet) ready to explicitly affirm the right to same-sex adoption or *a fortiori* a hypothetical right to same-sex parenthood. In this situation, European judges may try to put forward the right for same-sex parents and their children to enjoy at least some 'core' rights allowing the flourishing of the adult–child relationship. To our knowledge, only the

[118] Koffeman (n 116), para 5.

[119] Directive 2011/24/EU (n 116).

[120] Opinion of Advocate General Kokott in *V.M.A. v Stolichna obshtina, rayon 'Pancharevo'* (n 109), para 75.

[121] *Mennesson v France*, Application no 65192/11, para 62. See also *Paradiso and Campanelli v Italy*, Application no 25358/12, para 180.

[122] *S.H. and Others v Austria*, Application no 57813/00, para 114: 'the Court also observes that there is no prohibition under Austrian law on going abroad to seek treatment of infertility that uses artificial procreation techniques not allowed in Austria and that in the event of a successful treatment the Civil Code contains clear rules on paternity and maternity that respect the wishes of the parents'.

ECtHR has been asked to rule on the critical issues of parental responsibility and contacts in the specific context of rainbow families. Unfortunately, its decisions on the matter did not further much the cause of legal recognition and protection of the links established in such families.

In 2018, in *Bonnaud and Lecoq*,[123] the ECtHR decided that the impossibility for a couple of women to share parental responsibility over the two children that they were raising together was not contrary to the ECHR. Each of them had become mother of one of the children through ART in Belgium and they wished to exercise joint parental authority over both of them using a mutual 'delegation of parental authority' which under French law is a general possibility for (a) parent(s) to share parental responsibility with a third party. However, the domestic courts found that, as both women were already perceived as the children's mothers by family and friends and as they did not report any particular difficulties, the necessity of a delegation had not been demonstrated. The ECtHR endorsed this explanation observing that the refusal to grant the delegation was based on the factual circumstances of the case[124] and that the assessment by the French courts did not reveal any difference in treatment based on sexual orientation.[125]

In 2020, in *Honner*,[126] the Court similarly considered that the denial of a right to contact the mother's ex-partner who had assumed the role of a second mother for years was not in breach of the Convention. Here, again, the couple had travelled to a Belgian fertility centre, and the woman who had given birth had appointed her partner as the child's testamentary guardian and had also largely entrusted her with the child's daily upbringing. The two women had entered into a civil partnership in 2009 but separated in 2012, and the child's mother had subsequently refused contacts between the child and her ex-partner who had then applied for contact as a person having established lasting emotional ties with the child. The national judge, however, refused to order such right to contact as, due to the very sharp deterioration in the relationship between the two women, contacts did not appear to be in the child's best interest. The ECtHR ruled in favour of the defending State by considering that French courts had delivered a 'carefully reasoned' decision, taking into consideration all the relevant facts and prioritising the prevailing interest of the child who was in a traumatic and guilt-inducing situation.

[123] *Bonnaud and Lecoq v France*, Application no 6190/11.
[124] Ibid, para 44.
[125] Ibid, para 45.
[126] *Honner v France*, Application no 19511/16.

One may consider that *Bonnaud and Lecoq* as well as *Honner* did not give due consideration to the fact that the applicants were not ordinary 'third parties' but the child's co-mothers. There had been no possibility of officialising the relationship between the children and their mother's partner despite the joint parental project, as, at the time, they could not have recourse to intra-family adoption and no alternative parenting status had been designed to accommodate the specific needs of rainbow families. However, by applying the general provisions of the Civil Code to the applicants as if they were any 'third party' in relation to their children and eluding the fact that they were actually the children's second parents, the French decisions may certainly be considered as treating obviously different situations in a similar manner which, arguably, the Court should have considered contrary to Article 14 ECHR.[127]

Most recently, the ECtHR dealt with another French case, *Callamand*,[128] which concerned the refusal of post-separation contacts between a child and her mother's ex-wife. The Court decided that in that particular situation, the French courts had not given sufficient consideration to the co-mother's right to respect for her family life and had accordingly violated Article 8 ECHR. Specifically, the Court noted that 'the applicant sought only the opportunity to continue to see, from time to time, a child in respect of whom she had acted as a co-parent for more than two years since her birth'.[129] Unlike in *Honner*, the Court considered that 'it [was] not sufficiently clear from the reasoning of the domestic courts how they proceeded to investigate whether a fair balance was maintained between potentially conflicting interests'[130] and that 'the Court of Appeal did not show that the fact that [the child] was having difficulties was in consequence of his meetings with [the applicant]'.[131] Thus, while not formally departing from the *Honner* approach, *Callamand* may be considered a timid evolution towards an increased ECHR protection provided to social and affective ties established in the context of rainbow families.

[127] See P. Cannoot, 'Inadmissibility decision in Bonnaud and Lecoq v. France: Should the Court have recognized the specificity of a same-sex relationship?' (*Strasbourg Observers*, 11 April 2018) <https://strasbourgobservers.com/2018/04/11/inadmissibility-decision-in-bonnaud-and-lecoq-v-france-should-the-court-have-recognized-the-specificity-of-a-same-sex-relationship/>; A. Margaria, 'Honner v France: Damage prevention and/or damage control?' (*Strasbourg Observers*, 12 January 2021) <https://strasbourgobservers.com/2021/01/12/honner-v-france-damage-prevention-and-or-damage-control/>.

[128] *Callamand v France*, Application no 2338/20.

[129] Ibid, para 41 (free translation).

[130] Ibid, para 39 (free translation).

[131] Ibid, para 43 (free translation).

9.3.4 *Social Benefits: The Work–Life Balance of Same-Sex Parents*

As regards parenting-associated social benefits, so far, the ECtHR does not appear very inclined to require states to treat same-sex parents similarly to different sex-parents, which may seem consistent with the approach taken in *Bonnaud* and *Honner* but which may change in the post-*Callamand* context.

Indeed, in *Hallier and others*,[132] the Court considered that refusing a co-mother the benefit of a paternity leave was not in breach of the Convention. The Court did consider that a lesbian co-mother 'is in a situation comparable to that of a biological father in a heterosexual couple'; however, it noted that legislation on paternity leave 'was intended to strengthen fathers' responsibility for their children's upbringing ... and to bring about a change in the sharing of domestic tasks between men and women'.[133] According to the Court, granting fathers eleven days of paid leave was proportionate to such a legitimate aim. Moreover, the Court said that the differentiated treatment was not based on sex or sexual orientation but on the existence or absence of a biological link with the child. Finally, the Strasbourg judges considered that 'making the benefit of this leave dependent on a parenthood link with the child could, at the time in question, fall within the margin of appreciation granted to the State in this area'.[134]

The Court's reasoning may be considered unsatisfying. First, the aim of strengthening fathers' responsibility would not be undermined in any way by providing the parental leave also to co-mothers. Then, the justification based on biological links may be considered weak as some legal fathers are not their child's biological fathers. Conversely, there are situations where a co-mother is biologically related to her partner's child, such as in the circumstances of *R.F. and others*. Finally, as concerns the distinction based on legal parenthood as such, the reasoning may be considered flawed as it neglects the fact that, at the time, it was impossible for the applicants to have such tie legally established because of their sexual orientation. Once again, this amounts to denying a specific benefit to same-sex couples blaming them for not having established a legal relationship that had been impossible for them to establish.

This decision of the ECtHR seems to be based on broadly the same premises as the EU directive 2019/1158 on work–life balance for parents

[132] *Hallier and Others v France*, Application no 46386/10.
[133] Ibid, para 31 (free translation).
[134] Ibid, para 32 (free translation).

and carers.[135] Indeed, whereas the directive officially 'acknowledges the existence of non-traditional family types',[136] it does not include any provision referring directly to same-sex parents or prohibiting discrimination based on sexual orientation. There might thus be a 'heteronormative bias' here, in the way in which families are perceived and described.[137] As a consequence, directive 2019/1158 may be considered as not paying sufficient attention to the need of families that do not reflect traditional gender norms, such as rainbow families.[138] It shall be seen whether the CJEU might be able to increase inclusiveness in EU parental leave law through interpretation, notably in the light of the Charter provisions.

9.3.5 *Family Reunification: The Landmark* V.M.A. v Stolichna Obshtina *Case*

One important step in favour of rainbow families was taken by the CJEU in the *V.M.A. v Stolichna obshtina* case.[139] The applicant in the main proceedings was a Bulgarian woman married to a British woman. They had resided together in Spain since 2015 and had a daughter in 2019. The Spanish birth

[135] Directive (EU) 2019/1158 of the European Parliament and of the Council of 20 June 2019 on work-life balance for parents and carers and repealing Council Directive 2010/18/EU PE/20/ 2019/REV/1 [2019] OJ L188/79.

[136] European Commission, Directorate-General for Employment, Social Affairs and Inclusion, N. Picken and B. Janta, *Leave Policies and Practice for Non-traditional Families* (Publications Office 2020) <http://data.europa.eu/doi/10.2767/276102>.

[137] E. Chieregato, 'A work-life balance for all? Assessing the inclusiveness of EU Directive 2019/ 1158' (2020) 36 International Journal of Comparative Labour Law and Industrial Relations 59.

[138] Ibid. See also Chapter 2 by Alina Tryfonidou.

[139] *V.M.A. v Stolichna obshtina, rayon 'Pancharevo'* (n 107). See C. De Capitani, 'Rainbow families and the right to freedom of movement – the V.M.A. v Stolichna Obshtina, Rayon 'Pancharevo' Case' (*EU Law Analysis*, 11 January 2022) <http://eulawanalysis.blogspot.com/ 2022/01/rainbow-families-and-right-to-freedom.html>; H. Hardy, 'Court of Justice of the European Union's landmark decision on the cross-border recognition of the relationship of same-sex parents and their children' (*Global Human Rights Defence*) <https://ghrd.org/article-detail.php?id=82>; J. Meeusen, 'Functional recognition of same-sex parenthood for the benefit of mobile Union citizens – Brief comments on the CJEU's Pancharevo judgment – GEDIP' (*GEDIP-EGPIL*, 2022) <https://eapil.org/2022/02/03/functional-recognition-of-same-sex-parenthood-for-the-benefit-of-mobile-union-citizens-brief-comments-on-the-cjeus-pancharevo-judgment/>; D. Thienpont and G. Willems, 'Le droit à la libre circulation des familles homoparentales consacré par la Cour de justice de l'Union européenne' (2022) 132 Revue trimestrielle des droits de l'homme 925; A. Tryfonidou, 'The cross-border recognition of the parent–child relationship in rainbow families under EU law: A critical view of the ECJ's V.M.A. ruling' (*European Law Blog*, 21 December 2021) <https:// europeanlawblog.eu/2021/12/21/the-cross-border-recognition-of-the-parent-child-relationship-in-rainbow-families-under-eu-law-a-critical-view-of-the-ecjs-v-m-a-ruling/>. See also Chapter 7 by Michael Bogdan.

certificate mentioned the applicant's wife as 'mother' and the applicant as 'mother A'. In 2020, the couple asked the Bulgarian administration to issue a Bulgarian birth certificate to the child but their request was rejected based on the fact that Bulgarian birth certificates only have one box for 'mother' and one for 'father'. Only one name may be entered in each box.

The Court noted that despite not recognising the applicant's parenthood, national courts had found that the child was to be considered a Bulgarian national. While this position could seem inconsistent, it implied that as an EU citizen, the child was entitled to identity documents recognising her parents as established in another member state which allowed her to be accompanied by them when exercising her freedom of movement.[140] As the national position allowing nationality while refusing parenthood felt somewhat unconvincing (the latter normally flowing from the former), the CJEU also considered the alternate hypothesis where the child would not be granted Bulgarian nationality based on its *Coman* reasoning. Just as the term 'spouse' in Directive 2004/38 must be interpreted as to include same-sex spouses legally married in a Member State, the term 'descendant' in the same Directive must be read as applying to children whose relationship with their same-sex parents has been validly established somewhere in the EU.[141] The CJEU specifically added, exactly as in *Coman*, that 'the obligation ... to recognise the parent-child relationship between [a child] and [their same-sex parents] in the context of the child's exercise of her rights under Article 21 TFEU and secondary legislation relating thereto, does not undermine the national identity or pose a threat to the public policy of that Member State'.[142]

While such consecration of the right to free movement of rainbow families is undeniably a very significant achievement, the scope of *V.M.A. v Stolichna obshtina* is limited.[143] On the one hand, it only covers birth certificates issued by a Member State and does not apply to same-sex legal parenthood established in a third country.[144] On the other hand, the obligation of recognition

[140] *V.M.A. v Stolichna obshtina, rayon 'Pancharevo'* (n 107), paras 40–50.

[141] Ibid, paras 67–68.

[142] Ibid, para 56.

[143] Tryfonidou (n 139).

[144] In this respect, see *S.-H. v Poland*, Application nos 56846/15 and 56849/15; S. Ganty, 'Surrogacy as citizenship deprivation in S.-H. v. Poland' (*Strasbourg Observers*, 14 March 2022) <strasbourgobservers.com/2022/03/14/surrogacy-deprives-from-citizenship-in-s-h-v-poland%EF%BF%BC/#:~:text = –%20H.,of%20the%20Polish%20legal%20system>. In this decision relating to two men who became parents through surrogacy in California and live in Israel with the children, the Court accepts the government's position that directive 2004/38 confers them a right to family reunification based on one of the co-fathers' Polish

is limited to the exercise of the right to free movement and does not involve the other legal effects of legal parenthood.

9.3.6 *Recognition of Parenthood Established Abroad: Towards an EU Regulation?*

V.M.A. v Stolichna obshtina has set up a very important milestone but family reunification as such is not sufficient to guarantee the real freedom of movement of mobile rainbow families. Unless the ties of legal parenthood are fully or entirely recognised, the latter will still be confronted with awkward and complicated situations where, while being allowed to settle together, rainbow families will not be considered as legal families for most aspects of parent–child relationships such as parental responsibility, social benefits, tax law, inheritance, and so on. Also, it is not certain whether and how states that are obliged to welcome same-sex parents' families in their legal order may progressively be inclined or constrained – through the operation of a 'contagion or percolation' dynamic – to grant them the full range of rights and duties normally arising from legal parenthood.

Notably, in her 2020 State of the Union address,[145] the president of the Commission Ursula von der Leyen expressly declared that 'to make sure that we support the whole community, the Commission will soon put forward a strategy to strengthen LGBTQI rights' and that, as a part of this, she would 'push for mutual recognition of family relations in the EU' because 'if you are parent in one country, you are parent in every country'. In its subsequent 'Union of Equality: LGBTIQ Equality Strategy 2020–2025' (LGBTIQ Equality Strategy), the Commission effectively committed to '[proposing] a horizontal legislative initiative on the mutual recognition of parenthood between Member States'.[146] After an impact assessment,[147] a formal proposal

citizenship despite the lack of recognition of parenthood itself and despite the fact that parenthood was established in a third country.

[145] European Commission, 'State of the Union Address by President von der Leyen at the European Parliament Plenary' Press release (16 September 2020) <https://ec.europa.eu/commission/presscorner/detail/ov/SPEECH_20_1655>.

[146] European Commission, Communication from the Commission to the European Parliament, the Council, the European Economic and Social Committee and the Committee of the Regions. Union of Equality: LGBTIQ Equality Strategy 2020–2025, COM(2020) 698 final.

[147] European Commission, 'Cross-border family situations – Recognition of parenthood: Inception impact assessment' Ares(2021)2519673 <https://ec.europa.eu/info/law/better-regulation/have-your-say/initiatives/12878-Cross-border-family-situations-recognition-of-parenthood_en>.

for a Council regulation on the cross-border recognition of parenthood was published in December 2022.[148]

As regards the issue of the recognition of family ties established abroad, some important developments recently occurred in the case law of the ECtHR related to the specific context of international surrogacy. In *D.B. and others v Switzerland*,[149] the Court decided that two men who became parents through surrogacy in California, one of them providing his sperm for the conception, should be able to have their legal parenthood established in the United States recognised in Switzerland. The Court thus expanded its *Mennesson* approach to same-sex parents, explicitly considering that the fact that the applicants are a same-sex couple does not justify departing from the principles identified in the French case. Another, currently pending ECtHR case *A.D.-K. v Poland*[150] also relates to the recognition of same-sex parenthood. The applicants are two women who became parents together in the UK and were registered there as the child's 'mother' and 'parent' on the British birth certificate. They complain that the Polish authorities refused to recognise their daughter's legal parenthood as established in the UK, insisting that the decision had an impact not only on the child's citizenship (as one of her co-mothers is Polish) but also on her inheritance rights and, more generally, on 'their right to be considered parents'. The facts are thus very similar to those at issue in V.M.A. and, in the light of the decision in *D.B. and others*, it seems likely that the court will require that parentage be recognised, except if the difference between the Swiss and the Polish contexts is considered sufficient to justify a different approach. If this is confirmed, the ECtHR will deserve to be credited for a really significant contribution to strengthening the position of international rainbow families.

9.4 CONCLUSION

The above developments show a fairly strong convergence of the two European legal orders as regards the rights of same-sex couples and rainbow families.

In the first place, the European (supranational) Courts currently refrain from forcing states to abandon their traditional conception of the fundamental institutions of family law – marriage and parentage. There is a clear link

148 European Commission, Proposal for a Council Regulation on jurisdiction, applicable law, recognition of decisions and acceptance of authentic instruments in matters of parenthood and on the creation of a European Certificate of Parenthood, COM(2022) 695 final.

149 *D.B. and Others v Switzerland*, Application nos 58817/15 and 58252/15.

150 *A.D.-K. and Others v Poland*, Application no 30806/15.

between the 'deep-rooted social and cultural connotations' of *Schalk and Kopf*, and the idea expressed by the Advocate General in *V.M.A.* that the rules on parentage represent 'the essence of the conception which the State is seeking to protect as its national identity'. The common underlying idea is that marriage and parentage are so deeply connected to the States' social and cultural identity that it is not (yet) possible to impose a distinct, uniform, and inclusive European approach that would guarantee the right to marry and to become a parent irrespective of sexual orientation.

It can be considered that, as a compensation for not affirming the right to same-sex marriage or same-sex parenthood, the ECtHR tends to require that family relationships be recognised and protected in alternative ways. The *Fedotova* Grand Chamber decision puts it very clearly as regards couple relationships by requiring States to provide at least the option of registered partnership. Things are less clear as regards parent–child relationships, but *Callamand* may be cautiously considered as a step towards a similar requirement to offer minimal recognition and protection to parenting relationships in rainbow families through parental responsibility and contact rights. For its part, the CJEU contributes to the advancement of equality by requiring a non-discriminatory allocation of family-related social benefits. By affirming that registered same-sex partners should enjoy the same social benefits as heterosexual spouses, the *Hay* decision provides a significant addition to the right to a partnership affirmed by the ECtHR. Hopefully, the Court will adopt a similar approach when applying directive 2019/1158 on work–life balance and make sure that same-sex parents are not discriminated against in the allocation of parenting-related benefits.

Arguably, the most significant developments in recent years have occurred in relation to mobile families. In this respect, the *Coman* and *V.M.A.* decisions clearly affirm an obligation of European States to guarantee the right to family reunification in a way that affirms the right to be together as the core of the right to family life. Yet the recent decisions of the ECtHR go even further as, on the one hand, *Orlandi* requires States to recognise same-sex marriages celebrated abroad as at least a registered partnership and, on the other hand, *D.B. v Switzerland* requires the recognition of same-sex parenthood established abroad at least when one of the co-parents is biologically linked to the child.

Thus, while being careful not to directly confront the most conservative states by forcing the recognition of same-sex couples and rainbow families through marriage and parentage, the ECtHR and the CJEU use, in a complementary way, different strategies to strengthen their legal position. Taken together, developments regarding registered partnerships, parental responsibility and contacts, social benefits, family reunification, and cross-border recognition lead to the conclusion that the current European recognition and protection of same-sex families is admittedly incomplete or imperfect, but quite significant, especially considering the still fragmented European context. At some point in the future, new families' increased visibility and legitimacy should lead to the ultimate step of imposing a European and inclusive understanding of marriage and parenthood.

10

Surrogacy before European Courts

The Gender of Legal Fictions

ALICE MARGARIA*

10.1 INTRODUCTION

In Europe, the landscape of surrogacy continues to be quite diverse. Whilst the practice is allowed in a few jurisdictions, the majority of legal frameworks prohibit it or leave it unregulated.[1] Regardless of the legal approach taken, surrogacy has always raised a multiplicity of legal questions, some of which have reached European supra-national courts. The European Court of Human Rights (ECtHR) has been mostly concerned with the determination of legal parenthood, in particular the recognition of the parent–child relationship between children born from surrogacy abroad and their intended parents. The Court of Justice of the European Union (CJEU) has so far dealt with the issue of maternity leave for intended mothers of children born from surrogacy. The different thematic focus – and the significantly more frequent interventions by the ECtHR – is explained by the European Union's (EU) lack of competence in substantive family law issues, which limits its contact with surrogacy to questions of equality and employment rights.[2] In spite of addressing different questions, both European courts ground their construction of

* This work has been supported by the Volkswagen Foundation as part of the project 'Who Is the Court for? Bringing the Human (back) into Human Rights' and by the University Research Priority Program 'Human Reproduction Reloaded' of the University of Zurich, Switzerland.

[1] See, for example, J. M. Scherpe, C. Fenton-Glynn, and T. Kaan (eds), *Eastern and Western Perspectives on Surrogacy* (Intersentia 2019); K. Trimmings, S. Shakargy, and C. Achmad (eds), *Research Handbook on Surrogacy and the Law* (Edward Elgar Publishing 2024).

[2] See also the recent proposal for a Regulation aimed at harmonising the rules of private international law relating to parenthood at the EU level: European Commission, Proposal for a Council Regulation on jurisdiction, applicable law, recognition of decisions and acceptance of authentic instruments in matters of parenthood and on the creation of a European Certificate of Parenthood, COM(2022) 695 final.

legal motherhood in gestation and birth, thus failing to reflect the lived realities of those involved in surrogacy arrangements and placing intended mothers in a precarious position, especially compared to intended fathers. This differential treatment, I argue in this chapter, reveals the gender of legal fictions in the determination of legal parenthood in Europe.[3]

The analysis is divided into three main sections. Sections 10.2 and 10.3 explore the CJEU and ECtHR case law on surrogacy with the aim of reconstructing the emerging understandings of motherhood and fatherhood and, more broadly, the gendered assumptions underlying the attribution of legal parenthood and related parental rights. It will be shown that one of the assumptions which remains central and uncontested in both systems is the conflation of gestation and motherhood.

This will give rise to reflections on the broader issue of legal fictions in the attribution of legal parenthood in Section 10.4 of the chapter. In Western jurisdictions, legal fictions have played a central role in the legal architecture of parenthood. Whilst the attribution of motherhood follows the *mater semper certa est* rule, according to which the person who gives birth is the child's mother, the marital presumption provides that the father of a child born during marriage is the husband of the child's mother. Section 10.4 sheds light on the gendered lives of these rules and foregrounds the immutability of the *mater semper certa est* rule in contrast with the adoption of various context-specific tests to determine legal fatherhood following social and technological developments. In the context of surrogacy, the gendered lives of these presumptions help explain the imbalance between intended mothers and intended fathers, and the different ways in which their claims for legal parenthood are handled by courts in general. Whilst genetics suffice for intended fathers to establish legal fatherhood, birth-givers are bound to legal motherhood regardless of the circumstances, even if someone else actually *mothers* or *parents* the child.

10.2 SURROGACY BEFORE THE CJEU

In 2014, the CJEU was confronted with two preliminary references that raised the question of whether a woman is entitled to maternity leave with respect to her child born from a surrogate. Whilst surrogacy as such does not fall within

3 I borrow this expression from H. Charlesworth and C. Chinkin, 'The gender of jus cogens' (1993) 15 Human Rights Law Review 63, later adopted by Ç. Başak and L. Helfer, 'The gender of treaty withdrawal: Lessons from the Istanbul Convention' (*EJIL: Talk!*, 28 November 2022) <www.ejiltalk.org/the-gender-of-treaty-withdrawal-lessons-from-the-istanbul-convention/>.

the competence of the EU, maternity leave is regulated by EU law. In *CD v ST*, the intended mother (CD) had a child conceived with her partner's sperm and the eggs of the surrogate.[4] CD breastfed the newborn until the age of three months, and both she and her partner were granted parental responsibility. Before the child was born, CD had unsuccessfully applied for paid time off for surrogacy under her employer's adoption policy. Subsequent to the birth, her employer eventually granted CD paid leave on a discretionary basis. The Employment Tribunal in Newcastle upon Tyne (UK) referred the issue of whether the refusal to grant paid leave equivalent to adoption and maternity leave to an intended mother was contrary to the Pregnant Workers Directive,[5] and constituted discrimination on the grounds of sex, contrary to the Equality Treatment Directive.[6] The second case, *Z v Government Department and the Board of Management of a Community School*, stems from similar facts.[7] Before the child was born, Z, the intended genetic mother, applied to her employer for leave equivalent to adoption leave.[8] The employer rejected her request but offered unpaid leave to attend the child's birth in California, and statutory parental leave for the period subsequent to birth. Just like in *CD*, the Irish Equality Tribunal asked the CJEU whether a failure to provide for surrogacy leave was a breach of EU gender equality law.[9]

Interestingly, the CJEU did not join the two preliminary references, and Advocate General Kokott in *CD* and Advocate General Wahl in Z took quite different approaches. Following a 'contextual and teleological' approach to interpretation, Advocate General Kokott argued in favour of an EU right to maternity leave for intended mothers.[10] She explained that, just like a woman

4 Case C-167/12 *CD v ST* EU:C:2014:169.

5 Council Directive 92/85/EEC of 19 October 1992 on the introduction of measures to encourage improvements in the safety and health at work of pregnant workers and workers who have recently given birth or are breastfeeding (tenth individual Directive within the meaning of Article 16 (1) of Directive 89/391/EEC) [1992] OJ L348/1.

6 Directive 2006/54/EC of the European Parliament and of the Council of 5 July 2006 on the implementation of the principle of equal opportunities and equal treatment of men and women in matters of employment and occupation (recast) [2006] OJ L204/23.

7 Case C-363/12 *Z v Government Department and the Board of Management of a Community School* EU:C:2014:159.

8 In Ireland, surrogacy was and is still unregulated, but draft legislation is currently being discussed.

9 See n 6, and Council Directive 2000/78/EC of 27 November 2000 establishing a general framework for equal treatment in employment and occupation [2000] OJ L303/16. In Z, the intended mother suffered a rare condition where she had no uterus and therefore could not undertake a pregnancy. She complained also of a discrimination on the grounds of disability, but without success.

10 M. Finck and B. Kas, 'Surrogacy leave as a matter of EU law: *CD* and *Z*' (2015) 52 Common Market Law Review 281, 284.

who has given birth to her child, 'an intended mother has in her care an infant for whose best interests she is responsible'.[11] Precisely because she had not been pregnant herself, the intended mother is confronted with 'the challenge of bonding with that child, integrating it into the family and adjusting to her role as mother'.[12] Advocate General Kokott, therefore, concluded that in light of recent medical advances, the personal scope of the Pregnant Workers Directive is to be understood in 'functional rather than monistic biological terms'.[13] Advocate General Wahl, on the contrary, argued in Z that the protection of the special relationship between mother and child was to be interpreted 'as a logical corollary of childbirth (and breastfeeding)'.[14] Broadening the personal scope of the Directive would result in a contradictory situation whereby an employed intended mother would be entitled to paid (maternity) leave, but an adoptive mother or a father would not have such a right.[15]

The Grand Chamber held that, under EU law, maternity leave presupposes that the worker was pregnant and gave birth.[16] The fact that, in the first case, CD was breastfeeding the child did not make any difference.[17] The CJEU clarified the twofold goal of maternity leave: the protection of the health of the mother 'in the especially vulnerable situation arising from her pregnancy';[18] and, the protection of the special relationship between a woman and her child, which applied 'only [in] the period after pregnancy and childbirth'.[19] It was therefore concluded that the Member States are not required to extend maternity leave to intended mothers but may, of course, adopt more favourable provisions.[20] Also, according to the CJEU, the exclusion of intended mothers from maternity leave did not constitute direct or indirect discrimination on the ground of sex because an intended father would be treated in the same way, and there was no evidence that the refusal at stake placed working women in a disadvantageous position compared to working men.[21]

[11] Opinion of Advocate General Kokott in Case C-167/12 *CD v ST* EU:C:2013:600, para 46.
[12] Ibid.
[13] Ibid, para 48.
[14] Opinion of Advocate General Wahl in Case C-363/12 *Z v Government Department and the Board of Management of a Community School* EU:C:2013:604, para 47.
[15] Ibid, para 51.
[16] *CD v ST* (n 4), para 37; *Z v Government Department and the Board of Management of a Community School* (n 7), para 58.
[17] *CD v ST* (n 4), para 40.
[18] Ibid, para 35.
[19] Ibid, para 36.
[20] Ibid, para 42.
[21] Ibid, paras 47–50.

The decisions in *CD* and *Z* lay bare the decisive role given to gestation and birth in defining what is meant by 'being a mother' under EU law, and the resulting gap between the realities of contemporary families and EU law. As observed by Caracciolo di Torella and Foubert, the EU framework on the protection of maternity at work is firmly grounded in the assumption that the person who is pregnant and gives birth is the child's legal mother, in line with the *mater semper certa est* rule.[22] The CJEU rulings in *CD* and *Z* are cases in point: the Pregnant Workers Directive, as interpreted by the Grand Chamber, incorporates a gestational understanding of motherhood, whereby pregnancy is the trigger for its application. Whilst it is true that the EU has over the years succeeded in developing a framework where pregnancy and maternity in the workplace are protected, this framework remains nonetheless ill-equipped to deal with the diversity of contemporary families, including those created through surrogacy.

CD and *Z* also reveal 'the gendered character' of EU conceptions of parenthood.[23] Through these decisions, the CJEU supports and 'further entrenches the protection of the special relationship between a woman and her child … as a natural addendum of the Directive's health and safety protection'.[24] By excluding intended mothers from the personal scope of the Directive, the CJEU reserves this protection to women and newborns who have a gestational link, thus ignoring the experiences of CD and Z as actual carers of their children. On this point, the Opinion of Advocate General Wahl takes an important step forward. In spite of concluding against a broad interpretation of the personal scope, he suggested that the 'special relationship' objective should be given 'independent significance', namely detached from pregnancy and birth.[25] In his words, 'the scope of protection afforded by Article 8 of Directive 92/85 could not … be meaningfully limited only to women who have given birth, but would necessarily also cover adoptive mothers or indeed, any other parent who takes full care of his or her new-born child'.[26] In spite of supporting an undesirable practical outcome, the reasoning offered by Advocate General Wahl has the potential to challenge the gendered assumption that gestational mothers, and mothers more broadly, always have a stronger connection with the child and should therefore take

[22] E. Caracciolo di Torella and P. Foubert, 'Maternity rights for intended mothers? Surrogacy puts the EU legal framework to the test' (2014) 2 European Gender Equality Law Review 5, 5.

[23] Finck and Kas (n 10) 291.

[24] Caracciolo di Torella and Foubert (n 22) 8.

[25] Opinion of Advocate General Wahl in Z v *Government Department and the Board of Management of a Community School* (n 14), para 47.

[26] Ibid, para 47.

more leave to look after their newborns than fathers. One could therefore argue that Advocate General Wahl subtly calls for a 'commitment to the social value of parenthood'[27] and suggests care as the ground for attributing paid leave from work. The CJEU, on the contrary, remains anchored to the *mater semper certa est* rule and, accordingly, continues to treat pregnancy and maternity as a continuum.

The next section argues that a gestational understanding of motherhood runs also through the case law of the ECtHR. In that context, where the case law offers more insight into the Court's reasoning, the precarious position of intended mothers is closely connected to – and actually a consequence of – a genetic understanding of fatherhood.

10.3 SURROGACY BEFORE THE ECTHR

10.3.1 *The Relevance of Genetics*

Transnational surrogacy has become a matter of frequent discussion at the ECtHR. Widespread legal bans at the domestic level have led some intended parents to resort to surrogacy abroad, with the aim of benefitting from more permissive legal frameworks and intention-based regulations of legal parenthood. Even in cases of transnational surrogacy, however, the journey to fulfil one's wish to have a child often comes with significant challenges. Regarding legal challenges, it is not uncommon for intended/social parents and their children born from surrogacy to encounter difficulties when demanding legal recognition of their parent–child relationships, lawfully formed abroad, in their country of residence. The ECtHR has been an important agent in strengthening the legal protection of family relationships created through transnational surrogacy: through its rapidly growing case law, this Court has created space for the experiences of (some of) these families within domestic legal frameworks which prohibit surrogacy arrangements.

The trajectories along which this process has developed have benefitted some intended parents more than others. One of these trajectories lies in the relevance attributed to genetics, which can be traced back to the ECtHR decision in the early case of *Mennesson v France*.[28] This case was the first to bring the issue of recognition of foreign birth certificates following transnational surrogacy to the ECtHR's table. The couple's twins, who were

[27] S. Fredman, 'Reversing roles: Bringing fathers into the frame' (2014) 10 *International Journal of Law in Context* 442, 442.

[28] *Mennesson v France*, Application no 65192/11 (extracts). See also *Labassee v France*, Application no 65941/11.

conceived using the gametes of the intended father and donor eggs, were born from a surrogate in California. French authorities had refused to transcribe the Californian birth certificates indicating Mr and Mrs Mennesson (the intended parents) as parents of their daughters. They reasoned that doing so would be against public order due to the domestic prohibition of surrogacy.

In the view of the ECtHR, the position of legal uncertainty in which the children were placed as a consequence of non-recognition of their family ties compromised their ability to establish 'details of their identity as individual human beings, which include[d] the legal parent–child relationship'.[29] This assumed 'special' relevance, the Court emphasised, because one of the intended parents was also genetically linked to the children, and genetic parentage constitutes an 'importan[t] … component of identity'.[30] Non-recognition was therefore considered to breach the children's right to respect for private life. In contrast, no violation of the applicants' right to respect for their family life was found on the ground that they could settle in France and enjoy their daily family life 'in conditions broadly comparable to those of other families' with no risk of being separated, even in the absence of legal recognition.[31] As explained below, the ECtHR's emphasis on genetics ended up marginalising the experience and claim of Mrs Mennesson, even if she had been involved in the surrogacy arrangement and later in the children's upbringing as much as her husband, thus legitimising an imbalance between intended fathers and intended mothers.

Even if the intended parents' rights under Article 8 ECHR were not formally considered to be breached, the relevance attributed to genetics in finding a violation of the child's right to respect for private life eventually had positive consequences for the legal position of Mr Mennesson. At the domestic level, the French Court of Cassation tempered its stance, allowing for the registration of the intended genetic father in accordance with the foreign birth certificate, unless evidence indicated that the document was irregular, falsified, or that the facts did not reflect biological reality.[32] As concerns the intended mother, the Court of Cassation reiterated its commitment to the *mater semper certa est* rule and, in 2017, clarified that if the mother was married to the father, she could nonetheless seek to adopt the child, provided that the statutory requirements were met and adoption was in the child's best interests.[33]

29 *Mennesson* (n 28), para 96.
30 Ibid, para 100.
31 Ibid, para 92.
32 Cour de Cassation, Assemblée plénière, Nos 619 and 620 of 3 July 2015.
33 Cour de Cassation, 1ère Chambre Civile, Nos 824–827 of 5 July 2017.

The issue of legal recognition of intended motherhood, in particular of Mrs Mennesson, came under the spotlight again in 2019, when the Grand Chamber issued its first advisory opinion under Protocol 16 upon a request by the French Court of Cassation.[34] The Grand Chamber clarified that domestic law is required to provide a possibility of recognition to the relationship lawfully established abroad between the child and the intended mother, who is designated as the legal mother on the birth certificate. The principle of the child's best interests was a decisive factor in reaching this conclusion. The Grand Chamber noted that the lack of legal recognition of the intended mother–child relationship had negative consequences on several aspects of the child's respect for private life, ranging from nationality and inheritance rights to the risk of the relationship being discontinued in case of parental separation or the father's death.[35] In the Grand Chamber's view, the child's best interests also entailed 'the legal identification of the persons responsible for raising him or her, meeting his or her needs and ensuring his or her welfare, as well as the possibility for the child to live and develop in a stable environment'.[36] Hence, the general and absolute impossibility of obtaining legal recognition of the intended mother–child relationship was incompatible with the child's best interests, which required at a minimum that each situation be examined on a case-by-case basis.[37]

As concerns the choice of the means of recognition, the ECtHR held that states are not obliged to register the details of the foreign birth certificate nor to recognise the relationship between a child and their intended mother *ab initio*.[38] Considering the child's best interests as paramount, recognition has to be possible 'at the latest when [the relationship between a child and their intended mother] has become a practical reality'.[39] It follows that, depending on the circumstances of the specific case, adoption may offer a valid legal avenue for recognising the relationship between the child and the intended mother, as long as 'the procedure enables for a decision to be taken rapidly'.[40]

After reading the Advisory Opinion, one would expect intended fathers and intended mothers to be on a more equal footing when seeking recognition of

34 Advisory Opinion concerning the recognition in domestic law of a legal parent–child relationship between a child born through a gestational surrogacy arrangement abroad and the intended mother [GC], request no P16–2018–001, French Court of Cassation, 10 April 2019.

35 Ibid, para 40.

36 Ibid, para 42.

37 Ibid, para 42.

38 Ibid, paras 50 and 52.

39 Ibid, para 52.

40 Ibid, para 54.

their parent–child relationships following transnational surrogacy – especially because Mrs Mennesson was considered to deserve recognition in spite of having no genetic link with her children. Subsequent case law, however, suggests the opposite. In fact, whilst the Advisory Opinion has served to extend legal recognition to, for instance, the intended non-genetic father in a registered partnership with the intended genetic father,[41] the original imbalance between intended mothers and intended fathers in different-sex couples has been left untouched.

10.3.2 *The Gendered Effects of Genetics*

This section takes the above argument on the relevance of genetics further, and traces the gendered effects of genetics with respect to the determination of legal motherhood and legal fatherhood following transnational surrogacy. To do so, it focuses on the ECtHR decision in the case of *D. v France*, where – in contrast to previous cases – both intended parents were genetically linked to their child born from surrogacy in Ukraine.[42] The foreign birth certificate indicated the intended parents as legal parents, with no mention of the surrogate. Whilst French authorities registered the legal relationship between the child and the intended father, the mother was offered the possibility to apply for step-child adoption.

The applicants argued that the refusal to register the Ukrainian birth certificate with respect to the relationship between the intended mother and the child breached the child's right to respect for private life, and amounted to discrimination on the grounds of birth contrary to Article 14.[43] No violation was found. Given the likelihood of a positive and speedy decision,[44] the ECtHR considered step-child adoption to meet the requirements set by the Advisory Opinion. As it will be shown, this decision adds nuance to what Levi defines as the ECtHR's 'genetic essentialism' by bringing the gendered effects

[41] *D.B. and Others v Switzerland*, Application nos 58817/15 and 58252/15. In this case, the Court considered the absolute impossibility for the non-genetic intended father to have his ties with the child born from surrogacy in the United States recognised for a period of seven years and eight months in violation of the child's right to respect for private life.

[42] *D. v France*, Application no 11288/18. The text of the judgment is available only in French. All translations are my own.

[43] More specifically, they argued that their daughter was in an analogous position to any other French child born abroad, but was treated less favourably (i.e. with only partial recognition of the foreign birth certificate) because she was born from surrogacy.

[44] *D. v France* (n 42), para 67.

of genetics to the fore.[45] In particular, it foregrounds the different degree of decisiveness that genetics holds for obtaining the recognition of legal fatherhood and legal motherhood, respectively.

In *D. v France*, the ECtHR began by clarifying its approach in *Mennesson*. In particular, it explained that genetics does not give rise to an obligation to recognise the relationship between the intended father and the child specifically by means of the transcription of the foreign birth certificate.[46] The Court also reiterated the legal principle established in the Advisory Opinion, according to which domestic law must offer a possibility of recognition of a legal parent–child relationship with the intended mother, although the choice of means falls within the state's margin of appreciation.[47]

According to the ECtHR, there was no reason to depart from these principles in the case at hand, even if the intended mother was genetically linked to the child.[48] Requiring the intended genetic mother to initiate adoption proceedings was considered compatible with Article 8 ECHR. Even if – the Court acknowledged – the intended mother might have difficulties envisaging adoption as the route to be legally recognised given her genetic link, step-child adoption constituted an 'effective and sufficiently rapid mechanism' of recognition, which did not exceed the state's margin of appreciation.[49]

On the surface, the reasoning presents the situation of intended fathers and intended mothers as equal, but when transposed into practice, the state's obligation to allow for recognition of the relationship between intended parents in different-sex couples de facto brings unequal benefits to intended mothers and intended fathers.[50] Whilst intended genetic fathers tend to enjoy automatic recognition of the foreign birth certificate, intended genetic mothers still need to initiate adoption proceedings to be recognised as legal mothers. In the case at hand, the ECtHR explicitly acknowledged the existence of a differential treatment between intended genetic fathers and intended genetic mothers, but did not rule on this aspect because the application exclusively concerned the rights of the child.[51] Even if the Court does not

45 M. Levy, 'Surrogacy and parenthood: A European saga of genetic essentialism and gender discrimination' (2022) 29 Michigan Journal of Gender and Law 121, 130.

46 *D. v France* (n 42), para 50.

47 Ibid, para 51.

48 Ibid, para 59.

49 Ibid, paras 63 and 64.

50 A. Margaria, 'Genetics and the construction of parenthood: The ECtHR jurisprudence on transnational surrogacy' in N. Dethloff and K. Kaesling (eds), *Between Sexuality, Gender and Reproduction – On the Pluralisation of Family Forms* (Intersentia 2023) 197.

51 *D. v France* (n 42), para 61. Moreover, the applicants had not informed French authorities and courts that the intended mother was genetically linked to the child; that circumstance had

formally take a position on the gender discriminatory dimension of the case, *D. v France* shows that an imbalance between intended fathers and intended mothers still persists after the Court's Advisory Opinion. As will be explained in the next subsection, this imbalance is due to the status of genetics as a decisive marker of legal fatherhood and, at the same time, the uncontested primacy of gestation and birth in determining legal motherhood.

10.3.3 *The Trumping Effects of Genetics*

This imbalance between intended fathers and intended mothers emerges even more clearly from the case of *A.M. v Norway*, decided in March 2022.[52] The Court was confronted with a novel factual scenario, which the Grand Chamber had already contemplated in the Advisory Opinion, when reflecting on the negative impact of non-recognition of the intended mother–child relationship on the child's private life: that of an intended non-genetic mother whose relationship with the child born from transnational surrogacy is at risk because of her separation from the intended father.[53] In this case, X was born from surrogacy in 2014, with A.M. (the intended mother) and E.B. (the intended father) recorded as legal parents on the Texan birth certificate. Although their relationship had ended well before the birth, E.B. and A.M. had remained in contact and carried on with their joint surrogacy plan. The sperm of E.B. and donor eggs were used for conception.

In the weeks following the birth and upon their return to Norway, X lived with the applicant A.M. whilst E.B. (who had meanwhile bought a new flat and was living with a new partner) visited daily. E.B.'s acknowledgment of paternity was recognised. A.M., however, could not be registered in the National Population Register as X's mother in the absence of a valid adoption because the Norwegian Children Act provides that the woman who gives birth is to be regarded as legal mother. For a period of time, since A.M. and E.B. could not reach an agreement on the child's residence, X moved between their houses on a daily basis. In August 2015, when the child was around seventeen months old, E.B. decided to cut off contact between A.M. and X, who has since lived with E.B. and his new partner. A.M. initiated administrative proceedings to be recognised as X's mother or, alternatively, to adopt the child, but her application was dismissed. According to Norwegian law, the

become known only before the ECtHR, following a request for clarification by the Chamber: see para 81.

52 *A.M. v Norway*, Application no 30254/18.

53 Advisory Opinion (n 34), para 40.

surrogate is to be regarded as X's mother in accordance with the *mater semper certa est* rule. Adoption was not a viable alternative because E.B., who had sole parental responsibility, did not consent.

In April 2016, A.M. initiated further legal proceedings before the Oslo City Court to be recognised as X's legal mother or, alternatively, to be granted contact rights. The City Court held that the guiding factor in deciding upon A.M.'s request for recognition was the child's best interests.[54] In that regard, it noted that 'X had been living in a safe, adequate environment since then, with E.B. as his father, H. as his stepmother, and with his halfsibling and other family members'.[55] It followed that, even if A.M. had 'everything necessary to offer X a safe and good relationship', this was not a sufficient ground for taking the risk of going back to a situation characterised by conflict between A.M. and E.B.[56] As to A.M.'s request for contact rights, the City Court dismissed it on the ground that there was no legal basis to grant contact rights to a person in her position. The City Court's ruling was upheld by the High Court, and the Supreme Court refused the applicant leave to appeal.

The ECtHR considered the lack of recognition of A.M. as X's mother compatible with Article 8 ECHR alone and in conjunction with Article 14 ECHR.[57] Whilst acknowledging that the applicant's situation was 'particularly harsh since E.B. had prevented her from maintaining her relationship with X and essentially put an end to [her] parental project', the Court was of the view that this could not be attributed to the authorities.[58] Domestic courts had, according to the Court, carried out a close examination of the case and ascertained that the child's best interests did not require a solution different from what the Children Act and adoption legislation mandated.[59] Therefore, even if 'the applicant acted as a mother for X ... with the intention that she would continue to do so in the future' and they had 'forged emotional bonds',[60] the *status quo* established by the father's unilateral decision to keep the child away from the intended mother coupled with the passage of time (the child was eight years old at the time of the ECtHR proceedings) ultimately prevailed and left the intended mother with no legal protection at all.

54 *A.M. v Norway* (n 52), para 49.

55 Ibid, para 54.

56 Ibid, para 55.

57 The issue of denial of contact rights was not examined by the ECtHR because A.M. had raised it before the City Court and the High Court, but failed to include it in the appeal before the Supreme Court. See ibid, para 104.

58 *A.M. v Norway* (n 52), para 133.

59 Ibid.

60 Ibid, para 108.

If read against the background of previous case law, two factors may explain why the impossibility for A.M. to establish legal parenthood was considered not to breach Article 8 ECHR. First, X was not a party before the Court. A.M.'s long struggle to obtain legal recognition of motherhood or at least contact – though recognised by Judge O'Leary in her concurring opinion as 'a testament to her commitment to [the child]'[61] – did not provide a legal basis to represent the child's interests and right to family ties before domestic courts. Therefore, the applicant could not benefit from the centre-stage position given to the interests of children in previous case law.[62] Second, unlike in previous cases, the intended mother's request for recognition was opposed – rather than supported – by the intended and legal father.[63]

The ECtHR's decision lays bare not only the gendered effects but also the trumping power of genetics. Apart from confirming the precarious (legal) position of intended mothers, *A.M.* displays their (legal) subordination to the will of intended fathers. As expressed by Judge Jelić in her dissenting opinion, 'E.B. ha[d] exclusive power to decide over the applicant becoming the mother of a child who was intended to be hers, when she had been unable to procreate biologically'.[64] By finding no violation, the Court's majority turns a blind eye on the far-reaching consequences of a genetic understanding of fatherhood which – in case of tension between the intended parents – may go so far as to permanently exclude the intended mother from the life of the child she took care of and intended to raise.

To be sure, the intended mother's *mediated* right to recognition can be traced back to the Advisory Opinion, where the Grand Chamber found it important to contextualise the relationship between Mrs Mennesson and her daughters before delving into the issue of recognition of intended motherhood. In the ECtHR's own words, the question at stake 'explicitly includes the factual element of a father with a biological link to the child in question' and 'the Court will limit its answer accordingly'.[65] This contextual remark seems to suggest that, in *Mennesson*, the intended mother was given a possibility for recognition because of her involvement in the children's lives, but also in her capacity as the wife of the genetic father.[66] This helps to explain why the

[61] Concurring Opinion of Judge O'Leary in *A.M. v Norway*, Application no 30254/18, para 19.

[62] Ibid, para 15. See also *Paradiso and Campanelli v Italy*, Application no 25358/12.

[63] This was also pointed by Judge O'Leary in her Concurring Opinion in *A.M. v Norway* (n 61), para 16.

[64] Dissenting Opinion of Judge Jelić in *A.M. v Norway*, Application no 30254/18, para 44.

[65] Advisory Opinion (n 34), para 36.

[66] A. Margaria, 'Parenthood and cross-border surrogacy: What is 'new'? The ECtHR's first Advisory Opinion' (2020) 28 Medical Law Review 412, 424.

Court found no violation in *A.M.*, especially considering the close emotional bonds the applicant had established with X before their contact was terminated by E.B., as well as her uncontested parental suitability.

Apart from reflecting a preference for stability in the form of the intact bi-parental heterosexual family, the outcome in *A.M.* is closely interwoven with the automatic recognition of genetic intended fathers following transnational surrogacy. Genetics places intended fathers in a position of privilege over intended mothers from the very beginning – an imbalance that is legally fortified if the relationship deteriorates.

10.4 GOING TO THE ROOTS: EXPLAINING THE PRECARIOUS POSITION OF INTENDED MOTHERS

The decision in *A.M. v Norway* is paradigmatic of a stratified access to legal parenthood following transnational surrogacy. In particular, to quote Judge O'Leary's concurring opinion, it demonstrates that the journey of resorting to transnational surrogacy to avoid domestic bans is 'particularly precarious for non-biological parents and even genetic (not gestational) mothers, in relation to whom the law has not kept apace either of social reality or of science'.[67] As mentioned above, the central role given to genetics in establishing legal fatherhood places intended genetic fathers in a privileged position as compared to mothers, as they obtain automatic recognition of their ties and, as a result, their legal presence in their child's life is guaranteed *ab initio*. This section seeks to dig deeper into the roots of this imbalance, and reflects on two interrelated reasons: (1) an enduring fear of disaggregating (legal) motherhood; and (2) the immutable character of the *mater semper certa est* rule, in contrast with a concomitant openness to rethinking legal fatherhood in times of social change and family diversity. The combination of these two reasons underpins what I call 'the gender of legal fictions' governing the attribution of legal parenthood.

10.4.1 *Normative Legal Fictions and the Attribution of Legal Parenthood*

This section connects the imbalance between intended mothers and intended fathers supported by the ECtHR case law on transnational surrogacy to the broader regulation of motherhood and fatherhood in Western legal systems. Two basic rules have traditionally informed the attribution of legal motherhood and legal fatherhood, respectively: *mater semper certa est*, according to

[67] Concurring Opinion of Judge O'Leary in *A.M. v Norway* (n 61), para 23.

which legal motherhood is attributed to the person giving birth, and therefore on the grounds of gestation and birth; and *pater est quem nuptiae demonstrant*, also called the marital presumption, according to which when a child is born during marriage, the mother's husband is presumed to be the father. Whilst these rules may often reflect the social reality, they are grounded in legal fictions, namely in 'presumptions created by law because it is socially and legally convenient to assume that they are true'.[68]

Legal fictions are common devices in legal architecture and serve different purposes. They can be 'devices of pragmatism and efficiency, aimed at saving costs and avoiding time wasting'.[69] In some contexts, legal fictions are 'deliberately generated in response to uncertainty' – like in the case of the marital presumption.[70] Whilst the marital presumption may simply confirm the genetic father's identity, it also allows the system to conceal the issue of extramarital conception, which is considered to transgress the norm of the nuclear family.[71] Like any legal fiction, therefore, the *pater est quem nuptiae demonstrant* rule is not used to represent an actual reality but is rather a technique to successfully reach certain ends:[72] first, to give uncertainty the appearance of certainty, and second, to safeguard the traditional family unit.[73] More than a reflection on genetic truth, therefore, the marital presumption is an 'expression of a normative [legal] standpoint . . . towards transgressive sexual relationships'.[74]

Even if the determination of legal parenthood has been conventionally presented as a 'neutral, objective and purely factual enquiry', it actually involves judgement.[75] It presupposes making decisions about who deserves recognition as legal parent, even in the paradigm case of a child conceived through sexual intercourse and raised by both their genetic parents. Jackson explains that requiring the surrogate to relinquish all parental rights over the child is 'a choice which is obscured by the law's insistence that gestation – as

68 N. Milanich, 'Certain mothers, uncertain fathers – Placing assisted reproductive technologies in historical perspective' in Y. Ergas, J. Jenson, and S. Michel (eds), *Reassembling Motherhood: Procreation and Care in a Globalised World* (Columbia University Press 2017) 22.

69 Z. Rathus, 'Social science or "Lego science"? Presumptions, politics, parenting and the new family law' (2010) 10 QUT Law Review 164, 178.

70 Milanich (n 68) 24.

71 E. Jackson, 'What is a parent?' in A. Diduck and K. O'Donovan (eds), *Feminist Perspectives on Family Law* (Routledge 2006) 62.

72 R. Michaels and A. Riles, 'Law as technique' in M.-C. Foblets and others, *The Oxford Handbook of Law and Anthropology* (Oxford University Press 2022) 872.

73 Jackson (n 71) 59.

74 Milanich (n 68) 26.

75 Jackson (n 71) 73.

opposed to genetic relatedness or the intention to raise the child – is the defining feature of motherhood'.[76] *Mater semper certa est* is therefore 'more [a] normative dogma than a descriptor of a social, much less natural, reality'.[77] This in turn reveals not only the 'purposeful' nature of legal fictions, but also their power as 'tool[s] for governing' society.[78] In the context of legal parenthood, legal fictions may serve as instruments of reproductive politics by providing a mechanism for the implementation of specific policy objectives,[79] such as the primacy of the heterosexual and cisgender biological family and the exclusion of LGBTIQ+ persons from the realm of family relationships.

This risk becomes particularly 'real' when the temporality of legal fictions, and therefore their fictitious nature, is forgotten or not taken seriously.[80] By definition, a fiction does not resolve the ultimate question at stake; 'it simply creates a provisional solution subject to future re-evaluation'.[81] In practice, however, protracted provisionality may turn into continuous – quasi automatic – applicability, as the tenacity and immutability of the *mater semper certa est* rule demonstrates. As will be explained later, when the social forces and ideals which have shaped filiation rules are forgotten, left unquestioned, or interiorised, legal fictions may pose a real harm to those falling outside the paradigm case.

10.4.2 *The Gendered Life of Legal Fictions*

Social and scientific developments, such as assisted reproductive technologies, surrogacy, DNA testing, and the proliferation of de facto cohabitation, have foregrounded the temporality of both *mater semper certa est* and *pater est quem nuptiae demonstrant*, and de facto jeopardised their validity and reliability. De jure, however, these two rules have not been subject to the same degree of questioning and contestation. Whilst legal frameworks have shown an increased openness to depart from the marital presumption when determining legal fatherhood, *mater semper certa est* remains 'one of the most immutable facts' of Western family laws.[82] As will be elaborated upon later, this is

76 Ibid, 68.
77 Milanich (n 68) 24.
78 Michaels and Riles (n 72) 873.
79 Rathus (n 69) 179.
80 Ibid, 166.
81 Michaels and Riles (n 72) 873.
82 Z. Mahmoud and E. C. Romanis, 'On gestation and motherhood' (2023) 31 Medical Law Review 109, 109 (referring specifically to English family law).

attributable to the 'trope of maternal certainty'[83] that treats gestation, motherhood, and mothering as a continuum.

Over the decades, legal frameworks have demonstrated a certain flexibility and attention to context in determining legal fatherhood. In fact, the marital presumption has always been rebuttable by proof that the mother's husband could not be the child's genetic father. Before DNA testing became available, the type of evidence which could displace the presumption was that the husband was sterile, impotent, or outside the country at the time of conception (*extra quatuor maria* in English law, 'beyond the four seas of England').[84] Since the 1940s, DNA technology has assisted in identifying a child's legal father with an increasing degree of accuracy, now close to full certainty. In the context of rising divorce rates and non-formalised adult relationships, this technological development has enabled legal frameworks to react to the steadily diminishing pre-eminence of marriage by adopting genetics as the primary vehicle for grounding legal fatherhood.

Genetics, however, does not work as a father–child connector in all contexts. In the case of sperm donation, for instance, genetics is trumped by the intention to become a father. When fertility treatment is provided by licenced clinics, legal fatherhood is attributed to the consenting husband or heterosexual partner of the woman undergoing treatment, rather than to the sperm donor. Outside the paradigm case, therefore, the determination of legal fatherhood rests on different tests depending on the specific circumstances.

In sharp contrast, the definition of legal motherhood continues to be 'rigidly inflexible and inattentive to the different contexts in which children are conceived'.[85] Even if there have long been multiple paths to motherhood, such as adoption and fostering, a 'mother' has been conventionally understood to be a woman who both bears and cares for a child.[86] Shifts in social and legal norms, technological advances, and the development of markets in both procreation and care have made motherhood 'a choice for more women'.[87] In *social* terms, therefore, we have witnessed a certain 'liberalisation of motherhood'[88] entailing greater possibilities to choose how to mother, although not everywhere and for everyone. When it comes to *legal*

83 Milanich (n 68) 28.

84 Jackson (n 71) 62.

85 Ibid, 66.

86 Y. Ergas, J. Jenson, and S. Michel, 'Introduction' in Y. Ergas, J. Jenson, and S. Michel (eds), *Reassembling Motherhood: Procreation and Care in a Globalised World* (Columbia University Press 2017) 1.

87 Ibid, 2.

88 Ibid.

motherhood, however, the attribution of this status continues to be shaped by a sort of 'biological determinism'[89] and parturition tends to remain the 'non-negotiable criterion for motherhood'.[90] Law fails to distinguish between the physical act of 'giving birth and being a mother';[91] rather, it tends to equate the physical act of giving birth with motherhood.

Whilst motherhood may subsequently be transferred by adoption, at the moment of birth, a child's legal mother will generally be the birth-giver.[92] As Mahmoud and Romanis put it, legal motherhood is perceived as '*innately* existing within a particular individual' and therefore '*truly* irrebuttable'.[93] Even if there are other ways to obtain the status of legal mother, they are predicated on the primary ascription of the maternal status to the birth-giver.[94] Adoption, for example, presupposes the consent of the birth mother and/or a court decision establishing that the birth mother is unavailable, unable, or unwilling to take care of the child.[95] From this perspective, adoption does not contradict, but rather presupposes and confirms the *mater semper certa est* rule.[96] The same holds true for surrogacy. Even in jurisdictions where surrogacy is allowed and surrogacy contracts are valid, the structure of that contract tends to presuppose the birth mother's priority. The intended parents acquire legal parenthood because and only if the birth mother agrees to waive her rights; and if she does not agree, she will be the child's legal mother regardless of the child's genetic origins and mode of conception.[97] These examples demonstrate that motherhood and procreation have been historically difficult to disassemble, potentially more than motherhood and care.[98]

The inflexibility of the *mater semper certa est* rule leads to many problematic outcomes. In the context of surrogacy, one of the practical consequences of the gestation-based test is that the child is born into a legal limbo which, depending on the specific case, will characterise at least their first moments of life. To identify the surrogate as legal mother *ab initio* may bring the practical

89 Mahmoud and Romanis (n 82) 114.
90 F. Swennen, 'Motherhoods and the law' in H. Willekens, K. Scheiwe, T. Richarz, and E. Schumann (eds), *Motherhood and the Law* (Göttingen University Press 2019) 103.
91 K. O'Donovan, 'Constructions of maternity and motherhood in stories of lost children' in J. Bridgeman and D. Monk (eds), *Feminist Perspectives on Child Law* (Routledge 2000) 73.
92 H. Willekens, 'Motherhood as a legal institution: A historical-sociological introduction' in H. Willekens and others (eds), *Motherhood and the Law* (Göttingen University Press 2019).
93 Mahmoud and Romanis (n 82) 118.
94 Willekens (n 92) 31.
95 Ibid.
96 Ibid.
97 Ibid, 33.
98 Ergas, Jenson, and Michel (n 86) 7.

advantage of ensuring the child's survival *on paper*, but 'the price to pay for this simplicity is a fundamental misrepresentation of a reality of this child's parentage'.[99] Far from creating certainty, therefore, the application of the *mater semper certa est* rule creates uncertainty and instability from a child's (rights) perspective and for the whole family.

Apart from the practical inconveniences identified by the Grand Chamber in the Advisory Opinion, the non-recognition of the relationship between the intended mother and the child amounts to denying weight to and, consequently, devaluing the social aspects of parenthood, in particular of motherhood. Moreover, conflating gestation with motherhood ignores the experience of many surrogates who do not see their undertaking of gestational labour as an act of mothering, do not consider themselves as 'mothers', and – even more importantly – do not intend to mother, thus harming their autonomy.[100] Outside the context of surrogacy, the current conceptualisation of legal motherhood also poses real harm to birthing parents who do not identify as women.[101] With few exceptions, the predominant trend is to register trans birthing men as legal mothers of their children by virtue of their biological role in gestation and childbirth, in contrast with their male (legal) gender identity and lived experience as 'fathers'.[102]

Overall, the rigid application of the *mater semper certa est* rule fails to reflect contemporary diversity in family formation. This concern was also raised by Judge Jelić in her dissenting opinion in *A.M. v Norway*.[103] Considering recent developments in reproductive rights and the diversity of motherhoods in the twenty-first century, she considers the conflation of gestation and legal motherhood 'overly simplistic', and wishes for 'a more lenient law which is able to assess individual situations of mothers and which determines the legal status of a mother on a case-by-case basis'.[104] Judge Jelić's opinion echoes scholarly calls for rethinking the 'single-static-status approach' to legal

99 Jackson (n 71) 68.

100 Z. Mahmoud, 'Surrogates across the Atlantic: Comparing the impact of legal and health regulatory frameworks on surrogates' autonomy, health and wellbeing' (PhD thesis, University of Exeter 2022).

101 Mahmoud and Romanis (n 82) 31.

102 See, for example, the case of Freddy McConnell decided by English courts: *Re TT and YY* [2019] EWHC 2384, 25 September 2019; *R (McConnell and YY) v Registrar General* [2020] EWCA Civ 559, 29 April 2020. See also *O.H. and G.H. v Germany*, Application nos 53568/18 and 54741/18.

103 Dissenting Opinion of Judge Jelić in *A.M. v Norway* (n 64).

104 Ibid, para 34.

motherhood, which does not account for the multiple ways in which motherhoods – as fluid kinship nodes – are actually practiced.[105]

10.4.3 *Explaining the Gender of Legal Parenthood*

The previous section showed that, whilst the marital presumption and the broader regulation of legal fatherhood have proven adaptable, the definition of legal motherhood as grounded in gestation and birth has proven largely resistant to social and technological changes. This section takes a step further and identifies two structural factors underlying the asymmetrical evolution of the *mater semper certa est* and *pater est quem nuptiae demonstrant* rules: (1) a long-standing socio-legal desire to preserve the unitary status of motherhood, and (2) gendered notions of care and parenting underlying the regulation of legal parenthood, which remain largely uncontested.

In Western legal systems, the regulation of parent–child relationships is based on the 'unalterable two-parent paradigm', according to which a child can only have two parents: one father and one mother.[106] This goes hand in hand with the unitary nature of legal motherhood. As explained by Swennen, motherhood has traditionally been understood as an 'indivisible bundle of parentage, parenthood and parenting rights and obligations', which is conferred solely upon the birth-giver.[107] Accordingly, and in spite of the pluralisation and fragmentation of motherhood on the ground, Western legal frameworks have generally shown resistance to disaggregating motherhood, not only from gestation but also from care. In other words, gestation, motherhood, and mothering tend to be treated as a continuum in law and society.

An enlightening example of this supposed continuum is the prohibition of egg donation as compared to the typically more permissive attitude towards sperm donation, which persists in some Western jurisdictions.[108] The case of *S.H. and Others v Austria*, decided by the Grand Chamber of the ECtHR in 2011, triggers some important reflections in this regard.[109] This case stemmed

[105] Swennen (n 90) 101. See also Chapter 3 by David Archard and Chapter 4 by Ségolène Barbou des Places.

[106] J. Scherpe, 'Breaking the existing paradigms of parent–child relationships' in G. Douglas, M. Murch, and V. Stephens (eds), *International and National Perspectives on Child and Family Law: Essays in Honour of Nigel Lowe* (Intersentia 2018) 345.

[107] Swennen (n 90) 103.

[108] See C. M. Romeo Casabona, R. Paslack, and J. W. Simon, 'Reproductive medicine and the law: Egg donation in Germany, Spain and other European countries' (2013) 38 Revista de derecho y genoma humano 15. Egg donation is still prohibited in Germany and Switzerland. In Norway, Italy, and Austria, previous bans have been lifted in recent years.

[109] *S.H. and Others v Austria*, Application no 57813/00.

from the complaint of two couples who needed *in vitro* fertilisation (IVF) treatment, the first with the use of donor sperm and the second with the use of donor eggs, to have children genetically linked with at least one of the prospective parents. Under Austrian law at that time, egg donation was prohibited in all circumstances, while sperm donation was allowed only for *in vivo* fertilisation. The Grand Chamber considered the restrictions imposed by Austrian law to be compatible with Article 8 ECHR.[110] The margin of appreciation doctrine played a central role in reaching this conclusion. Given that IVF raised sensitive moral and ethical issues on which an 'emerging',[111] but 'not yet clear common ground' existed, states enjoyed a wide margin of appreciation in regulating the fast-moving field of assisted reproduction.[112]

The Austrian Government had put forward various justifications for its restrictions, including the need to protect women from exploitation and humiliation, and the fear of selective reproduction.[113] The Austrian legislature had also been guided by the idea that the *mater semper certa est* principle effectively prevents the possibility of tension between a biological and a genetic mother, both of whom could claim the status of legal mother.[114] This was considered a 'valid wish' by the Grand Chamber,[115] which appreciated the legislature's attempt to reconcile the desire to make assisted reproductive technologies available and the unease among large parts of society as to the ethically and morally sensitive issues triggered by these technologies.[116]

When hearing the applicants' complaint, the Austrian Constitutional Court held that allowing *in vitro* fertilisation with donor sperm but not with egg donation did not amount to discrimination, because sperm donation 'was not considered to give rise to a risk of creating unusual family relationships which might adversely affect the well-being of a future child'.[117] The German Government, intervening as a third party, similarly explained that in Germany, the prohibition of egg donation was necessary 'to protect the child's

[110] Before, the Chamber had found the Austrian regulation in violation of Article 8 taken in conjunction with Article 14: ibid.

[111] Ibid, para 96.

[112] Ibid, para 97.

[113] Ibid, para 101.

[114] Ibid, para 104.

[115] A. Timmer, 'S.H. and Others v Austria: Margin of appreciation and IVF' (*Strasbourg Observers*, 9 November 2011) <https://strasbourgobservers.com/2011/11/09/s-h-and-others-v-austria-margin-of-appreciation-and-ivf/>. See also W. Van Hoof and G. Pennings, 'The consequences of S.H. and Others v Austria for legislation on gamete donation in Europe: An ethical analysis of the European Court of Human Rights judgments' (2012) 25 Reproductive BioMedicine Online 667.

[116] *S.H. and Others v Austria* (n 109), para 104.

[117] Ibid, para 25.

welfare from the unambiguous identity of the mother'.[118] According to the German Government, 'splitting motherhood might jeopardise the development of the child's personality and lead to considerable problems in his or her discovery of identity'.[119] More radically, the Italian Government – also a third-party intervener – argued that 'to call maternal filiation into question by splitting motherhood would lead to a weakening of the entire structure of society'.[120]

As these quotes suggest, egg donation was and, in some contexts, still is considered to generate 'a problematic situation of unmanageable uncertainly and destabilisation'.[121] Whilst it is true that legal frameworks have already had to deal with a fragmentation of motherhood in the context of adoption, the Grand Chamber of the ECtHR acknowledged that egg donation brings about a split of motherhood which 'differs significantly from adoptive parent–child relations and … add[s] a new aspect to this issue'.[122] By disaggregating the genetic and the gestational components, egg donation breaks away from the understanding of gestation and motherhood as coterminous and turns maternal certainty into ambiguity.

Interestingly, in *S.H. and Others*, similar concerns were not raised in relation to the potential fragmentation of fatherhood following sperm donation. Split fatherhood seems not to give rise to uncertain and problematic situations or, as Palumbo frames it, the resolution of the situations it is perceived to trigger is more straightforward.[123] In the case of sperm donation, the father is simply the person who has consented to the treatment, and this is not considered to negatively affect the child's welfare.[124] Reflecting upon Norwegian law, which prohibited egg donation but allowed (and still allows) sperm donation, Melhuus observes that the reason for accepting sperm donation has to do with an 'intrinsic uncertainty about paternity': unlike eggs, sperm comes from outside the body, thus creating no different situation from sexual intercourse.[125]

As pointed out by Willekens in his historical-sociological account of motherhood, the universal function of the *mater semper certa est* rule is to

118 Ibid, para 70.
119 Ibid.
120 Ibid, para 73.
121 L. Palumbo, 'The borders of legal motherhood: Rethinking access to assisted reproductive technologies in Europe' in Y. Ergas, J. Jenson, and S. Michel (eds), *Reassembling Motherhood: Procreation and Care in a Globalised World* (Columbia University Press 2017) 82.
122 *S.H. and Others v Austria* (n 109), para 105.
123 Palumbo (n 121) 82.
124 Ibid.
125 M. Melhuus, 'Better safe than sorry: Legislating assisted conception in Norway' in C. Krohn-Hansen and K. Nustad (eds), *State Formation: Anthropological Perspectives* (Pluto 2005) 227.

ensure children's and group survival.[126] Since children are unable to survive without the care provided by adults for a number of years, a responsible person must be allocated to them at birth. Because the woman giving birth is considered most likely to take care of the child spontaneously,[127] it is efficient for legal frameworks to place the primary responsibility for childcare on her.[128]

That being said, when reflecting upon the rationale of *mater semper certa est*, it is also important to keep in mind the normative character inherent in the allocation of legal parenthood mentioned in Section 10.3.1, and in particular its gendered substrate. As observed by McCandless, the allocation of parenthood has always been informed by gendered perceptions of the two-parent family model.[129] The 'normative politics of family life'[130] rests on the notion that children have, at most, two different-sex parents, and is grounded in a 'principle of gender asymmetry assigning different and complementary roles to men and women'.[131] That explains why, throughout history, legal mothers have been granted rights and duties different from those attributed to legal fathers. It also explains why legal efforts to keep fathers in the family picture, especially in the post-separation/divorce context, have often aimed at ensuring men's role as breadwinners rather than their emotional presence. The principle of gender asymmetry underlying the allocation of legal parenthood also helps explain why the *mater semper certa est* rule was established in the first place, and why it retains its primacy in spite of increasing family diversity on the ground. The person giving birth has been considered the most likely to take responsibility for the newborn not only due to her gestational involvement but also, and especially, in her capacity as a woman.

The continuous application of the *mater semper certa est* rule over the centuries has only consolidated this notion. As argued by Mahmoud and Romanis, the automatic attribution of motherhood to those who give birth 'binds and confines women to a biological destiny, assuming that caring responsibilities after birth innately accompany gestation'.[132] People who do not gestate and give birth enjoy greater freedom to make social determinations

[126] Willekens (n 92) 41.
[127] Ibid 42.
[128] Ibid.
[129] J. McCandless, 'Reforming birth registration law in England and Wales?' (2017) 4 Reproductive BioMedicine and Society Online 52, 56.
[130] Ibid.
[131] Willekens (n 92) 23.
[132] Mahmoud and Romanis (n 82) 119. Of course, adoption is always a possibility. Yet, apart from involving delicate decisions at a personal level, from a technical-legal point of view, it presupposes the prior registration of the birth-giver as 'mother'.

about their parental legal status.[133] This applies *in primis* to legal fathers, who, in Czapanskiy's terminology, have often been constructed as 'volunteer parents', with limited parental duties but extensive protection of their autonomy to take part (or not) in a child's upbringing.[134] Legal mothers, on the contrary, have been defined as 'draftees'.[135] They can walk away less easily, if at all, from their extensive parental duties, and their autonomy with respect to mothering is given little and marginal protection.

In spite of a shift to gender neutrality on the face of family laws, legal parenthood remains a highly gendered institution in the fine grains of legal practice. The different evolution that the *mater semper certa est* and *pater est quem nuptiae demonstrant* rules have undergone largely attests to this. The inflexible application of the *mater semper certa est* rule to establish legal motherhood supports and reinforces traditional notions about gender roles: most of all, the notion that it is ideal for the newborn to be taken care of by the birthing person and, relatedly, that 'at the moment of birth, the person who is ready and able to become responsible for the care of a newly born child is who we call a "mother"'.[136] At the same time, the more context-specific approach to determining legal fatherhood and, in the context of surrogacy, the emphasis on the genetic link of intended fathers confirm that men's intention to parent or not to parent is taken more seriously than women's, and therefore that intention is supportive of a 'male approach to parenthood'.[137] More generally, Western legal frameworks seem to have more easily accepted the fragmentation of fatherhood than of motherhood because mothers continue to be perceived as, and to a great extent still are, the primary caregivers.[138]

10.5 CONCLUSION

In spite of the many social and technological changes which have transformed and diversified how family ties are created and experienced, the legal definition of motherhood endorsed by European supranational courts remains grounded in gestation and birth. As a result, intended mothers of children

133 Ibid.

134 K. Czapanskiy, 'Volunteers and draftees: The struggle for parental equality' (1991) 38 UCLA Law Review 1415, 1415–1416.

135 Ibid.

136 A. Margaria, 'Trans men giving birth and reflections on fatherhood: What to expect?' (2020) 34 International Journal of Law, Policy and the Family 225, 235.

137 G. Douglas, 'The intention to be a parent and the making of mothers' (1994) 57 Modern Law Review 636, 638.

138 See also Chapter 2 by Alina Tryfonidou.

born through surrogacy are often placed in a precarious or disadvantaged legal position, being denied legal rights reserved for birth-givers, such as maternity leave, and the legal recognition of their parent–child relationship – at least *ab initio*.

The immutability of the *mater semper certa est* rule and the precarious position of intended mothers are not solely indicative of a wider socio-legal reluctance to accept the fragmentation of motherhood. They are tangible outcomes of the gender of the legal fictions governing the attribution of legal parenthood. Different from the *mater semper certa est* rule, the *pater est quem nuptiae demonstrant* rule has undergone greater scrutiny and reevaluation. This has resulted in a context-sensitive approach to determine legal fatherhood, wherein also mere genetics or the intention to be a father count as legitimate and sufficient grounds for establishing legal fatherhood. By demonstrating less flexibility and adaptability to the determination of legal motherhood, legal systems reinforce the expectation that (gestational) mothers bear the primary responsibility for childcare, whilst fathers may determine their degree and type of involvement without necessarily jeopardising their legal status. These gendered expectations, which are reflected in current practices of attributing legal parenthood, act as stumbling blocks to meeting the needs and realities of many contemporary families.

PART IV

The EU Family in Internal and External Crises

11

The Abused and Neglected Child in the EU Family: Risk, Borders, and Public Law Child Protection

RUTH LAMONT

11.1 INTRODUCTION

Discussion of European family law and the conception of the European family originally focussed on the rights of free movement, the processes of migration, and experience of cross-national difference or convergence.[1] As the European Union (EU) secured competence over private international family law and adopted a range of legislation governing jurisdiction, choice of law, and the recognition of judgments in various contexts, including divorce, matrimonial property, and maintenance, the scope of European family law broadened considerably.[2] It directly addresses children within the family, regulating both the consequences of international child abduction, and the jurisdiction, and recognition of judgments in parental responsibility matters,[3] making the child and the child's welfare a direct subject of European family law.[4] The child is also the subject of direct rights protections under Article 24[5] of the EU Charter of Fundamental Rights.[6]

1 See, for example, E. Caracciolo di Torella and A. Masselot, 'Under construction: EU family law' (2004) 29 European Law Review 32; L. Ackers, *Shifting Spaces: Women, Citizenship and Migration within the European Union* (Policy Press 1998).

2 European Commission, Proposal for a Council Regulation on jurisdiction, applicable law, recognition of decisions, and acceptance of authentic instruments in matters of parenthood and on the creation of a European Certificate of Parenthood, COM(2022) 695 final is the latest proposal in this field and would regulate the cross-border recognition of parental status, however acquired, in relation to a child.

3 Council Regulation (EU) No 2019/1111 of 25 June 2019 on jurisdiction, the recognition and enforcement of decisions in matrimonial matters and the matters of parental responsibility and on international child abduction (recast) [2019] OJ L178/1.

4 H. Stalford, *Children and the European Union: Rights, Welfare and Accountability* (Hart Publishing 2012).

5 See R. Lamont, 'Article 24' in S. Peers and others (eds), *The Charter of Fundamental Rights of the European Union* (Hart Publishing 2021).

6 [2012] OJ C326/2.

The migration of families with children between Member States has meant that children, for the purposes of EU law, may be caught between two (or sometimes more) legal systems. The private international law rules developed by the EU are intended to address this directly, providing certainty of jurisdiction and recognition and enforcement of judgments between the Member States. These rules were conceptualised as mainly dealing with private law disputes between family members, normally parents, disputing arrangements for custody or access in the aftermath of a relationship breakdown. However, the public law aspects of cross-border family life have also become highly significant to the operation of EU family law. Children abused or neglected by their family have also been caught between legal systems: whilst identified as being at risk of harm in one legal system, they may have close links (through nationality or other reason) to another legal system.

This chapter will examine how the scope of European private international law now encompasses child protection and will consider the status of the abused and neglected child within the European concept of family. The child protection system and legal framework in each Member State may be very different, making legal borders still highly important in this legal context. The chapter will examine the evolution of the private international law rules in this context, the particular problems evident in practice, and will then seek to explore the tension that still exists in regulating the family between European law and the domestic law of the Member States. It will be argued that the child as a victim of abuse or neglect within the family is not clearly 'seen' within EU international family law, in associated policy or legal frameworks. Whilst children as victims are paid close attention in cross-border criminal contexts[7] and asylum law,[8] the role of the state in combatting violence against children through public family law has received little attention despite evident but legitimate differences in national legal systems managing child protection issues.

11.2 CROSS-BORDER PUBLIC LAW CHILD PROTECTION WITHIN THE EUROPE UNION

Family law is often identified as an area of law quintessentially domestic in character and closely related to the religious, cultural, and legal history of the

[7] See, for example, P. Fussey and P. Rawlinson, *Child Trafficking in the EU: Policing and Protecting Europe's Most Vulnerable* (Routledge 2017).

[8] C. Smyth, *European Asylum Law and the Rights of the Child* (Routledge 2014).

State concerned.[9] The harmonisation of private international family law rules within the EU[10] has opened the debate on potential for convergence or even eventual harmonisation of substantive family laws across Europe. In relation to the harmonisation of private international law rules on divorce, the particular emphasis on civil law approach to divorce and procedure has been identified as having an influence on the common law legal systems.[11] The private international law rules and the migration of persons opens up new cross-border understandings of family law and how disputes should be managed and resolved. This can have an impact on the content of Member State family law,[12] though it has arguably had relatively limited impact on child law. The primacy of the child's best interests as the basis for decision-making over children allows for legitimate broad-ranging difference. The open-textured nature of an assessment of the child's best interests, and application of the concept to the facts of a case, provides significant flexibility to domestic courts.[13]

The role of the European Court of Human Rights in adjudicating on Article 8 of the European Convention on Human Rights 1950 (ECHR), the right to respect for private and family life, has arguably been more influential on the convergence of family law standards and the expectations placed on signatory States in relation to family life across Europe.[14] The ECHR has placed positive obligations on signatory States to intervene to prevent the abuse of a child under Article 3, the prohibition on torture and inhuman and degrading treatment, and this includes abuse originating from within the family structure.[15] The law of each EU Member State will contain measures

[9] M. Antokolskaia, 'Harmonisation of substantive family law in Europe: Myths and reality' (2010) 22 Child and Family Law Quarterly 397, 399.

[10] The influence of EU law on domestic family law is also broader than just private international law rules. The free movement of citizens within the Union has based family migration on specific categories of family relationship, requiring Member States to adapt their domestic law to accept certain categories of relationship as the basis of free movement rights for children; see C-129/18 SM EU:C:2019:248 on the kafala form of adoption of a child. See also Chapter 2 by Alina Tryfonidou, Chapter 7 by Michael Bogdan, and Chapter 9 by Geoffrey Willems.

[11] M. Harding, 'The harmonisation of private international law in Europe: Taking the character out of family law?' (2011) 7 Journal of Private International Law 203.

[12] See, for example, *Radmacher v Granatino* [2010] UKSC 42 on enforceability of prenuptial agreements in English law on division of assets on divorce. The prenuptial agreement under dispute was concluded in Germany, where it would have been enforceable and the parties expected it to be binding, a factor accounted for in the decision of the Supreme Court regarding the influence of the agreement on the division of assets under English law.

[13] Stalford (n 4) 37.

[14] For a full assessment, see C. Fenton-Glynn, *Children and the European Court of Human Rights* (Oxford University Press 2021).

[15] *E v the United Kingdom*, Application no 33218/96.

for child protection in some form to provide a method of intervention in the family to prevent or stop abuse and neglect. The child protection framework will respond in accordance with particular standards defined in domestic law. The methods and processes of intervention, along with the terminology and standards upon which intervention is legitimated by national law vary considerably, consequently making comparison and cooperation between national systems highly challenging.[16]

In general, practical terms, once a child has been identified as at potential risk of harm within the family, the state will engage with the child and the wider family through social service provision and support for the family to address sources of harm. If the risk cannot be ameliorated or addressed within the family structure, the state may take legal measures, usually through public law civil proceedings, but also potentially through the criminal law. Measures will often provide for the removal of the child from the situation of risk within their family and place the child, often in a kinship placement (frequently with grandparents), or with other carers, such as foster carers and/or, in some systems, pursue formal adoption of the child, potentially severing ties with the child's birth family. It is important to acknowledge this role of the state in relation to the family, and the potentially very serious consequences if there are failures in intervention. However, both the standards determining the point at which intervention may take place and the forms interventions take will be different depending on the Member State.

In terms of how we perceive the family, families subject to state intervention for the protection of a child are not susceptible to our common conception of family and family life. Family as the primary site of care and affection for children does not conform with the reality of a child abused within the family, and child protection practice is set apart from other aspects of family law. This has also led to difficulties surrounding the definition of issues such as parental chastisement of children, where physical harm by parents is legitimated by law.[17] Traditional conceptions of divided and gendered parental roles have also led to problematic characterisation of parental action, particularly for mothers,[18] and different characterisation dependent on legal context, either private law disputes over parenting, or intervention in the family to protect the

[16] See N. Parton, 'Comparing child protection systems' in P. Dolan and N. Frost (eds), *The Routledge Handbook of Global Child Welfare* (Routledge 2017).

[17] Fenton-Glynn (n 14) 164.

[18] E. Kuskoff and others, 'Of good mothers and violent fathers: Negotiating child protection interventions in abusive relationships' (2023) Violence Against Women (online first).

child through public law.[19] In families of different cultural origins, understanding and responses to state intervention may also vary enormously, posing particular problems in the context of children with links abroad to other legal systems.

This context, along with the increasingly cross-border nature of family life, has meant that it is relatively common, particularly in some Member States with high levels of inward migration, for children to be subject to care proceedings in a State other than that of the child's nationality.[20] The protection of the welfare of the at-risk or abused child is now a challenge for EU private international family law where it regulates the cross-border family. The International Court of Justice in the 1958 *Boll* case observed that the social purpose of child protection law applies to all children, not just nationals of a particular state.[21] As such, the abused or at-risk child has to lie within the conception of cross-border family in law, and, more importantly, identified as having specific needs for the promotion of their welfare.

11.2.1 *The Significance of the Foundations of EU Family Law to Child Protection*

The adoption of private international family law measures by the EU originated in the desire to address the consequences of the free movement of persons between the Member States. The fundamental freedom to migrate within the physical European space had promoted the movement of not just workers, but their families[22] and consequentially, between legal systems and legal spaces. In the European context, the family has been recognised as 'pivotal' to migration choices, and the increasingly less uniform and homogeneous nature of family life has an impact on the social, cultural, and legal structures regulating such migration.[23]

[19] L. Thompson, 'Impossible expectations? Abused mothers' experiences of the child protection and family court systems' (2020) 32 Child and Family Law Quarterly 31, 34.

[20] R. Lamont, 'Care proceedings with a European dimension under Brussels II*a*: Jurisdiction, mutual trust and the best interests of the child' (2016) 28 Child and Family Law Quarterly 67, 69.

[21] *Netherlands v Sweden (Application of the Convention of 1902 Governing the Guardianship of Infants)* [1958] I.C.J. Reports 55.

[22] Now: Directive 2004/38/EC of the European Parliament and of the Council of 29 April 2004 on the right of citizens of the Union and their family members to move and reside freely within the territory of the Member States [2004] OJ L158/77. See also Chapter 7 by Michael Bogdan.

[23] A: Bailey and P. Boyle, 'Untying and retying family migration in the New Europe' (2004) 30 Journal of Ethnic and Migration Studies 229, 234.

Beyond regulating the structural elements of family relationships legitimising the key entitlement to free movement in European law,[24] the EU did not clearly seek to regulate the reasons for migration. Since the introduction of the concept of European citizenship[25] by the Treaty of Maastricht in 1993, individuals are able to move with motivations beyond purely the economic. This is of interest to family lawyers where motivations for migration were directly related to maintaining or breaking family relationships through the use of legal borders and differences. It has particular significance in relation to children who do not necessarily have control over their migration and the reasons for it,[26] which can take a number of forms. For example, migration may constitute an unlawful attempt to separate a child from a parent through parental child abduction, or moving a child across an international border may form part of an attempt to avoid intervention by child protection agencies by moving abroad.[27]

One of the ways in which European law acknowledged the impact that the free movement of persons was having on family life was to seek to regulate private international law rules, alongside the internal EU migration framework. McEleavy has highlighted that the integration of private international family law rules in the EU was motivated to specifically and directly affect the life of the European citizen, making the legal status and familial consequences of their migration to another Member State simpler.[28] In family law (as opposed to commercial law, where there was a clearer link to facilitating litigation associated with the creation of the internal market), the initial interventions were controversial. The economically derived basis for seeking to address the consequences of the free movement of persons and potentially encourage future migration was regarded as problematic.[29] Family law was

[24] F. Banda and J. Eekelaar, 'International conceptions of the family' (2017) 66 International and Comparative Law Quarterly 833, 834.

[25] Article 20 TFEU (ex Article 17 of the Treaty establishing the European Community (TEC)).

[26] See M. Moskal and N. Tyrrell, 'Family migration decision-making, step-migration and separation: Children's experiences in European migrant worker families' (2016) 14 Children's Geographies 453.

[27] R. Lamont, 'The development of child protection across international borders for children at risk of harm' in G. Douglas, M. Murch, and V. Stephens (eds), *International and National Perspectives on Child and Family Law* (Intersentia 2018) 242.

[28] P. McEleavy, 'The Brussels II Regulation: How the European Community has moved into family law' (2002) 51 International and Comparative Law Quarterly 883, 892.

[29] P. McEleavy, 'Private international law: Brussels II*bis* matrimonial matters, parental responsibility, child abduction and mutual recognition' (2004) 53 International and Comparative Law Quarterly 503, 505.

regarded as having been 'instrumentalised'[30] in achieving the internal market goals of the Union, along with giving further substance to the emerging concept of European citizenship derived from Article 20 of the Treaty on the Functioning of the EU (TFEU). However, for the EU to assume competence over private international family law, it is necessary to demonstrate a link to the needs of the internal market.[31]

The consequence of this foundation for European family law was a particular emphasis in the underlying policies towards cross-border families, which informed the determination of the international family 'problems' to be addressed by EU law. The conception of the 'problem' to which economic family migration may give rise was centred on the consequences of migration for family ties, primarily parental ties. It was noted that, in potentially placing extra pressure on family relationships, the migration context may contribute to relationship breakdown between the parents, with associated consequences for any children of the family. The legal framework developed by the EU then focused on addressing the consequences of the breakdown of relationships between parents in a previously extant family, and the resulting cross-national movement and litigation.[32] The potential for abuse or neglect of children within the family structure, and the impact on children of having links to more than one Member State as a result of their family's migration, was not clearly in focus.

This has had a significant impact in relation to public law child protection, where it is the state intervening to protect a child and seeking legal authority to provide for their welfare, rather than the anticipated dispute between holders of parental responsibility over their obligations towards the child between one another. Despite a long history of public law disputes over children between countries,[33] the academic engagement and research into the cross-border links of children subject to child protection proceedings is of relatively recent origin.[34] It is an area where national law and policies may vary widely and the children subject to public law intervention by the state may face

30 J. Meeusen, 'Instrumentalisation of private international law in the European Union: Towards a European conflicts revolution? (2007) 9 European Journal of Migration and Law 287, 300.

31 Article 81 TFEU (ex Article 65 TEC).

32 The regulation of matrimonial property regimes, choice of law on divorce, and on cross-border maintenance claims affecting children could be said to add to this focus on the practical consequences of cross-border relationship breakdown between parents.

33 *Netherlands v Sweden (Application of the Convention of 1902 Governing the Guardianship of Infants)* (n 21).

34 S. Mustasaari, 'Introduction to Special Issue on transnational child protection' (2022) 34 Child and Family Law Quarterly 333, 333.

enormously different surrounding circumstances and personal histories.[35] The increasingly global links maintained by children within their family networks means that the potential for a child to have family members abroad, or significant familial links to another country, is higher. The law and the procedures for providing outcomes for children deemed at risk of neglect or abuse from their family have to be able to respond to these global links to effectively secure the welfare of the child. This is the context in which European family law has operated.

11.2.2 *Developing Cross-Border Child Protection within the EU Family Law Framework*

Regulation 2201/2003,[36] or Brussels II*bis*, was the first significant and effective piece of EU legislation impacting on family law between the Member States. It created jurisdiction rules for divorce and disputes over parental responsibility including contact and custody within the EU. On the assumption that jurisdiction would be uniformly assumed, recognition of the resulting judgments was almost automatic. The Regulation also created an additional framework for child abduction, building on the Hague Convention on the Civil Aspects of International Child Abduction 1980, to encourage the return of a child unlawfully removed or retained between Member States. These rules are now embodied in the updated and revised Regulation 2019/1111, known as Brussels II*bis* Recast.[37] The legal framework centres on the consequences of this process of breakdown in relationships between parents, that is, the private law aspects of family conflict.

After the adoption of Regulation 2201/2003, the first question posed to the Court of Justice of the European Union (CJEU) regarding the interpretation of the Regulation was regarding its material scope. In Case C-435/06 C,[38] the mother of two children appealed against the decision of the Finnish court to transfer legal responsibility for her children from the Finnish court to the

[35] S. Mustasaari, 'Children abroad: A relational analysis of cross-border child protection cases in the Finnish Central Authority' (2022) 34 Child and Family Law Quarterly 361, 365.

[36] Council Regulation (EC) No 2201/2003 of 27 November 2003 concerning jurisdiction and the recognition and enforcement of judgments in matrimonial matters and the matters of parental responsibility [2003] OJ L338/1. For an assessment of the Regulation, see T. Kruger and L. Samyn, 'Brussels II*bis*: Successes and suggested improvements' (2016) 12 Journal of Private International Law 132.

[37] Council Regulation (EC) No 2019/1111 on jurisdiction, the recognition, and enforcement of decisions in matrimonial matters and the matters of parental responsibility and on international child abduction (recast) [2019] OJ L 178/1.

[38] Case C-435/06 C EU:C:2007:714.

Swedish authorities. The two children both had Finnish nationality, and the elder child also had joint Swedish nationality. They had been taken into care in Sweden in February 2005, but their mother had moved them to Finland in March 2005. The Swedish authorities sought the enforcement of the decision to take the children into care in Finland.[39] The CJEU confirmed that since the decision related to the attribution, exercise, delegation, restriction, or termination of parental responsibility under Article 1(1)(b), Regulation 2201/2003, it was within the material scope of the Regulation.[40] This meant that EU law relating to jurisdiction and the recognition of judgments under Regulation 2201/2003 applied to the public law judgment to take the children into the care of the Swedish state, since this decision affected the exercise of parental responsibility over the child.

The available European family law legislation was not clearly directed at governing jurisdiction over these children. Both Brussels II*bis* and the updated Brussels II Recast create a distinction between jurisdiction over disputes affecting parental responsibility, including placement in foster or educational placements, and decisions on adoption which are expressly excluded from the material scope of the Regulation.[41] Adoption, either in kinship placements or outside the birth family, can be a common outcome from care proceedings in some Member States. This makes the initial decision to assume jurisdiction over a child identified as at risk of harm within the family extremely important because it affects the potential outcome for the child in determining the available family arrangement options when the court makes substantive decisions in relation to the child's future. The preparatory proposals for Brussels II*bis* did not envisage that public law proceedings would feature heavily in cross-border disputes, instead focusing on clarity in divorce jurisdiction and resulting private law disputes over children.[42] Arising from the evidence in practice under the original Regulation, the Commission's proposals for the Recast Regulation after ten years of operation of Brussels II*bis* acknowledged specific challenges in the effective and efficient placement of children abroad for their welfare required revisions to the legislative framework.[43] Despite this

[39] Ibid, paras 14–23.

[40] Ibid, para 26.

[41] Article 1(4) of Regulation 2019/1111 (n 3).

[42] See European Commission, Proposal for a Council Regulation concerning jurisdiction and the recognition and enforcement of judgments in matrimonial matters and in matters of parental responsibility repealing Regulation 1347/2000, COM(2002) 222 final.

[43] Problems in securing timely consent for placement in the foreign jurisdiction were specifically identified. European Commission, Proposal for a Council Regulation on jurisdiction, the recognition and enforcement of decisions in matrimonial matters and the matters of parental responsibility, and on international child abduction (recast), COM(2016) 411 final.

acknowledgment and amendments to the governing framework, the risks posed to children within the family and the need for state intervention for the child's protection are incidental to the conception of family life.

The focus on the breakdown of parental relationships meant that circumstances affecting the child within the extant family, and the role of the state in intervening in family life, had not been fully considered. The increasing movement of families and children has meant that children involved in child protection proceedings, governed by the domestic public law of the Member State, often have links to foreign jurisdictions. Even if the child was born in the country where they are made subject to care proceedings, their parents may be nationals of other countries and they may have significant close family members in other countries, for example, grandparents. Alternatively, the child may have been born abroad and migrated along with the family, or there may be an attempt to avoid domestic child protection proceedings by moving the children to another state (as appears to have been the case in C-435/06 C[44]). In other circumstances, a child at risk of harm may have been placed with institutions abroad for specialist care and support unavailable in their home country.[45]

This aspect of cross-border family life had emerged as a serious concern in practice under the Brussels II*bis* Regulation.[46] Article 15 of the Regulation, allowing transfers of jurisdiction over parental responsibility proceedings in the best interests of the child between the Member States assumed particular importance in relation to child protection where the child had links to another Member State. When the host state instituted proceedings for their protection, the question arose as to the circumstances where the case should be transferred to the foreign court, usually the court of the child's nationality. In Case C-428/15 *Child and Family Agency*,[47] the CJEU made it clear that Article 15 of Regulation 2201/2003 could apply to the transfer of public law proceedings to a different Member State than to that first seised. In determining whether the alternative court with a particular connection to the child was 'better placed' to hear the case, the CJEU directed that the analysis should focus on whether it provided 'genuine and specific added value',[48] accounting for rules of procedure that justifies transferring jurisdiction from the child's habitual residence, the primary ground of jurisdiction.[49] The assessment of

[44] C (n 38).
[45] See Case C-92/12 *HSE* EU:C:2012:255.
[46] Lamont (n 20).
[47] Case C-428/15 *Child and Family Agency* EU:C:2016:819.
[48] Ibid, para 57.
[49] Article 8 of Regulation 2201/2003 (n 36).

whether the transfer of jurisdiction is in the child's best interests is a truncated assessment, limited to whether the transfer will be 'detrimental to the situation of the child'.[50] This can include whether the transfer will affect the child's right of freedom of movement within the EU, but not how the interests of other parties, for example, the child's parent, may be affected by the transfer.[51]

Much of the litigation in relation to transfers of jurisdiction under Article 15 occurred in England and Wales, partly because it was a common migration destination country within the EU, and partly because it maintains a system of closed adoptions where the child does not maintain links with the birth family without the consent of the child's birth parent(s) where this is deemed to be in the child's best interests.[52] In England and Wales, if a foreign national child was habitually resident in England under Article 8 Brussels II*bis*, the English court could adopt orders under Children Act 1989 to protect the child[53] in England.[54] The question of whether jurisdiction over the care proceedings should be transferred to the Member State of the child's nationality under Article 15 of the Regulation should always be considered in care proceedings involving a foreign national child.[55] Under Article 15, the court had to consider whether the foreign court was better placed to hear the proceedings and whether the transfer was in the child's best interests, accounting for the impact of the transfer on the welfare of the child, but not the potential outcome of substantive proceedings, that is, the long-term future of a child deemed to be at risk if care is maintained in their family.[56]

Concerns were expressed within the EU over the differences in law and practice in relation to child protection in the different Member States.

50 *Child and Family Agency* (n 47), para 63.

51 Ibid, paras 66–67.

52 Children and Adoption Act 2002 (England and Wales).

53 If the threshold criteria under s.31(2), Children Act 1989 are met, a range of possible disposals are available.

54 Since the UK's withdrawal from the EU, jurisdiction in England and Wales would be assumed on the basis of the child's habitual residence under Article 5 the Hague Convention on Jurisdiction, Applicable law, Recognition, Enforcement and Cooperation in Respect of Parental Responsibility and Measures for the Protection of Children 1996 which also allows for transfers of jurisdiction under Article 8: see R. Lamont, 'Child protection in international family law and the determination of where the child 'belongs' for the purpose of jurisdiction' (2022) 34 Child and Family Law Quarterly 401. Regulation 2201/2003 was informed by the terms of the 1996 Convention in drafting, but arguably the 1996 Convention is clearer in defining the process of transfer of jurisdiction over a parental responsibility case: see P. Beaumont 'Private international law concerning children in the UK after Brexit: Comparing Hague Treaty Law with EU Regulations' (2017) 29 Child and Family Law Quarterly 214, 220.

55 *In Re E (A Child) (Care Proceedings: European Dimension) Practice Note* [2014] EWHC 6 (Fam).

56 *Re J (Children) (Brussels II Revised: Article 15)* [2016] UKSC 15.

In English care proceedings there has been increasing willingness to transfer jurisdiction over a child national to another Member State to respect the interest of the other country in protecting their nationals, but this transfer should only occur when transfer is in the child's best interests.[57] Where a child is at risk, the English court is obliged to act for the child's protection, but other countries regard the English law approach of placing children removed from their parents' care in adoption and preventing contact with the birth parents as highly problematic.[58] This approach to adoption as an outcome from child protection proceedings in England and Wales attracted significant criticism from other Member States[59] and encouraged the English court to consider transfer of jurisdiction to enable the Member State of which the child was a national to determine the long-term future of the child.

There have also been practical difficulties in the execution of the process for transferring jurisdiction to the foreign court which will hopefully be addressed to some degree by Regulation 2019/1111, the Recast Regulation.[60] Between EU Member States, transfers of cases between jurisdictions are now managed under Article 12, Regulation 2019/1111, which now contains specific time limits for informing the foreign jurisdiction of a potential transfer and instituting proceedings, and jurisdiction can be accepted by the foreign court if it is in the best interests of the child. Practical concerns relating to the production of social workers reports regarding issues such as assessment and organisation of kinship placements in the foreign state, and cooperation between social work services between the Member States may however still be difficult to coordinate.[61]

The experience of cross-border family disputes in the EU has demonstrated that the impact of family violence and child abuse has a significant cross-border dimension. However, the legal framework, along with systems of cooperation between key actors in child protection services such as social workers, has not been conceptualised with this issue in mind. EU private international family law has been developed with private law disputes as the

[57] Ibid.

[58] C. Fenton-Glynn, 'Adoption without consent', Report for the European Parliament PETI Committee (2015) <www.europarl.europa.eu/RegData/etudes/STUD/2015/519236/IPOL_STU(2015)519236_EN.pdf>.

[59] R. Lamont and C. Fenton-Glynn, 'Cross-border care and adoption proceedings in the European Union' (2016) 38 Journal of Social Welfare and Family Law 94.

[60] *Re HA (A Child) (Brussels IIA Art. 15)* [2015] EWHC 1310 (Fam).

[61] M. Wright, 'Working the international child protection case: A snapshot of local authorities' experiences within an evolving legal context' (2019) 41 Journal of Social Welfare and Family Law 15, 28.

focus, where it is most often the case that the best interests of the child are secured through protecting and supporting family relationships post relationship breakdown between the parents. The complexity of the child's circumstances where the child is at risk of abuse or neglect poses additional challenges when a cross-border link is also evident and the role of the state in intervening in the family changes the nature of the dispute. The substantive outcomes for the child themselves, and their wider family, may be significantly different depending on the country where the dispute is heard and the available options for a child deemed to be at risk of abuse or neglect.

11.3 THE EUROPEAN CHILD AND THE ABUSIVE OR NEGLECTFUL FAMILY

In recent years, there has been far greater focus within the EU on the rights of the child and how these can be protected and mainstreamed throughout EU law.[62] The European Commission's recently published 'Strategy on the Rights of the Child'[63] identifies combatting violence against children and ensuring child protection as a priority. The impact of violence occurring within the family is highlighted as a concern. The Commission seeks the promotion of integrated child protection systems, working together to protect and support the child in their best interests.[64] They direct attention to prevention measures, particularly family support designed to maintain and safeguard the child in their family environment. These are key factors for effective cross-border child protection, since there should be a framework for clear routes of cooperation between state authorities for the welfare of the child. The Commission also asks Member States to promote national strategies for family- and community-based care with a focus on preparing children to leave public care.[65] Despite this engagement at a policy level, the child as a victim of abuse and neglect within the family is not clearly defined within the European conception of the family and remains an oblique factor in developing European family law rules.

The key factor for the EU in building child protection mechanisms is its limited competence to do so in this field. Children as victims of violence or

[62] See Lamont, 'Article 24' (n 5).

[63] European Commission, Communication from the Commission to the European Parliament, the Council, the European Economic and Social Committee and the Committee of the Regions: EU Strategy on the Rights of the Child, COM(2021) 142 final.

[64] Ibid 11.

[65] Ibid 12.

risk of harm has been an issue in other legal contexts, particularly the trafficking of children,[66] and the child as a victim of crime.[67] These measures are based on the EU competence in relation to cross-border criminal law under Title V TFEU.[68] It has engaged with violence against children in the context of the Daphne research funding programme which supported research projects that aimed to protect children, young people, and women against violence.[69] The funding calls included transnational projects seeking to build professional capacity in child protection,[70] but had very broad scope covering a range of different research priorities. The Fundamental Rights Agency has produced a guide to the protection of children found outside of parental care in a Member State other than that of their nationality, although this largely focuses the specific and specialised needs of children trafficked within the Union.[71]

The recognition that the child may face significant abuse and violence within the family environment is partial and fragmented across the EU legal competence and policy framework. The child harmed within the family is a victim of crime, yet state intervention through social work support and monitoring, and family law child protection frameworks is usually the priority response where a child is identified at risk of abuse or neglected within this environment. The nature and approach of this framework in responding to child abuse and neglect obviously lies within the competence of the Member State. However, the experience of abuse and neglect by children with family

66 Directive 2011/36/EU of the European Parliament and of the Council of 5 April 2011 on preventing and combating trafficking in human beings and protecting its victims, and replacing Council Framework Decision 2002/629/JHA [2011] OJ L101/1.

67 Directive 2012/29/EU of the European Parliament and of the Council of 25 October 2012 establishing minimum standards on the rights, support, and protection of victims of crime, and replacing Council Framework Decision 2001/220/JHA [2012] OJ L315/57; Directive 2011/93/EU of the European Parliament and of the Council of 13 December 2011 on combating the sexual abuse and sexual exploitation of children and child pornography, and replacing Council Framework Decision 2004/68/JHA [2011] OJ L335/1.

68 Article 83(1) TFEU.

69 Decision No 779/2007/EC of the European Parliament and of the Council of 20 June 2007 establishing for the period 2007–2013 a specific programme to prevent and combat violence against children, young people, and women and to protect victims and groups at risk (Daphne III programme) as part of the General Programme Fundamental Rights and Justice.

70 See European Commission, Action grants to support transnational projects aiming to build capacity for professionals in child protection systems and legal professionals representing children in legal proceedings – JUST/2015/RCHI/AG/PROF <https://ec.europa.eu/justice/grants1/calls/2015_action_grants/just_2015_rchi_ag_prof_en.htm>.

71 EU Fundamental Rights Agency, 'Children deprived of parental care found in an EU Member State other than their own' (2019) <https://fra.europa.eu/en/publication/2019/children-deprived-parental-care-found-eu-member-state-other-their-own>.

links in more than one country may add a distinct European dimension to child protection in the cross-border family, strongly in evidence in the practice of the Brussels II*bis* Regulation. The family as an abusive environment is out-of-focus, only obliquely acknowledged by European law in fragmented diverse contexts. This is partly due to the significant differences in child protection regimes across the Member States and the challenges associated with assessment of risk and cultures of protection.

11.3.1 *Differences in Family Laws and Understandings of Child Protection*

Despite elements of harmonisation within the EU and Council of Europe legal frameworks, it is evident that family laws across the European legal space remain different. This is the case in relation to both their underlying approach (beyond the distinctions between common law and civil law systems) and in decision-making processes in disputes relating to children. This is particularly the case in public law and arrangements for children under child protection measures provided by the state, broadly conceived. In this context, methods of cooperation are not closely developed between states, despite the existence of International Social Services,[72] designed to assist children and families with social problems arising from migration, and the work of charities such as Children and Families across Borders within this framework.[73] The potential for intra-State controversies over the differences in approach have been made evident in the EU context, with significant political concern expressed over the English practice of adoption as an outcome of child protection proceedings by other EU Member States.[74] The approach to child protection across the Member States is highly variable with different emphasis on family engagement, placement, and use of adoption in different legal systems within different underlying political legal cultures.[75]

The perception and understanding of risk to children exposed to violence, abuse, and neglect is heavily influenced by culture. The response to evidence of risk can differ both in the broader legal culture and regulatory environment, but also on the ground practice and experience of the social workers and, if necessary, legal actors. Weston and Mythen have explored how professions involved in child protection understand and perceive the risks posed to

72 <www.iss-ssi.org/index.php/en/>.

73 <http://cfab.org.uk>.

74 Lamont and Fenton-Glynn (n 59) 98.

75 T. Spratt and others, ‘Child protection in Europe: Development of an international cross-comparison model to inform national policies and practices’ (2015) 45 British Journal of Social Work 1508, 1513.

children in the context of child sexual exploitation.[76] In a localised domestic study, they found that interactions with children and perceptions of the risks to their welfare are influenced by the practitioners' background assumptions and the context of the decision-making. In particular, they found that personal opinions seeped into professional assessments and decisions relating to children, in assessing the nature of the risks posed, its source, and appropriate interventions. They demonstrate that in assessing risk, and choosing state intervention in the family, the influence of localised legal and professional culture is very strong. Walklate and Mythen identify (in relation to domestic abuse) that: '... those deemed at risk are not forensically measured ... they are constructed within a logic of norms and values that are felt'.[77] The tendency within child protection practice has been to broaden the understanding of what poses a risk to a child since the turn of the century,[78] but the assessments determining risks posed to children remain strongly individualised.

The response of the domestic legal system to a child at risk in the family is therefore heavily informed by (potentially highly) localised cultures and practices. It has been suggested that perceptions of risk in determining abuse are too individualised and localised, rather than addressing the general causes of harm to children.[79] However, these broader contextual factors could also have an influence on how the professionals involved regard and interpret the parenting practices of a non-national family, or assess a placement for the child in another Member State. How to effectively coordinate these systems at both a social work and legal level has been left largely unexamined, remaining a sub-concern in the management of cross-border cases though there is a rising number. The EU conception of family life, in obscuring and only partially engaging with family violence and abuse of children in this context, has meant these concerns are left outside of the scope of policy formation for effective consideration and engagement.

Private international family law has always operated to partially obscure the differences between legal systems. As a system of law that is designed to accommodate and manage the impact one legal system may have on another,

76 S. Weston and G. Mythen, 'Disentangling practitioners' understandings of child sexual exploitation: The risks of assuming otherwise?' (2022) 22 Criminology and Criminal Justice 618, 630.

77 S. Walklate and G. Mythen, 'Beyond risk theory: Experiential knowledge and "knowing otherwise"' (2011) 11 Criminology and Criminal Justice 99, 108.

78 N. Parton, 'Child protection and safeguarding in England: Changing and competing conceptions of risk and their implications for social work' (2011) 41 British Journal of Social Work 854, 867.

79 B. Featherstone, A. Gupta, K. Morris, and J. Warner, 'Let us stop feeding the risk: Towards a social model of "child protection"' (2018) 7 Families, Relationships and Societies 7, 10.

private international law rules are often designed to limit the focus on differences between both substantive legal rules and processes for dispute resolution. However, the EU has sought to use private international law as a means to *encourage* migration and integration within Europe. The emphasis on uniform assumption of jurisdiction is to encourage the mutual recognition of resulting judgments within the European judicial space. However, Meeusen has questioned the extent to which this approach is suitable for family law, pointing out, 'The very strict regime of mutual recognition now obliges Member States to accept the content of family law decisions originating in other Member States as if they were indifferent to the substantive outcome of these cases.'[80] He argues that European private international law '... radically liberalizes international family law in a somewhat hidden way, while Member States are at the same time unable to reach agreement on common substantive principles and rules of family law'.[81] In the context of children at risk of abuse within the family, this criticism is particularly pertinent. This aspect of European private international family law has placed the tension between assumption of jurisdiction over children and the legal indifference to substantive outcomes for the child under particular pressure.

11.4 CONCLUSIONS

The European Commission's Strategy on the Rights of the Child states that its '... overarching ambition is to build the best possible life for children in the European Union and across the globe'.[82] The range of policy and legal engagement with children across the breadth of EU competence demonstrates an ongoing strong commitment to securing children's rights within Europe, even if there are difficulties in practice for the achievement of this ambition.

The limitations on this ambition and of European engagement with children in the family are demonstrated by considering cross-border child protection where a child is identified in one Member State as at risk of abuse or neglect in their family environment. Legal borders are still significant for these children and families. There are considerable differences between the Member States in the practice of child protection and the perception and understanding of risk and risk management. In this sphere, the substantive

80 Meeusen (n 30) 303.

81 Ibid 304.

82 European Commission, Communication from the Commission to the European Parliament, the Council, the European Economic and Social Committee and the Committee of the Regions: EU Strategy on the Rights of the Child, COM(2021) 142 final.

outcomes of legal systems still really matter and are significantly different. Parents who abuse or neglect their children have not been perceived as an aspect of the EU conception of family life, where rights are associated with securing opportunities, rather than also recognising a concomitant need to prevent and protect children from harm by the family. The tension between the indifference of private international law rules, and the significance of the substantive decision for the child and family concerned, deserves further reflection and consideration in the future practice of EU law and development of cross-border policies on cooperation over children and their welfare.

12

The EU Family

Surviving Ideological Familism in Times of Illiberalism

NAUSICA PALAZZO*

12.1 INTRODUCTION

Reflections around European Union (EU) family law start off by noting that the EU has no exclusive or shared power to regulate substantive family law.[1] This might induce one to think that the family is not a privileged object of regulation for EU law.[2] However, the family is not absent from the EU legal framework.[3]

The legal regulation of the family is currently dispersed across the extensive body of EU laws. We can find fragments in legal acts that result from the EU power to harmonise private international law rules applying to such families as enshrined in Article 81(3) of the Treaty on the Functioning of the EU (TFEU), the only Treaty provision granting an explicit EU competence over

* For providing thoughtful comments or leads at various stages of this chapter, I am grateful to the editors of the volume, Kim Lane Sheppele, and Katinka Linnamäki. I am grateful to Filipe Gama for assistance in technical editing, Nathalie Kornet for her valuable research assistance and to Fondazione Cariplo for its generous support of this research.

1 The term 'EU Family Law' refers to relevant provisions in primary and secondary EU law as well as initiatives of the EU in the area of family. See C. McGlynn, *Families and the European Union – Law, Politics and Pluralism* (Cambridge University Press 2006) 152; E. Caracciolo di Torella and A. Masselot, 'Under construction: EU Family Law' (2004) 29 European Law Review 32. The European Convention of Human Rights and constitutional traditions common to the Member States should also be included amongst such sources under Article 6 (3) TEU.

2 M. Antokolskaia, *Harmonisation of Family Law in Europe: A Historical Perspective* (Intersentia 2006) 3–5.

3 See also Chapter 4 by Ségolène Barbou des Places.

family law.[4] Yet, the current 'architecture' of EU family law is more complex than that.[5]

Particularly, the development of the case law in the area of family-related discrimination[6] and fundamental rights attests to the growing constitutional relevance of the family in the Union.[7] The regulation of the family can be found in a series of documents of constitutional significance, such as the Charter of Fundamental Rights of the European Union (the Charter). However, its constitutional status should be taken to refer to a larger notion of constitutional relevance that certain EU legal provisions possess. As De Baere and Gutman put it:

> it is remarkable the extent to which European family law is a constitutional topic par excellence, taking into account its linkage to the subjects of Union citizenship, discrimination and fundamental rights, as well as to recent

4 Such a power has been exercised in a series of regulations on divorce, property, and registered partnerships, as well as in matters of matrimonial property regimes. Council Regulation (EC) 2201/2003 of 27 November 2003 concerning jurisdiction and the recognition and enforcement of judgments in matrimonial matters and matters of parental responsibility [2003] OJ L338/1; Council Regulation (EU) No 2016/1104 of 24 June 2016 implementing enhanced cooperation in the area of jurisdiction, applicable law, and the recognition and enforcement of decisions in matters of the property consequences of registered partnerships [2016] OJ L183/30; Council Regulation (EU) No 2016/1103 of 24 June 2016 implementing enhanced cooperation in the area of jurisdiction, applicable law, and the recognition and enforcement of decisions in matters of matrimonial property regimes [2016] OJ L183/1.

5 C. Kilpatrick, 'The Court of Justice and Labour Law in 2010: A new EU discrimination law architecture' (2011) 40 Industrial Law Journal 280.

6 The examples are numerous. They include the Court's intervention in the area of employment benefits for same-sex couples, the free movement of same-sex spouses and cohabitants, to mention but a few. See A. Tryfonidou, 'Law and sexual minority rights in the EU: Navigating a political minefield' in P. Cardwell and M.-P. Granger (eds), *Research Handbook on the Politics of EU Law* (Edward Elgar Publishing 2020); N. Palazzo, 'The EU family: Is marital status emerging as a prohibited ground of discrimination?' in E. Bernard, M. Cresp, and M. Ho-Dac (eds), *La famille dans l'ordre juridique de l'Union européenne: Family within the legal order of the European Union* (Bruylant 2020); J. Rijpma and N. Koffeman, 'Free movement rights for same-sex couples under EU law: What role to play for the CJEU?' in D. Gallo, L. Paladini, and P. Pustorino (eds), *Same-Sex Couples before National, Supranational and International Jurisdictions* (Springer 2014); D. Kochenov, 'Gay rights in the EU: A long way forward for the Union of 27' (2007) 3 Croatian Yearbook of European Law and Policy 469. A seminar decision in the area of free movement is the *Coman* decision (Case C-673/16 *Coman and others* EU:C:2018:385). See also Chapter 7 by Michael Bogdan and Chapter 9 by Geoffrey Willems. In the context of discrimination in employment, see Case C-267/06 *Maruko* EU:C:2008:179; Case C-147/08 *Römer* EU:C:2011:286; Case C-267/12 *Hay* EU:C:2013:823.

7 D. Martiny, 'Is unification of family law feasible or even desirable?' in A. S. Hartkamp and others (eds), *Towards a European Civil Code* (Kluwer 2011) 435. On the limited relevance of human rights protection acquired within the EU, see B. de Witte, 'The past and future of the European Court of Justice in the protection of human rights' in P. Alston (ed), *The EU and Human Rights* (Oxford University Press 1999).

> institutional developments that are of 'constitutional' importance to the EU, such as the recourse to enhanced cooperation for the first time in connection with the 'Rome III Regulation' on divorce ...[8]

This doctrinal circle lies further from the 'centre' of family law[9] in the sense that for historical reasons it is less intuitive to think of the legal regulation of the family as falling under the purview of constitutional law.[10] This chapter contributes to the literature on this larger circle, commenting on recent developments that point to a growing constitutional relevance of the family. As they started to attract the (LGBTQ) family in the controversial area of the EU's common values, these developments could not easily be predicted.[11] This shift, as will be shown, is manifesting itself in conjunction with the rise of illiberalism across the Union. In the same way in which, in illiberal regimes in Europe, the traditional family is becoming a focal point in the construction of national identity,[12] the EU is prepared to mobilise the protection of LGBTQ people and families from discrimination as a matter of 'identity' and common

[8] G. De Baere and K. Gutman, 'The impact of the European Union and the European Court of Justice on European Family Law' in J. M. Scherpe (ed), *European Family Law Vol. I – The Impact of Institutions and Organisations on European Family Law* (Edward Elgar Publishing 2016) 10–11 [citations omitted].

[9] One could think of family law as a series of concentric circles. The first, narrower, circle is the core of family law or family law *stricto sensu*, and encompasses issues relating to marital relationships and parent–child relationships. These two categories have a broad material scope that spans issues such as entry into and exit from marriage, registered partnerships, cohabitation, the legal recognition of same-sex or other non-traditional families, and matters concerning parental responsibility, adoption, child custody and support, and so on. This definition aligns with the scope of major works in EU family law, which cover matrimonial issues or issues related to parent–child relationships. See, for example, K. Boele-Woelki, 'Cross-border family relations in Europe: Towards a common European matrimonial property law based upon cooperation between private international law and substantive law' in A. L. M. Keirse and M. B. M. Loos (eds), *Alternative Ways to Ius Commune – The Europeanisation of Private Law* (Intersentia 2012) 33.

[10] Foregrounding the family into this area requires gradually overcoming ingrained assumptions in civil law systems around family law as an object of private law. On this point, see É. Millard, *Famille et droit public. Recherches sur la construction d'un objet juridique*, Tome 182 (LGDJ 1995). See also Editors' introduction (referring to an idea of the family as a 'traditionally private-law governed institution').

[11] For a criticism of introducing values into Treaties, see J. Lacroix, 'Does Europe need common values?' (2009) 8 European Journal of Political Theory 141.

[12] K. Lane Scheppele, D. Kochenov, and B. Grabowska-Moroz, 'EU values are law, after all: Enforcing EU values through systemic infringement actions by the European Commission and the Member States of the European Union' (2020) 39 Yearbook of European Law 3, 21 (arguing that 'sometimes claims of constitutional identity constitute rejections of European values in the name of a conflicting ideology that poses a much more fundamental challenge to European unity as well as the survival of liberal democratic constitutionalism in the Member State in question').

values. Looking at the role of family in similar European culture wars and how it reflects on the constitutional relevance of the family in EU law is essential to understand the contemporary moment.

After exploring the notions of illiberalism and familism in Section 12.1, the chapter proceeds to explore the case studies of Hungary and Poland to assess how an ideological usage of the family is mobilised within illiberal discourse (Sections 12.2 and 12.3). In Section 12.4, the chapter explores the reaction that similar developments have triggered on the part of the EU and assesses the actual and likely repercussions of such developments on the ways in which the EU treats the 'family' as an object of EU constitutional law. The central claim of the chapter is that similar developments attest to a tentative yet discernible expansion of the constitutional relevance of the family in the space of the EU which occurs as a result of increased protection of LGBTQ families.[13]

12.2 ILLIBERALISM, FAMILISM, AND THE EUROPEAN FAMILY

The family as a social formation continues to attract much attention by illiberal actors and assumes special relevance in European-style culture wars. In these ongoing culture wars, a certain 'fatigue' of some Member States towards the EU is becoming increasingly visible,[14] and the family is one of the areas that illiberal political actors focus on to catalyse an anti-European sentiment. Hence, the role of the family within illiberal political agendas deserves more sustained reflection in socio-legal scholarship and EU law scholarship.[15]

[13] See Section 12.5.

[14] Z. Hesová, 'Three types of culture wars and the populist strategies in Central Europe' (2021) 28 Czech Journal of Political Science/Politologick 130; K. Stöckl, 'The European culture wars' (*ZOiS Spotlight* 13/19, 3 April 2019) <https://en.zois-berlin.de/publications/zois-spotlight/archiv-2019/the-european-culture-wars>. Other features of European culture wars include historical revisionism and civilizationism overtones (Hesová (n 14) 137).

[15] For instance, the *magnum opus* on illiberalism, the *Routledge Handbook on Illiberalism*, contains sixty-one chapters. Amongst them there are two chapters covering the role of 'gender' within illiberal agendas, while the family is not the object of a separate chapter. A. Sajó, R. Uitz, and S. Holmes (eds), *Routledge Handbook of Illiberalism* (Routledge 2021). The Oxford Handbook of Illiberalism, while not including a chapter explicitly focused on the role of the family, contains numerous chapters relevant to the topic. See especially, A. Graff, and E. Korolczuk, 'Gender and Illiberal Politics' in M. Laruelle (ed), Oxford Handbook of Illiberalism (Oxford University Press 2023). The topic is, however, drawing growing attention, as attested by important works recently published. See K. Linnamäki, 'Not in front of the child: Illiberal familism and the Hungarian anti-LGBTQ+ "Child Protective Law"'(2022) 10 Politics and Governance 16; L. Balogh, A. László Pap, and E. Pásztor, 'Hungary: The concept of family within the framework of "illiberal democracy"' in N. Yassari and M.-C. Foblets (eds), *Normativity and Diversity in Family Law* (Springer 2022).

'Illiberal democracy' is the tag that Hungarian Prime Minister Viktor Orbán attached to his plan to dismantle liberal democracy as we know it.[16] After he publicly committed to building an illiberal democracy in 2015, Jarosław Kaczyński, the leader of the Polish populist party Law and Justice winked at him and pledged to build a 'Budapest in Warsaw'.[17] It was straightforward for Kaczyński to deliver on his promise: meanwhile, he had been waging a war on 'gender' in 2012–2014 and spreading seeds of gender conservativism throughout the country.[18]

In academic usage, 'illiberalism' refers to a political movement that rejects the key traits of liberal democracy.[19] It is a specific sceptical posture that accuses liberal democracies of failing on several fronts, including the political, the cultural, and the economic.[20] At present, there are contrasting views regarding whether illiberalism has a core ideology or whether it constitutes an empty signifier in semiotic terms. However, in the area of human rights, it displays a clearer *ex negativo* content across illiberal agendas (in their rejecting certain specific features of political liberalism), and in this sense it could be seen as a thin-centred ideology. Specifically, illiberalism displays a revulsion for pluralism and individualism.[21] These traits are supposedly atomising society and disrupting meaningful social bonds by replacing the communal order with a 'chilly, egoistical, and morally hollow one'.[22]

As illiberals rally around conservative understandings of gender and family and partake in that kind of 'gender policy backsliding',[23] or 'war on gender',[24] the family becomes the stage where critical, almost eschatological, identity

[16] M. Laruelle, 'Illiberalism: A conceptual introduction' (2022) 38 East European Politics 306.

[17] N. Buckley and H. Foy, 'Poland's new government finds a model in Orban's Hungary' *Financial Times* (6 January 2016) <www.ft.com/content/0a3c7d44-b48e-11e5-8358-9a82b43f6b2f>.

[18] On which, see W. Grzebalska, 'Poland', in E. Kováts and M. Põim (eds), *Gender as Symbolic Glue: The Position and Role of Conservative and Far Right Parties in the Anti-gender Mobilizations in Europe* (FEPS – Foundation for European Progressive Studies 2015).

[19] See Laruelle (n 16) 303. See also J. Dawson and S. Hanley, 'What's wrong with East-Central Europe? The fading mirage of the "liberal consensus"' (2016) 27 Journal of Democracy 21.

[20] A. Jakab and D. Kochenov, 'Introductory remarks' in A. Jakab and D. Kochenov (eds), *The Enforcement of EU Law and Values: Ensuring Member States' Compliance* (Oxford University Press 2017), describing a 'spectrum of non-compliance'.

[21] See generally, M.-L. Frick, 'Illiberalims and human rights' in Sajó, Uitz, and Holmes (n 15) 861.

[22] S. Holmes, 'The antiliberal idea' in Sajó, Uitz, and Holmes (n 15) 3–15.

[23] A. Krizsan and C. Roggeband, 'Towards a conceptual framework for struggles over democracy in backsliding states: Gender equality policy in Central Eastern Europe' (2018) 6 Politics and Governance 90.

[24] E. Korolczuk, '"The war on gender" from a transnational perspective: Lessons for feminist strategising' in *Anti-gender Movements on the Rise? Strategising for Gender Equality in Central*

struggles are waged.[25] The illiberal script explicitly attributes the collapse of national identity to the collapse of traditional gender and family norms.[26] It flatly rejects interpretations of family and women's roles in society that allegedly contradict nature.[27] It is to these distorted and 'unnatural' understandings of family, gender, and sexual orientation that, for example, Polish illiberal actors refer to as the 'ebola from Brussels'.[28]

Similar discourses derive nourishment from opposition to Brussels. More broadly, they tend to stress the existence of an external power that seeks to impose exotic legal reforms which clash with local *mores*. Such external powers are dubbed differently depending on the geographical context and the aim that the invoked opposition is seeking to achieve. They are variously labelled as 'the West', 'the Communist regime', 'the European Union', and 'liberal élites'.[29] A recurring criticism is, for instance, that these powerful elites are carrying out a global 'sexual revolution' to reduce population growth and destroy traditional societies.[30]

To assess the role of the family within illiberal agendas, one also has to look at how illiberalism welds together with the notion of familism. Familism is a polysemous term that inter alia refers to an ideology that values the family over other social bonds.[31] It furthermore refers to discursive construction of an abstract family model that acts as an ideal for other social institutions,

and Eastern Europe (Heinrich Böll Stiftung 2014) <https://pl.boell.org/sites/default/files/uploads/2014/10/war_on_gender_korolczuk.pdf>.

25 A. Pető, 'Gender and illiberalism' in Sajó, Uitz, and Holmes (n 15) 313–325. Interestingly, some authors point to the replacement of the rights of the individual with the rights of a narrowly defined family as part and parcel of a larger systematic attempt to weaken democracy through anti-gender policies. See, for example, E. Lombardo, J. Kantola, and R. Rubio-Marin, 'De-democratization and opposition to gender equality politics in Europe' (2021) 28 Social Politics 521.

26 See, for example, N. Yuval-Davis, 'Gender and nation' (1997) 16 Ethnic and Racial Studies 621.

27 By now it is becoming established that 'gender' is integral to illiberal projects although the centrality of these norms slipped under the radar of research for many years. See R. Kuhar and D. Paternotte, *Anti-Gender Campaigns in Europe: Mobilizing against Equality* (Rowman & Littlefield 2017); S. Mancini and N. Palazzo, 'The body of the nation: Illiberalism and gender' in Sajó, Uitz, and Holmes (n 15) 406.

28 E. Korolczuk and A. Graff, 'Gender as "Ebola from Brussels": The anticolonial frame and the rise of illiberal populism' (2018) 43 Signs: Journal of Women in Culture and Society 797.

29 Ibid.

30 G. Kuby, *The Global Sexual Revolution: Destruction of Freedom in the Name of Freedom* (James Patrick Kirchner tr, Angelico Press 2015).

31 E. Ochiai, 'Introduction: Reconstruction of intimate and public spheres in Asian modernity' in E. Ochiai and L. Aoi Hosoya (eds), *Transformation of the Intimate and the Public in Asian Modernity* (Kyoto University Press 2013) (describing how it simply refers to policies that emphasise family obligations, such as care work). But see Linnamäki (n 15) 18 on the different nuances of the term.

including the state.[32] Familism per se is not necessarily problematic. Illiberal actors across Europe, however, seem to be appropriating the ideology of familism to achieve objectives that often transcend family politics – and are more connected to those majoritarian aspirations that characterise illiberalism. Diluting the rights of family members therein, especially women, is one of such aspirations. As Korolczuk and Graff put it, illiberalism is 'constructing a new universalism … that replaces individual rights with rights of the family as a basic societal unit'.[33] An instrumental recourse to familism is evidenced by the fact that this family-centred ideology does not always translate into actual family policies. By and large, it 'acts as an ideological base to which states and policy makers can refer to, to justify their decisions in matters that often exceed the scope of family politics'.[34]

Illiberal ideological familism[35] is detrimental to non-traditional families, particularly LGBTQ families. For example, research shows how ideological familism was discursively mobilised in the debate preceding the enactment of the new Hungarian law on 'paedophilia' targeting the LGBTQ community.[36] On that occasion, through this strategic embrace, Hungary's ruling Fidesz–KDNP Party Alliance sought to demonise the LGBTQ community by depicting it as a threat to innocent children and LGBTQ families as more prone to child abuse.[37] It is also potentially detrimental to families that align with the illiberal model of family to the extent that illiberal attitudes are reproduced *within* this type of traditional family and can prove harmful to women and children.

A second analytically useful notion to understand the illiberal enterprise is that of familialism. If familism emphasises the centrality of the family in rights talk, this second notion – 'familialism' – links the family to national demographics and reproductive needs. German sociologist Andreas Kemper refers

32 O. Tóth and C. Dupcsik, 'Trust in people and conservatism of family and gender roles in Hungary and in some other European countries' (2011) 1 Journal of Intimate and Public Spheres 152, 153.

33 Korolczuk and Graff (n 28) 789.

34 Linnamäki (n 15) 16, citing D. Szikra and D. Szelewa, 'Do Central and Eastern European countries fit the "Western" picture? The example of family policies in Hungary and Poland' in C. Klenner and S. Leiber (eds), *Welfare States and Gender Inequality in Central and Eastern Europe: Continuity and Post-socialist Transformation in the EU Member States* (European Trade Union Institute 2010).

35 By the term, I refer to the strategic embrace of ideological familism by illiberal actors.

36 LXXIX Act of 2021 on stricter measures against paedophile offenders and amending certain laws to protect children, entered into force in January 2022.

37 For a description of the political background that led to the adoption of the law, see A. Pető, 'Three readings of one law: Reregulating sexuality in Hungary' (*LSE EUROPP blog*, 8 July 2021) <https://blogs.lse.ac.uk/europpblog/2021/07/06/three-readings-of-one-law-reregulating-sexuality-in-hungary/>.

to familialism as a form of biopolitics that takes 'a strictly standardised image of a 'functioning family'' as a foundational unit of the nation.[38] This ideology simultaneously subordinates individual choice to the normative demands of the reproduction of the nation. It comes across as a new form of gender conservativism that singles out a 'limited, population-biological-national, and normative idea of the family' to pursue national population policy.[39]

Below I offer an overview of the ideological usage of the family in the two textbook cases of Hungary and Poland. As it will be noted, these developments pose a direct challenge to the EU and its attempt to uphold in its *acquis* more progressive understandings of family that include protection of LGBTQ couples.

12.3 HUNGARY

With Fidesz's 2010 Manifesto (*Nemzeti ügyek politikája*), the family gained a new centrality in the illiberal discourse in Hungary.[40] The Manifesto suggests that past liberal governments neglected families, giving in to the allure of the sirens of modernity, progressivism, and neoliberalism. According to Orbán, who repeatedly referred to a failure of the state to prevent families from 'falling into debt slavery', the collapse of the family is visible both at the conceptual and the financial level.[41] Its conceptual and financial breakdown contributed to the weakening of the nation.[42] The restoration of the centrality of families and family policies hence goes hand in hand with a conviction that working families contribute to the well-functioning of the nation, so policies 'should be directed there'.[43] It furthermore operates within the larger project of 'symbolic-constitutive rejection of the liberal left as illegitimate to rule or participate in (defining "real") democracy'.[44]

Fidesz's discourse around gender and family has evolved over time. Scholarship has identified two phases, 2010–2014 and 2014–2018, in which

38 A. Kemper, 'Foundation of the nation. How political parties and movements are radicalising others in favour of conservative family values and against tolerance, diversity, and progressive gender politics in Europe' (Friedrich Ebert Stiftung 2016) <http://library.fes.de/pdf-files/dialog/12503.pdf>.

39 Ibid 60.

40 See, for example, Fidesz, *Nemzeti ügyek politikája* (2010) <www.langzsolt.hu/upl/files/nemzeti_ugyek_politikaja_8481.pdf>, 10, 12, 20, 74.

41 N. V. T. Lugosi, 'Radical right framing of social policy in Hungary: Between nationalism and populism' (2018) 34 Journal of International and Comparative Social Policy 224.

42 Ibid.

43 Ibid 223, citing Fidesz's 2010 Manifesto (n 40) 76.

44 E. Palonen, 'Performing the nation: The Janus-faced populist foundations of illiberalism in Hungary' (2018) 26 Journal of Contemporary European Studies 316.

the party emphasised different aspects to create a structural link between the Hungarian national identity and the family.[45] From 2010 to 2014, a first connection was established between the people of Hungary and Christianity, seen as the origin of morals and social norms. According to Orbán, the economic crisis of 2008 was caused by a moral crisis, and addressing the former required first and foremost addressing the latter.[46] Noting a worrisome disentanglement of work, credit, family, and nation from the moral foundations of the 'Christian' nation, Orbán pledged to reconstruct the link between the two by foregrounding families as the central target of state policy. According to Robert Sata, a researcher who conducted a systematic discourse analysis of Orbán's speeches from 2010 to 2018:

> [u]sing this logic, the Fidesz government has not only enshrined 'the family' as a marriage between a man and a woman into the constitution but it also clearly defines the role of women in its vision for Hungary and the ideal Hungarian family – they should stay at home to rear enough children to form a strong Hungarian nation. This is because, for Orbán, the demographic downturn in Hungary is as important as fighting the economic crisis, because it threatens the future of the community, making Hungarians 'an endangered species'.[47]

Between 2014 and 2019, another aspect gained traction, namely the strong anti-immigration stance of the ruling Fidesz–KDNP Party Alliance. This posture was achieved by linking Christianity more closely with national identity – beyond a mere matter of personal faith. It was, furthermore, achieved by reconstructing the role of women within society. Women were notably called upon to restore their traditional function as the bearers of reproductive capacities.[48] They were reminded of their larger responsibility towards the continuation of the Hungarian nation. In the last few years, gender-related rights in the country suffered from a setback, as exemplified by the replacement of gender mainstreaming policies with family mainstreaming policies and by the reconceptualisation of the role of women in society into mere mothers. A setback was furthermore illustrated by the observed

45 R. Sata, 'In the name of the family' (Gunda Werner Institut – Heinrich Böll Stiftung 2022) <www.gwi-boell.de/en/2022/01/31/im-namen-der-familie-wie-populistinnen-ungarn-gegen-geschlechtergleichstellung>.

46 Ibid 7–8.

47 Ibid 10, n 55.

48 On the link between women and the biological reproduction of the nation, see A. McClintock, 'Family feuds: Gender, nationalism and the family' (1993) 44 Feminist Review 61.

decline in women's reporting of sexual violence, due to a hostile environment created through genderphobic policies.[49]

In this second phase, the opposition against Brussels elites also became more overt. The EU, feminism, and liberalism have been blamed for low birth rates, and for imposing a 'gender agenda' that blurs natural boundaries by 'creating a third gender, ... ridiculing faith, and regard[ing] families as redundant, and nations as obsolete'.[50]

A key year in this phase is 2019. Fidesz dubbed 2019 as 'the year of the family'.[51] In 2019, Fidesz passed the Family Protection Action Plan.[52] The reform came as the outgrowth of the described centrality of family in the project of national reconstruction launched with the 2010 party's Manifesto. The Plan included a vast array of social welfare policies aimed at supporting families, spanning preferential housing loan or 'baby-expecting allowance' ('babaváró támogatás'), tax breaks for mothers of at least four children, crèche service, and childcare allowance for working grandparents.[53] While these policies pursue commendable goals, the European Commission, in its assessment of the measures, expressed some concerns. Especially, it pointed to the fact that the baby-expecting allowance was only available to married couples, and that in case of divorce the loan contract must be terminated (since marriage is an eligibility condition).[54]

By and large, whereas public spending on family policies has doubled since 2010,[55] it is targeted at very specific groups, such as large families. Roma families do not profit from the different family programmes, even though they are the group most affected by poverty.[56] Their exclusion is premised on the ruling party's aspiration to link family policies with anti-immigration policies. It also seems consistent with the state objective of boosting Hungarian demographic indicators. These exclusionary policies seem to dovetail with the notion of 'welfare chauvinism' under which welfare spending can be appropriated

[49] K. Parti, 'Illiberal and populist political narratives on gender and underreporting of sexual violence: A case study of Hungary' (2022) 10 Politics and Governance 26. For a description of the gender-phobic climate, see J. Takács, K. Fobear, and S. Schmitsek, 'Resisting genderphobia in Hungary' (2022) 10 Politics and Governance 38.

[50] See Sata (n 45) 16, n 99.

[51] E. Zimanyi, 'Family b/Orders: Hungary's campaign for the "family protection action plan"' (2020) 20 Feminist Media Studies 305.

[52] Ibid 305.

[53] See Sata (n 45) 16, n 99.

[54] Ibid 3.

[55] A. Irion, 'Family first: Exclusionary social policy in Orban's Hungary' (*Illiberalism.Org*, 31 March 2022) <www.illiberalism.org/family-first-exclusionary-social-policy-in-orbans-hungary/>.

[56] See Lugosi (n 41) 210.

to draw the boundaries of authentic citizens and exclude 'others'[57] – a posture that aligns with the idea of a 'ethno-exclusionary welfare state'.[58]

Even more than welfare law, it is constitutional law that has been at the heart of the illiberal promotion of the traditional family. The year 2021 marks the entry into force of major constitutional amendments aimed at entrenching traditional notions of family. The ideological context in which the amendments were passed made explicit the intent of relying on biological evidence in constructing family ties and not international trends or ideologies in relation to childbearing.[59] The 2011 text elevated the family and the nation to the status of 'cornerstones of co-existence, with loyalty, faith and love constituting the principal values of unity',[60] and attempted to recast the family as an institution of national relevance.[61] The 2020 Ninth Amendment of the Fundamental Law claims that '[t]he mother shall be a woman, the father shall be a man'[62] in an attempt to render the gender identity of the parents of a child immutably linked to their biological sex. Under Article XVI, 'Hungary shall protect the right of children to a self-identity corresponding to their sex at birth, and shall ensure an upbringing for them that is in accordance with the values based on the constitutional identity and Christian culture of our country'. Ultimately, the definition of family refers to the heteronormative relationship of two adults of different sex founded on marriage complemented by the nuclear component. The entrenchment of the traditional family is hence total and covers both the sexual orientation of the parents, the gender identity of family members, and the nuclear imperative.

These brief notes should explain the broader context of the emergence of the Hungarian child protective law that targets LGBTQ people equating them to paedophiles, recently challenged by the EU.[63] It furthermore illustrates the marked centrality of the family in the Hungarian illiberal discourse.

57 J. Mewes and S. Mau, 'Unraveling working-class welfare chauvinism' in S. Svallfors (ed), *Contested Welfare States: Welfare Attitudes in Europe and Beyond* (Stanford University Press 2012) 136 (noting that this approach is consistent with generally held views amongst the population aimed at restricting benefits to Hungarians). See also N. Lendvai-Bainton and D. Szelewa, 'Governing new authoritarianism: Populism, nationalism and radical welfare reforms in Hungary and Poland' (2021) 55 Social Policy & Administration 559.

58 Lendvai-Bainton and Szelewa (n 57) 563.

59 At the same time, the amendment argued that the new definition is without prejudice to existing same-sex registered partnerships and the rights thereof, reaffirming as it does only a different conception of marriage that defies current ideological trends exogenous to the country's culture.

60 Fundamental Law 25 April 2011 (Government of Hungary), 2&5.

61 D. Szikra, 'Democracy and welfare in hard times: The social policy of the Orbán Government in Hungary between 2010 and 2014' (2014) 24 Journal of European Social Policy 486.

62 Article 1, Ninth Amendment to the Fundamental Law (Magyarország Alaptörvényének kilencedik módosítása) 15 December 2020 (Government of Hungary).

63 See Section 12.5.

12.4 POLAND

> The Polish tradition, the Polish republican tradition, the Polish tradition of freedom, so Poland is an island of freedom, because this freedom in Western Europe today is retreating. Today, for saying the obvious, that there can be no children from a homosexual couple, you can face a criminal trial in some countries. This will not be accepted in Poland under any circumstances, as they say in Podhale.[64]

Podhale is a conservative region in the South Polish mountains where the Górale population live. By referring to it, Kaczynski suggests that something will never be accepted due to the conservativism of the region. In a series of statements delivered in September 2019, Kaczynski foregrounded the family as the centrepiece of Polish society. In his view, families should be understood to refer to a self-evident entity comprising 'one man, one woman, in a lasting relationship, and their children. This is a family'.[65]

The rhetoric employed by the ruling party in Poland follows a script similar to that employed in Hungary. First, the welfare system is crucial for re-establishing the lost centrality of the family. Its rediscovered centrality is best exemplified by the so-called 500+ Policy. The program is the 'the most expensive and wide-scale redistribution policy in post-1989 Poland'[66] and was introduced to reverse negative trends in demographics.[67] Under the program, every family receives a 500 Zloty (around 105 euro) tax-free monthly payout per each second and subsequent children under eighteen, independent of the family income. Under certain conditions, non-citizen residents can join the program.[68] The program received generally positive reviews due to its contribution to increasing fertility and combating poverty. At the same time,

[64] 'Jarosław Kaczyński uzupełnił definicję rodziny i przyznał, co w Polsce się nie przyjmie' (*Ofeminin*, 9 September 2019) <www.ofeminin.pl/swiat-kobiet/zycie-rodzinne/jaroslaw-kaczynski-uzupelnil-definicje-rodziny-na-konwencji-w-krakowie/5y1crvr>.

[65] It was reported that, after receiving criticism, Kaczynski responded by extending his definition of family to include single parents and families with adopted children with adoption being accepted as a gracious and selfless act. 'Jarosław Kaczyński o Rodzinie: Kobieta,Mężczyzna i Ich Dzieci' *Politika* (7 September 2019) <https://wpolityce.pl/polityka/462852-jaroslaw-kaczynski-o-rodziniekobietamezczyzna-i-ich-dzieci>. See E. Korolczuk and A. Graff, '"Worse than Communism and Nazism put together": War on gender in Poland' in Kuhar and Paternotte (n 27).

[66] W. Grzebalska and A. Pető, 'The gendered modus operandi of the illiberal transformation in Hungary and Poland' (2018) 68 Women's Studies International Forum 164.

[67] Ibid 167.

[68] 'Rodzina 500 plus – Ministerstwo Rodziny i Polityki Społecznej' (*Portal Gov.pl*, 22 March 2023) <www.gov.pl/web/rodzina/rodzina-500-plus>; '500+ Child Benefit in Poland | Kids in the City' (*Kidsinthecity.pl*, 6 February 2022) <https://kidsinthecity.pl/500-plus-child-benefit-in-poland/>.

however, the EU Commission expressed concerns over the effects an additional non-work income can yield on the participation in the labour market. The Commission noticed that, according to the most recent statistics, the program incentivised workers with low wages to stay at home,[69] and that women find themselves at higher risk of dropout from the labour force as they bear the highest burden of caregiving duties.[70]

A second common trait between Poland and Hungary is the idea that families are entrusted with a host of communitarian goals, including the goal of transmitting the 'culture of civilization, for the sustainability of larger communities'.[71] Notwithstanding their important social function, family units are seen as being systematically under attack.[72]

Recasting the family as the central target of state policy first entails a reconceptualisation of the role of women in society. A recent report of the United Nations (UN) notes the 'pervasive and flagrant stereotyping of women, including by some political leaders, as unsuited to political power and the insistence on a woman's role as primarily wife and mother' ensuing from similar policies.[73] It secondly leads to a new emphasis on family mainstreaming, similarly to what occurred in Hungary, and to erasing the term 'gender' from the government agenda. Grzebalska and Petö describe 'family mainstreaming and anti-gender policies [as] one of the main pillars on which the illiberal state has been erected, and through which security, equality and human rights have been redefined'.[74] The Family 500 Plus policy described above can also be interpreted through a similar lens.

A key battle of illiberal actors in the area of sexuality and reproduction is also waged on the scholastic front.[75] In Poland, a new school subject called 'History and the Present' was recently introduced. The subject aims at better portraying Polish history and society and will soon be taught in schools all over Poland with a (controversial) mandatory handbook.[76] One specific section in

69 European Commission, 'First results of Poland's Family 500+ programme released' (16 May 2018) <https://ec.europa.eu/social/main.jsp?langId=en&catId=1246&newsId=9104&furtherNews=yes>.

70 Ibid.

71 Ibid.

72 See also 'Jarosław Kaczyński: dla PiS najważniejsze są rodzina oraz naród' (*PR24 Portal – polskieradio24.pl*, 7 September 2019) <https://polskieradio24.pl/5/1222/artykul/2365079,jaroslaw-kaczynski-dla-pis-najwazniejsze-sa-rodzina-oraz-narod>.

73 UN Working Group on the issue of discrimination against women in law and in practice, 'Mission report' (United Nations 2016) <www.ohchr.org/EN/NewsEvents>.

74 See Grzebalska and Pető (n 66) 164 (abstract).

75 See N. Palazzo and M. Tomasi, 'I referendum in materia di diritti delle coppie omosessuali: Minoranze e vox populi' (2016) 1 GenIUS 89.

76 The handbook is authored by historian Wojciech Roszkowski.

the book drew the criticism of the opposition parties and civil society, since it frames in-vitro fertilisation as human breeding. The contested passages refer to 'the creation of arbitrary groups of people sometimes of the same sex, who will bring children into the world separately from the natural union of man and woman, most preferably in a laboratory'.[77] The book voices a larger criticism to Western ideology and its embedded trends affecting family relationships. The main targets of criticism are the contemporary separation of sex from love and fertility (i.e. reproduction), and the degrading of sex to a mere leisure activity. These trends are in turn described as damaging for children who are, as a consequence, left stranded and deprived of the love of parents.[78]

Ultimately, constitutional discourse is also mobilised by Polish illiberal actors. The concept of family appears in numerous provisions of the Constitution. Relevant provisions state that the family is under the protection and guardianship of the Republic of Poland. The family is constructed narrowly as comprising a man and a woman who are married,[79] as well as their children and relatives on both sides. Furthermore, the Constitution enshrines the right of parents to raise their children according to their personal convictions,[80] and the right of the child to be protected against demoralisation.[81]

With conservative family norms being entrenched at the constitutional level, regressive policies are mostly advocated for at the local level, where a form of 'regressive' experimentation occurs. The main example in this regard is the Charter of Family Rights drafted by the influential far-right, Catholic think tank Ordo Iuris Institute for Legal Culture.[82] The Charter of Family Rights supplies a model law for local governments to enact local policies aimed at combating fake news informed by an 'LGBT ideology' – as well as the 'political correctness' of the EU. According to Ordo Iuris, similar deplorable ideas are spread by the EU and other international organisations, such as OSCE.[83] In the aftermath of the European Parliament resolution

77 J. Dobrosz-Oracz, '"Jest świetny, bo niepolscy Polacy się denerwują". Jak Rydzyk wychwalał HiT, a Czarnek kiwał głową' (*wyborcza.pl*, 8 December 2022, <https://wyborcza.pl/7,82983,28784865,jest-swietny-bo-niepolscy-polacy-jak-sie-denerwuja-jak-rydzyk.html>.

78 Ibid.

79 Article 18 of the Constitution of the Republic of Poland (Konstytucja Rzeczypospolitej Polskiej) of 1997 (Constitution of Poland).

80 Article 48(1) of the Constitution of Poland.

81 Article 72(1) of the Constitution of Poland.

82 O. Iuris, 'Local government charter of the rights of the family' (*ordoiuris.pl*, 29 March 2019) <https://en.ordoiuris.pl/family-and-marriage/local-government-charter-rights-family>.

83 See, for example, O. Iuris, 'Fake news about "LGBT-free zones" results in a proliferation of lies about Poland. Ordo Iuris Steps In' (*ordoiuris.pl*, 22 July 2020) <https://en.ordoiuris.pl/family-and-marriage/fake-news-about-lgbt-free-zones-results-proliferation-lies-about-poland-ordo>.

condemning the Charter and the creation of LGBT-free zones – outlined in the section below – the Deputy Director of Ordo Iuris Center of International Law firmly defended this model law placing emphasis on familism, and on the Charter's ability to foster 'family-friendly law'.[84]

12.5 THE EU'S RESPONSE TO ILLIBERAL EROSION

In recent years, the Commission has taken legal action to protect the rights of the LGBTQ community in Hungary and Poland.[85] In Poland, the mentioned creation of 'zones free from LGBT ideology' has been at the centre of the EU's criticism. The problem was successfully linked to the possibility for Poland to receive European Structural and Investment Funds. In March 2021, the European Parliament voted in favour of a second resolution declaring the EU an 'LGBTIQ Freedom Zone',[86] and called upon the Polish government to revoke those local discriminatory declarations patterned after the Charter of Family Rights.[87] The Commission, furthermore, initiated talks with Polish local authorities expressing concerns for the adoption of similar declarations hostile to LGBTQ families. According to the Commission, these declarations especially run counter to the values enshrined in Article 2 of the Treaty on European Union (TEU) – respect for human dignity, freedom, democracy, equality, the rule of law, and respect for human rights, including the rights of persons belonging to minorities, as well as Article 7 of Regulation 1303/2013 on EU funding, prohibiting discrimination on several grounds, including sex and sexual orientation, 'during the preparation and implementation of programmes'.[88]

84 M. Olek, 'Ideological document attacking Poland – Ordo Iuris comment on European Parliament Resolution' (*ordoiuris.pl*, 2 January 2020) <https://en.ordoiuris.pl/family-and-marriage/magdalena-olek-ideological-document-attacking-poland-ordo-iuris-comment>.

85 European Commission, 'Commission takes legal action for discrimination LGBTIQ' Press release (July 2021) <https://ec.europa.eu/commission/presscorner/detail/en/ip_21_3668>.

86 European Parliament Resolution of 11 March 2021 on the declaration of the EU as an LGBTIQ Freedom Zone (2021/2557(RSP)). See also, European Parliament Resolution of 18 December 2019 on public discrimination and hate speech against LGBTI people, including LGBTI free zones (2019/2933(RSP)).

87 Recitals C–H of European Parliament Resolution of 11 March 2021 (n 86).

88 Article 7(2) of Regulation (EU) No 1303/2013 of the European Parliament and of the Council of 17 December 2013 laying down common provisions on the European Regional Development Fund, the European Social Fund, the Cohesion Fund, the European Agricultural Fund for Rural Development and the European Maritime and Fisheries Fund and laying down general provisions on the European Regional Development Fund, the European Social Fund, the Cohesion Fund and the European Maritime and Fisheries Fund and repealing Council Regulation (EC) No 1083/2006 [2013] OJ L347/320.

The Resolution of the European Parliament furthermore contains an important declaration of intent that points to the main advancements that the Union pledges to make in the forthcoming years. Recital X refers to 'the lack of legal provisions for the mutual recognition of a birth certificate with two same-sex parents' and a legislative initiative to close this legal gap, as well as 'a revision of the 2009 guidelines on free movement, both scheduled for 2022'.[89]

At the beginning of December 2022, the European Commission proposed new rules on the recognition of parenthood amongst Member States which would demand, inter alia, recognition of the parenthood of children of same-sex couples.[90] The proposal was submitted as part of the EU's strategy for the rights of the child as well as the EU's LGBTIQ Equality Strategy 2020–2025.[91] While the proposal does not explicitly link the reform to the deterioration of the rule of law in Poland and Hungary, its approval would inevitably limit the ability of the Member States to pass laws that adversely affect the legal status of children and parents in LGBTQ families by preventing the recognition of family ties established abroad.[92] For this reason, one can anticipate an obstruction of the proposal by countries like Poland and Hungary.[93] Given the requirement of unanimity in the Council, Poland and Hungary can exercise their veto power and prevent the proposal from ever becoming legally binding.[94]

89 Recital X of EP Resolution of 11 March 2021 (n 86).

90 European Commission, Proposal for a Council regulation on jurisdiction, applicable law, recognition of decisions and acceptance of authentic instruments in matters of parenthood and on the creation of a European Certificate of Parenthood, COM (2022) 695 final.

91 Ibid 1 (Explanatory Memorandum). See European Commission, Communication from the Commission to the European Parliament, the Council, the European Economic and Social Committee and the Committee of the Regions. EU Strategy on the rights of the child, COM (2021) 142 final; European Commission, Communication from the Commission to the European Parliament, the Council, the European Economic and Social Committee and the Committee of the Regions. Union of Equality: LGBTIQ Equality Strategy 2020–2025, COM (2020) 698 final.

92 C. Bennett, 'European Commission seeks to enshrine same-sex parents' rights' *Politico* (7 December 2022) <www.politico.eu/article/european-commission-try-to-enshrine-same-sex-parental-right> (describing the regulation as an 'initiative [which] is particularly targeted at protecting the rights of same-sex parents who move through the EU with their children – a goal that could irk EU countries like Hungary and Poland, which have passed anti-LGBTQ+ resolutions in recent years').

93 A legal obligation to mutually recognise the parenthood of a child by two persons of the same sex for the purpose of rights derived from EU law already derives from the case law of the CJEU. Case C-490/20 *V.M.A. v Stolichna obshtina, rayon 'Pancharevo'* EU:C:2021:1008. See also Chapter 9 by Geoffrey Willems.

94 Article 81(3) TFEU.

A surprising development is the recent decision of the Commission to launch an infringement procedure against Hungary and its child protective anti-LGBTQ law. The reform introduced a prohibition to expose minors to content related to homosexuality and gender reassignment, restricted daytime display on TV on content related to these topics, and limited the ability to provide sex education in school to only certain listed organisations. The Children Protection Act's declared objective is to increase sanctions against paedophile offenders. At the time of the enactment of the law, the European Commission noted that '[t]he protection of children is an absolute priority for the EU and its Member States. However, the Hungarian law contains provisions which are not justified on the basis of promoting this fundamental interest or are disproportionate to achieve the stated objective'.[95] Similarly, Ursula von der Leyen expressed concerns in relation to the reform, noting that it 'clearly discriminates against people on the basis of their sexual orientation and ... goes against all the values, the fundamental values, of the European Union'.[96]

The most problematic aspect of the law is that it conflates paedophilia with homosexuality.[97] During the parliamentary discussion preceding its enactment, an analogy was drawn between exposing children to queer gender and the issue of child abuse by LGBTQ families, thereby 'evok[ing] the historically widespread myth that non-heteronormative sexualities and child abuse are inevitably connected'.[98] As argued by conservative member of the Hungarian National Assembly János Volner, 'the LGBTQ movement has more than once been involved in similar scandals'.[99]

A new law passed in April 2023 further corroborates the idea that the hidden objective of the reform is to harm the LGBTQ community, particularly LGBTQ families: the Whistleblowing Act would have allowed citizens to anonymously report to authorities gay and lesbian couples who raise children,

95 'Brussels Takes Hungary to Court on Anti-LGBT Law and Klubrádió' *Euronews* (15 July 2022) <www.euronews.com/my-europe/2022/07/15/european-commission-takes-hungary-to-court-over-anti-lgbt-law-and-klubradio-closure>.

96 L. Hutchinson, 'EU Member States express 'grave concern' over Hungary's LGBTIQ discrimination' *The Parliament* (23 June 2021) <www.theparliamentmagazine.eu/news/article/eu-member-states-express-grave-concern-over-hungarys-lgbtiq-discrimination>.

97 See n 36, 37 and accompanying text.

98 See Linnamäki (n 16) 21.

99 Government of Hungary, 'A pedofil bűnelkövetőkkel szembeni szigorúbb fellépésről, valamint a gyermekek védelme érdekében egyes törvények módosításáról szóló előterjesztés általános vitája a lezárásig' ['General Debate on the proposal for stricter measures against paedophile offenders and amending certain laws to protect children until its closure'], Parliamentary Diary, 206(1), 2021, 30309.

and any family arrangement that offends the traditional family as enshrined in the Constitution.[100] The law has then been vetoed by the president of Hungary, Katalin Novak.

What is relevant to the present analysis is that, for the first time, in February 2023, the Commission proposed a standalone plea based on Article 2 TEU, which lists the values of the Union, to challenge the Hungarian law. The toolkit aimed at countering rule of law deterioration is expanding. The nuclear option[101] under Article 7 TEU did not prove so nuclear in the end due to its burdensome and lengthy procedures, including the vote of the European Council by unanimity to establish 'the existence of a serious and persistent breach'. In the face of a failure to utilise this procedure, the EU has been seeking workarounds. Amongst them is the use of infringement actions,[102] and of Regulation 2020/2092 on a general regime of conditionality for the protection of the Union budget, which makes EU funds contingent on the respect of the rule of law.[103] The budget Conditionality Regulation has been 'validated' by the Court and – acting in tandem with a 'multitude' of other existing conditionality mechanisms – is likely to constitute an important tool for ensuring compliance with rule of law values through the powerful leverage of withholding EU funds.[104]

As to the infringement actions, these are proving the barycentre of the EU's response to illiberal erosion. In a first phase, the Commission brought 'indirect' infringement actions to counter democratic backsliding in Hungary – in the sense that it did not explicitly link these actions to the rule of law.[105]

[100] V. Gulyas and M. Kasnyik, 'Hungary's new law lets locals report on same-sex families' *Bloomberg* (13 April 2023) <www.bloomberg.com/news/articles/2023-04-13/hungary-s-new-law-allows-locals-to-report-on-same-sex-families>. The veto could have been overruled by Parliament. L. Kijewski, 'Hungarian president vetoes anti-LGBTQ law' *Politico* (22 April 2023) <www.politico.eu/article/hungary-president-katalin-novak-vetoes-viktor-orban-anti-lgbtq-law/>.

[101] Gulyas and Kasnyik (n 100). The law has recently been vetoed by the president of Hungary, Katalin Novak. The veto can be overruled by Parliament. Kijewski (n 100).

[102] M. Schmidt and P. Bogdanowicz, 'The infringement procedure in the rule of law crisis: How to make effective use of Article 258 TFEU' (2018) 55 Common Market Law Review 1061.

[103] Regulation (EU, Euratom) No 2020/2092 of the European Parliament and of the Council of 16 December 2020 on a general regime of conditionality for the protection of the Union budget [2020] OJ L433/1.

[104] Case C-156/21 *Hungary v Parliament and Council* EU:C:2022:97; Case C-157/21 *Poland v Parliament and Council* EU:C:2022:98. On how the EU is effectively using a series of conditionality mechanisms in parallel to the conditionality regulation, see K. Lane Sheppele and J. Morijn, 'Frozen, how the EU is blocking funds to Hungary and Poland using a multitude of conditionalities' (*VerfBlog*, 4 April 2023) <https://verfassungsblog.de/frozen/>.

[105] M. Dawson and E. Muir, 'Hungary and the indirect protection of EU fundamental rights and the rule of law' (2013) 14 German Law Journal 1959. See also G. Halmai, 'The early retirement age of the Hungarian judges' in F. Nicola and B. Davis (eds), *EU Law Stories:*

Recently, however, the Commission has pursued 'direct' infringement actions that more explicitly counter rule of law deterioration,[106] based on the Charter or Article 19 TEU (protecting judicial independence).[107]

The use of a standalone plea based on Article 2 is a new move, described by commentators as nothing short of 'revolutionary'.[108] The move occurs against the backdrop of a lively scholarly debate on whether this plea was possible and, if so, normatively desirable.[109] The plea is included in a *prima facie* routine infringement proceeding against the child protective anti-LGBQT law. It points to Hungary's failure to comply with the Audiovisual Media Services Directive (AVMSD)[110] – protecting minors from inappropriate content in on-demand media audiovisual services – and certain EU law provisions on

Contextual and Critical Histories of European Jurisprudence (Cambridge University Press 2017) 471.

106 European Commission, 'Strengthening the rule of law within the Union – A blueprint for action' COM (2019) 343 final.

107 M. Bonelli, 'Infringement Actions 2.0: How to protect EU values before the Court of Justice' (2022) 18 European Constitutional Law Review 31. See Case C-619/18 *Commission v Poland* EU:C:2019:531; on which see L. Pech and D. Kochenov, 'Respect for the rule of law in the case law of the European Court of Justice: A casebook overview of key judgments since the Portuguese judges case' SIEPS 2021:3 <www.sieps.se/globalassets/publikationer/2021/sieps-2021_3-eng-web.pdf?>, 74; see also Case C-791/19 *Commission v Poland* EU C:2021:596.

108 L. D. Spieker, 'Berlaymont is back: The Commission invokes Article 2 TEU as self-standing plea in infringement proceedings over Hungarian LGBTIQ rights violations' (*EU Law Live*, 22 February 2023) <https://eulawlive.com/op-ed-berlaymont-is-back-the-commission-invokes-article-2-teu-as-self-standing-plea-in-infringement-proceedings-over-hungarian-lgbtiq-rights-violations-by-luke-dimitrios-spieker/>. See also L. Kaiser, 'A new chapter in the European rule of law saga?' (*VerfBlog*, 4 March 2023) <https://verfassungsblog.de/a-new-chapter-in-the-european-rule-of-law-saga/>.

109 As to scholars voicing support for bringing systemic infringement actions based on Article 2, see K. Lane Scheppele, 'Enforcing the basic principles of EU law through systemic infringement actions' in C. Closa and D. Kochenov (eds), *Reinforcing Rule of Law Oversight in The European Union* (Cambridge University Press 2021); A. von Bogdandy and L. D. Spieker, 'Countering the judicial silencing of critics: Article 2 TEU values, reverse Solange, and the responsibilities of national judges' (2019) 15 European Constitutional Law Review 391; Schmidt and Bogdanowicz (n 102). As to positions sceptical towards this option due to the indeterminacy of the provision, see Bonelli (n 107) 57; P. Pohjankoski, 'Rule of law with leverage: Policing structural obligations in EU law with the infringement procedure, fines, and set-off' (2021) 58 Common Market Law Review 1341; T. Boekestein, 'Making do with what we have: On the interpretation and enforcement of the EU's founding values' (2022) 23 German Law Journal 431; Editorial Comments, 'Safeguarding EU values in the Member States – Is something finally happening?' (2015) 52 Common Market Law Review 625.

110 Directive 2010/13/EU of the European Parliament and of the Council of 10 March 2010 on the coordination of certain provisions laid down by law, regulation or administrative action in Member States concerning the provision of audiovisual media services (Audiovisual Media Services Directive) [2010] OJ L95/1.

services and e-commerce.[111] The pleas pivoting on the AVMSD also point to a violation of Articles 1, 7, 11, and 21 of the Charter, which protect the value of dignity, the respect for private and family life, the freedom of expression and information, and, ultimately, the right to non-discrimination inter alia based on sex and sexual orientation. Then, there is the mentioned succinct passage in the press statement according to which 'by adopting the legislation cited in the first paragraph, Hungary has infringed Article 2 TEU'.[112] It is unclear whether the Commission will link the Article 2 plea to the gravity of the Charter violations since the argument is not developed further. According to Bonelli, '[f]or the time being, it is sufficient to point out that the two formulations, taken at face value, seem to go in two slightly different directions: one where a violation of Article 2 TEU would result from a serious breach of several Charter rights; and one where the alleged infringement of the values of Article 2 TEU would constitute the actual alleged violation.'

This passage attests to the growing determination of the EU to tackle rule of law deterioration with a bite. The issue of protecting LGBTQ families as such looms over these developments, while failing to be openly foregrounded as central in the ongoing European culture wars. However, LGBTQ families seem to have gained enhanced constitutional relevance as a result of such developments. First, although the content of the Article 2 plea is not yet available, the infringement procedure summons the right to respect for private and family life and, hence, a negative sphere where LGBTQ people and, potentially, families should be protected. Second, the objective of the child protective law as one that seeks to 'shield' children from being exposed to LGBTQ populations is also flatly inconsistent with the ways in which the EU interprets the objective of protecting children as stated by Ursula von der Leyen.[113] Third, the move comes after the mentioned EU Parliament resolution discursively engaging Article 2 to discourage the adoption of the Charter of Family Rights in Poland, and previous attempts at using Article 2 as an interpretative device in the letter of formal notice against Hungary's child protective anti-LGBQT law.[114]

[111] Other invoked provisions include Article 3(2) of Directive 2000/31/EC of the European Parliament and of the Council of 8 June 2000 on certain legal aspects of information society services, in particular electronic commerce, in the Internal Market [2000] OJ L178/1; Articles 16 and 19 of Directive 2006/123/EC of the European Parliament and of the Council of 12 December 2006 on services in the internal market [2006] OJ L376/36; Article 56 TFEU.

[112] Action brought on 19 December 2022 in Case C-769/22 *Commission v Hungary* [2023] OJ C54/16.

[113] See n 95 and n 96.

[114] See Bonelli (n 107) 48.

The latest move of Orbán's government, allowing the reporting of LGBTQ couples with children and all families that offend the traditional model of family enshrined in the Constitution, as well as the emphasis placed during parliamentary debates on LGBTQ families being inherently abusive, could induce the Commission to lay focus on the delicate repercussions that the so-called child protective law has on LGBTQ relationships per se, not just on LGBTQ individuals. Put differently, the Commission is faced with the choice of either treating these parallel developments as mere background noise or as expression of a larger pattern pointing to systemic attempt to curtailing the rights of LGBTQ families as such.

In sum, recent moves by the EU, such as the ground-breaking utilisation of Article 2 TEU as a legally justiciable principle, may serve to reinforce the constitutional significance of LGBTQ families by sublimating the protection of an LGBTQ-friendly family at a higher level, so as to speak: the level of EU's common values.

At present, this sublimation will likely primarily affect such negative sphere of freedom. The described steps attest to the gradual expansion of an emerging EU constitutional family law as a consequence of the attraction of the negative liberties of LGBTQ families in the foundational values of the EU. A separate question is whether the area of common values will become a tool to expand the EU's competences and confer increased protection to LGBTQ families. For example, one may ask whether, in the future, the recognition of the legal ties of LGBTQ families through legal-regulatory regimes such as registered partnerships will also become a question that engages the EU's common values.[115] While illustrating this (now remote) possibility, the chapter does not take a position on the normative desirability of such an expansion.

[115] There is an established pattern in the protection of LGBTQ families that might point to an additional centrality of the LGBTQ family in this area named in legal scholarship the 'theory of small changes' or 'incrementalism'. K. Waaldijk, 'Small change: How the road to same-sex marriage got paved in the Netherlands' in R. Wintemute and M. Andenæs (eds), *Legal Recognition of Same-Sex Partnerships: A Study of National, European, and International Law* (Hart Publishing 2001) 437; W. N. Eskridge, Jr. *Equality Practice: Civil Unions and the Future of Gay Rights* (Routledge 2002); Y. Merin, *Equality for Same-Sex Couples: The Legal Recognition of Gay Partnerships in Europe and the United States* (Rowman & Littlefield 2002). According to this incremental pattern, the decriminalisation of homosexual behaviour is usually followed by the introduction of anti-discrimination laws protecting the LGBTQ community, and ultimately by the legalisation of same-sex legal partnerships. While this pattern concerns domestic jurisdictions, it is also observable in the framework of the European Convention on Human Rights, in which the European Court of Human Rights (ECtHR) recently released a ground-breaking decision identifying a Convention right to same-sex registered partnerships. *Fedotova and Others v Russia*, Application nos 40792/10, 30538/14 and 43439/10; *Buhuceanu and Others v Romania*, Application nos 20081/19 and 20 others.

12.6 CONCLUSION

As illiberal movements gain momentum across Europe, the EU faces new challenges that require an accelerated process of self-reflection. This chapter explored the ideological manipulation of the concept of family within illiberal regimes in Europe, and examined the Union's response to this erosion of liberal values. Surprisingly, the ongoing 'culture wars' over family norms between the EU, Hungary, and Poland have served as a catalyst for increasing the constitutional significance of the family within the EU.

Following the rise of illiberalism, the EU found itself in a prolonged state of confusion, struggling with a sense of uncertainty. Recently, the EU seems to be moving beyond this phase in an attempt to supply clearer answers as to 'what we are and what we want'.[116] It is noteworthy that family and child protection issues have become an integral part of this endeavour to define EU identity and its foundational values. The protection of the rights and freedoms of LGBTQ families and communities, in particular, has emerged as a key area that increasingly engages EU common values in both discourse and legal frameworks, as evidenced by the reactions to the declarations of the Polish Charter and Hungary's anti-LGBTQ child protection law. Recent developments provide an opportunity to pause and reflect on the unpredictable progress that has been made in recent years.

See also *Oliari and Others v Italy*, Application nos 18766/11 and 36030/11 (however, this judgement placed greater emphasis on the special circumstances of the Italian legal, social, and political context). The EU, of course, has a unique history and distinctive mission that might prevent this pattern from ever applying, but would it be completely unthinkable to have, ten years from now, a declaration to the effect that LGBTQ families as such are something that pertains to and deserve protection as a matter that engages European common values? The prediction of the attraction of LGBTQ legal partnerships in the area of the common values would not operate in a *vacuum*: it is corroborated by a linear progression in the EU's approach regarding the protection of LGBTQ families. The introduction of the EU Commission proposal on the cross-border recognition of parenthood also attests to this shift. The prediction is further strengthened by the concomitant shift in the case law of the ECtHR, whose *acquis* on fundamental rights 'constitute[s] general principles of the Union's law' under Article 6(3) TEU. It is ultimately corroborated by the growingly visible determination with which the Union is resolved to counter illiberal erosion.

[116] E. Montale, *Ossi di seppia* (Piero Gobetti 1925). This point does not engage with the issue of whether the EU will forge through its Article 2 plea a negative identity – whereby it draws lines against unwanted developments – or a more positive one. See Spieker (n 108).

13

Epilogue to the Family in EU Law

Is There a European Family Law?

JENS M. SCHERPE*

13.1 INTRODUCTION

This volume on 'The Family in EU Law' is an important and very timely contribution to an important debate. It follows up on Clare McGlynn's ground-breaking 'Families and the European Union'. Much has happened since McGlynn's 2006 book, but some things have not changed. The European Union (EU) still does not have legislative competence in the area of family law, and it probably never will. Nevertheless, the EU institutions and especially the Court of Justice of the European Union (CJEU) have increasingly had to deal with family matters, especially in the context of free movement of workers and cross-border cases more generally, as well as equality and non-discrimination. The EU Charter of Fundamental Rights has also begun to make an impact on families and family law, but is arguably still applied with too much trepidation.[1] In any event, the EU institutions and the CJEU have progressively utilised the competences that they do have, particularly to ensure the free movement of workers and non-discrimination in labour and social laws, with increasing impact on families and family law. Moreover, and as also will be addressed below, the 2019–2024 strategy and policy priority 'Promoting our European way of life' probably comprises significant family law aspects as well.[2]

* This contribution is partly based on the author's previous work: in particular, 'Marriage and the family' in L. Corrias and R. Tinnevelt (eds), *European Ways of Life: Legal and Philosophical Perspectives* (Edward Elgar Publishing, forthcoming), and 'Is there a 'European Family Law'?' (2023) 54 Victoria University of Wellington Law Review 317.

1 On the latter, see, for example, Chapter 6 by Gunnar Thor Petursson, Xavier Groussot, and Alezini Loxa.

2 European Commission, 'Promoting our European way of life: Protecting our citizens and our values' <https://commission.europa.eu/strategy-and-policy/priorities-2019–2024/promoting-our-european-way-life_en>.

The absence of a true and direct legislative competence on family law matters can explain that the family receives very little mention in the EU Treaties. Nevertheless, 'family' plays an important role in the above-mentioned contexts and is hugely relevant in many areas of EU law, as shown in many of the chapters in this book. This regularly necessitates a debate on what 'family' actually is, as well as what family-related terms like spouse, child, parent, and so on mean in the contexts in which they are used. It is fair to say that there is a significant divergence amongst Member States when it comes to understandings of 'family' and family law issues generally, making this an even more complicated and politicised area for the EU organs and institutions. Therefore, this book can make an important contribution to the development of this area of law.

This epilogue will first look at the 'dividing lines' in Europe, which have shifted significantly over the last decades. It then asks whether families are part of what (for better or worse) has been termed the 'European way of life', and if so, which families. Following this, this contribution then discusses whether despite the absence of a direct legislative competence, there are elements of a European or EU Family Law by looking at the notions of 'Institutional' and 'Organic' European/EU Family Law, concluding that while there is no universal definition of what is a 'family', there are elements of such definitions and indeed elements of a European Family Law and an EU Family Law.

13.2 FROM NORTH–SOUTH DIVIDE TO EAST–WEST DIVIDE

Historically, the dividing lines in family law used to be a reasonably clear divide between the 'progressive North' (leaving aside the Republic of Ireland and, to a certain extent, the jurisdictions of the UK) and the 'conservative South'. This can best be seen when examining the development of the law of divorce, where predominantly Protestant jurisdictions had a more liberal approach and introduced divorce (much) earlier compared to those that were/are predominantly Catholic. Even permitting divorce as such was controversial in the latter until relatively recently, with divorce only being possible in Italy since 1970, in Spain since 1981, and in the Republic of Ireland since 1996. Malta, the last European jurisdiction to introduce divorce, did so as late as 2011.[3] The development of divorce law in Europe has been described

[3] Thereby depriving private international law teachers of the last European example to easily create cases involving 'limping marriages'. While the Vatican, of course, still does not permit divorce, it is factually nearly impossible to construct good examples involving the Vatican for teaching purposes.

expertly by Masha Antokolskaia[4] and thus need not be repeated here. Unsurprisingly, although today there still is no uniformity as to the bases of divorce/divorce grounds, there are clear trends towards an understanding of marriage and the divorce process that gives the spouses greater autonomy to regulate their own affairs, including divorce. What also unites all European jurisdictions today is the move beyond allowing divorce exclusively based on fault.[5] Moreover, the trend towards greater autonomy of the spouses not only extends to the substantive divorce laws but also to the divorce process as such. In many jurisdictions in Europe, divorces no longer need to be pronounced by a court but are dealt with by administrative bodies or lawyers/notaries, thus dejuridifying the divorce process and removing it even further from state influence.[6] It is also interesting to note that the arguably most 'liberal' (i.e. permissive) divorce laws that allow divorce on the mere basis that one of the spouses requests this can be found in the North (e.g. Sweden and Finland), South (e.g. Spain), East (e.g. Russia), and West (e.g. England and Wales) of Europe. The development of the law of divorce thus exemplifies not only the withdrawal of the state from trying to control marriage by setting moralistic divorce requirements, but also the end of the 'classic' North–South divide in family law in Europe.

Arguably, this divide has now been replaced with an East–West divide as regards the institution of marriage and what often has been termed (wrongly, as these relationships have always existed) as 'new' family forms, especially same-sex relationships with or without children. The development of the recognition of same-sex relationships has been described elsewhere in greater depth.[7] For present purposes, it is sufficient to point out that this official recognition began with the emphatic statement of the Swedish *lagutskottet*

4 M. Antokolskaia, 'Divorce in a European perspective' in J. M. Scherpe (ed), *European Family Law Vol. III – Family Law in a European Perspective* (Edward Elgar Publishing 2016); M. Antokolskaia, *Harmonisation of Family Law in Europe: A Historical Perspective* (Intersentia 2006); M. Antokolskaia, 'The search for a common core of divorce law: State intervention v. spouses' autonomy' in M. Martín-Casals and J. Ribot (eds), *The Role of Self-determination in the Modernisation of Family Law in Europe* (Documenta Universitaria 2006); M. Antokolskaia, 'Convergence and divergence of divorce laws in Europe' (2006) 18 Child and Family Law Quarterly 307.

5 D. Martiny, 'Divorce and maintenance between former spouses – Initial results of the Commission in European Family Law' in K. Boele-Woelki (ed), *Perspectives for the Unification and Harmonisation of Family Law in Europe* (Intersentia 2003) 534.

6 On this, see the national reports in A. Dutta and others (eds), *Scheidung ohne Gericht?* (Gieseking 2017).

7 On this, see, for example, K. Boele-Woelki and A. Fuchs, *Same-Sex Relationships and Beyond* (Intersentia 2017); S. Cretney, *Same Sex Relationships from 'Odious Crime' to 'Gay Marriage'* (Oxford University Press 2006). For brief overviews, see, for example, J. M. Scherpe, 'Gleichgeschlechtliche Lebensgemeinschaften' in J. Basedow, K.-J. Hopt, and R. Zimmermann (eds), *Handwörterbuch des Europäischen Privatrechts* (Mohr Siebeck 2009);

(committee on legal affairs) in 1973 that 'from society's point of view, two persons of the same sex living together as a couple is a perfectly acceptable form of family life'.[8] The process continued with the introduction of registered partnerships in Denmark in 1989,[9] and culminated with the opening up of marriage to same sex couples twenty-eight years later with the Netherlands being the first jurisdiction to do so. Unlike in many non-European jurisdictions such as Canada,[10] the United States,[11] South Africa,[12] and Taiwan,[13] in Europe, this change was usually brought about through political and parliamentary initiatives[14] and not by court challenges,[15] although the motivation was the same: to end the discrimination against same-sex relationships.

J. M. Scherpe, 'Same-sex relationships' in J. Basedow, K.-J. Hopt, and R. Zimmermann (eds), *Max Planck Encyclopedia of European Private Law* (Oxford University Press 2012); J. M. Scherpe, 'From 'odious crime' to family life – same-sex couples and the ECHR' in A. Verbeke and others (eds), *Confronting the Frontiers of Family and Succession Law – Liber amicorum Walter Pintens* (Intersentia 2012); J. M. Scherpe, 'The legal recognition of same-sex couples in Europe and the role of the European Court of Human Rights' (2013) 10 The Equal Rights Review 83. See also the contributions in J. M. Scherpe and A. Hayward (eds), *The Future of Registered Partnerships – Family Recognition beyond Marriage?* (Intersentia 2017).

8 'Utskottet vill dock betona alt en samlevnad mellan två parter av samma kön är från samhällets synpunkt en fullt acceptabel samlevnads-form.': *Lagutskottets betänkande* (LU) 1973:20 <www.riksdagen.se/sv/dokument-och-lagar/dokument/betankande/lagutskottets-betankande-i-anledning-av-kungl_FW01LU20/html>, 116.

9 On this, see I. Lund-Andersen, 'Registered partnerships in Denmark' in Scherpe and Hayward (eds) (n 7); J. M. Scherpe, 'Zehn Jahre registrierte Partnerschaft in Dänemark - Zur Novellierung des Gesetzes von 1989' (2000) Deutsches und Europäisches FamilienRecht 32; J. M. Scherpe, 'Erfahrungen mit dem Rechtsinstitut der registrierten Lebenspartnerschaft in Dänemark' (2001) Familie Partnerschaft Recht 439; P. Dopffel and J. M. Scherpe, 'Gleichgeschlechtliche Lebensgemeinschaften im Recht der nordischen Länder' in J. Basedow, K. J. Hopt, H. Kötz, and P. Dopffel (eds.), *Die Rechtsstellung gleichgeschlechtlicher Lebensgemeinschaften* (Mohr Siebeck 2000).

10 *Halpern v Canada* (AG), [2003] O.J. No. 2268 (10 June 2003), followed by *Reference Re Same-Sex Marriage* [2004] 3 S.C.R 698 which led to the Civil Marriage Act being passed in 2005.

11 *Obergefell v Hodges* (576 U.S._ (2015)).

12 *Minister of Home Affairs and Another v Fourie and Another; Lesbian and Gay Equality Project and Others v Minister of Home Affairs and Others* [2005] ZACC 19.

13 Judicial Yuan Interpretation No. 748 of 24 May 2017.

14 In the case of the Republic of Ireland, after a referendum on 22 May 2015, leading to the Marriage Act 2015.

15 Slovenia being a notable exception, where same-sex marriage came into being after a Supreme Court decision in 2022. See also Latvia's introduction of a functional equivalent to marriage after a Supreme Court decision in December 2021. The subsequent failure of Parliament to pass a civil union Bill means that such unions can now be registered by the administrative courts and have the same legal effect as marriages. On this, see, for example, 'Saeima's Legal Affairs Committee throws away initiative for legal protection of all families' (*BNN*, 6 December 2022) <https://bnn-news.com/saeimas-legal-affairs-committee-throws-away-initiative-for-legal-protection-of-all-families-240703>.

Interestingly, the introduction of same-sex marriage defied the traditional North–South divide, with, for example, Spain introducing it in 2005, and thus before Norway (2008), Sweden (2009), and Denmark (2012). However, a new divide was also created. The recognition of same-sex marriages is largely restricted to Western European jurisdictions, with the notable exception of Slovenia and Estonia, with the latter opening up marriage to same-sex couples by an Act of Parliament in June 2023 (while this chapter was originally written!), with the law coming into effect in 2024.[16] Several Eastern European jurisdictions have even gone so far as to amend their constitutions to define marriage as a union between a man and a woman only to prevent legislation that may allow same-sex marriages without a further constitutional amendment.[17] By contrast, the Republic of Ireland went in the opposite direction and amended the Constitution to *allow* same-sex marriages after a public referendum. Regrettably, in some Eastern European countries the discussion on the recognition of same-sex relationships is 'weaponised' to further other political means and ostensibly a 'national identity'.[18] As a result, Europe and the EU Members States are at least as divided on the issue of same-sex marriage (and indeed same-sex parenting) as they were in the past on divorce except that the dividing line is now between the East and the West. These widely divergent views obviously make it even more difficult to establish what 'family' means in EU Law.

13.3 DO FAMILIES HAVE A PLACE IN THE 'EUROPEAN WAY OF LIFE'? AND IF SO, WHICH FAMILIES?

How then do the European Institutions and EU law deal with the conflicting understandings of 'family' between Eastern and Western European jurisdictions?

In the first instance, arguably by avoiding it, or at least not addressing it directly. In her manifesto 'A union that strives for more – My agenda for Europe', the candidate, now-President of the European Commission Ursula

[16] For the situation in Latvia, see n 17.

[17] See, for example, Article 46 of the Constitution of Bulgaria; Article 28 of the Constitution of Lithuania; Article 18 of the Constitution of Poland; Article 110 of the Constitution of the Republic of Latvia; Article 62 of the Constitution of Serbia; Article L of the Constitution of Hungary; Article 62(2) of the Constitution of Croatia; Article 41 of the Constitution of Slovakia.

[18] See, for example, Chapter 12 by Nausica Palazzo; V. Todorova, 'Gender wars in Bulgaria' in J. M. Scherpe and S. Gilmore (eds), *Family Matters – Essays in Honour of John Eekelaar* (Intersentia 2022); and L. Vaige, *Cross-Border Recognition of Formalized Same-Sex Relationships* (Intersentia 2022).

von der Leyen used the word 'family' only twice and in the contexts of work–life balance and health.[19] Given the central importance of families for the functioning of the Union and Member States, this was disappointing but perhaps can be explained by the fact that candidates for office tend to avoid topics of greater controversy to be more electable.

Moreover, neither the somewhat controversially named strategy and policy priority 'Promoting our European way of life'[20] nor the Commission President's Mission letter to Margaritis Schinas, the Vice-President for Promoting our European Way of Life, dated 1 December 2019, in which the latter is entrusted with his new role, contain direct mentions of family matters. With a little good will, one could read into the tasks that the Vice-President was given, namely 'Ensuring coherence of the external and *internal* dimensions of migration' (emphasis added) and 'Coordinating work on inclusion and building a genuine Union of equality and diversity', that the remit of the portfolio implicitly includes families generally, that is, also non-traditional families, and ensuring their unhindered right to free movement. Read that way, families must then be included in the 'European Way of Life' – but what families? How do families fit into the European way of life, what role do they play, and how are they composed? What is a 'European family', if there is such a thing? Are they different from other families, and if so, how? What would be the point of identifying a 'European family' – to treat them differently from non-European families? And is 'European' different from 'EU' in this context? Here is where the chapters of this book make an important contribution to explore this difficult, and controversial, area of law.

Remarkably, and to her credit, the Commission President later made it absolutely crystal-clear that she very much considers the recognition of all family forms as part of the *Mission in her State of the Union Address 2020*.[21] Towards the end of the address, she made this point with astonishing directness:

[19] European Commission, Directorate-General for Communication, U. von der Leyen, *A Union that Strives for More – My Agenda for Europe – Political Guidelines for the Next European Commission 2019–2024* (Publications Office 2019) <https://data.europa.eu/doi/10.2775/018127>.

[20] European Commission (n 2). For a debate on the supposed 'European way of life', see the contributions in L. Corrias and R. Tinnevelt (eds), *European Ways of Life: Legal and Philosophical Perspectives* (Edward Elgar Publishing, forthcoming).

[21] European Commission, U. von der Leyen, *State of the Union Address 2020 – Building the World We Want to Live In: A Union of Vitality in a World of Fragility* (Brussels, 16 September 2020) <https://ec.europa.eu/commission/presscorner/detail/en/SPEECH_20_1655>.

> Honourable Members,
>
> I will not rest when it comes to building a Union of equality.
>
> A Union where you can be who you are and love who you want – without fear of recrimination or discrimination.
>
> Because **being yourself is not your ideology.**
>
> **It's your identity.**
>
> **And no one can ever take it away.**
>
> So I want to be crystal clear – **LGBTQI-free zones are humanity free zones. And they have no place in our Union.**
>
> And to make sure that we support the whole community, the Commission will soon put forward a strategy to strengthen LGBTQI rights.
>
> As part of this, I will also push for mutual recognition of family relations in the EU. **If you are parent in one country, you are parent in every country.**[22]

That these are not just empty words could be seen in the subsequent initiative *Proposal for a Council Regulation on jurisdiction, applicable law, recognition of decisions and acceptance of authentic instruments in matters of parenthood and on the creation of a European Certificate of Parenthood*.[23] However, given the resistance of many Eastern European Member States to the recognition of parenthood of same-sex couples, evidenced by the positions taken by the respective Member States in the decisions of *V.M.A.*[24] and *Rzecznik Praw Obywatelskich*,[25] it is unlikely that the required unanimity for the passing of the regulation will be achieved.[26] This means that, at best, an enhanced cooperation may be the outcome – which is far from what the Commission President said she would work for in her Address and also would not fulfil the express LGBTIQ Equality Strategy 2020–2025 of the EU.[27]

Objectively speaking, there is no general 'European Way of Life' when it comes to marriage, and the recognition of families and parent–child

[22] Ibid 22–23. Bold print in the original.

[23] COM(2022) 695 final.

[24] Case C-490/20 *V.M.A. v Stolichna obshtina, rayon 'Pancharevo'* EU:C:2021:1008.

[25] Case C-2/21 *Rzecznik Praw Obywatelskich* EU:C:2022:502.

[26] On this, see also Chapter 2 by Alina Tryfonidou, Chapter 9 by Geoffrey Willems, and Chapter 12 by Nausica Palazzo, as well as the references in n 18, and A. Tryfonidou, 'The ECJ recognises the right of rainbow families to move freely between EU Member States: The V.M.A. ruling' (2022) 47 European Law Review 534; D. Thienpont and G. Willems, 'Le droit à la libre circulation des familles homoparentales consacré par la Cour de justice de l'Union européenne' (2022) 132 Revue trimestrielle des droits de l'homme 925; L. Bracken, 'Recognition of LGBTQI+ parent families across European borders' (2022) 29 Maastricht Journal of European and Comparative Law 399.

[27] European Commission, Communication from the Commission to the European Parliament, the Council, the European Economic and Social Committee and the Committee of the Regions. Union of Equality: LGBTIQ Equality Strategy 2020–2025, COM(2020) 698 final.

relationships. On the contrary, these issues have deliberately been turned into a battleground by some politicians. The language used by the latter usually entails claims to 'protect our nation's values' and 'our way of life'.[28] Unsurprisingly, those who have embraced these new family forms likewise demand that *their* values and *their* way of life is accepted and recognised. Achieving political consensus is, therefore, unlikely if not impossible. However, in the past, the same was said about divorce and probably holds true for most 'controversial' family law topics at the time.[29] Future generations will likely shake their heads in disbelief that this has actually been seriously debated.

For the nearer future, the matter will likely continue to lie in the hands of the judiciary and the application of human rights law.[30] In light of the European human rights jurisprudence,[31] it seems fairly obvious that the denial of the existence (and refusal of recognition) of same-sex relationships and same-sex families cannot prevail. Moreover, the EU's LGBTIQ Equality Strategy 2020–2025 at its core aims to ensure that 'everybody in the European Union should be safe and free to be themselves' and thus in reality mandates the recognition of these families.[32] This inevitably creates huge tension within the EU and is a cause for great concern. As the author of this epilogue has written elsewhere:

[28] See the examples cited by Todorova (n 18) and Vaige (n 18).

[29] For a particularly readable and enjoyable account of this in England, see, S. Cretney, *Family Law in the Twentieth Century: A History* (Oxford University Press 2004), particularly the passages on the – then very controversial – Deceased Wife's Sister's Marriage Act 1907, which was followed by protracted debate of what ultimately became the Deceased Brother's Widow's Marriage Act 1921 (41–49).

[30] See, for example, Chapter 9 by Geoffrey Willems, Chapter 10 by Alice Margaria, and Chapter 12 by Nausica Palazzo.

[31] Space precluded an engagement with the ECtHR's case law and even referring the abundance of cases on what the Court calls 'sexual orientation issues'. An overview of the cases can be found on the Court's Factsheet: European Court of Human Rights, Press Unit, Factsheet – Sexual orientation issues (December 2023) <www.echr.coe.int/documents/d/echr/FS_Sexual_orientation_ENG>. Outside of Europe, the jurisprudence is developing along similar lines: see for the USA, *Obergefell v Hodges* (576 U.S. _ (2015)); for South Africa, *Minister of Home Affairs and Another v Fourie and Another; Lesbian and Gay Equality Project and Others v Minister of Home Affairs and Others* [2005] ZACC 19; for Canada, *Reference re Same-Sex Marriage* [2004] 3 S.C.R. 698, 2004 SCC 79; for Taiwan, the *Constitutional Interpretation No. 748*, <https://tapcpr.org/english/statement/2017/11/30/no-748-same-sex-marriage-case>; and for Latin America the ruling by the Inter-American Court of Human Rights, Advisory Opinion (Opinión Consultativa) 24/17 of 24 November 2017 in a case concerning Costa Rica <https://corteidh.or.cr/docs/opiniones/seriea_24_eng.pdf>.

[32] See n 27.

In the absence of a common 'European way of life' on these issues, sadly the very best one currently can hope for – and even that seems doubtful – is the acceptance or tolerance of other jurisdictions' 'ways of life'. The Gordian knot of course is that both sides of the debate claim this acceptance. As it stands, the sword that is most likely to cut the knot is wielded by the human rights obligations of the European nations, but the danger is that it might cut too deeply for the Union to prevail.[33]

13.4 IS THERE A EUROPEAN FAMILY LAW? OR AN EU FAMILY LAW?

It has been and still is being doubted whether, in the absence of a body with legislative competence in family law (be it a European or EU one), there can actually be such a thing as European or EU family law. Yet this view laboured under the assumption that this family law would have to be embodied in a 'European Family Law Code',[34] that is, comprehensive legislation, to be recognised as such. But why would such a code be required? After all, nobody disputes the existence of European Consumer Law, even though there is no European Consumer Code. Neither does the absence of a specific legislative power for European/EU family law, and consequently family statutes, necessarily preclude the existence of a European Family Law or EU Family Law. Instead, there are bits and pieces of family law on a European level, which either have grown organically (so-called 'Organic European Family Law') as a result of similar national legal developments, or have been created by institutions such as the CJEU and the European Court of Human Rights (ECtHR) (so-called 'Institutional European Family Law').

Organic European/EU Family Law consists of elements of a common family law that have 'grown', that is, developed similarly in the European jurisdictions (if speaking of European Family Law) and/or EU Member States (if speaking of EU Family Law).[35] That, as outlined above, the law of marriage is hugely divergent between jurisdictions does not rule out the existence of other

[33] J. M. Scherpe, 'Marriage and the family', in L. Corrias and R. Tinnevelt (eds), *European Ways of Life: Legal and Philosophical Perspectives* (Edward Elgar Publishing, forthcoming).

[34] Which to Sir Gerald Fitzmaurice, one of the dissenting judges in the ground-breaking decision *Marckx v Belgium* (1979–80) 2 EHRR 14, apparently was something of great concern, when he accused the majority of reading (or rather introducing) 'a whole code of family law into Article 8' of the European Convention on Human Rights. On this, see W. Pintens and J. M. Scherpe, 'The Marckx case: A "whole code of family law"?' in S. Gilmore, J. Herring, and R. Probert (eds), *Landmark Cases in Family Law* (Hart Publishing 2011).

[35] For a more detailed description of Institutional and Organic European Family Law, see J. M. Scherpe, *The Present and Future of European Family Law* (Edward Elgar Publishing 2016) ch 2 and 3.

elements of European Family Law. Moreover, even in the law of marriage, a core of joint elements can be identified (e.g. that a marriage is restricted to two persons; certain prohibited degrees; or that the spouses – at least nominally – are equals) that can be identified as European/EU Family Law.

For the purposes of this volume, and as shown expertly by the preceding chapters, what can be termed 'Institutional European Family Law' and specifically 'Institutional EU Family Law' are of greater relevance. This 'Institutional' Family Law is created through binding family law rules by multilateral agreements or treaties such as the EU Treaties or the European Convention on Human Rights or (as is more often the case) their interpretations by the CJEU or the ECtHR.

As the contributions in this volume have shown, there are undoubtedly growing areas of family law emanating indirectly from EU laws or from CJEU decisions. The driving force behind these is the free movement of persons, the principles of equality and non-discrimination, and the legal competences to regulate cross-border issues through private international law instruments. A typical example for this is the way Council Directive 2000/78/EC of 27 November 2000 establishing a general framework for equal treatment in employment and occupation[36] was applied to same-sex couples. In *Maruko v Versorgungsanstalt der deutschen Bühnen*,[37] the surviving partner of a same-sex registered partnership had been denied a survivor's pension in Germany as the law only extended these benefits to spouses (marriage not being available to same-sex couples at the time). The Court held that this would amount to direct discrimination within the meaning of Council Directive 2000/78/EC, provided that the couples were in comparable situations.[38] Even though the Member States were free to legislate on adult relationships (and especially marriage) in principle, they were obliged to do so without discrimination.[39]

[36] OJ L303/16.

[37] Case C-267/06 *Maruko* EU:C:2008:179. On this, see also G. De Baere and K. Gutman, 'The impact of the European Union and the European Court of Justice on European Family Law' in J. M. Scherpe (ed), *European Family Law Vol. I – The Impact of Institutions and Organisations on European Family Law* (Edward Elgar Publishing 2016) especially 39 ff. See also Chapter 6 by Gunnar Thor Petursson, Xavier Groussot, and Alezini Loxa.

[38] Which they were, according to Verwaltungsgericht München 1.6.2006 – M 2 K 05.1595.

[39] See also, European Network of Legal Experts in the non-discrimination field, C. O'Cinneide, *The Evolution and Impact of the Case-Law of the Court of Justice of the European Union on Directives 2000/43/EC and 2000/78/EC* (European Commission 2012) <www.equalitylaw.eu/downloads/1452-evolution-and-impact-en-final>; and European Network of Legal Experts in the non-discrimination field, K. Liu and C. O'Cinneide, *The Ongoing Evolution of the Case-Law of the Court of Justice of the European Union on Directives 2000/43/EC and 2000/78/EC* (European Commission 2019) <http://5009-the-ongoing-evolution-of-the-case-law-of-the-court-of-justice-of-the-european-union-on-directives-2000-43-ec-and-2000-78-ec-pdf-766-kb>.

In *Römer v Freie und Hansestadt Hamburg*,[40] the Court decided along similar veins holding that receiving a lower supplementary pension benefit because the applicant had been in a registered partnership rather than a marriage was directly discriminatory and, thus, a violation of the Directive. Although pensions and comparable benefits are not what is generally seen as the 'core' of family law, these decisions nevertheless accepted a family form other than marriage, at least for some purposes. Admittedly, this result was only reached because the relationship in question resembled that of a heteronormative marital relationship. While this generally seems to be the approach of EU Law,[41] it is highly questionable whether it still is the appropriate yardstick for family relationships. Nevertheless, this recognition of same-sex relationships can be seen as creating an element of Institutional EU Family Law just as, for example, the decision in *Coman*.[42] None of the decisions mentioned create a right to same-sex marriage nor the necessity for general recognition of such relationships in the EU. Given the legal and institutional constraints, this has never been a possible outcome. However, these decisions establish elements of an EU Family Law, a minimum standard under which the Member States must not fall, as well as a steppingstone towards full(er) recognition of more diverse family forms in general and same-sex relationships and families in particular.

In addition to the EU Institutions, the ECtHR is probably the most potent source for Institutional European Family Law, given that the EU and all Member States are Contracting States of the Convention. Although decisions based on the ECHR often concern the substantive family law of the Contracting State immediately involved, they nevertheless set a minimum standard for all others. The prime example, and arguably the starting point of European Family Law, is the *Marckx* decision of 1979 on the legal status of

[40] Case C-147/08 *Römer* EU:C:2011:286.

[41] On this, see, for example, Chapter 2 by Alina Tryfonidou, Chapter 4 by Ségolène Barbou des Places, Chapter 9 by Geoffrey Willems, Chapter 10 by Alice Margaria, and Chapter 12 by Nausica Palazzo.

[42] Case C-673/16 *Coman and others* EU:C:2018:385. On this case, see, for example, A. Tryfonidou, 'The ECJ recognises the right of same-sex spouses to move freely between EU Member States: The Coman ruling' (2019) European Law Review 663; and D. V. Kochenov and U. Belavusau, 'After the celebration: Marriage equality in EU Law post-Coman in eight questions and some further thoughts' (2020) 27 Maastricht Journal of European and Comparative Law 549 as well as Chapter 7 by Michael Bogdan and Chapter 9 by Geoffrey Willems.

children born out of wedlock.[43] As a result of the decision, which held that these children must be treated equally to those born in marriage, numerous European jurisdictions had to change their family laws.[44]

Another example is the decision of *Christine Goodwin v United Kingdom*, which similarly and powerfully established a minimum standard for all Contracting States, namely that there must be the possibility to change one's legal gender from the one allocated at birth and to marry under that gender.[45] This did not only lead to a string of further cases, each of which clarified the legal position of transgender persons,[46] but also meant that the Contracting States had to adapt their laws in this area.

All of these are just examples, and one could list many more, including parenthood and especially surrogacy,[47] parental responsibility,[48] and the right to know one's origin,[49] of how elements of European Family Law have been created by the ECtHR.

43 *Marckx v Belgium*, Application no 6833/74.

44 See, for example, Law Commission of England and Wales, *Illegitimacy* (Law Com No 118, 1982); Scottish Law Commission, *Report on Illegitimacy* (Scot Law Com No 82, 1984); Law Commission, *Illegitimacy (Second Report)* (Law Com No 157, 1986); Hoge Raad case no 463, 181.1980, Nederlands Jurisprudentie 1980, 1460. See also F. Sturm, 'Das Straßburger Marckx-Urteil zum Recht des nichtehelichen Kindes und seine Folgen' (1982) FamRZ - Zeitschrift für das gesamte Familienrecht 1151; M. Salzberg, 'The Marckx case' (1983–1984) 13 Denver Journal for International Law and Policy 283; C. Forder, 'Legal protection under Article 8 ECHR: Marckx and beyond' (1990) 37 Netherlands International Law Review 162.

45 Application no 28957/95. On this, see, for example, Scherpe (n 35) 11 ff, as well as the contributions in J. M. Scherpe, *The Legal Status of Transsexual and Transgender Persons* (Intersentia 2015).

46 In *Goodwin*, the Court did not stipulate which legal requirements must be fulfilled by the individual for this, since that was not the issue in the case. The question had to, therefore, be dealt with by national legislation (for example, in the UK's case by the Gender Recognition Act 2004 (UK)) and subsequent litigation). See, for example, *L v Lithuania*, Application no 27527/03; *Schlumpf v Switzerland*, Application no 29002/06; *Hämäläinen v Finland*, Application no 37359/09; *YY v Turkey*, Application no 14793/08; *AP, Garçon and Nicot v France*, Application nos 79885/12, 52471/13 and 52596/13; *YT v Bulgaria*, Application no 41701/16; *X and Y v Romania*, Application no 2145/16 and 20607/16; and *AD and others v Georgia*, Application nos 57864/17, 79087/17 and 55353/19.

47 In the field of surrogacy and parenthood, for example, see Chapter 10 by Alice Margaria. For a wider analysis of surrogacy laws, see, for example, J. M. Scherpe, C. Fenton-Glynn, and T. Kaan (eds), *Eastern and Western Perspectives on Surrogacy* (Intersentia 2019); N. Espejo-Yaksic, C. Fenton-Glynn, and J. M. Scherpe (eds), *Surrogacy in Latin America* (Intersentia 2023).

48 For example, *Zaunegger v Germany*, Application no 22028/04 (2019) FamRZ - Zeitschrift für das gesamte Familienrecht 108, with notes by D. Henrich and J. M. Scherpe. See also the later decision in *Sporer v Austria*, Application no 35637/03.

49 For example, *Odièvre v France*, Application no 42326/98, and *Godelli v Italy*, Application no 33783/09.

13.5 CONCLUSION: AN EU/EUROPEAN FAMILY LAW FOR EUROPEAN FAMILIES?

A fragmentary European and EU Family Law has begun to develop, creating elements and pockets of family law in very diverse and often unconnected areas. At the heart of these developments, especially in the EU context, there lies the central question which this volume addresses: What is a family?

'Family' means different things to different people, and is also likely to mean different things in different legal and social contexts. But that families, whatever form they take, are part of the basic European fabric cannot be denied. It is, therefore, not surprising that organic and institutional elements of European Family Law have begun and continue to grow. For now, most of them are separate little islands; but in the distant future they may grow together and form a more coherent and more recognisable body of European and EU Family Law.

Ultimately, it is to be hoped (to paraphrase the abovementioned statement by Commission President Ursula von der Leyen) that at least in Europe, if you are a family in one country, you are family in every country. Nobody's family is any less a family just because somebody else's family also is a family in the eyes of the law. Because love is love, and caring is caring.

Bibliography

Ackers, L. 'Citizenship, gender and dependency in the EU: Women and internal migration' in K. H. Hervey and D. O'Keeffe (eds), *Sex Equality Law in the European Union* (Wiley 1996).

Shifting Spaces: Women, Citizenship and Migration within the European Union (Policy Press 1998).

Ackers, L., and H. Stalford, 'Children, migration and citizenship in the European Union: Intra-community mobility and the status of children in EC law' (1999) 21 Children and Youth Services Review 987.

Adam, S., and P. Van Elsuwege, 'EU citizenship and the European federal challenge through the prism of family reunification' in D. Kochenov (ed), *EU Citizenship and Federalism – The Role of Rights* (Cambridge University Press 2017).

Almond, B. *The Fragmenting Family* (Oxford University Press 2008).

Antokolskaia, M. 'Convergence and divergence of divorce laws in Europe' (2006) 18 Child and Family Law Quarterly 307.

Harmonisation of Family Law in Europe: A Historical Perspective (Intersentia 2006).

'The search for a common core of divorce law: State intervention v. spouses' autonomy' in M. Martín-Casals and J. Ribot (eds), *The Role of Self-Determination in the Modernisation of Family Law in Europe* (Documenta Universitaria 2006).

'Harmonisation of substantive family law in Europe: Myths and reality' (2010) 22 Child and Family Law Quarterly 397.

'Divorce in a European perspective' in J. M. Scherpe (ed), *European Family Law Vol. III – Family Law in a European Perspective* (Edward Elgar Publishing 2016).

Archard, D. *The Family: A Liberal Defence* (Palgrave Macmillan 2010).

'Family and family law: Concepts and norms' in E. Brake and L. Ferguson (eds), *Philosophical Foundations of Children's and Family Law* (Oxford University Press 2018).

Azoulai, L. 'Transfiguring European citizenship: From Member State Territory to Union Territory, in EU citizenship and federalism: The role of rights' in D. Kochenov (ed), *EU Citizenship and Federalism* (Cambridge University Press 2015).

'The European individual and collective entities' in L. Azoulai, S. Barbou des Places, and E. Pataut (eds), *Constructing the Person in EU Law: Rights, Roles, Identities* (Hart Publishing 2016).

Bailey, A., and P. Boyle, 'Untying and retying family migration in the New Europe' (2004) 30 Journal of Ethnic and Migration Studies 229.

Balogh, L., A. László Pap, and E. Pásztor, 'Hungary: The concept of family within the framework of "illiberal democracy"' in N. Yassari and M.-C. Foblets (eds), *Normativity and Diversity in Family Law* (Springer 2022).

Banda, F., and J. Eekelaar, 'International conceptions of the family' (2017) 66 International and Comparative Law Quarterly 833.

Barbou des Places, S. 'The integrated person in EU law' in L. Azoulai, S. Barbou des Places, and E. Pataut (eds), *Constructing the Person in EU Law: Rights, Roles, Identities* (Hart Publishing 2016).

'La famille du ressortissant d'État tiers: une famille désinstituée?' in H. Fulchiron (ed), *La famille du migrant* (Lexis Nexis 2020).

Barnard, C. S. *The Substantive Law of the EU* (Oxford University Press 2022).

Barrett, G. 'Family matters: European Community law and third country national family members' (2003) 40 Common Market Law Review 369.

Başak, Ç., and L. Helfer, 'The gender of treaty withdrawal: Lessons from the Istanbul Convention' (*EJIL: Talk!*, 28 November 2022) <www.ejiltalk.org/the-gender-of-treaty-withdrawal-lessons-from-the-istanbul-convention/>.

Beaumont, P. 'Private international law concerning children in the UK after Brexit: Comparing Hague Treaty Law with EU Regulations' (2017) 29 Child and Family Law Quarterly 214.

Beck-Gernsheim, E. *Reinventing the Family: In Search of New Lifestyles* (Polity Press, 2002).

Beqiraj, J., and F. Ippolito, 'Conceptualizing an 'association citizenship' for children of Turkish workers' in D. Thym and M. H. Zoetewij-Turhan (eds), *Rights of Third-Country Nationals under EU Association Agreements* (Brill 2015).

Bernardes, J. *Family Studies: An Introduction* (Routledge 1997).

Berneri, C. *Family Reunification in the EU* (Hart Publishing 2017).

'Family reunification between static EU citizens and third country nationals' (2018) 20 European Journal of Migration and Law 289.

Boekestein, T. 'Making do with what we have: On the interpretation and enforcement of the EU's founding values' (2022) 23 German Law Journal 431.

Boele-Woelki, K. 'Cross-border family relations in Europe: Towards a common European matrimonial property law based upon cooperation between private international law and substantive law' in A. L. M. Keirse and M. B. M. Loos (eds), *Alternative Ways to Ius Commune – The Europeanisation of Private Law* (Intersentia 2012).

Boele-Woelki, K., and A. Fuchs (eds), *Same-Sex Relationships and Beyond* (Intersentia 2017).

Bonelli, M. 'Infringement Actions 2.0: How to protect EU values before the Court of Justice' (2022) 18 European Constitutional Law Review 30.

Bonelli, M., and M. Claes. 'Crossing the Rubicon? The Commission's use of Article 2 TEU in the infringement action on LGBTIQ+ rights in Hungary' (2023) 30 Maastricht Journal of European and Comparative Law 3.

Bottomley, A., and S. Wong, 'Shared household: A new paradigm for thinking about the reform of domestic property relations' in A. Diduck and K. O'Donovan (eds), *Feminist Perspectives on Family Law* (Routledge 2006).

Bracken, L. 'Recognition of LGBTQI+ parent families across European borders' (2022) 29 Maastricht Journal of European and Comparative Law 399.
Bradley, D. 'Family law' in J. M. Smits (ed), *Elgar Encyclopedia of Comparative Law* (Edward Elgar Publishing 2006).
Bribosia, E., and I. Rorive, 'L'arrêt Coman: Quand la Cour de justice contribue à la reconnaissance du mariage homosexuel' (2018) n 253 Journal de droit européen 344–347.
Brighouse, H., and A. Swift, *Family Values: The Ethics of a Parent–Child Relationship* (Princeton University Press 2014).
Brown, A. *What Is the Family of Law? The Influence of the Nuclear Family* (Hart 2019).
Burke, C., and Ó. Í. Hannesson, 'Citizenship by the backdoor? Gunnarsson' (2015) 52 Common Market Law Review 1111.
Burke, E. *Reflections on the Revolution in France* (first published 1790) (Penguin 1968).
Caiola, A. 'Une acception large de la notion de "conjoint" pour garantir la liberté de séjour des citoyens européens' (2018) Revue des affaires européennes 335.
Camus, A. *Resistance, Rebellion and Death* (Wintage 1974).
Cannoot, P. 'Inadmissibility decision in Bonnaud and Lecoq v. France: Should the Court have recognized the specificity of a same-sex relationship?' (*Strasbourg Observers*, 11 April 2018) <https://strasbourgobservers.com/2018/04/11/inadmissibility-decision-in-bonnaud-and-lecoq-v-france-should-the-court-have-recognized-the-specificity-of-a-same-sex-relationship/>.
Caracciolo di Torella, E., and A. Masselot, 'Under construction: EU family law' (2004) 29 European Law Review 32.
Caracciolo di Torella, E., and P. Foubert, 'Maternity rights for intended mothers? Surrogacy puts the EU legal framework to the test' (2014) 2 European Gender Equality Law Review 5.
Caring Responsibilities in European Law and Policy (Routledge 2020).
Carlier, J.-Y. 'Vers un ordre public européen des droits fondamentaux – L'exemple de la reconnaissance des mariages de personnes de même sexe dans l'arrêt Coman' (2019) *Revue trimestrielle des droits de l'homme* 220.
Carrera, S. *In Search of the Perfect Citizen?* (Martinus Nijhoff 2009).
Carrera, S., and A. Wiesbrock, 'Civic integration of third-country nationals: Nationalism versus Europeanisation in the Common EU Immigration Policy', CEPS 2009.
Charlesworth, H., and C. Chinkin, 'The gender of jus cogens' (1993) 15 Human Rights Law Review 63.
Cheal, D. *Sociology of Family Life* (Blackwell 2002).
Chieregato, E. 'A work-life balance for all? Assessing the inclusiveness of EU Directive 2019/1158' (2020) 36 International Journal of Comparative Labour Law and Industrial Relations 59.
Choudhry, S. 'Right to respect for private and family life (family life aspects)', in S. Peers, T. Hervey, and A. Ward (eds), *The EU Charter of Fundamental Rights: A Commentary* (Hart Publishing 2014).
Coltrane, S. *Gender and Families* (Rowman & Littlefield 1998).
Corrias, L., and R. Tinnevelt (eds), *European Ways of Life: Legal and Philosophical Perspectives* (Edward Elgar Publishing, forthcoming).
Costello, C. 'Article 33 family and professional life' in S. Peers, T. Hervey, and A. Ward (eds), *The EU Charter of Fundamental Rights: A Commentary* (Hart Publishing 2014).

Craig, P., and G. de Búrca, *EU Law: Text, Cases and Materials (UK Version)* (Oxford University Press 2020).

Cretney, S. *Family Law in the Twentieth Century: A History* (Oxford University Press 2004).

Same Sex Relationships from 'Odious Crime' to 'Gay Marriage' (Oxford University Press 2006).

Czapanskiy, K. 'Volunteers and draftees: The struggle for parental equality' (1991) 38 UCLA Law Review 1415.

Dąbrowska-Kłosińska, P. 'The right to family reunion vs integration conditions for third-country nationals' (2018) 20 European Journal of Migration and Law 251.

Dailey, A. 'Federalism and families' (1995) 143 University of Pennsylvania Law Review 1787.

Dawson, J., and S. Hanley, 'What's wrong with East-Central Europe? The fading mirage of the "Liberal Consensus"' (2016) 27 Journal of Democracy 21.

Dawson, M., and E. Muir, 'Hungary and the indirect protection of EU fundamental rights and the rule of law' (2013) 14 German Law Journal 1959.

De Baere, G., and K. Gutman, 'The impact of the European Union and the European Court of Justice on European Family Law' in J. M. Scherpe (ed), *European Family Law Vol. I – The Impact of Institutions and Organisations on European Family Law* (Edward Elgar Publishing 2016).

De Capitani, C. 'Rainbow families and the right to freedom of movement – the V.M.A. v Stolichna Obshtina, Rayon 'Pancharevo' Case' (*EU Law Analysis*, 11 January 2022) <http://eulawanalysis.blogspot.com/2022/01/rainbow-families-and-right-to-freedom.html>.

de Witte, B. 'The past and future of the European Court of Justice in the protection of human rights' in P. Alston (ed), *The EU and Human Rights* (Oxford University Press 1999).

Derave, C., and H. Ouhnaoui, 'C.E. & al. v. France: Legal recognition of intended parenthood from previous same-sex relationships (between women)' (*Strasbourg Observers*, 7 October 2022) <http://strasbourgobservers.com/2022/10/07/c-e-al-v-france-legal-recognition-of-intended-parenthood-from-previous-same-sex-relationships-between-women/>.

Dermott, E., and T. M. Fowler, 'What is a family and why does it matter' (2020) 9 Social Sciences 1.

Diduck, A. *Law's Families* (Cambridge University Press 2003).

'Shifting familiarity' (2005) 58 Current Legal Problems 235.

Diduck, A., and F. Kaganas, *Family Law, Gender and the State* (Hart Publishing 2012).

Dopffel, H. P. and J. M. Scherpe 'Gleichgeschlechtliche Lebensgemeinschaften im Recht der nordischen Länder' in J. Basedow, K. J. Hopt, H. Kötz, and H. P. Dopffel (eds), *Die Rechtsstellung gleichgeschlechtlicher Lebensgemeinschaften* (Mohr Siebeck 2000).

Dougan, M. 'So long, farewell, aufwiedersehen, goodbye: The UK's withdrawal package' (2020) 57 Common Market Law Review 631.

Douglas, G. 'The intention to be a parent and the making of mothers' (1994) 57 Modern Law Review 636.

Dubout, E. 'The European form of family life. The case of EU citizenship' (2020) 5 European Papers 3.

Dutta, A., and others (eds), *Scheidung ohne Gericht?* (Gieseking 2017).

Editorial Comments, 'Safeguarding EU values in the Member States – Is something finally happening?' (2015) 52 Common Market Law Review 625.

Editorial Comments, 'Who are the "peoples of Europe"?' (2023) 60 Common Market Law Review 305.

Edwards, R., J. McCarthy, and V. Gillies, 'The politics of concepts: Family and its (putative) replacements' (2012) 63 British Journal of Sociology 730.

Eeckhout, P. 'The EU Charter of Fundamental Rights and the federal question' (2002) 39 Common Market Law Review 945.

Ergas, Y., J. Jenson, and S. Michel, 'Introduction' in Y. Ergas, J. Jenson, and S. Michel (eds), *Reassembling Motherhood: Procreation and Care in a Globalised World* (Columbia University Press 2017).

Eskridge, W. N., Jr. *Equality Practice: Civil Unions and the Future of Gay Rights* (Routledge 2002).

Espejo-Yaksic, N., C. Fenton-Glynn, and J.M. Scherpe (eds), *Surrogacy in Latin America* (Intersentia 2023).

Fabbrini, F. *Fundamental Rights in Europe: Challenges and Transformations in Comparative Perspectives* (Oxford University Press 2014).

Fallon, M. 'Observations sous CJUE, 5 juin 2018, Gr. Ch., Coman, C-673/16, EU: C:2018:385' (Cahiers de l'EDEM, June 2018) <http://uclouvain.be/fr/instituts-recherche/juri/cedie/actualites/observations-sous-cjue-5-juin-2018-gr-ch-coman-c-673-16-eu-c-2018-385.html>.

Featherstone, B., A. Gupta, K. Morris, and J. Warner, 'Let us stop feeding the risk monster: Towards a social model of "child protection"' (2018) 7 Families, Relationships and Societies 7.

Featherstone, B. *Children and the European Court of Human Rights* (Oxford University Press 2021).

Ferri, D., and G. Martinico, 'Revisiting the Ruiz Zambrano Doctrine and exploring the potential for its extensive application' (2021) 27 European Public Law 685.

Finch, J. 'Displaying families' (2007) 41 Sociology 65.

Finck, M., and B. Kas, 'Surrogacy leave as a matter of EU law: CD and Z' (2015) 52 Common Market Law Review 281.

Forder, C. 'Legal protection under Article 8 ECHR: Marckx and beyond' (1990) 37 Netherlands International Law Review 162.

Fredman, S. 'Reversing roles: Bringing fathers into the frame' (2014) 10 International Journal of Law in Context 442.

Frick, M. L. 'Illiberalims and human rights' in A. Sajó, R. Uitz, and S. Holmes (eds), *Routledge Handbook of Illiberalism* (Routledge 2021).

Fulchiron, H. 'Un modèle familial européen?' in H. Fulchiron and C. Bidaut-Garon (eds), *Vers un statut européen de la famille* (Dalloz 2014).

'Citoyenneté européenne, liberté de circulation et reconnaissance des situations familiales créées dans un État membre: Un petit pas pour de grandes enjambées?' (2018) Recueil Dalloz 1678.

'La CEDH et la reconnaissance des mariages entre personnes de même sexe célébrés à l'étranger: Avis de tempête ou signal brouillé?' (2018) Recueil Dalloz 446.

Fussey, P., and P. Rawlinson, *Child Trafficking in the EU: Policing and Protecting Europe's Most Vulnerable* (Routledge 2017).

Ganty, S. 'Silence is not (always) golden: A criticism of the ECJ's approach towards integration conditions for family reunification' (2021) 23 European Journal of Migration and Law 176.

'Surrogacy as Citizenship Deprivation in S.-H. v. Poland' (*Strasbourg Observers*, 14 March 2022) <http://strasbourgobservers.com/2022/03/14/surrogacy-deprives-from-citizenship-in-s-h-v-poland%EF%BF%BC/#:~:text= – %20H.,of%20the%20Polish%20legal%20system>.

Gheaus, A. 'Is the family uniquely valuable?' (2012) 6 Ethics and Social Welfare 120.

Gilding, M. 'Reflexivity over and above convention: The new orthodoxy in the sociology of personal life, formerly sociology of the family' (2010) 61 British Journal of Sociology 757.

Gittins, D. *The Family in Question* (Macmillan 1985).

González Pascual, M., and A. Torres Pérez (eds), *The Right to Family Life in the European Union* (Routledge 2018).

Goudappel, F. *The Effects of EU Citizenship* (T.M.C. Asser Press 2010).

Graff, A., and E. Korolczuk, 'Gender and Illiberal Politics' in M. Laruelle (ed), Oxford Handbook of Illiberalism (Oxford University Press 2023).

Groussot, X., and E. Gill-Pedro, 'Old and new human rights in Europe – The scope of EU rights versus that of ECHR rights' in E. Brems and J. Gerards (eds), *Shaping the Rights in ECHR – The Role of the European Court of Human Rights in Determining the Scope of Human Rights* (Cambridge University Press 2013).

Groussot, X., and G. T. Petursson, 'The EU Charter of Fundamental Rights five years on – The emergence of a new constitutional framework' in S. de Vries, U. Bernitz, and S. Weatherill (eds), *The EU Charter of Fundamental Rights as a Binding Instrument – Five Years Old and Growing* (Hart Publishing 2015).

Grzebalska, W. 'Poland' in E. Kováts and M. Põim (eds), *Gender as Symbolic Glue: The Position and Role of Conservative and Far Right Parties in the Anti-gender Mobilizations in Europe* (FEPS – Foundation for European Progressive Studies 2015).

Grzebalska, W., and A. Pető, 'The gendered modus operandi of the illiberal transformation in Hungary and Poland' (2018) 68 Women's Studies International Forum 164.

Guild E., C. J. Gortázar Rotaeche, and D. Kostakopoulou (eds), *The Reconceptualization of European Union Citizenship* (Brill Nijhoff 2014).

Guild E., S. Peers, and J. Tomkin, *The EU Citizenship Directive: A Commentary* (Oxford University Press 2019).

Guth, J. 'When is a partner not a partner? Conceptualisations of "family" in EU Free Movement Law' (2011) 33 Journal of Social Welfare and Family Law 193.

Gutman, K. 'The essence of the fundamental right to an effective remedy and to a fair trial in the case law of the Court of Justice of the European Union: The best is yet to come?' (2019) 20 German Law Journal 884.

Halmai, G. 'The early retirement age of the Hungarian judges' in F. Nicola and B. Davis (eds), *EU Law Stories: Contextual and Critical Histories of European Jurisprudence* (Cambridge University Press 2017).

Hammje, P. 'Obligation de reconnaissance d'un mariage entre personnes de même sexe conclu dans un État membre aux fins d'octroi d'un droit de séjour dérivé' (2018) Revue critique de droit international privé 816.

Hantrais, L. 'What is a family or family life in the European Union?' in E. Guild (ed), *The Legal Framework and Social Consequences of Free Movement of Persons in the European Union* (Kluwer 1999).

Harding, M. 'The harmonisation of private international law in Europe: Taking the character out of family law?' (2011) 7 Journal of Private International Law 203.

Hart, H. L. A. 'Positivism and the separation of law and morals' (1958) 71 Harvard Law Review 593.

Hayward, A. 'Same-sex registered partnerships – A right to be recognized' (2016) 75 Cambridge Law Journal 27.

Herring, J., R. Probert, and S. Gilmore, *Great Debates in Family Law* (Macmillan 2015).

Herring, J. *Family Law* (Pearson 2017).

Hervey, T. H. 'A gendered perspective on the right to family life in European Community law' in N. Neuwahl and A. Rosas (eds), *The European Union and Human Rights* (Martinus Nijhoff 1995).

Hesová, Z. 'Three types of culture wars and the populist strategies in Central Europe' (2021) 28 Czech Journal of Political Science/Politologick 130.

Hodson, L. 'Ties that bind: Towards a child-centred approach to lesbian, gay, bi-sexual and transgender families under the ECHR' (2012) 20 International Journal of Children's Rights 501.

Holmes, S. 'The antiliberal idea' in A. Sajó, R. Uitz, and S. Holmes (eds), *Routledge Handbook of Illiberalism* (Routledge 2021).

Honorati, C., and M. C. Baruffi, *EU Private International Law in Family Matters: Legislation and CJEU Case Law* (Intersentia 2022).

Hyltén-Cavallius, K. 'Who cares? Caregivers' derived residence rights from children in EU free movement law' (2020) 57 Common Market Law Review 399.

Iglesias Sanchez, S. 'Fundamental rights and citizenship of the Union at a crossroads: A promising alliance or a dangerous liaison?' (2014) *European Law Journal* 107.

Irwin, S. 'Resourcing the family: Gendered claims and obligations and issues of explanation' in E. B. Silva and C. Smart (eds), *The New Family?* (Sage 1999).

Jackson, E. 'What is a parent?' in A. Diduck and K. O'Donovan (eds), *Feminist Perspectives on Family Law* (Routledge 2006).

Jacobs F. G. (ed), *European Law and the Individual* (North Holland 1976).

Jakab, A., and D. Kochenov, 'Introductory remarks' in A. Jakab and D. Kochenov (eds), *The Enforcement of EU Law and Values: Ensuring Member States' Compliance* (Oxford University Press 2017).

Kaganas, F., and S. Day Sclater, 'Contact disputes: Narrative constructions of "good" parents' (2004) 12 Feminist Legal Studies 1.

Kaiser, L. 'A new chapter in the European rule of law saga?' (*VerfBlog*, 4 March 2023) <https://verfassungsblog.de/a-new-chapter-in-the-european-rule-of-law-saga/>.

Kemper, A. 'Foundation of the nation: How political parties and movements are radicalising others in favour of conservative family values and against tolerance, diversity, and progressive gender politics in Europe' (Friedrich Ebert Stiftung 2016) <http://library.fes.de/pdf-files/dialog/12503.pdf>.

Kiernan, K. 'Changing European families: Trends and issues' in J. Scott, J. Treas, and M. Richards (eds), *The Blackwell Companion to the Sociology of Families* (Blackwell 2004).

Kilpatrick, C. 'The Court of Justice and Labour Law in 2010: A new EU discrimination law architecture' (2011) 40 Industrial Law Journal 280.

Knowles, E. *Oxford Dictionary of Quotations* (Oxford University Press 2009).

Kochenov, D. 'Gay rights in the EU: A long way forward for the Union of 27' (2007) 3 Croatian Yearbook of European Law and Policy 469.

'Mevrouw de Jong Gaat Eten: EU citizenship and the culture of prejudice' EUI Working Paper RSCAS 2011/06 <https://cadmus.eui.eu/handle/1814/15774>.

(ed), *EU Citizenship and Federalism: The Role of Rights* (Cambridge University Press 2017).

Kochenov, D., and U. Belavusau, 'After the celebration: Marriage equality in EU Law post-Coman in eight questions and some further thoughts' (2020) 27 Maastricht Journal of European and Comparative Law 549.

'Same-sex spouses: More free movement, but what about marriage? Coman' (2020) 57 Common Market Law Review 227.

Kochenov, D., and M. van den Brink, 'Pretending there is no union: Non-derivative *Quasi*-citizenship rights of third-country nationals in the EU' in D. Thym and M. H. Zoetewij-Turhan (eds), *Rights of Third-Country Nationals under EU Association Agreements* (Brill 2015).

Koffeman, N. *Morally Sensitive Issues and Cross-Border Movement in the EU: The Cases of Reproductive Matters and Legal Recognition of Same-Sex Relationships* (Intersentia 2015).

'Taddeucci and McCall v. Italy: Welcome novelty in the ECtHR's case-law on equal treatment of same-sex couples' (*Strasbourg Observers*, 27 July 2016) <https://strasbourgobservers.com/2016/07/27/taddeucci-and-mccall-v-italy-welcome-novelty-in-the-ecthrs-case-law-on-equal-treatment-of-same-sex-couples/>.

Korolczuk, E. '"The war on gender" from a transnational perspective: Lessons for feminist strategising' in *Anti-gender Movements on the Rise? Strategising for Gender Equality in Central and Eastern Europe* (Heinrich Böll Stiftung 2014) <https://pl.boell.org/sites/default/files/uploads/2014/10/war_on_gender_korolczuk.pdf>.

Korolczuk, E., and A. Graff, '"Worse than Communism and Nazism put together": War on gender in Poland' in R. Kuhar and D. Paternotte (eds), *Anti-gender Campaigns in Europe: Mobilizing against Equality* (Rowman & Littlefield 2017).

'Gender as "Ebola from Brussels": The anticolonial frame and the rise of illiberal populism' (2018) 43 Signs: Journal of Women in Culture and Society 797.

Koslowski R., 'A constructive approach to understanding the European Union as a federal polity' (1999) 4 Journal of European Public Policy 561.

Krizsan, A., and C. Roggeband, 'Towards a conceptual framework for struggles over democracy in backsliding states: Gender equality policy in Central Eastern Europe' (2018) 6 Politics and Governance 90.

Kruger, T., and L. Samyn, 'Brussels IIbis: Successes and suggested improvements' (2016) 12 Journal of Private International Law 132.

Kuby, G. *The Global Sexual Revolution: Destruction of Freedom in the Name of Freedom* (Angelico Press 2015).

Kuhar, R., and D. Paternotte, *Anti-gender Campaigns in Europe: Mobilizing against Equality* (Rowman & Littlefield 2017).

Kuskoff, E., and others, 'Of good mothers and violent fathers: Negotiating child protection interventions in abusive relationships' (2023) Violence Against Women (online first).

Lacroix, J. 'Does Europe need common values?' (2009) 8 European Journal of Political Theory 141.

Lambinet, F., and S. Gilson, 'Arrêt "Hay": Les partenaires (de même sexe) pacsés doivent-ils être traités comme des (hétérosexuels) Mariés' 2014 Journal de droit européen 243.

Lamont, R. 'Care proceedings with a European dimension under Brussels II*a*: jurisdiction, mutual trust and the best interests of the child' (2016) 28 Child and Family Law Quarterly 67.

'Not a European family: Implications of Brexit for international family law' (2017) 29 Child and Family Law Quartely 267.

'The development of child protection across international borders for children at risk of harm' in G. Douglas, M. Murch, and V. Stephens (eds), *International and National Perspectives on Child and Family Law* (Intersentia 2018).

'Article 24' in S. Peers and others (eds), *The Charter of Fundamental Rights of the European Union* (Hart Publishing 2021).

'Child protection in international family law and the determination of where the child "belongs" for the purpose of jurisdiction' (2022) 34 Child and Family Law Quarterly 401.

Lamont, R., and C. Fenton-Glynn, 'Cross-border care and adoption proceedings in the European Union' (2016) 38 Journal of Social Welfare and Family Law 94.

Lane Scheppele, K. 'Enforcing the basic principles of EU law through systemic infringement actions' in C. Closa and D. Kochenov (eds), *Reinforcing Rule of Law Oversight in The European Union* (Cambridge University Press 2021).

Lane Scheppele, K., D. Kochenov, and B. Grabowska-Moroz, 'EU values are law, after All: Enforcing EU values through systemic infringement actions by the European Commission and the Member States of the European Union' (2020) 39 Yearbook of European Law 3.

Lane Scheppele, K., and J. Morijn, 'Frozen, how the EU is blocking funds to Hungary and Poland using a multitude of conditionalities' (*VerfBlog*, 4 April 2023) <https://verfassungsblog.de/frozen/>.

Laruelle, M. 'Illiberalism: A conceptual introduction' (2022) 38 East European Politics 303.

Łazowski, A. 'When *Cives Europae* became bargaining chips: Free movement of persons in the Brexit negotiations' (2018) 18 ERA Forum 469.

Lebret, A. 'The European Court of Human Rights and the framing of reproductive rights' (2020) Droits Fondamentaux <www.crdh.fr/revue/n-18–2020/the-european-court-of-human-rights-and-the-framing-of-reproductive-rights/>.

Leeder, E. *The Family in Global Perspective: A Gendered Journey* (Sage 2004).

Leib, E. J. 'Friendship and the law' (2007) 54 UCLA Law Review 631.

Lenaerts, K. 'Exploring the limits of the EU Charter of Fundamental Rights' (2012) 8 European Constitutional Law Review 375.

Lendvai-Bainton, N., and D. Szelewa, 'Governing new authoritarianism: Populism, nationalism and radical welfare reforms in Hungary and Poland' (2021) 55 Social Policy & Administration 559.

Levy, M. 'Surrogacy and parenthood: A European saga of genetic essentialism and gender discrimination' (2022) 29 Michigan Journal of Gender and Law 121.

Lievens, J. 'EHRM opent deur naar europese erkenning homohuwelijk' (2018) Juristenkrant 1.

Linnamäki, K. 'Not in front of the child: Illiberal familism and the Hungarian anti-LGBTQ+ "Child Protective Law"' (2022) 10 Politics and Governance 16.

Lombardo, E., J. Kantola, and R. Rubio-Marin, 'De-democratization and opposition to gender equality politics in Europe' (2021) 28 Social Politics 521.

Loxa, A. 'Analysis: "Cross-border recognition of parenthood for rainbow families"' (*EU Law Live*, 14 December 2021) <https://eulawlive.com/analysis-cross-border-recognition-of-parenthood-for-rainbow-families-by-alezini-loxa/>.

Lugosi, N. V. T. 'Radical right framing of social policy in Hungary: Between nationalism and populism' (2018) 34 Journal of International and Comparative Social Policy 210.

Lund-Andersen, I. 'Registered partnerships in Denmark' in J. M. Scherpe and A. Hayward (eds), *The Future of Registered Partnerships – Family Recognition beyond Marriage?* (Intersentia 2017).

Mahmoud, Z. 'Surrogates across the Atlantic: Comparing the impact of legal and health regulatory frameworks on surrogates' autonomy, health and wellbeing' (PhD thesis, University of Exeter 2022).

Mahmoud, Z., and E. C. Romanis, 'On gestation and motherhood' (2023) 31 Medical Law Review 109.

Mancini, S., and N. Palazzo, 'The body of the nation: Illiberalism and gender' in A. Sajó, R. Uitz, and S. Holmes (eds), *Routledge Handbook of Illiberalism* (Routledge 2021).

Margaria, A., 'Parenthood and cross-border surrogacy: What is "new"? The ECtHR's First Advisory Opinion' (2020) 28 Medical Law Review 412.

'Trans men giving birth and reflections on fatherhood: What to expect?' (2020) 34 International Journal of Law, Policy and the Family 225.

'Honner v France: Damage prevention and/or damage control?' (*Strasbourg Observers*, 12 January 2021) <https://strasbourgobservers.com/2021/01/12/honner-v-france-damage-prevention-and-or-damage-control/>.

'Genetics and the construction of parenthood: The ECtHR jurisprudence on transnational surrogacy' in N. Dethloff and K. Kaesling (eds), *Between Sexuality, Gender and Reproduction – On the Pluralisation of Family Forms* (Intersentia 2023).

Marguénaud, J.-P. 'Le refus de la procréation médicalement assistée à un couple d'homosexuelles mariées ou la subsidiarité otage de la proportionnalité.' (2018) Revue trimestrielle de droit civil 349.

Marshall, T. H. *Citizenship and Social Class, and Other Essays* (Cambridge University Press 1950).

Martens, P. 'L'égalité dans l'adoption' (2013) Revue de jurisprudence de Liège, Mons et Bruxelles 1404.

Martiny, D. 'Divorce and maintenance between former spouses – Initial results of the Commission in European family law' in K. Boele-Woelki (ed), *Perspectives for the Unification and Harmonisation of Family Law in Europe* (Intersentia 2003).

'Is unification of family law feasible or even desirable?' in A. S. Hartkamp and others (eds), *Towards a European Civil Code* (Kluwer 2011).

Marzano, V. J. 'Oliari and the European Court of Human Rights: Where the court failed' (2017) Pace International Law Review 241.

McCandless, J. 'Reforming birth registration law in England and Wales?' (2017) 4 Reproductive BioMedicine and Society Online 52.

McClintock, A. 'Family feuds. Gender, nationalism and the family' (1993) 44 Feminist Review 61.

McEleavy, P. 'The Brussels II Regulation: How the European community has moved into family law' (2002) 51 International and Comparative Law Quarterly 883.

'Private international law: Brussels IIbis matrimonial matters, parental responsibility, child abduction and mutual recognition' (2004) 53 International and Comparative Law Quarterly 503.

McGlynn, C. 'A family law for the European Union?' in J. Shaw (ed), *Social Law and Policy in an Evolving European Union* (Hart Publishing 2000).

'Ideologies of motherhood in European community sex equality law' (2000) 6 European Law Journal 29.

'Families and the European Union Charter of Fundamental Rights: Progressive change or entrenching the status quo' (2001) 26 European Law Review 582.

'Reclaiming a feminist vision: The reconciliation of paid work and family life in European Union law and policy' (2001) 7 Columbia Journal of European Law 262.

'The Europeanisation of family law' (2001) 13 Child and Family Law Quarterly 35.

Families and the European Union: Law, Politics and Pluralism (Cambridge University Press 2006).

Meeusen, J. 'Instrumentalisation of private international law in the European Union: Towards a European conflicts revolution?' (2007) 9 European Journal of Migration and Law 287.

'Functional recognition of same-sex parenthood for the benefit of mobile Union citizens – Brief comments on the CJEU's Pancharevo judgment – GEDIP' (*GEDIP-EGPIL*, 2022) <https://eapil.org/2022/02/03/functional-recognition-of-same-sex-parenthood-for-the-benefit-of-mobile-union-citizens-brief-comments-on-the-cjeus-pancharevo-judgment/>.

Melhuus, M. 'Better safe than sorry: Legislating assisted conception in Norway' in C. Krohn-Hansen and K. Nustad (eds), *State formation: Anthropological perspectives* (Pluto 2005).

Menendez, A. 'Which free movement? Whose free movement?' in S. Borelli and A. Guazzarotti (eds), *Labour Mobility and Transnational Solidarity in the European Union* (Jovene editore 2019).

Merin, Y. *Equality for Same-Sex Couples: The Legal Recognition of Gay Partnerships in Europe and the United States* (Rowman & Littlefield 2002).

Mewes, J. and S. Mau, 'Unraveling working-class welfare chauvinism' in S. Svallfors (ed), *Contested Welfare States: Welfare Attitudes in Europe and Beyond* (Stanford University Press 2012).

Michaels, R., and A. Riles, 'Law as technique' in M.-C. Foblets and others, *The Oxford Handbook of Law and Anthropology* (Oxford University Press 2022).

Milanich, N. 'Certain mothers, uncertain fathers – Placing assisted reproductive technologies in historical perspective' in Y. Ergas, J. Jenson, and S. Michel (eds), *Reassembling Motherhood: Procreation and Care in a Globalised World* (Columbia University Press 2017).

Milios, G. 'Defining "family members" of EU citizens and the circumstances under which they can rely on EU law' (2020) 39 Yearbook of European Law 293.

Millard, É. *Famille et droit public. Recherches sur la construction d'un objet juridique*, Tome 182 (LGDJ 1995).

Moebius, I., and E. Szyszczak, 'Of raising pigs and children' (1998) 18 Yearbook of European Law 125.

Montale, M. *Ossi Di Seppia* (Piero Gobetti 1925).

Morgan, D. H. J. *Family Connections* (Polity Press 1996).

Moskal, M., and N. Tyrrell, 'Family migration decision-making, step-migration and separation: Children's experiences in European migrant worker families' (2016) 14 Children's Geographies 453.

Müller-Freienfels, W. 'The unification of family law' (1968) 16 The American Journal of Comparative Law 175.

Murat, P. 'Article II-69' in L. Burgorgue-Larsen, A. Levade, and F. Picod (eds), *Traité établissant une Constitution pour l'Europe. Commentaire article par article. Partie II: La Charte des droits fondamentaux de l'Union* (Bruylant 2005).

Mustasaari, S. 'Introduction to Special Issue on transnational child protection' (2022) 34 Child and Family Law Quarterly 333.

'Children abroad: A relational analysis of cross-border child protection cases in the Finnish Central Authority' (2022) 34 Child and Family Law Quarterly 361.

Naldini, M., and J. Long. 'Geographies of families in the European Union: A legal and social policy analysis' (2017) 31 International Journal of Law, Policy and the Family 94.

Nic Shuibhne, N. 'The right to move and reside: Disentangling the dual dynamics of fundamental rights in EU citizenship law' in S. Douglas-Scott and N. Hatzis (eds), *Research Handbook on EU Law and Human Rights* (Edward Elgar Publishing 2017).

O'Brien, C. 'Between the devil and the deep blue sea: Vulnerable EU citizens cast adrift in the UK post-Brexit' (2021) 58 Common Market Law Review 431.

O'Donovan, K. 'Constructions of maternity and motherhood in stories of lost children' in J. Bridgeman and D. Monk (eds), *Feminist Perspectives on Child Law* (Routledge 2000).

O'Leary, S. *The Evolving Concept of Community Citizenship: From the Free Movement of Persons to Union Citizenship* (Kluwer 1996).

Öberg, M.-L. 'From EU citizens to third country nationals: The legacy of *Polydor*' (2016) 22 European Public Law 97.

'Internal market acquis as a tool in EU external relations: From integration to disintegration' (2020) 47 Legal Issues of Economic Integration 151.

Ochiai, E. 'Introduction: Reconstruction of intimate and public spheres in Asian modernity' in E. Ochiai and L. Aoi Hosoya (eds), *Transformation of the Intimate and the Public in Asian Modernity* (Kyoto University Press 2013).

Palazzo, N. 'The EU family: Is marital status emerging as a prohibited ground of discrimination?' in E. Bernard, M. Cresp, and M. Ho-Dac (eds), *La famille dans l'ordre juridique de l'Union européenne / Family within the Legal Order of the European Union* (Bruylant 2020).

Palazzo, N., and M. Tomasi, 'I referendum in materia di diritti delle coppie omosessuali: Minoranze e vox populi' (2016) 1 GenIUS 89.

Palonen, E. 'Performing the nation: The Janus-faced populist foundations of illiberalism in Hungary' (2018) 26 Journal of Contemporary European Studies 308.

Palumbo, L. 'The borders of legal motherhood: Rethinking access to assisted reproductive technologies in Europe' in Y. Ergas, J. Jenson, and S. Michel (eds), *Reassembling Motherhood: Procreation and Care in a Globalised World* (Columbia University Press 2017).

Parti, K. 'Illiberal and populist political narratives on gender and underreporting of sexual violence: A case study of Hungary' (2022) 10 Politics and Governance 26.

Parton, N. 'Child protection and safeguarding in England: Changing and competing conceptions of risk and their implications for social work' (2011) 41 British Journal of Social Work 854.

'Comparing child protection systems' in P. Dolan and N. Frost (eds), *The Routledge Handbook of Global Child Welfare* (Routledge 2017).

Paskalia, V. *Free Movement, Social Security and Gender in the EU* (Hart Publishing 2007).

Pastre-Belda, B. 'La Cour européenne des droits de l'homme, entre promotion de la subsidiarité et protection effective des droits' (2013) Revue trimestrielle des droits de l'Homme 256.

Pataut, E. 'La famille saisie par l'Union' in E. Bernard, M. Cresp, and M. Ho-Dac (eds), *La famille dans l'ordre juridique de l'Union européenne / Family within the Legal Order of the European Union* (Bruylant 2020).

Pech, L., and D. Kochenov, 'Respect for the rule of law in the case law of the European Court of Justice: A casebook overview of key judgments since the Portuguese judges case' SIEPS 2021:3 <www.sieps.se/globalassets/publikationer/2021/sieps-2021_3-eng-web.pdf?>.

Pető, A. 'Gender and illiberalism' in A. Sajó, R. Uitz, and S. Holmes (eds), *Routledge Handbook of Illiberalism* (Routledge 2021).

'Three readings of one law: Reregulating sexuality in Hungary' (*LSE EUROPP blog*, 8 July 2021) <https://blogs.lse.ac.uk/europpblog/2021/07/06/three-readings-of-one-law-reregulating-sexuality-in-hungary/>.

Pintens, W. 'Family law in Europe: Developments and perspectives' (2008) 41 The Comparative and International Law Journal of Southern Africa 155.

Pintens, W., and J. M. Scherpe, 'The Marckx case: A "whole code of family law"?' in S. Gilmore, J. Herring, and R. Probert (eds), *Landmark Cases in Family Law* (Hart Publishing 2011).

Pohjankoski, P. 'Rule of law with leverage: Policing structural obligations in EU law with the infringement procedure, fines, and set-off' (2021) 58 Common Market Law Review 1341.

Popenoe, D. 'American family in decline, 1960–1990: A review and appraisal' (1993) 55 Journal of Marriage and the Family 527.

Poppelwell-Scevak, C. 'Oliari, Orlandi and homophobic dissenting opinions: The Strasbourg approach to the recognition of same sex marriages' (*Strasbourg Observers*, 2 February 2018) <https://strasbourgobservers.com/2018/02/02/oliari-orlandi-and-homophobic-dissenting-opinions-the-strasbourg-approach-to-the-recognition-of-same-sex-marriages/>.

Prechal S., and R. Widdershoven, 'Redefining the relationship between "Rewe-effectiveness" and effective judicial protection' (2011) 4 Review of European Administrative Law 41.

Puppinck, G. 'X. and Others v. Austria (Part I): Had the woman been a man ...' (*Strasbourg Observers*, 4 March 2013) <https://strasbourgobservers.com/2013/03/04/x-and-others-v-austria-part-i-had-the-woman-been-a-man/>.

Ragone, S., and V. Volpe, 'An emerging right to a "gay" family life? The case Oliari v. Italy in a comparative perspective' (2016) 17 German Law Journal 451.

Rathus, Z. 'Social science or 'Lego science'? Presumptions, politics, parenting and the new family law' (2010) 10 QUT Law Review 164.

Rawls, J. *A Theory of Justice* (revised edition, Oxford University Press 1999).

Réveillère, V. 'Family rights for naturalized EU citizens: Lounes' (2018) 55 Common Market Law Review 1855.

Rijpma, J. J. 'You gotta let love move: ECJ 5 June 2018, Case C-673/16, Coman, Hamilton, Accept v. Inspectoratul General pentru Imigrări' (2019) 15 European Constitutional Law Review 324.

Rijpma, J. J., and N. Koffeman, 'Free movement rights for same-sex couples under EU law: What role to play for the CJEU?' in D. Gallo, L. Paladini, and P. Pustorino (eds), *Same-Sex Couples before National, Supranational and International Jurisdictions* (Springer 2014).

Rodean, N. 'Adoption and same-sex couples: New rights in European constitutional space after the ruling X and Others v. Austria' (2014) 29 Direitos Fundamentais & Justiça 30.

Romeo Casabona, C. M., R. Paslack, and J. W. Simon, 'Reproductive medicine and the law: Egg donation in Germany, Spain and other European countries' (2013) 38 Revista de Derecho y Genoma Humano 15.

Sajó, A., R. Uitz, and S. Holmes (eds), *Routledge Handbook of Illiberalism* (Routledge 2021).

Salzberg, M. 'The Marckx case' (1983–1984) 13 Denver Journal for International Law and Policy 283.

Sata, R. 'In the name of the family' (Gunda Werner Institut - Heinrich Böll Stiftung 2022) <www.gwi-boell.de/en/2022/01/31/im-namen-der-familie-wie-populistinnen-ungarn-gegen-geschlechtergleichstellung>.

Scheiwe, K. 'EU law's unequal treatment of the family: The case law of the European Court of Justice on rules prohibiting discrimination on grounds of sex and nationality' (1994) 3 Social and Legal Studies 243.

Scherpe, J. M. 'Zehn Jahre registrierte Partnerschaft in Dänemark - Zur Novellierung des Gesetzes von 1989' (2000) Deutsches und Europäisches FamilienRecht 32.

'Erfahrungen mit dem Rechtsinstitut der registrierten Lebenspartnerschaft in Dänemark' (2001) Familie Partnerschaft Recht 439.

'Gleichgeschlechtliche Lebensgemeinschaften' in J. Basedow, K.-J. Hopt, and R. Zimmermann (eds), *Handwörterbuch des Europäischen Privatrechts* (Mohr Siebeck 2009).

'From 'odious crime' to family life – Same-sex couples and the ECHR' in A. Verbeke and others (eds), *Confronting the Frontiers of Family and Succession Law – Liber amicorum Walter Pintens* (Intersentia 2012).

'Same-sex relationships' in J. Basedow, K.-J. Hopt, and R. Zimmermann (eds), *Max Planck Encyclopedia of European Private Law* (Oxford University Press 2012).

'The legal recognition of same-sex couples in Europe and the role of the European Court of Human Rights' (2013) 10 The Equal Rights Review 83.

(ed), *The Legal Status of Transsexual and Transgender Persons* (Intersentia 2015).
The Present and Future of European Family Law (Edward Elgar Publishing 2016).
'Breaking the existing paradigms of parent–child relationships' in G. Douglas, M. Murch, and V. Stephens (eds), *International and National Perspectives on Child and Family Law: Essays in Honour of Nigel Lowe* (Intersentia 2018).
'Is there a 'European Family Law'?' (2023) 54 Victoria University of Wellington Law Review 317.
'Marriage and the family' in L. Corrias and R. Tinnevelt (eds), *European Ways of Life: Legal and Philosophical Perspectives* (Edward Elgar Publishing, forthcoming).
Scherpe, J. M., C. Fenton-Glynn, and T. Kaan (eds), *Eastern and Western Perspectives on Surrogacy* (Intersentia 2019).
Scherpe, J. M., and A. Hayward (eds), *The Future of Registered Partnerships – Family Recognition beyond Marriage?* (Intersentia 2017).
Schmidt, M., and P. Bogdanowicz, 'The infringement procedure in the rule of law crisis: How to make effective use of Article 258 TFEU' (2018) 55 Common Market Law Review 1061.
Schönberger, C. 'European citizenship as federal citizenship, some citizenship lessons of comparative federalism' (2007) 19 European Review of Public Law 63.
Schütze, R. *European Union Law* (Cambridge University Press 2018).
Shaw, J. *The Transformation of Citizenship in the European Union* (Cambridge University Press 2007).
Shenfield, F., and others, 'Cross border reproductive care in six European countries' (2010) 25 Human Reproduction 1367.
Smart, C. *Personal Life: New Directions in Sociological Thinking* (Polity 2007).
Smet, S. 'X. and others v. Austria (Part II): A narrow ruling on a narrow issue' (*Strasbourg Observers*, 6 March 2013) <https://strasbourgobservers.com/2013/03/06/x-and-others-v-austria-part-ii-a-narrow-ruling-on-a-narrow-issue/>.
Smyth, C. *European Asylum Law and the Rights of the Child* (Routledge 2014).
Snell, J. 'Do fundamental rights determine the scope of EU law?' (2018) 43 European Law Review 475.
Somek, A. 'The individualisation of liberty: Europe's move from emancipation to empowerment' (2013) 4 Transnational Legal Theory 258.
'Alienation, despair and social freedom' in L. Azoulai, S. Barbou des Places, and E. Pataut (eds), *Constructing the Person in EU Law: Rights, Roles, Identities* (Hart Publishing 2016).
Spaventa, E. 'Mice or horses? British citizens in the EU 27 after Brexit as "former EU citizens"' (2019) 44 European Law Review 589.
Spieker, L. D. 'Berlaymont is back: The Commission invokes Article 2 TEU as self-standing plea in infringement proceedings over Hungarian LGBTIQ rights violations' (*EU Law Live*, 22 February 2023) <https://eulawlive.com/op-ed-berlaymont-is-back-the-commission-invokes-article-2-teu-as-self-standing-plea-in-infringement-proceedings-over-hungarian-lgbtiq-rights-violations-by-luke-dimitrios-spieker/>.
Spratt, T., and others, 'Child protection in Europe: Development of an international cross-comparison model to inform national policies and practices' (2015) 45 British Journal of Social Work 1508.

Stacey, J. *Brave New Families: Stories of Domestic Upheaval in Late Twentieth Century America* (Basic Books 1990).
Stalford, H. 'Concepts of family under EU law – Lessons from the ECHR' (2002) 16 International Journal of Law, Policy and the Family 410.
Children and the European Union: Rights, Welfare and Accountability (Hart Publishing 2012).
'The UK referendum on membership of the EU: Whither social welfare and family law?' (2016) 38 Journal of Social Welfare and Family Law 115.
Stehlík, V. 'The CJEU crossing the Rubicon on the same-sex marriages? Commentary on Coman case' (2018) 18 International and Comparative Law Review 85.
Stevenson, C. 'Persuasive definitions' (1938) 47 Mind 331.
Stöckl, K. 'The European culture wars' (*ZOiS Spotlight* 13/19, 3 April 2019) <https://en.zois-berlin.de/publications/zois-spotlight/archiv-2019/the-european-culture-wars>.
Strumia, F. 'The family in EU law after the SM ruling: Variable geometry and conditional deference' (2019) 4 European Papers 389.
Sturm, F. 'Das Straßburger Marckx-Urteil zum Recht des nichtehelichen Kindes und seine Folgen' (1982) Zeitschrift für das gesamte Familienrecht 1151.
Swennen, F. 'Motherhoods and the law' in H. Willekens and others (eds), *Motherhood and the Law* (Göttingen University Press 2019).
Szikra, D. 'Democracy and welfare in hard times: The social policy of the Orbán Government in Hungary between 2010 and 2014' (2014) 24 Journal of European Social Policy 486.
Szikra, D., and D. Szelewa, 'Do Central and Eastern European countries fit the "Western" picture? The example of family policies in Hungary and Poland' in C. Klenner and S. Leiber (eds), *Welfare States and Gender Inequality in Central and Eastern Europe: Continuity and Post-socialist Transformation in the EU Member States* (European Trade Union Institute 2010).
Takács, J., K. Fobear, and S. Schmitsek, 'Resisting genderphobia in Hungary' (2022) 10 Politics and Governance 38.
Thienpont, D., and G. Willems, 'Le droit à la libre circulation des familles homoparentales consacré par la Cour de justice de l'Union européenne' (2022) 132 Revue trimestrielle des droits de l'Homme 925.
Thompson, L. 'Impossible expectations? Abused mothers' experiences of the child protection and family court systems' (2020) 32 Child and Family Law Quarterly 31.
Thym, D., and M. H. Zoetewij-Turhan, 'Introduction: Free movement between membership and partnership' in D. Thym and M. H. Zoetewij-Turhan (eds.), *Rights of Third-Country Nationals under EU Association Agreements* (Brill 2015).
Timmer, A. 'S.H. and Others v Austria: Margin of appreciation and IVF' (*Strasbourg Observers*, 9 November 2011) <https://strasbourgobservers.com/2011/11/09/s-h-and-others-v-austria-margin-of-appreciation-and-ivf/>.
Tobler, C. 'Equality and non-discrimination under the ECHR and EU law: A comparison focusing on discrimination against LGBTI persons' (2014) 74 Heidelberg Journal of International Law 521.
'Free movement of persons in the EU v. in the EEA: Of effect-related homogeneity and a reversed Polydor principle' (2018) 3 European Papers 1429.
Todorova, V. 'Gender wars in Bulgaria' in J. M. Scherpe and S. Gilmore (eds), *Family Matters – Essays in Honour of John Eekelaar* (Intersentia 2022).

Torres Pérez, A. *Conflicts of Rights in the European Union – A Theory of Supranational Adjudication* (Oxford University Press 2009).

'Rights and powers in the European Union: Towards a Charter that is fully applicable to the Member States' (2020) 22 Cambridge Yearbook of European Legal Studies 279.

Tóth, O., and C. Dupcsik, 'Trust in people and conservatism of family and gender roles in Hungary and in some other European countries' (2011) 1 Journal of Intimate and Public Spheres 152.

Trimmings, K., S. Shakargy, and C. Achmad (eds), *Research Handbook on Surrogacy and the Law* (Edward Elgar Publishing 2024).

Tryfonidou, A. '(Further) signs of a turn of the tide in the CJEU's citizenship jurisprudence: Case C-40/11, *Iida*, Judgment of 8 November 2012' (2013) 20 Maastricht Journal of European and Comparative Law 302.

'Another failed opportunity for the effective protection of LGB rights under EU law: Dr David. L. Parris v. Trinity College Dublin and Others' (*EU Law Analysis*, 1 December 2016) <http://eulawanalysis.blogspot.com/2016/12/another-failed-opportunity-for.html>.

'EU free movement law and the children of rainbow families: Children of a lesser god?' (2019) 38 Yearbook of European Law 220.

'The ECJ recognises the right of same-sex spouses to move freely between EU Member States: The Coman ruling' (2019) 44 European Law Review 663.

'Law and sexual minority rights in the EU: Navigating a political minefield' in P. Cardwell and M.-P. Granger (eds), *Research Handbook on the Politics of EU Law* (Edward Elgar Publishing 2020).

'Positive state obligations under European law: A tool for achieving substantive equality for sexual minorities in Europe' (2020) 13 Erasmus Law Review 98.

'The cross-border recognition of the parent–child relationship in rainbow families under EU law: A critical view of the ECJ's V.M.A. Ruling' (*European Law Blog*, 21 December 2021) <https://europeanlawblog.eu/2021/12/21/the-cross-border-recognition-of-the-parent-child-relationship-in-rainbow-families-under-eu-law-a-critical-view-of-the-ecjs-v-m-a-ruling/>.

'The ECJ recognises the right of rainbow families to move freely between EU Member States: The V.M.A. ruling' (2022) 47 European Law Review 534.

'The impact of right-wing populism on the family rights of sexual minorities in Europe' (2022) EU-POP Working Paper Series 2.

'Cross-border recognition of parenthood in the EU: Comments on the Commission proposal of 7 December' (2023) 24 ERA Forum 149.

'Surrogacy in the ECHR and the European institutions' in K. Trimmings, S. Shakargy, and C. Achmad (eds), *Research Handbook on Surrogacy and the Law* (Edward Elgar Publishing forthcoming).

Vaige, L. *Cross-Border Recognition of Formalized Same-Sex Relationships* (Intersentia 2022).

Van Eijken, H. *EU Citizenship and the Constitutionalisation of the European Union* (Europa Law Publishing 2015).

Van Hoof, W., and G. Pennings, 'Extraterritorial laws for cross-border reproductive care: The issue of legal diversity' (2012) 19 European Journal of Health Law 187.

'The consequences of S.H. and Others v Austria for legislation on gamete donation in Europe: an ethical analysis of the European Court of Human Rights judgments' (2012) 25 Reproductive BioMedicine Online 667.

Van Middelaar, L. *The Passage to Europe: How a Continent Became a Union* (Yale University Press 2014).

von Bogdandy, A., and L. D. Spieker, 'Countering the judicial silencing of critics: Article 2 TEU values, reverse Solange, and the responsibilities of national judges' (2019) 15 European Constitutional Law Review 391.

Waaldijk, K. 'The gender-neutrality of the International Right to Marry: Same-sex couples may still be excluded from marriage, but their exclusion – and their foreign marriages – must be recognised' (23 July 2018) <https://papers.ssrn.com/abstract=3218308>.

'Small change: How the road to same-sex marriage got paved in the Netherlands' in R. Wintemute and M. Andenæs (eds), *Legal Recognition of Same-Sex Partnerships: A Study of National, European, and International Law* (Hart Publishing 2001) 437.

Walklate, S., and Mythen, G. 'Beyond risk theory: Experiential knowledge and "knowing otherwise"' (2011) 11 Criminology and Criminal Justice 99.

Weiler J. 'Editorial: Does the European Union truly need a Charter of Rights?' (2000) 6 European Law Journal 95.

Weston, S., and G. Mythen, 'Disentangling practitioners' understandings of child sexual exploitation: The risks of assuming otherwise?' (2022) 22 Criminology and Criminal Justice 618.

Willekens, H. 'Motherhood as a legal institution: A historical-sociological introduction' in H. Willekens and others (eds), *Motherhood and the Law* (Göttingen University Press 2019).

Willems, G. 'Orientation sexuelle et adoption: L'Autriche condamnée par la Cour européenne des droits de l'homme' (2013) Revue trimestrielle des droits de l'homme 1037.

'Droits de l'homme et procréation médicalement assistée: La Cour de Strasbourg face aux évolutions biomédicales et aux mutations de la filiation' in N. Massager, *Procréation médicalement assistée et gestation pour autrui: Regards croisés du droit et de la pratique médicale* (Anthemis 2017).

'Le droit au regroupement familial des époux homosexuels consacré par la Cour de justice de l'Union européenne' (2018) La semaine juridique (édition générale).

Williams, R. *Keywords: A Vocabulary of Culture and Society* (Croom Helm 1976).

Wollenschläger, F. 'A new fundamental freedom beyond market integration: Union citizenship and its dynamics for shifting the economic paradigm of European integration' (2011) 17 European Law Journal 1.

Woods, L. 'Family rights in the EU – Disadvantaging the disadvantaged?' (1999) 11 Child and Family Law Quarterly 17.

Wright, M. 'Working the international child protection case: A snapshot of local authorities' experiences within an evolving legal context' (2019) 41 Journal of Social Welfare and Family Law 15.

Yuval-Davis, N. 'Gender and nation' (1997) 16 Ethnic and Racial Studies 621.

Zimanyi, E. 'Family b/Orders: Hungary's campaign for the "Family Protection Action Plan"' (2020) 20 Feminist Media Studies 305.

Index

For EU product safety concerns, contact us at Calle de José Abascal, 56–1°, 28003 Madrid, Spain or eugpsr@cambridge.org.

www.ingramcontent.com/pod-product-compliance
Lightning Source LLC
LaVergne TN
LVHW010055220926
848484LV00005BA/1080
* 9 7 8 1 0 0 9 4 9 8 8 2 1 *